The Residential Is Racial

Post 45 Loren Glass and Kate Marshall, Editors
Post•45 Group, Editorial Committee

The Residential Is Racial
A Perceptual History
of Mass Homeownership

Adrienne Brown

Stanford University Press
Stanford, California

Stanford University Press
Stanford, California

©2024 by Adrienne Brown. All rights reserved.

Publication is made possible in part by a grant from the Barr Ferree Foundation Publication Fund, Department of Art and Archaeology, Princeton University.

No part of this book may be reproduced or transmitted in any form or by any means, electronic or mechanical, including photocopying and recording, or in any information storage or retrieval system, without the prior written permission of Stanford University Press.

Printed in the United States of America on acid-free, archival-quality paper

Library of Congress Cataloging-in-Publication Data
Names: Brown, Adrienne, author.
Title: The residential is racial : a perceptual history of mass
    homeownership / Adrienne Brown.
Other titles: Post 45.
Description: Stanford, California : Stanford University Press, 2024. |
    Series: Post*45 | Includes bibliographical references and index.
Identifiers: LCCN 2023025433 (print) | LCCN 2023025434 (ebook) |
    ISBN 9781503636941 (cloth) | ISBN 9781503638648 (paperback) |
    ISBN 9781503638655 (ebook)
Subjects: LCSH: American literature—20th century—Themes, motives. |
    Race discrimination in literature. | Home ownership in literature. |
    Home ownership—United States—History—20th century. | Discrimination in
    housing—United States—History—20th century.
Classification: LCC PS228.R32 B75 2024 (print) | LCC PS228.R32 (ebook) |
    DDC 810.9/355—dc23/eng/20230915
LC record available at https://lccn.loc.gov/2023025433
LC ebook record available at https://lccn.loc.gov/2023025434

Cover design: Michele Wetherbee
Cover collage: *Homebodies #5*, Zoë Charlton, 2013. Image courtesy of the artist.
Typeset by Newgen in Minion Pro 10/15

Contents

Acknowledgments vii

Introduction 1

Part I The Road to Mass Homeownership

1 Empire Builders 45
The Racial Longings of Modern Real Estate

2 Scoring Housing's Modern Jazzy Sound at the Rent Party 85

3 Making Ownership Feel Good Again 123
Rewriting the Land Man after the Great Depression

Part II A Nation of Homeowners

4 Appraisal Manuals 177
Looking at Residential Looking on the Midcentury Block

5 Feeling Racial Attachments to Property with John Cheever and Lorraine Hansberry 215

6 What Does Institutional Racism Look Like? 263
The Investigative Aesthetics of Fair Housing

Epilogue 305
Resurrection City and Beverly Hills, Chicago

Notes 315

Index 375

Acknowledgments

THE ACT OF WRITING CONTINUALLY reveals the precarity of ownership. While my name is listed on the cover of this book, its writing would not have been possible without the vast amount of scholarship preceding me as well as the vast amount of care and generosity that has always held me and, if I'm lucky, will continue to do so. While I hope my footnotes point to most—if certainly not all—of my scholarly debts, I'm grateful to have a place to recognize the people and networks that have buoyed me beyond copyrighted material. This book follows heartily from ideas left unworked out in the last, and so I continue to be grateful to my dissertation advisors at Princeton, Diana Fuss, Bill Gleason, and Valerie Smith, and the many people I met and learned from there who continue to be so kind, smart, and generous. At the University of Chicago, if anyone understood the dispossessive nature of writing, it was Lauren Berlant—it was from them that I learned new ways for weathering its tumults and finding new joys and forms through it. Thank you to the members of More Than Diversity—your solidarity boosted me more than you could ever know. I thank my colleagues in the English Department and my colleagues in the Department of Race, Diaspora, and Indigeneity—I continually learn new ways of making, doing, and thinking from you all. Special thanks to C. Riley

Snorton for always knowing the right time to call. Gratitude to the entire staff at Arts + Public Life who have cheered me on to the end of this project and whose work inspires me daily. Ongoing thanks to David Simon, Gerard Passannante, Zachary Samalin, and Sonali Thakkar for talking me through. Thanks to Gabe Winant for helping me think through some sticky points around the 1930s. Gratitude to Monica Huerta for being such a great partner in property thought. Thank you to Katie Kahal, Anna Dobrowolski, Kimberly McGee, and Joshua Stapleton for your support. Harris Feinsod, Leah Feldman, Nasser Mufti, and Christopher Taylor read early drafts of this material and helped me hold the faith that it would become a book. Thank you to Sarah Lewis and the incredible writing group she brought into existence including Nell Painter, Leigh Raiford, Courtney Baker, Jeneé Osterheldt, and Kimberly Drew. Thank you to all the graduate students I've had the opportunity to teach and advise—all of our conversations have made my thinking sharper. Thank you to the Black Reconstructions team, especially Mabel Wilson, for so much inspiration. Thank you to the staff and fellows at the Schomburg Center for Research in Black Culture—being a 2018 Schomburg Scholar-in-Residence was transformative to this project. Particular thanks to Brent Hayes Edwards, Aisha Al-Adawiya, Michelle Commander, Brian Jones, Naomi Lorrain, Margaret Odette, Denisse Andrade, Dan Berger, Jasmine Johnson, Christopher Willoughby, Hasna Muhammad, Gaiutra Bahadur, and Garrett Felber. I also want to thank Hathaway Hester and the National Association of Realtors for granting me access to their archives.

Thanks to the audiences of all the lectures I gave on this material. Thanks to the reviewers and editors of the articles and chapters drawing from material included here. An early version of Chapter 2 appeared in *Paths to Prison: Histories on the Architecture of Carcerality,* edited by I. Kirkham-Lewitt (Columbia University Press, 2020). An early version of Chapter 3 was published in *Timelines of American Literature,* edited by Cody Marrs and Chris Hager (Johns Hopkins University Press, 2019), and in *Reconstructions Exhibition Field Guide* (Museum of Modern Art, 2021). An early version of Chapter 4 was published in *American Quarterly*: "Appraisal Narratives: Reading Race on the Midcentury Block," 70.2 (June 2018), copyright © 2018 American Studies Association, and an early version of Chapter 5 appeared in *Modern Fiction Studies*: "We Wear the Mask: John Cheever Writes Race," 63.4 (March 2018), copyright © 2018 Purdue University. Thank as well to the anonymous reviewers of this manuscript and very big thanks to Caroline McKusick and Erica Wetter at Stanford University Press for believing in this book and helping me see it through.

Thanks to all the babies and not so babies anymore whose snuggles made finishing each page worth it (and thanks to the parents who made such amazing kids possible)—Jacks (all three that I hold dear), Niloufer, Felix, Marlow, Delia, Mina, Asa, Moses, Irene, Noah, Sadie, and more. Thank you to Adom Getachew and Natacha Nsabimana for so much joy. Same to Wendy Lee and Jacky Shin. Thanks to my neighbors, the Carters, for being the best neighbors. Ongoing gratitude to the Williams family—Sally, Bob, Jocelyn, Tan, Megan, Matt, and Jack. Thanks to my UK family, Brian, Marion, Donald, Harriet, Kurt, and Lyra. Thanks to Rachel Karish, Sarah Balagtas, and Brittany Williams for decades of the weirdest fun. Thanks to Anthony Brown. Thank you to Tony and Michelle Brown and Deli. So much love to Evelyn and Adrianna. Thank you, Marilyn Brown—this book is finally done and we can have fun again. And thanks to Andrew Ferguson—once more, this book is for you with love. You'd better like this one, too.

The Residential Is Racial

INTRODUCTION

WHO HAS A FEEL FOR ownership, a touch for property, an aptitude for owning and valuing ownership? The notion that some have an inherent *sense* for ownership—an orientation equal parts ability and feeling, marking one's talents to both own and appreciate owning's merits—has historically propelled the mutual formation of race and property. The interdependence of these concepts has been most visible in the coevolved philosophical, economic, and legal systems used to legitimate chattel slavery, native dispossession, and real property beginning in the 17th century—projects collectively anchored by an understanding of whiteness as the laudable and superior penchant to own. But the mutual remaking of race and property endured into the twentieth century, if along increasingly more bureaucratic channels in the United States, as homeownership surpassed the ownership of arable land and enslaved people to become Americans' most prized form of possession. Endorsed by the state and embraced by many of its citizens by the mid-twentieth century as the surest path to wealth creation, homeownership became the lingua franca of the American Dream. Yet, as many histories of homeownership have shown, the materialization of this dream for most white Americans depended upon the exclusion of those deemed racially incapable of cherishing homeownership, performing its idioms and, most importantly, conserving its value on a market built on such presumptions about racialized ownership.

This book recovers how the modern case for mass homeownership wielded the long-standing belief that caring for property was an inherent racial capacity even as homeownership was remaking how Americans sensed and defined race and valued racial evidence. More than deepening established grooves of racial inequity or recalibrating a few of its categories, mass homeownership reconstructed the American racial sensorium—the embodied habits and learned procedures used to detect, perceive, and orient one's self in relation to race—to better secure the value of whiteness within the new physical, aesthetic, and actuarial environments comprising the residential.¹ Becoming residential—a spatial category catalyzing new modes of sensing, moving, and being organized around the superiority of homeownership—involved reshaping where and how Americans looked for race, the methods and forms they used to perceive, experience, and describe it, and the shifting stakes of its interpretation. *The Residential Is Racial* traces homeownership's racialized touch to understand the extent of its reach, why its grip has remained so firm upon so many across the color line, and what other forms of residential feeling might be limned from the cultural and bureaucratic archives of the twentieth century.

That the U.S. would become a nation of homeowners in the twentieth century was not preordained. Most Americans did not own their own homes nor necessarily desired to do so for much of the nation's history. Though aspirations for the U.S. to be populated by property owners originated in Jeffersonian agrarianism, by 1920 less than half of Americans were. As more Americas moved to cities where they worked jobs outside of their homes in the early twentieth century, homeownership did not as readily appeal to their hearts, minds, or pocketbooks as owning land once had. Americans continued to sing out about the comforts of home, sweet, home, but the owned one was not necessarily all that sweeter.²

The case for homeownership required conscious construction in the early twentieth century before it could become naturalized as the base of the American Dream. As the fields of real estate, appraisal, and land economics professionalized in tandem with currents of race science, the specific rationale for homeownership as an economic benefit, civic duty, and racial imperative solidified. The state first partnered with the real estate industry to encourage homeownership as a defensive response to the 1917 Russian Revolution.³ The dispossessions of the Great Depression further set the stage for the state's more substantial remaking of the housing market through mortgage insurance subsidizing affordable thirty-year mortgages for white Americans while devaluing black space and occupancy. The federal government's interventions in the mortgage market helped a majority of Americans, mostly white, to own their homes for the first time in 1950, mostly located in all-white neighborhoods. Homeownership rates for minorities also rose in this period but at a far slower clip, helping cement the story—albeit a segregated one—of America as a nation of homeowners.

This achievement of mass homeownership for white Americans in the midcentury is, by now, a well-plumbed story. And each year, through the work of historians and social scientists who have served as this history's primary investigators, we more deeply understand the extent of the collaboration between the state and the real estate industry in creating and maintaining a discriminatory housing market.[4] Yet, even as our knowledge of the racial project of mass homeownership and its attendant mechanisms of redlining, contract-buying, blockbusting, and rental exploitation expands, the core of the story of housing and race in the twentieth century remains largely intact—that the transformation of the U.S. into a majority homeowning nation depended upon the ongoing devaluation of black neighborhoods and residents.[5]

While housing experts and activists have attended to the foundational role that race played in the creation of mass homeownership, this book most insistently tracks the inverse: the role mass homeownership played in altering the definition, perception, and value of race. As the residential emerged as a distinct spatial typology and, by extension, a way of life, codified through law, custom, academic research, and the economy, visions of the ideal residential subject also took shape. And like most typologies in the late nineteenth and early twentieth centuries, the emergence of the residential subject was informed by scientific, philosophical, and aesthetic theories of race—most keenly those positing ownership as a racial capacity of both intellect and feeling. Whites were not only more capable of managing ownership's complexities, these arguments went, but inherently valued ownership more fiercely than other races. As realtors and, eventually, the state built the case for homeownership in the early twentieth century, this older rhetoric about the racial sensibility of property dating back to the Enlightenment shaped maxims of modern homeownership's feel as well as electing who was most suited to its repertoire. But as the fever for homeownership took hold in the 1920s, aided by state incentives, and the home increasingly became the largest investment most Americans would ever make, imperatives to make race more cleanly legible and easier to appraise grew, too. Whiteness broadened to assimilate those once deemed on its borders. Italian, Eastern European, and Irish homeowners invested in whiteness by purchasing homes requiring the exclusion of those deemed unfit to own—a category increasingly synonymous with blackness as the century marched on. Whiteness was increasingly understood as not merely a trait belonging to specific persons but as a neighborhood's most valuable amenity, to be preserved at all costs, while blackness was deemed illiquid, presumed to devalue all it touched, neighbored, or possessed. This transposition of race into a quality of space changed what counted as racial evidence as well as the methods for gathering, tallying, and appraising it. The visual apperception of whiteness and the fidelity of one's performance of it superseded hidden blood and invisible ancestry as useful racial measures within the bureaucratic systems developed to appraise home values via maps, forms, and what one could glimpse while driving through a neighborhood.

Telling this story of homeownership—treating race not as a constant being responded to but as a malleable concept continually recalibrated by residential space and markets—entails reading the practices of realtors and bureaucrats alongside the work of artists and writers as they learned to newly represent the racial sensorium in the age of mass homeownership. Rather than understanding redlining as mere policy—naming the practice of devaluing certain neighborhoods in relation to their racial makeup—this book approaches redlining as a mode of perception altering what it meant to sense race and assign it value. Far from stable documents accurately depicting the racial makeup of neighborhoods, redlining maps are better understood as projections of numerous subjective hypotheses about how race might be read and adjudicated on the scale of the block. Such an approach enables us to denaturalize the countless and often quotidian assumptions, decisions, and interpretations about what race was and how to read and value it to recover the growing importance of neighborhood scale to race's perception and appraisal. Unsettling weak formulations like "white flight" that flatten the co-constitutive relationship between race and the residential, I track how mass homeownership more fulsomely remade the rubrics of race from the early cases realtors made for its essentialness in the early 1900s through the passage of the Fair Housing Act in 1968.

If we consider race not as a fact marked and plotted by bureaucrats and realtors but as a category being actively remade within the public sphere in accordance with the growing civic and financial value of residential investments, both race and the residential appear less stable and more multiply constituted as a result, even as the racism perpetuated by these systems remained largely intact. To observe these changes, the archives for gauging the fluctuating measures of race and its alleged capacities must shift, as well as our ways of reading them. Who had the capacity to be an ideal resident, how to best measure this capacity, and should ownership be the horizon of the good life were inquiries being answered in affective and sensorial terms across a host of cultural, academic, and bureaucratic works: in novels, plays, films, and songs; magazines and newspapers; academic institutes, conferences, and journals of new disciplines like land economics and planning; and professional and trade publications where realtors and appraisers honed and shared their craft. Cases made for and against homeownership relied on prescriptions about how homeownership should feel, what kind of perception appraisers should adopt when assessing a home's value, and the reliability of one's racial sensorium in making judgments about the present and future worth of a neighborhood. Determining the value of a home or of homeownership more broadly, despite being draped in the language of the free market, relied on perceptual, aesthetic, and phenomenological evidence of race and its sensations exceeding discourses of empiricism or laws of value. Resituating residential discrimination as a key moment within the history of perception and aesthetics as well as of policy, demography, and democracy, we get an even more expansive picture of both its origins and its impacts. In the twentieth century, neighborhood formation was also a mode of racial formation. These processes together forged new norms for perceiving, marking, and measuring race on the residential scale. This book tracks the racial honing of the residential sensorium—perceiving race like a bureaucrat, an appraiser, and a homeowning neighbor—central to the functioning of the residential itself.

In considering the mutual formation of racial and residential perception, this book also charts a fuller range of ways that black writers and artists in particular weighted the value of property rights and residential integration to projects of equality. A strategic focus on winning full property rights as a means of gaining full citizenship has propelled civil rights projects organized by race from Emancipation forward. Following the increasing urbanization of the black population in the U.S. and the growing movement of economic and symbolic power away from landownership and toward homeownership, civil rights and nondiscriminatory property rights have long been coupled as correlated struggles.

Yet, within a broad archive of black property thought—including figures like Martin Luther King Jr. and Lorraine Hansberry, but also restless freedmen and rent party hosts, blockbusters, scammers, and the bourgeois-aspirant—we find more erratic, conflicted, and inventive responses to property's position as the horizon of freedom, rights, or liberation writ large. While considering the ways whiteness has centered conceptions of residential subjectivity, this book also tunes in to the complex ways that black writers and artists imagined a future for blackness untethered from visions of either property lost or gained, reckoning with property's promises but also its bonds, burdens, and limits. Critical theories about whiteness's discursive invisibility are best understood in relation to redlining's success in making whiteness a requirement for optimal housing financing while expunging its vocabulary. At the same time, writers cataloging urban black enclaves, including Gwendolyn Brooks, James Baldwin, Lorraine Hansberry, and Thomas Pynchon, grappled with what it meant to ask readers to survey black neighborhoods when the origins of urban inequity were located outside the black belt itself. Even as homeownership was becoming synonymous with the American Dream in the twentieth century, the relationship of Americans across the color line with homeownership was far rockier than this revery-oriented shorthand suggests. If "real estate governs," as Reinhold Martin contends, this book attends to the range of narratives that gave shape to this governance while considering how narrative and perceptual forms themselves facilitate and disrupt the correlated reigns of both property and race in moments of boom, stagnation, and crisis.[6]

The Racial History of the Propertied Subject of Feeling

Mass homeownership in the twentieth century belongs to the history of property more broadly. And as with property at large, mass homeownership not only shaped racial outcomes, but helped to remake race itself as a concept and category. Mass homeownership could be said to qualify as a racial project, defined by Michael Omi and Howard Winant as "an effort to reorganize and redistribute resources along particular racial lines."[7] Yet, because property has also helped to produce and give value to the category of race, it seems most apt to consider race and property as mutually constitutive projects: property functions a racial project even as race is also always being produced in and through property. Or, as Brenna Bhandar puts it, "racial subjects and modern property laws are produced through one another."⁸ Theories of property, in other words, did not merely develop in reaction to race but shaped how race was itself theorized, defined, and perceived. Modes of feeling, moreover, played an outsize role in how the co-formations of race and property evolved. To position mass homeownership in relation to the ongoing mutual constitution of property and race, some background on the history of this co-formation and the centrality of feeling to its operation is in order.

The definition of property has been contested and continually retheorized since its invention.⁹ In describing the complex that is property, contemporary legal theory has most regularly conceptualized it as a "bundle of sticks," an image conjuring property's status as "not a single unitary thing but rather a group of rights, some of which may be added or removed under appropriate conditions."¹⁰ This constellation of property, moreover, has long anchored theorizations of states, societies, and individuals. As Athena Athanasiou notes, ownership sits squarely "at the heart of the onto-epistemologies of subject formation" in the West. Within this tradition, Athanasiou continues, "being and having are constituted as ontologically imbricated with each other: being is defined as having; having is constructed as an essential prerequisite of proper human being."¹¹ In England, private property began to garner new and specific legal definition in the seventeenth century and its rights and rules and proved pivotal to the Enlightenment philosophy that followed. From John Locke's definition of property as including one's own body and freedom—"every man has a property in his own person"—and his belief that the right to property preexists and supersedes politics itself, to Adam Smith's insistence on the superiority of societies organized around property's protection, the idea that political institutions should fundamentally center the rights of property owners was, and is, the cornerstone of liberalism.¹²

Rationales of property's sanctity drew heavily from speculations that the desire to own was not learned but innate. While David Hume, like Thomas Hobbes before him, argued that the desire for property was a convention and a product of utility rather than a natural predilection, the most impactful Enlightenment theories of properties naturalized its allure.¹³ For Adam Smith, the moral justification for property derived from the notion that people inherently experience feelings of loss when deprived of something they believed they possessed. In his outline of the most sacred laws of justice, laws that "guard his property and possessions" follow only after prohibitions against murder in importance.[14] Jurist William Blackstone would linger even longer on property sentiment in his influential *Commentaries on the Laws of England* in 1765: "There is nothing which so generally strikes the imaginations and engages the affections of mankind as the right to property; or that sole and despotic dominion which one man claims and exercises over the external things of the world, in total exclusion of the right of any other individual in the universe."[15] Like Adam Smith, Blackstone approached property as a natural driver of desire, linking the power of land to the power of dominion writ large.

Debates over property's nature, definition, and function took shape at the same as expansions of settler colonialism and the transatlantic slave trade. As Brenna Bhandar captures in her description of ownership as a racial regime, "there cannot be a history of private property law as the subject of legal studies and political theory in early modern England that is not at the same time a history of land appropriation."[16] "The evolution of modern property laws and justifications for private property ownership," she notes, "were articulated through the attribution of value to the lives of those defined as having the capacity, will, and technology to appropriate, which in turn was contingent on prevailing concepts of race and racial difference."[17] Early modern theories about private property as a capacity made it possible for English settlers to conceive of indigenous populations as occupants rather than owners of the land and to render black bodies as property to be dispossessed from their lands, repossessed and exchanged.

The difference between race and indigeneity has most centrally hinged on the distinction between an identity rooted in the body versus one forged from place; or focusing more specifically about the distinction between black and indigenous identities, as resulting from discrete, if always intersecting, processes of enslavement and genocidal dispossession. Such a schema has also dictated how the divergent political agendas of these groups have been glossed, with representation and inclusion being most often attributed to the struggles of racial minorities while demands for sovereignty and decolonization anchor indigenous concerns. But for all their differences, race and indigeneity prove porous categories.[18] Enlightenment efforts to codify the characteristics of non-Europeans used their alleged disinterest in or incapacity for property to rationalize their subjugation, be it through enslavement, exploitation, or dispossession. When the capacity for property is treated as a defining trait of a people and used to determine that people's aptitude for sovereignty over either their own bodies or their land, it is a tool of racialization.[19] This is not to collapse the distinctions between race and indigeneity in all contexts, especially since both are not only produced in relation to property but also continually remake definitions of property and determinations of its value. But it is to insist upon the flexibility of property as a tool, used by white settlers to variously create and enforce categories of race and indigeneity depending on which concept best served their interests at a given time. Claiming property feeling as a tool of racialization captures the manifold ways settlers used theories of property to justify the subjugation of others, at times racializing indigenous and other non-white populations alike as similarly unfit for property while creating treaties and laws justifying indigenous dispossession in terms best understood through the lens of sovereignty and colonization.[20]

John Locke's labor theory of property was perhaps most influential as a rationale for subjugation. Locke's notion that "as much land as a man tills, plants, improves, cultivates, and can use the product of, so much is his property" incentivized European settlers to the Americas to view the land as unimproved and, thus, open to be claimed.[21] As governor of Massachusetts James Sullivan wrote in 1801, "as property is defined by Mr. Locke, and other great men, there may be a question, how far the savages had acquired one in the soil of this wilderness." For Sullivan, the "precarious and transient occupancy" of Indians did not equate to ownership.[22] By the early nineteenth century, the idea that Indians only had a right of occupancy and not full ownership of the land dominated settler ideology. Fueling this belief was the faulty assumption that Indians were disinterested farmers who had failed to enclose the land for private use, rendering them inherently incapable of improving the land in Lockean terms. Such justifications undergirded settler imaginaries and legal arguments rationalizing the treaties and wars dispossessing Indians of the land. While some European settlers in the U.S. believed Indians lacked a natural capacity for ownership, others in the nineteenth century insisted that a love for private property was what would ultimately save the Indian by bringing the untethered "savage" into a vision of "civilization" synonymous with the rule of private property. As President James Madison insisted in 1816, "divided and individual ownership" would be "the true foundation for a transit from the habits of the savage to the arts and comforts of social life."²³ Within this "white possessive logic," to cite Aileen Moreton-Robinson, property was framed as both an inherent capacity fueled by a natural drive to possess as well as a learned convention that could transform one's capacities and desires.²⁴ Belief in the civilizing power of private property would culminate in the Dawes Act of 1887, legislating the parceling up of tribal lands into individual private plots that ultimately led to further catastrophic loss of land for Native peoples in the U.S.

Justifications for and against slavery also mobilized arguments about property rights. Here, Locke's theory of self-property—that "every man has a Property in his own Person" that "no Body has any Right to but himself"—often took center stage.²⁵ Abolitionists cited Locke to argue for slavery's unnaturalness, with Frederick Douglass most prominently invoking the philosopher to insist "every man is the original, natural, rightful, and absolute owner of his own body, and he can only part from his self-ownership, by the commission of a crime."²⁶ Proslavery arguments, by contrast, anchored themselves in the natural right to property claimed as "the first element of civilization," as Judge William Harper argued in his 1837 defense of slavery.²⁷ Given that "the coercion of Slavery alone is adequate to form man to habits of labor," Harper insisted, "without it, there can be no accumulation of property, no providence for the future, no tastes for comfort or elegancies, which are the characteristics and essentials of civilization."²⁸ Echoing proslavery rhetoric more broadly, Harper's conviction that Negroes were "incapable of European aspirations" in terms of both their civilizational and emotional capacities extended to their alleged lack of feel for property.²⁹ As sociologist George Fitzhugh maintained of whites in 1854, "no people on earth love property more, will go greater lengths, so far as danger is concerned to obtain it, or take better care of it after it is obtained."³⁰ What distinguished whites from non-whites, Fitzhugh insists, was not any actual possession of property but rather one's measurable *affection* for it and the will to want to possess—a formulation crucial to ensuring that unpropertied whites could continue to claim what W. E. B. Du Bois would call the "public and psychological wage" of whiteness in the absence of any actual land claims.³¹ It was the thought (and feeling) about property that counted most for the white supremacists doing the counting.

After Emancipation, "the Negro's capacity as a property gainer and owner" became a focal point for sociologists, economists, politicians, and race scientists.[32] Despite Reconstruction's broken promise to freepersons of forty acres and a mule giving them title to land they had "improved" without wages, social scientists in the early twentieth century insisted on measuring African American progress in terms of the quantity of property they had acquired since being free. As one sociologist warned in 1910, "taking into consideration the corresponding conditions of the whites and the improved opportunities for gaining property, the Negro appears to be going backwards."[33] He attributes this failure not to the social and civic conditions continuing his subjugation but as a failure of feeling: "The average Negro seems to be moved by neither by a desire to accumulate property nor to prepare for a day of need."[34] Another economic study sought to understand whether the Negro's alleged flagging commitment to property was "attributable to the training and steadying influences of the period of slavery."[35] The characteristics ascribed to the Negro as well as most other non-white races in the nineteenth and twentieth centuries—sloth, an inability to save or invest in the future, a lack of self-control, disrespect for others' property, and an overall low standard of living—were used to insist upon their general unfitness to either purchase or maintain property of their own, a claim that bolstered any number of disenfranchisements, from voting and sharecropping to alien land laws prohibiting those of Chinese and Japanese descent from owning property.

While nineteenth-century arguments about property most often centered on landownership and the ability to make the land produce, these arguments were extended to homeownership in the twentieth. As black educator H. T. Kealing woefully lamented of his own people while making the case for Negro education, the Negro "is loath to buy a house, because he has no taste for responsibility nor faith in himself to manage large concerns."[36] He is willing to spend "large sums on expensive clothing and luxuries," Kealing continues, "while going without things necessary to a real home."[37] While white supremacists argued that blacks had a natural incapacity for managing property, Kealing and others who considered themselves sympathetic to the Negro cause framed their alleged property failings as a matter of culture, capable of correction, rather than as a biological deficiency. Part of the ongoing project of Emancipation, insisted Kealing and others, involved teaching Negroes to become stewards of property rather than objects of it after centuries of enslavement. Because slavery "did not teach him the meaning of home," as Kealing put it, "to do this is the burden of freedom."[38] As white supremacist economist Albert Stone would insist in his study of the Negro's property failures, the owned home was not merely the foundation of the Negro's prosperity or a marker of racial progress; rather, what most mattered when assessing the Negro's civilizational progress was "the extent to which these houses possess for their owners the true significance of homes."[39] It was the Negro's demonstrable feeling for property—not what he owned but his feelings for owning itself—that would most powerfully signal his advancement.

Du Bois would also approach property affect as a racial pathology. But rather than valorizing the drive to own as a marker of a people's capacity for civilization, Du Bois would flip this formulation to insist instead on the tyranny of ownership embedded within whiteness. Describing what Ella Myers terms "whiteness as dominion," Du Bois famously defined whiteness in his 1920 essay "The Souls of White Folk" as "the ownership of the Earth forever and ever, Amen."[40] Casting this belief as "this new religion of whiteness," Du Bois dwells on ownership's affective and embodied operations.[41] Not only does this credence manifest itself in the "strut," "arrogance," and "whoop" of the faithful, but Du Bois also notes how such property faith also led to the "chilling of generous enthusiasm" for the freedom of others to occupy and govern their lands without white interference.[42] Du Bois's framing of whiteness as the right to universal ownership sharply diverged from that of his onetime teacher, William James. James's belief in ownership's importance to subject formation led him to prioritize its study within the emergent field of psychology. Like "the blind impulse to watch over our body," as James wrote in 1890, an "equally instinctive impulse drives us to collect property."[43] As James insisted, "between what a man calls *me* and what he simply calls *mine* is difficult to draw."[44] Du Bois denaturalizes what James treats as impulse and racializes what James universalizes. But both agreed that property's absorption into identity was a foundational problem for the study of modern life, even as the methods for studying this relation transitioned from Enlightenment fields of philosophy and political economy to the newer disciplines of sociology and psychology. Whether wielded as a compliment or a critique, an asset or a pathology, the notion of whiteness's privileged relationship to ownership remained alive and well in this period as homeownership came to compete with, and eventually overtake, landownership as the foundational form of property anchoring the American imaginary.

The affective logic of racialized ownership shaped the emerging project of mass homeownership into the twentieth century that was first forwarded by the real estate industry and later embraced by the state. While most studies of residential discrimination focus on the period after the New Deal when the state began to subsidize homeownership for the white masses, I follow historian Paige Glotzer in connecting this story instead to the nineteenth century to bring "the deeper connections between American suburbs, slavery, and colonialism" into view.[45] As the platonic ideal of the propertied subject transitioned from the landowner to the homeowner in the twentieth century, ideas of racial capacity and feeling continued to undergird this formation. Recovering mass homeownership's inheritance of centuries' worth of theories defining whiteness *as* ownership allows us to better limn the stakes of maintaining property's racial pedigree into the twentieth.[46] The racial case for homeownership made in real estate trade publications was articulated and resisted in novels, films, and magazines negotiating and reframing the racial logic of homeownership as increasingly synonymous with citizenship, happiness, and security. At some point in the early twentieth century, as David Freund notes, white Americans stopped talking about residential discrimination in terms of personal feeling—as hatred, discomfort, or capacity—and started talking about it more consistently using the seemingly impersonal rubric of value—framing segregation as the protection of one's financial investment in property rather than as a matter of personal amity. And yet, what is value but the enshrinement of feeling into the collectivity ascribed to the free market? As Keeanga-Yamahtta Taylor puts it, while "people talk about the free market as this racially neutral, color-blind space within which the invisible hand of supply and demand dictates what does and doesn't happen," such descriptions conveniently overlook the fact that "the market is us."[47] "The American housing market," she writes, "was an expression of the prevailing racial consciousness of the society in which it operated."[48] Older racial theories of property capacity did not dissipate but were transformed and absorbed into the financial truisms about blackness's devaluing function that residents, realtors, lenders, and state agencies were quick to accept as fact, no matter how distasteful they claimed to find them.

If racial feeling is the cornerstone of property rights, and property rights are the cornerstone of liberalism, the changing strictures of liberalism at midcentury transformed and, by extension, further codified the racial dimensions of property if in more systemic and depersonalized ways. Of course, many midcentury realtors and landlords still openly described their reticence to lend or sell to blacks using the language of diminished capacity to properly care for property. A survey of white Chicago realtors from 1955 showed that many believed Negro tenants to be noisier, less tidy, and more destructive than white tenants. A common sentiment among these realtors was that the Negro "should develop a sense of concern for property, in particular, other people's property" before "making demands for acceptance."[49] While realtors in the survey insisted that "the Negro homeowner cares for his home as well as or better than the white homeowners," others claimed that "the Negro tenant is not as good as the white."[50] But as this framework of capacity became more and more unwieldy and impolitic at midcentury, it became easier to embrace the consequences of this centuries-held belief—namely the devaluation of black residents and black neighborhoods—as an inherent economic truth attributable to the free market itself. As the author of a 1963 appraisal manual laments, "despite educational and legal efforts to bring about the acceptance of true democratic doctrines," the "mixing of residents with diverse historical backgrounds within a neighborhood has immediate and depressing influences on value."[51] This appraiser presents the free market as an uneducable force to be obeyed, no matter how unjust its mores.

This book uses a broad cultural and bureaucratic archive to trace the transition from the white subject of property feeling—integral to conceptions of both whiteness and property before the twentieth century—to the modern residential subject structured by the racial truisms of the conveniently disembodied and unfeeling free market. As this book argues, the housing market rationalized and institutionalized the much older idea that whites felt most deeply for property in circulation since the Enlightenment. Moreover, the property that blacks did acquire failed to "accrue in value the same way or at the same rate," as Taylor observes. No matter its condition, "property in white hands is valued more than property in black hands."[52] The changing racial alchemy inherent to the property form in the age of mass homeownership, as well as the forms of feeling and perception used to secure its contours, is my focus. Even as older housing stock became modernized and marketed to the masses in the twentieth century, the modern housing market's creation via philosophies about hierarchies of racial feeling persisted even as these ideas were newly packaged as an economic rule rather than a biological fact.

The Residential Sensorium

"There comes a time in the life of every normal man whose lot is cast in a busy city when he longs to get away from the bustle and confusion of the crowd." These words appear in the inaugural 1903 issue of *The Suburbanite: A Monthly Magazine for Those Who Are and Those Who Ought to Be Interested in Suburban Homes*, published by the Passenger Department of the Central Railroad of New Jersey.[53] Targeting "insular" New Yorkers who snidely wondered "Can any good come of Jersey," *The Suburbanite* supplied a steady font of affirmative answers.[54] While the magazine promoted New Jersey's specific appeal, its insistence that the "normal man" longed to live residentially, protected from commercial, business, and industrial districts, was finding broad application across expanding urban and suburban residential areas alike.

Before the twentieth century, where you worked largely determined where you lived. If you worked on the land, you typically lived on or near to that land. And before the age of cars and commuter rail, workers and managers alike tended to live close to where they worked, shopped, and played.[55] The idea of the residential as a distinct spatial typology and by, extension, a way of life available to the masses became increasingly codified in law, custom, and economy in the early twentieth century. As urban migrations drew more people off the land and into cities where they generally worked outside of the home, zoning ordinances emerged in almost every metropolitan area to formally disaggregate living space from working space. Lest we naturalize zoning's uptake, scholars have noted the distinctiveness of Americans' embrace of land-use regulations compared to other nations. Enthusiasm for zoning in the U.S. is even more puzzling given its interference with the nation's other great obsession—individual property rights. Ernst Freund, an early scholar of municipal zoning, was one of the first to mark the "peculiarly American" passion for land-use regulations in 1926. Claiming Europeans were far more comfortable inhabiting multi-use neighborhoods—"people do not mind a little store around the corner a bit"—he notes that Americans, by contrast, had assumed the "extraordinary sensitiveness of property to its surroundings" to the point that zoning now formed part of the "national temperament."[56]

This new "temperament" for zoning quickly revolutionized American residential life. The first comprehensive zoning proposals appeared in the U.S. in 1905; by 1935, most American cities and suburbs were fully zoned.[57] Before municipal zoning, Americans largely relied on covenants to regulate both usage and future occupation. *Invasion* was a commonly deployed term to describe the advance of both unwanted industry and undesirable people within residential space. As William Dean Howells observed of "householders" fearful of the "calamitous" Irish in enclaves outside of Boston in 1871, the "encroachment of the Celtic army" makes "values tremble throughout that neighborhood." "Where the Celt, sets his foot," the Yankee "rarely, if ever returns."[58] Private covenants combatted "encroachments" of all kinds by restricting who a property could be sold to as well as its future uses. Building upon this tradition of covenants, municipal zoning worked to turn this patchwork of individual exclusions into district-wide laws. In addition to regulations around use, cities like Baltimore, Louisville, Richmond, and St. Louis passed ordinances in the early twentieth century sanctioning residential segregation by race. When the Supreme Court overruled racial zoning laws as unconstitutional in 1917 for overly constricting individual property rights, racial covenants became the next-best mechanism for maintaining segregation until they, too, were overturned in 1948.

Most residential municipalities in the U.S. favored the construction of single-family homes and implemented zoning laws to privilege this typology. Responding to the densely packed tenements appearing in late-nineteenth-century cities, housing reformers advocated for single-family homes in zoned residential districts as a matter of public health. Dense living spaces not only incubated physical illness, their arguments went, but also moral disease, as tenements and boardinghouses stood accused of exposing child occupants to sex and crime and facilitating the overall degeneration of the family unit. Arguments against residential density were also couched in racial terms. Paige Glotzer has charted how developers in Baltimore, for instance, used the prominence of typhoid outbreaks in black neighborhoods to promote residential segregation as a matter of public health.[59] The rise of zoning went hand in hand with the rise of mass homeownership, as zoning helped enshrine the owned single-family home as the most desirable and buildable form of residential architecture. As realtors began to craft the moral and financial argument for homeownership in the early twentieth century—an effort designed to reverse the steady decline of the U.S. homeownership rate since the 1890s, detailed in greater length in Chapter 1—zoning helped secure the financial value of the single-family home. Assuring homeowners that a meat-packaging plant wouldn't pop up next door—or an apartment complex, which owners increasingly feared as a vehicle bringing in undesirable new residents—zoning appealed to the increasing number of Americans staking their financial futures on the value of their homes.

While zoning covered a whole host of nuisance uses, the failure of district-wide racial segregation ordinances to pass legal muster drove realtors, lenders, and residents to hone other procedural and perceptual strategies to maintain—and profit from—segregation, including covenants, redlining, contract-buying, and steering. But while a pig farm or a factory could be demarcated as a nuisance with relative ease, reading and adjudicating races on a spectrum of desirability at the turn of the century proved a more complicated matter. How does one determine which races were "inharmonious" within certain neighborhoods, to quote the Federal Housing Administration's early underwriting manual, and which could blend into the preexisting racial symphony? Which assemblages of bodies could be assimilated into which racial and social units and which combinations translated into discordant drags on value? As scholars including Kenneth Jackson, Nell Painter, David Roediger, Matthew Frye Jacobson, Karen Brodkin, Dianne Harris, George Lipsitz, Eric Avila, and David Freund have described, mass homeownership broadened the category of whiteness in the twentieth century by recalibrating the measurement of the racially "harmonious" to more firmly include those once located on the bubble of whiteness.[60] Eastern Europeans, Italians, the Irish, and, in some cases, Jews, who once resided on the fringes of whiteness, became more decisively folded into this category in the twentieth century as it expanded to accommodate those willing and able to invest in homes requiring acts of racial maintenance. For instance, take the ranking of sixteen "racial and national groups" by their influence on land values included in Homer Hoyt's influential 1933 monograph, *One Hundred Years of Land Values in Chicago*.[61] Deemed "most favorable" to land values were the English, Germans, Scots, the Irish, and Scandinavians—ethnicities compatible with Nordic definitions of whiteness favored by white supremacists like Madison Grant and Lothrop

Stoddard—followed by a cluster of Eastern European nationalities and "Russian Jews of the lower class" located in the middle.[62] Ranked last as "those exerting the most detrimental effect" were South Italians, Negroes, and Mexicans. Hoyt's labeling of these groups as both "racial and national" in nature suggests his lack of concern about the distinction between race and nationality given its irrelevance for the purposes of valuation. Home values depended on appearances rather than truth, the perception of something's worth now and into the future over scientific, empirical, or ontological claims about the nature of difference. Whether the distinction between a Czech and a Serb was racial or ethnic in nature mattered far less than how the most valued group of residents ranked at the top of the list would read the bodies and behaviors of those ranked below them.

Because home values largely depended on the perceptual norms of white buyers whose desire to own was most encouraged and eventually subsidized by the public-private partnership managing the housing market, mechanisms of valuation altered the forms of racial measurement and definition deployed within the nation more broadly. Take the early-twentieth-century prominence of the one-drop rule as a racial measure based on the premise that any percentage of black blood rendered one legally and socially black. Within this formulation, beholders of the body approached its surfaces as faulty barometers of race; fair eyes and light skin that could allow someone to racially pass were not to be trusted given their potential to mask lineages undetectable through the external body itself. But the one-drop rule's skeptical approach to appearances was incompatible with the appearance-embracing modality of home valuation. Mass homeownership incentivized a mode of racial accounting that relied on exterior perception as a good-enough index of value. Fiction proves instructive in this regard. In 1925's *The Great Gatsby*, homeownership could not yet make Jay Gatsby appear fully white in the eyes of his Anglo-American neighbors; the racial taint of his origins as the non-Anglo James Gatz ultimately overrides the competing claim to ancestry announced by his castle-like manor. But by the 1950s, the fictional suburban banlieue of Shady Hill imagined by writer John Cheever hosted an assortment of Gatsby-esque residents whose pasts—and lineages—remain strategically uninterrogated as long as they look and act the part of white homeowners. As we move into the midcentury, neighbors did not actively hunt for undisclosed ancestors hiding within in a resident's bloodline; performing whiteness was good enough, even as both the appearance and performance of whiteness was itself being altered by mass homeownership.

The midcentury homogenization of whiteness, moreover, allowed neighbors, lenders, and appraisers to assess more quickly those deemed to fall short of it. As one Chicago realtor described of white home seekers in 1955, just the sight of "some colored" while driving through led them to "decide they didn't want to live in that neighborhood."[63] No conversation, interview, or interrogation was necessary; one didn't even have to stop the car. All the evidence one needed to assess the value of a neighborhood could be gathered in motion through the windshield. Hoyt's ranked list of sixteen became increasingly simplified by the midcentury as mass homeownership assimilated many of these once-distinctive groups into whiteness and inflated the peril associated with those who could not visually pass. Blockbusters would, in turn, learn to manipulate this glimpse-driven form of residential observation, sending identifiably black plants into white neighborhoods to scare homeowners into selling cheap. The residential sensorium was ripe for performances preying on its surface sensitivities.

By midcentury, if someone appeared white and was willing to commit to preserving white occupancy, then with only a small down payment, whiteness and homeownership could be theirs. For instance, while the mass dispossession of the "Okies" after the Dust Bowl placed their whiteness into question in the 1930s, as I describe in Chapter 3, mass homeownership became key to their reincorporation into whiteness in the 1950s. Social definitions of whiteness trumped legal definitions in the mass residential areas emerging in the postwar U.S. Almost everyone who moved to these neighborhoods was from somewhere else, their ancestry unspecified and unverified as they journeyed along the path to homeownership paved by federal subsidies. In this way, as I focus on in Chapter 5, the postwar suburban stories of John Cheever come to resemble stories of racial passing from decades prior given their shared interest in buried lineages and convenient forgettings. As the owned home became the most prized wage of whiteness at midcentury, the measure of whiteness adjusted to better suit its recent expansions as well as to more sharply police those who remained excluded from this category and its benefits.

As homeownership began to rival—and ultimately supersede—landownership as the American ideal, the residential emerged not just as a space but as a subjectivity. Enter once more *The Suburbanite*. Building from

William Dean Howells's diagnoses of the sensitivities of "householders" and anticipating Ernst Freund's assessments of these sensitivities as "peculiarly American," the magazine focused on how residential spaces could not only ease the nerves and pocketbooks of urban Americans but could remake their very habits of occupying and sensing. Its interest in limning the residential sensorium recurs across its early editions. An issue from 1905, for instance, quotes at length from an interview with "distinguished resident of New Jersey," inventor Thomas A. Edison, on "city life contrasted with suburban."[64] Edison derided urban living, insisting that "our senses are too acute for the life of the city." Claiming to be "thankful for my deafness" whenever forced to venture downtown, Edison longed for his vision to be similarly dulled: "if the eyesight would be blunted a little so that we would not have so many useless impressions recorded in the brain it would be well." Edison's comments ostensibly yoke the movie camera and residential living as modern technics for mediating the devastation wrought upon the senses in the industrial age. The movie camera and the residential alike modulate the overwhelming number of "useless impressions" threatening to overload the brain in urban space.

Edison's insistence on the suburb's perceptual superiority echoes the sentiments of another *Suburbanite* article, "The Camera in the Suburbs," published a month prior. As this article claims, one needn't trek to the Rockies or the Adirondacks to find scenery worth filming, for even "the exceeding small fry of the suburbs make pictures that are curious, and even valuable, as photographs of Nature in the outdoor magazines show."[65] The lower density and open air in the suburbs, this writer continues, allowed for a different relationship to technology and perception to emerge. "Photography, instead of the diversion or excitement of an occasional trip, as in the city, soon becomes a habit in the suburbs, or even a necessity."[66] The article concludes by pointing to the talent featured in the magazine's own pages as its greatest proof. "*The Suburbanite* has, from its first issue, been illustrated with the productions of amateur photographers in the suburbs" depicting "homes and home life, architecture and decoration, sylvan retreats and picturesque roads, cottages and palaces, repose and action, always clearly, artistically, and in a way to expound the charm, completeness and sanity of suburban living."[67]

What is not often featured in the amateur photographs illustrating the first few issues of *The Suburbanite* are pictures of people. Bucolic images of

FIGURE 1. Image from *The Suburbanite*, May 1903.

Afoot Through Lane and Field

By HENRY A. HOWARD

WITH the advance of spring, and the quickening of the pulse of Nature, comes the inclination to escape far from the madding crowd. The woodland path, the road by the river, and the broad expanse of field, all hold out beckoning hands. Who is there with soul so dulled but at this season of the year has experienced and welcomed this mysterious invitation of Nature? Even the President of the United States throws off the cares of state for a few days in order to commune with growing things and seek relaxation afield.

With different people the impulse takes different forms. The horse owner and the automobilist have the most luxurious method of outdoor exercise. The amateur photographer essays forth with his camera, the hunter with his gun and dog, while the humble German mechanic transports his entire family, from the in-

A SHADY ROAD.

erland. Whatever may be one's station in life, he is benefited physically and mentally by an aimless ramble through quiet roads and fields. Dame Nature has a certain restful and soothing influence which rejuvenates the tired business man. The physical benefit of the simple exercise of walking is too little appreciated in this country. The Englishman is a born cross-country walker, and he shows the results in his upright carriage and ruddy complexion. Americans may well learn a lesson from this hobby of the English. Within a short radius of New York are hundreds of inviting spots for a ramble. It is a good plan to start out with no definite object in view, and walk at a leisurely gait over whatever route appeals most. Then, when fatigue asserts itself, board a trolley car and ride home. To obtain the proper benefit from

Source: Central Railroad of New Jersey, *The Suburbanite: A Monthly Magazine for Those Who Are and Those Who Ought to Be Interested in Suburban Homes* 1, no. 2 (May 1903): 4.

glens, paths, lakes, and streams proliferate within the magazine, as do stately images of houses and tidy tree-lined streets. More occasionally punctuating this publication are images of hard-to-make-out figures on beaches, in lush gardens, golfing, or rowing canoes. Such images market the residential as a place where dwellers do not have to expend much energy making out people or faces; there are no masses of strangers to negotiate, only scenic milieus containing one or two lone users immersed within pastoral surroundings. By subordinating images of sociality to those of manors and meadows, *The Suburbanite* frames the residential as a space where strenuous acts of social adjudication and racial delineation are not necessary. Gone are both the "useless impressions recorded in the brain" that Edison described and the stress of needing to sift through them to ascertain the useful impressions from the useless ones emanating from the continual rush of bodies in growing urban spaces. The magazine frames the residential as a place that minimizes sensory input and thus frees up the perceptual apparati for less taxing pursuits. Whereas density, urban migration, and immigration scrambled the racial sensorium within crowded urban centers, as I chart in my first book, *The Black Skyscraper: Architecture and the Perception of Race*, the residential sensorium is framed here as a contrasting site of relief where one's senses would not be perpetually stressed by growing vertical vantage points, dense microecologies where smells and dialects confusingly intermingle, and the work of reading bodies, faces, and comportments to determine who one is encountering on the train, at the market, or as one of thousands of neighbors.[68] While *The Suburbanite*'s 1905 depictions of residential living's diminished perceptual demands vis-à-vis racial difference preceded later surges to these areas facilitated by mass homeownership—eventually bringing in more Gatsbys in the 1920s and more Gatzes after the New Deal—such a vision would continue to anchor representations of its most idyllic state. Lending institutions and realtors, moreover, would come to shoulder even more of the residential labor of racial discernment in the midcentury, assessing home seekers in offices and through loan applications before their presence on the block had the opportunity to disturb its perceptual milieu.

While few photographs of people appear in *The Suburbanite*, we do find brief racial portraits in its articles suggesting which kinds of people were most temperamentally fit for residential living while underscoring the importance of racial maintenance to the ongoing security of these spaces. For instance, in the magazine's inaugural issue heralding the pleasures of suburban driving, the article's author casually asks, "what more makes the blood of the Anglo-Saxon tingle than to get out on a beautiful day in June with a magnificent motor car beneath him."⁶⁹ This rhetorical question is left to hang, rhyming with nineteenth-century depictions of frontier settlement now giving way to leisurely drives. Other articles underscore the urgent stakes of suburbanization for the survival of Anglo-Saxon "blood." The author of "The Apartment House and Race Suicide" warns against apartment living's "deterrent influence on the multiplication of the species" as well as on how such dense occupation may lead to the "conversion of the race to methods of living that are not consonant with the teachings of the fathers."⁷⁰ Washington Irving and the habits of the Dutch burghers who settled New York are invoked by the author to accentuate "that atmosphere of domesticity, that desire for a home which has been the foundation on which the nation was built."⁷¹ Apartment living threatens to erode this racial-cultural foundation, this author warns, by increasing "the number of derelicts on the sea of life," leading to "more bachelors and more old maids," more working women, and more individuals unmoored at large from family.⁷² The future of white reproduction, the author warns, rests on residential communities steering its occupants toward traditional family structures. As another article in *The Suburbanite* more bluntly claims, "there is no 'race suicide' in the suburbs."⁷³

Historians and social scientists continue to reveal the extent to which racial policies and theories shaped almost every aspect of residential life in the twentieth century, from home construction and suburban developments to the subsidies offered by the state to white homeowners in the form of federally backed mortgage insurance. But these histories focused on policies and procedures have not fully captured how the project of mass homeownership in discrete residential spaces fundamentally altered how Americans perceived, full stop, but especially in relation to race. In endeavoring to tell this perceptual story, I build from David Freund's landmark work, *Colored Property: State Policy & White Racial Politics in Suburban America*, attending to "how white racial thinking itself changed during the years that the United States became a predominately suburban and home-owning nation."⁷⁴ But while Freund considers the evolution of theories of *racism* propelling segregation between 1920 and 1960, I find myself more interested in the changes in *racial phenomenology*—how people sensed, felt, and perceived both race and racism—but also *racial hermeneutics*—the practice of turning perceived racial evidence into knowledge and value. Becoming residential was also a form of racialization. And as is always true of processes of racialization, determining what counts as a race, who counts as which race, what measures of race prove most useful in which contexts, and the apertures of racial feeling are always more erratic processes than we often acknowledge, even when they reproduce familiar structures of racism.

What follows is not a history of homeownership or the residential per se, but rather a history of the feelings, perceptions, and values attached to residential living conditioned by the financial importance of race to mass homeownership's viability and uptake. I began writing this book with the hazard that while the social sciences have largely told the story of residential discrimination, a humanistic approach to this subject committed to looking closely at acts of looking and reading might shake loose a different dimension of this system and its production. In this effort, I'm indebted to Dianne Harris's approach in *Little White Houses: How the Postwar Home Constructed Race in America*, attending to "the role played by houses and material and visual culture attending to houses in the production of racial thinking."[75] But I also realized early on that telling this story would require deprioritizing the built environment in order to better see the property relations responsible for its outlay. Unlike my previous focus on the built environment's *material* effects on racial perception in *The Black Skyscraper*, I concentrate more persistently here on how the perceptual habits of property—never just a matter of its material manifestation as buildings and infrastructure but, as legal scholars insist, something that must also be understood in terms of rights, claims, and desires—continued to remake race into the age of mass homeownership as well as the utility of racial imaginaries in conceiving of other ways of dwelling. The work of legal scholars Cheryl Harris and Carol Rose, who underscore the historical import of property logics across periods while also considering the malleability of these logics as shaped by the expressiveness of embodiment and the habits and inventions of perception, have also shaped my approach. If race is "the story of visual habits, sightlines that allow the national popular to prescribe common sight," to cite Matthew Guterl, and "in property, vision and visual metaphor are essential modes of persuasion in the ways that human beings think they can and should interact with their environment" as Carol

Rose observes, I chart the ways property helps determine which racial sight lines advance and which recede in any given moment as well as the extent to which property's power to persuade relies upon its imbrication with racial sight.[76]

In what follows, I focus on residential archives where the affective and perceptual life of race appears as a problem or focal point. Cultural objects do a lot of this work, but so do real estate archives and appraisal textbooks figuring out how to "sell" the story of homeownership and teach its perceptual norms and standards of measurement. This book charts how the first generation of professional realtors' arguments used Enlightenment racial philosophy and eugenics to construct arguments for mass homeownership, follows descriptions of rent party acolytes in Northern cities devising other residential schemas, attends to the structures of repair enabling Americans across the color line to continue their love affair with property following the devastations of the Great Depression, and studies the post–New Deal transformations in appraisal, aesthetics, and observation appearing in real estate manuals, Broadway plays, *New Yorker* stories, and realist novels alike. Even when white writers described mass homeownership in self-pitying terms of "spiritual homelessness," to cite Catherine Jurca's pathbreaking work—overwriting the material dispossessions and housing precarity besetting those that ownership excluded—these bad feelings twistedly became one of "the hallmark[s] of the suburb's luxury and privilege," newly tacked on to ownership's affective profile.[77] Suburban disgruntlement failed to counteract property's financial incentives as homeownership rates continued to rise through the midcentury. This sourness was instead assimilated into homeownership's normal emotional register, updating the long-standing affective complex associated with the white man's burden. From this broad archive of feeling and description, we get a picture of the emergent residential sensorium as it both relied on and changed the measure and meaning of race.

Whiteness as Amenity, Blackness as Illiquidity

As the U.S. became a nation of segregated homeowners in the twentieth century, it also became a nation of debtors. Before the standardization of the thirty-year mortgage initiated by the New Deal, home financing was out of reach for most. In the late nineteenth century, buying a home generally required much larger down payments of up to 50 percent and shorter mortgage terms averaging five to ten years at variable rates, making default and second mortgages more common. After the ravages of the Great Depression, the state used mortgage insurance to subsidize fixed-rate, self-amortizing, long-term mortgages to stabilize the housing market. Decreasing both the initial down payment and subsequent monthly payments at set interest rates enabled more Americans than ever before to purchase their homes. For most, the home would become the largest purchase they would ever make. By midcentury, Americans were assuming an amount of house debt that would have been both financially unfeasible and morally unconscionable a half century prior.

Given the enormity of this purchase, choosing a neighborhood to buy in was not just a matter of preference or lifestyle but an act of financial speculation with high economic stakes As the mortgage evolved to become a greater part of American life for many Americans, so, too, did residential segregation. In the early nineteenth century, before the rise of mass homeownership, mixed-race neighborhoods were far more common. Between 1890 and the beginning of World War I, although racial and ethnic groups tended to concentrate in certain parts of the city, these areas were rarely exclusively segregated. Many urban blacks lived in concentrated neighborhoods, but others lived in immigrant districts and white neighborhoods. As one scholar describes of residential occupancy in the late nineteenth century, "The typical black in almost any Northern city had mostly white neighbors."[78] White occupants in this period tended to deem the nearby residential concentration of any population who was not firmly white—be they black, immigrant, or ethnic—as equally undesirable. But as the Great Migration began in earnest in the late 1910s—the same years when the number of homeowners in the U.S. increased for the first time in decades—black occupation was newly framed in urban centers as the foremost threat to home values that must be contained at all costs. As one scholar described this ideological shift, "the very consciousness of whites in the North seemed to change during the few years from 1917 to 1920 from an 'ethnic' view of urban diversity to one more centered on race" in which black occupancy became singularly feared. By 1920, widespread panic about black encroachment had taken hold in every Northern metropolitan area.[79]

Given the outsize role a neighborhood's racial makeup was alleged to play in the valuation of individual homes, realtors and lenders steadily instilled in homebuyers the idea that residential integration posed an existential threat to their financial stability. Though studies since the early twentieth century have challenged the idea that homes in integrated neighborhoods substantially lose value, black devaluation nonetheless became real estate gospel by the 1920s. Residents across the color line who sought to buy and invest in mixed-race or non-white neighborhoods were deterred by the difficulty of obtaining fair loans for mortgages in these "high risk" areas. The term *white flight* as a descriptor of midcentury residential movement flattens this story at best and misleads at worst; in addition to ensconcing whiteness as something static that then moved—obscuring how whiteness itself was being "renegotiated through residential movement," to cite historian Eric Avila—white flight also paints such movement as a mass act of panic-stricken choice alone.[80] The rhetoric of flight obscures the role that economic and state institutions played in subsidizing segregation by devaluing integrated neighborhoods.[81] Mass homeownership incentivized racism, couching residential segregation as an economic necessity for homeowners seeking to protect their investments. Whereas white ownership at the turn of the twentieth century was framed in eugenic and civilizational terms as a matter of survival, by midcentury the rationale for homeownership was more squarely economic but no less racialized as the benefits to be reaped from ownership were alleged to depend upon the preservation of the neighborhood as a racial unit. Home value, in other words, became a matter of linked racial fate; as the neighborhood went, so did the value of the home.

The linking of home value to neighborhood standing remade how people measured and perceived both race and neighborhoods given their growing correlation. To understand how racialization of the neighborhood unit changed how people saw and felt both race and space, I build from Cheryl Harris's transformational intervention in "Whiteness as Property." One of the central ways that whiteness comes to function as property, Harris outlays, is through their shared "conceptual nucleus" in the right to exclude.[82] Just as property is best understood not as things possessed but as a bundle of rights granting possessors the "absolute right to exclude," whiteness, too, is best conceptualized as a set of rights and assets rather than as a set of definable features or attributes. Since whiteness lacks an "inherent unifying characteristic," as Harris writes, as with property, the law has historically focused not on its definition but on protecting the rights that whiteness bestowed upon its claimants.[83] Further like property, one of whiteness's most powerful attributes is the right of its claimants to deny others its possession and privileges. As Harris writes, "the possessors of whiteness were granted the legal right to exclude others from the privileges inhering in whiteness," rendering it "an exclusive club whose membership was closely and grudgingly guarded."[84] As a legal scholar, Harris pays specific attention to the role the courts have historically played in "enforcing this right to exclude—determining who was or was not white enough to enjoy the privileges accompanying whiteness." "In that sense," Harris notes, "the courts protected whiteness as any other form of property."[85]

In the age of mass homeownership, however, protecting whiteness required not just excluding others from its legal categorization; it also required an increasing commitment to protecting its spatial concentration. Whiteness is not only tied to the right to exclude others from its categorization; it also entails the right to strategically expand who can claim whiteness when it is advantageous to do so. Membership in this club remained "closely and grudgingly guarded" but less exclusive as the twentieth century wore on. The broadening of whiteness through the assimilative mechanism of homeownership—helping to more fully incorporate those deemed on its boundaries only decades prior—proved strategic to maintaining whiteness and its attendant assets into the midcentury while more starkly guarding against its others. Those pulled more comfortably within the ranks of whiteness through homeownership had a new economic incentive to hold the racial line in the neighborhoods to which they moved, ensuring they would get the most out of their newly secured racial benefits. This social expansion of whiteness intensified its spatialization, devaluing blood and national origin as racial measures while inflating appearance and proximity as its most urgent battlegrounds.[86]

Within this changing measure of race driven by the linked fate of the neighborhood as a spatial and, increasingly, racial unit, whiteness expanded from being conceived of as a property to be protected, as Harris defines it, to adopting the characteristics of an *amenity*. The understanding of an amenity as a desirable and advantageous feature of a location enhancing a place's value came of age in the twentieth century. A feature ascribed as readily to trains and hotels as to neighborhoods, an amenity is something deemed to have near-universal value. Amenities are things assumed to appeal to the common user, from air-conditioning and increased leg space to park districts and good school systems. While the style of a home might be a matter of taste or personal preference, the desirable aspects of a neighborhood are treated as amenities any occupant is likely to want, helping enshrine the value of all the homes in its proximity. An amenity may be valuable because it is aesthetically pleasing, for the conveniences it offers, or for its effects on health and well-being. As largely timeless assets deemed to be generally desirable by most, the presence of amenities in a neighborhood raises the value of all adjacent homes.

In this way, whiteness became viewed not just as an attribute of certain occupants but as an amenity adhering within the neighborhood unit itself, securing its valuation. Lenders, insurers, realtors, policy makers, and occupants had a financial incentive to maintain this amenity through segregation. As the American Institute of Real Estate Appraisers insisted in 1951, homogeneity was integral to defining the neighborhood unit itself. In their estimation, a neighborhood was "a more or less unified area with somewhat definite boundaries and a fairly homogeneous population in which the inhabitants have a more than casual community of interests."[87] Since homogeneity proves constitutive of the neighborhood unit itself, "the character of one property affects the character of all others as though they were all cogs in a machine."[88] As whiteness became the most crucial amenity a neighborhood could offer, the upkeep of that amenity was seen as critical to the value of every home within in it. In this way, homeownership encouraged an investment in whiteness at the scale of the neighborhood.[89]

In the age of mass homeownership, the unit of the neighborhood came to rival that of the family in economic and social importance.[90] While a combination of legal rulings, executive orders, and legislative acts would strip away many of the legal protections for race-based residential exclusion across the twentieth century—between 1917 and 1968, racial zoning, covenants, discrimination in federally subsidized mortgages and housing, and eventually residential discrimination writ large would become illegal—the economic understanding of whiteness as a residential amenity and of the neighborhood unit as a racial unit would prove thornier to undo through state measures alone. As Paige Glotzer writes, "neither the liberal-driven fair-housing and antidiscrimination laws of the 1960s or conservative attempts to shrink the federal housing apparatus changed a core tenet of the American housing market: property value was linked to race."[91] Americans who for much of the twentieth century had invested the wages of whiteness into their homes learned to see, inhabit, and protect this investment in residential terms.

It is this story of how homeownership changed how Americans not only saw race but became beholden to its investment that I seek to unfurl. As whiteness transitioned from providing a "wage," to cite Du Bois, to becoming the source of home equity, or what Elaine Lewinnek calls "the mortgages of whiteness"—codifying the racial wealth gap for generations—how people felt about, described, and saw race also changed.[92] Literature proves to be a useful archive for studying these shifting norms of the racial sensorium since it is where racial feeling and perception find both direct and oblique forms of description and articulation. But we also see these shifts in narrative forms beyond the literary—in manuals where appraisers describe the imperative of racial measurement if not its techniques, in real estate trade journals where cases for racial ownership were tested and honed, and in theories of urban planning where the norms of racial sight shaped even the most progressive calls for residential integration. Residential description emerges as a critical subgenre of twentieth-century writing across literary, journalistic, and bureaucratic forms. From the forms appraisers filled out that were then used to create security maps to the decisions of writers like Gwendolyn Brooks, Ralph Ellison, John Steinbeck, and Thomas Pynchon to step away from fiction at moments in the midcentury to write essays about how to see and read neighborhoods, residential description was being produced and responded to across generic and formal divides. This outflow of residential description, I argue, was driven in part by the efforts of bureaucrats, appraisers, and writers alike to give form to the changes to racial perception occasioned by mass homeownership. We find writers weighing the utility of looking closely at residential space given the centrality of observation to segregation's maintenance.

Within this broad archive of twentieth-century residential description, we find writers grappling with whiteness's categorical expansion but also the hardening of blackness as an anti-residential force. As whiteness expanded in the twentieth century via homeownership, blackness became further differentiated and exceptionalized as the foremost threat to residential value. Whereas blacks were one of a host of undesirable racial others residentially feared by whites in the late nineteenth century—recall Howells on the Irish— the idea of black presence as absolutely devaluing and wholly unassimilable becoming a truism by the 1920s. Unlike labor markets in the early and mid-twentieth century that needed black workers to exploit and therefore necessitated their incorporation if in subordinated positions, the mass housing market became increasingly organized by total black exclusion from white residential districts. Although mixed-race residential districts were common in metropolitan areas in the late nineteenth century, housing policy and financing helped to dismantle such spaces as existential threats to economic value. Investing in either black neighborhoods or black residents became framed as a losing financial bet, while the profits to be made from segregation skyrocketed. Between 1920 and 1950, an astonishing amount of wealth was extracted from black residents unable to secure loans to either improve their homes or move to others, and the loans they received were often secured at exorbitant interest rates. Black renters were also exploited, often paying close to double what their white counterparts paid to rent in Northern cities, while contract-buying schemes dispossessed thousands of black families with no other road to ownership.

If whiteness was an amenity, blackness became explicitly associated with *illiquidity*. An illiquid asset cannot be moved or exchanged in the immediate future without a major loss of value. As one study of real estate from 1955 lays it out, "People fear the lack of liquidity of colored property."[93] Black occupancy was assumed to foster residential illiquidity wherever it went; once black residency was established and detected within a white neighborhood or too close to its borders, it was presumed that all the homes within its orbit would become difficult to sell without a major loss of value (even as many blacks ended up buying these quickly abandoned homes at exorbitant markups). "Black housing was valued differently from white housing," as Keeanga-Yamahtta Taylor observes, "thus stripping its supposed asset-like quality away."[94] Because of the alleged illiquidity of blackness, homeownership failed to fundamentally work the same for black holders as it did for white ones. By midcentury, the rationale for housing discrimination had transitioned from earlier theories about black incapacity for property to ones ensconcing white flight as an economic truism that came to function as a self-fulfilling prophecy. Black devaluation was modeled as a toxicity, assumed to contaminate the values of all the homes proximate to black occupancy. Within this logic, the residential quarantine of blacks became all the more urgent. This was not a matter of minimizing blackness in white residential settings or achieving black subordination therein; the priority was to secure its absolute elimination and exclusion from white blocks.[95]

Of course, Americans who did not fit into either the expanding category of whiteness or into blackness faced housing struggles of their own. As Wendy Cheng marks in *The Changs Next Door to the Diazes: Remapping Space in Suburban California*, "components of Asian and Latina/o racialization in the United States and their differential relationships to whiteness and property have been mutually constitutive."[96] Cheng calls for more attention to regional racial formations, allowing us to see the fullness of these "complex geographies of race." I take up Cheng's invitation when writing about California in Chapter 3, for instance, tracing how theories of racialized property incapacity that were mobilized against Asian, Latinx, and Native American populations were also applied to Okie migrants before their whiteness was resecured through residential property. As I argued in *The Black Skyscraper*, the measure and definition of race shifts depending on the historic, spatial, legal, and economic contexts occasioning its materialization. But even as racial perception undergoes continual readjustments, these shifts take place along a spectrum of racial difference framed by blackness and whiteness as opposing poles even as their measure may change. The housing market, moreover, proved central to reinforcing the extremity of this polarity due to the importance of visible racial difference to neighborhood assessment reasserting the importance of race's eased apprehension and the hardening of black illiquidity as a financial truism. Property shapes all processes of racialization, even as homeownership most centrally oriented itself around an understanding of whiteness as an amenity and blackness as an illiquidity.

I rehearse this shift here since the chapters that follow trace the accumulation of this shifting racial logic and its impacts as certain definitions of race and its measure fall in and out of favor according to the needs of the residential unit. We see this in early novels like *The Great Gatsby* and *Babbitt* grappling with the nascent power of the home to index race and its effects on the mechanics of racial perception, as well as in Great Depression novels like *The Grapes of Wrath* and *Gone with the Wind* querying how the decade's mass dispossessions affected the security of whiteness. The perceived illiquidity of blackness on the residential scene, moreover, shaped how black writers viewed property's prospects as a vehicle for prosperity or rights. In the face of property's continual disappointments for blacks failing to reap the same benefits as white property holders, black writers explored the affective stranglehold that property continued to have on black life and the limits of and possibilities for learning to let go of this bad object. While I recapitulate the mainstream arguments being forward by realtors and the state and making inroads in the public sphere at times in the book, at others I chart creative efforts to imagine housing untethered from homeownership and advancement defined in terms other than property.

The Homeowners of Fiction

In Henry James's 1908 description of the million-windowed "house of fiction," he wields the physical house as a model for the creative process. With this metaphor, James conjures a collective location from which writers perceive a shared social while accounting for the differences that also inevitably differentiate their output.[97] From within the metaphorical house of fiction, residents peer out from its distinctly shaped and varyingly spaced windows to behold the "scene" unfolding outside.[98] The style and shape of each window affects what and how each beholder sees, with "one seeing more where the other sees less, one seeing black where the other sees white, one seeing big where the other sees small, one seeing coarse where the other sees fine."[99] But despite their role in shaping perception, as James notes, these windows are "nothing without the posted presence of the watcher—without, in other words, the consciousness of the artist." "Tell me what the artist is," James concludes, "and I will tell you of what he has BEEN conscious."[100] The house of fiction helps James establish the liberty and limits guiding the writing process; or, as he puts it, the writer's "boundless freedom and his 'moral' reference."[101]

Already somewhat strained as a metaphor for literary production, the house of fiction makes for an even more tortured property relation.[102] Asking whether residents of the house of fiction rent their rooms or collectively own it is a likely daffy question given its seeming irrelevance to the metaphor's main commitment to demonstrating that those who share an origin point—be it a home, a neighborhood, a race, or a nation—will nonetheless represent the world differently. But when we consider the alleged thin line between being and having that has been crucial to theories of subjectivity since the Enlightenment, the house of fiction seems to reference not just a shared origin but a form of propertied personhood through which the universal—aka white—writer learns to perceive the rest of the world. Following Henry's brother, William, who in 1890 wrote that "between what a man calls me and what he simply calls mine is difficult to draw," we might posit a slightly modified version of Henry James's already-borrowed locution: tell me what the artist is, and I will tell you of what he has owned.

Whereas Anna Kornbluh uses James's famous formulation to ask, "what does realism build," I'm interested in how realism *owns* but also how writing more broadly facilitates ownership as an orientation.[103] In *The Black Skyscraper*, I considered James's writerly predilection for domestic spaces over uncontained sites of mass gathering he found challenging to bring into aesthetic form. James's commitment to the home's intimate scale, I argued, derived in part from its capacity to ease the perception of the racial sign as a vehicle for intrigue, secrets, and, by extension, narrative. But whereas the home materially alters how one perceives and from where, becoming a homeowner impacts the stakes of domestic perception as well as one's perceptual priorities. As the U.S. became a nation of homeowners—a transition, in turn, tied to the U.S. becoming a nation of debtors, appraisers, and redlined neighborhoods—what it meant to see, read, and feel changed most intensely in relation to the racial sign and its adjudication. I follow Chad Luck, who, in his rich plumbing of antebellum literature's theorization of the relationship between property and sensation, reclaims the importance of the sensate body to "our understanding and enactment of property practices" as well as the importance of literature as a site where "the persistent role of the body in the acquisition and exchange of property" is actively theorized.[104] Given the historic relationship between phenomenologies of race and property and mass homeownership's encouragement of their ongoing melding, literature remains a key tool for understanding the story of mass homeownership as constructed through racial feelings, drives, and sensations.

I also build upon John David Rhodes's insistence on deprioritizing the city to more fully attend to ownership's effects on the sensorium in excess of urbanity. "The modern is experienced and evoked not in terms of the 'shock' of the urban encounter," Rhodes explains, "but in terms of who owns what and where and how much—which is what the story of the modern is really about, after all."[105] Although one of this book's key interventions is to bring critical modes attentive to perception, affect, and form associated with humanistic disciplines to the archive of housing discrimination, the spatial canons traditionally used to organize literary output have limiting functions of their own that must be overcome. Literary canons of urban realism, cosmopolitan transnationalism, suburban literature of the melodramatic and postmodern varieties, and the residual modernist rural have made it difficult to observe homeownership's broader impact on the entwined histories of perception, race, property, and writing that supersede regional typologies.[106] By focusing instead on the residential—a concept spanning the urban, suburban, and rural that denotes the growing financial and ideological investment in housing across spaces and regions—homeownership's far-reaching influence across these canons can be better limned. The residential first emerged as a concept within bureaucratic discourses of zoning and real estate, but in what follows I seek to recover its function as an experiential category shaping how Americans perceived space, read both bodies and books, assessed value, and felt sovereign in relation to the spaces they called home. Although homeownership's ascension in the twentieth-century U.S. has primarily been charted by the social sciences, the mechanisms, observational modes, and genres both ordering and ordered by this property relation are a constructive part of the history of perception and American aesthetics.

Like its spatial frame, the time frame of this book—focusing on the first three-quarters of the twentieth century—also diverges from established canons of periodization. Beginning with the real estate industry's concerted efforts to construct and value the residential in racial terms, the book ends with the state's most definitive effort to disentangle the residential from the racial—the 1968 Fair Housing Act, which made overt acts of housing discrimination illegal. I end with the Fair Housing Act, however, not to position it as a triumphant close to the age of residential segregation, but because of its failure to function as such, pointing to the limits of legislation to undo the racialized logic of residential markets built upon modes of perception, description, and feeling produced over decades if not centuries. Seeing like a real estate agent at midcentury increasingly entailed seeing like a market and the depersonalization of racial sight. The literature featured in this book grapples with what it meant to see race under such obstructive, evasive, and often conflicting conditions. It also helps us consider the perplexing endurance of residential optimism across the color line given the frequent failures of the owned home to deliver on its financial and civic promises. But this book pays particular attention to the tightening stranglehold of homeownership's promise on the black literary imaginary through the midcentury despite its continual disappointments. Even as the black residential imaginary seemed to adjust to the dispiriting realities of segregation, moments of ownership disenchantment nonetheless flash into view within the literary archive, suggesting what it would take to let go of this dream to fashion new horizons of dwelling.

While literature and aesthetic production more broadly take precedence in parts of the book, its archive also exceeds the literary. Literature played an outsize role, for instance, in repairing Americans' misgivings about homeownership after the dispossessions of the Great Depression, helping re-cauterize white attachments to property. Literature, moreover, did not just represent new definitions and modalities of racial feeling and performance emerging at midcentury; it helped give form to the perceptual and affective norms of residential space for millions of Americans learning to be homeowners—and to inhabit the new cadence of whiteness it entailed—for the first time. Lastly, like most Americans, the lives of writers were deeply entangled with residential space. Not only did writers tend to work from homes they rented, borrowed, or bought, but their writing funded their ongoing relation to property. We find the everyday affective and economic burdens of property shaping the work of John Steinbeck, who sold one house and started building another while penning *The Grapes of Wrath*; Lorraine Hansberry, whose family used the success of *A Raisin in the Sun* to fuel their own property business; and Richard Wright, whose experience of discrimination when home shopping in New England led him to leave the U.S. for good. Recounting writers' own property entanglements allows us to better understand homeownership's effect on literary production.

But other modes of description, reportage, and instruction proved just as vital to understanding how the racial project of mass homeownership altered how race itself was seen, measured, and appraised. Residential literature encompasses literary fiction but also manuals, reportage, bureaucratic forms, professional journals, and maps representing descriptive processes of appraisal and valuation used to assess, maintain, and at times question the intertwined protocols for perceiving and assessing racial difference in residential space. The materials I take up here treat the work of seeing and knowing race on the block as a problem and as work—a matter of scientific, perceptual, historical, or financial deliberation requiring a variety of perceptual strategies at a time when racial categories themselves were being realigned.

Lastly, it is not coincidental that black women feature so prominently across many of this book's chapters. They include educator Nannie Burroughs, who chaired the Committee on Negro Housing for the President's Conference on Home Building and Home Ownership in 1931, as well as the more unruly rent party hosts and enthusiasts desiring to prolong its attendant forms of bodily dispossession and challenges to self-sovereignty. From the practices of residential observation honed by Gwendolyn Brooks in contradistinction to her more recognized planning peer, Jane Jacobs, to the interventions of Lorraine Hansberry and her lesser-known contemporary Kristin Hunter to reimagine the utility and the limits of racial solidarity to instigate new forms of dwelling, women populate the archive of mass homeownership's racial sensorium. Often tasked with upkeeping both white and black domestic space in the twentieth century, black women had perhaps the most complete view of both the privileges and burdens that homeownership could bestow. As Koritha Mitchell writes, black women "routinely recalibrate their conception of homemaking success" in ways that often exceeded ownership, heteronormativity, or the physical bounds of the home itself.[107] In line with Saidiya Hartman's excavation of the "aesthetical and riotous history of colored girls and their experiments with freedom" in *Wayward Lives, Beautiful Experiments*, we might consider homeownership as one more experiment that black women took up with varying results. It is their findings that most consistently anchor what follows.[108]

Chapter Summaries

Part 1 of this book, comprised of its first three chapters, focuses on the initial construction of the racial case for homeownership between 1900 and 1950, before America was a majority home-owning nation. During these decades, the idea that whites were more predisposed than others to own and own well more openly saturated economic and cultural arguments for mass homeownership and the construction of the residential sensorium. But we also find writers and thinkers in this period actively rebutting homeownership's value across the color line through imagining other forms of dwelling and, by extension, sensing and being. The first chapter, "Empire Builders: The Racial Longings of Modern Real Estate," establishes how a shared belief in property as a principally white capacity helped unite the real estate industry as a modern profession and paved the way for the state's eventual uptake of its theories. Focusing on the first two decades of the *National Real Estate Journal*, the house publication of the country's most prominent real estate guild, the National Association of Real Estate Boards, this chapter recovers the foundational function of race within the affective, social, and scientific arguments realtors constructed to insist upon homeownership's role in maintaining American white-settler identity into the residential age. I then turn to two of the era's most iconic novels—Sinclair Lewis's *Babbitt* (1922) and F. Scott Fitzgerald's *The Great Gatsby* (1925)—as they chart the changing racial sensorium produced through homeownership.

The book's second chapter, "Scoring Housing's Modern Jazzy Sound at the Rent Party," turns to the raucous archive of rental sounds and songs to recover black theories of dwelling in excess of ownership emerging from the early-twentieth-century rent party. Peaking in popularity in the 1920s and 1930s, rent parties helped working-class black residents in Northern cities afford the inflated rents in crowded enclaves. Often dark, damp, and noisy places resistant to technological capture, rent parties have left their traces in calling cards, jazz memoirs, sociological sketches, popular plays, and Duke Ellington's inventive portraits of urban utopia. Mining this archive, we find rent party documentarians and their protagonists—most notably black women—approaching housing not as a moral or civic duty but as a necessity around which social relations beyond ownership could emerge. The rent party appears in this chapter as a site where black Americans conceived of an alternative logic of dispossessive placemaking in direct contrast to the racialized arguments for homeownership.

The final chapter of this section, "Making Ownership Feel Good Again: Rewriting the Land Man after the Great Depression," begins by asking how

Americans across the color line came to reconcile with property following the devastating foreclosures of the Depression. While the subsidies of the New Deal provide an economic answer to this question, we must turn to the cultural archives of the 1930s to understand how Americans regained the ability to feel good about property and, by extension, its enduring racialization. I begin with a focus on John Steinbeck's long-standing investment in the idea of the white "land man," defined not by the fact of owning but rather by this figure's undying desire for ownership. In emphasizing a yearning for the land and the capacity for its care as a cornerstone of whiteness, Steinbeck charted a path toward a resolidified form of whiteness held together not by title to the land but by tenderness for it. Steinbeck's exploration of the racialized feeling of the "land man" culminated in his 1939 novel, *The Grapes of Wrath*, foreshadowing the Okies' eventual reincorporation into whiteness via their perceived capacity as homeowners. I conclude by turning from Steinbeck's "land men" to the work of black writers W. E. B. Du Bois and Richard Wright debating in the Depression's aftermath whether it was better to fight for the Negro's right to "land man" status or to cede this construct in favor of adopting other orientations toward dwelling. In revisiting the reanimated interest in the broken promise of forty acres and a mule following the Great Depression and the Great Migration as blacks left the land in droves, Wright and Du Bois highlight the differing roles land might play in antiracist struggle in an increasingly residential America.

The last three chapters of this book, making up Part II, focus on the period between 1950 and 1970, when federal subsidies directed largely toward white homeowners and segregated subdivisions helped turn the housing market into an incredibly effectual discrimination machine. The language of racial capacity buttressing early arguments for mass homeownership receded at midcentury as more neutral-seeming racial logics based on alleged market truisms advanced, supported by bureaucratic systems built to quietly maintain discrimination. These conditions led to a new configuration of whiteness deemphasizing blood for metrics of appearance, performance, and residential investment as well as the systemic disinvestment from black-owned property and black-majority neighborhoods left largely unaddressed by civil rights legislation. These chapters attend to how the fait accompli of segregated mass homeownership recalibrated forms of racial perception, observation, experience, and mobilization organized around the neighborhood unit as it increasingly hardened into a unit of racial measure.

In an echo of the first chapter's focus on the new field of professional real estate, the fourth chapter begins with a focus on another professional field developing the racial logic of mass homeownership: property appraisal. Appraisers approached the work of valuation as an empirical science. Yet, like most empirical practices, the science alleged to anchor this field in the twentieth century proves far more fungible, subjective, and aesthetic in practice. "Appraisal Manuals: Looking at Residential Looking on the Mid-Century Block" identifies several subgenres of "appraisal narratives" variously describing and obscuring procedures for perceiving and assessing race and property together. I begin by tracing the emergence of professional appraisal, paying particular attention to how manuals and textbooks designed to train burgeoning property valuators described the work of racial appraisal from the 1920s to the 1960s. I then turn to midcentury texts by Jane Jacobs, Gwendolyn Brooks, and Thomas Pynchon that at times reify and at others revise tactics for racial appraisal circulating within real estate and planning fields.

Chapter 5, "Feeling Racial Attachments to Property with John Cheever and Lorraine Hansberry," focuses on two of the foremost chroniclers of homeownership in the midcentury. Although Cheever and Hansberry shared a commitment to representing the emerging norms of residential life in the U.S., few have placed their residential fictions in direct conversation. Despite their differences in generation, race, class background, and preferred genres, Cheever and Hansberry each described the effects of the racial project of mass homeownership as it changed the contours of perception, affect, identification, and the possibility for racial solidarity. In his Shady Hill stories, Cheever foregrounds neighborhood formation at midcentury as a process of racial formation. His insistence on attending to whiteness as something requiring new descriptive attention following the expansion of suburban homeownership distinguishes his fiction from his peers often more willing to take whiteness for granted as something characters simply possessed rather than something they strove to maintain. Although Hansberry chafed at dismissive attempts to read *Raisin* as merely "about real estate," embracing this frame as a dynamic rather than a deadening descriptor allows us to better see her complex treatment of black attachment to property. Focusing on her depiction of George

Murchison, a character often read flatly by critics as an indictment of the black bourgeoisie, allows us to consider the varying forms black attachment to property takes in *Raisin*.

The book's final chapter, "What Does Systemic Racism Look Like? The Fair Housing Act's Aesthetic Riddles," tracks how activists and artists alike learned—or failed to learn—to bring the institutional racism associated with the housing market—designed to work impersonally and as a nonevent—into representation. This chapter first examines how activists from Martin Luther King Jr. to grassroot collectives in New York attempted to find a visual grammar for housing discrimination before turning to two works released on either side of the Fair Housing Act's 1968 passage—Kristin Hunter's 1966 novel, *The Landlord*, and its 1970 film adaptation written by Bill Gunn and directed by Hal Ashby—to consider how these works narrated the deindividualized forms of racism organizing the American housing market before and after this legal intervention. These representations falling on either end of the Fair Housing Act help us better see race and racism as evolving constructs differently calibrated across historical periods but also in relation to shifting physical and financial spaces.

In a brief epilogue, I consider the changing aesthetics of homeownership after the 1960s. While the ownership bug continues to persist within American culture and its representations, the stalwart setting of the single-family home at the center of a good deal of twentieth-century American literature is increasingly being usurped within the contemporary literary imagination by tent cities, refugee camps, military encampments, and reservations. The literature of dispossession—which I argue has always historically shadowed the residential literature in the twentieth-century U.S.—now seemingly occupies the center of twenty-first-century American fiction. I also read two closing cases—the 1969 erection of Resurrection City on the National Mall as part of the Poor People's Campaign and Gwendolyn Brooks's 1949 poem "Beverly Hills, Chicago"—as offering some lasting lessons and questions about ownership's place as the natural horizon of citizenship, security, or investment.

PART I

The Road to Mass Homeownership

Empire Builders
The Racial Longings of Modern Real Estate

HERBERT HOOVER'S 1931 PRESIDENTIAL ADDRESS to the President's Conference on Home Building and Home Ownership was filled with references to songs. Despite the conference's social science emphasis, the president's opening remarks—delivered live to three thousand delegates and broadcast to many more through the NBC and CBS radio networks—largely centered on the claim that "the sentiment for homeownership" was "embedded in the American heart."[1] To support this idea, Hoover turned to one of the great vehicles for sentimentality in the period, the American songbook:

> There is a wide distinction between homes and mere housing. Those immortal ballads, Home, Sweet Home; My Old Kentucky Home; and the Little Gray Home in the West, were not written about tenements or apartments. They are the expressions of racial longing which find outlet in the living poetry and songs of our people.[2]

Hoover went on to wryly contend that Americans "never sing songs about a pile of rent receipts," before concluding that "to own one's own home is a physical expression of individualism, of enterprise, of independence, and of the freedom of spirit."[3]

By 1931, Hoover was a decade into his project of homeownership boosterism, which he first began as secretary of commerce in 1921. Following the housing shortages caused by World War I and concerns about Bolshevism after the 1917 Russian Revolution, state officials worked alongside realtors and developers during the 1920s to zealously promote homeownership as America's greatest defense against social upheaval on the home front.[4] This initial public-private partnership, setting the stage for the more extensive collaborations enacted by the New Deal, endorsed homeownership as not just a savvy financial decision but as an innate yearning at the heart of American identity and, by extension, a requirement for a model civic and moral life.[5] Although the mass foreclosures instigated by the Great Depression interrupted these efforts to enshrine homeownership, Hoover's 1931 address finds the president nonetheless doubling down on its promotional rhetoric. His remarks, the most prominent endorsement of a version of the American Dream anchored by homeownership in this era, mark the pivotal role Hoover played in shaping the trajectory of mass homeownership in the U.S. for the rest of the century.

But Hoover also insists in his address that "the sentiment for homeownership" embedded in the "American heart" did not originate in America or with Americans. He instead identifies this sentiment as being first and foremost a "racial longing" that both precedes and supersedes the nation. Given Hoover's reputation as a technocrat who waged war on waste and inefficiency, his turn to affective evidence is somewhat surprising. The ravages of the Great Depression, still being uncovered in 1931, may have shaded Hoover's decision to offer a stirring aesthetic and affective rationale for homeownership. But his turn to the more specific tenor of racial emotion alleged to animate artistic production from "immortal ballads" of the past through the "living poetry and songs of our people" is more inexplicable. Hoover, who first came to national fame for his successful efforts in convincing Americans during World War I to curb their desires for sugar, fat, and meat on behalf of U.S. troops and allies, treats "racial longing" for ownership as an undeniable sacred truth that must be indulged.[6] The longing he finds enshrined in the aesthetic record allows Hoover to intimate that homeownership is most desired by—and perhaps desirable for—select Americans in possession of the right pedigree.

Although other papers and findings delivered at the 1931 White House Conference approached homeownership as a color-blind desire that should be attainable for all, Hoover's lyric symptomology of the racialized desire to own attests to the role that aesthetics, affect, and changing norms around racial perception were already playing in conceiving of and promulgating mass homeownership in the U.S. before the New Deal and its consequential embrace of redlining's technics. While the notion that black presence inherently lowered property values would become increasingly enshrined as the organizing principle of the American housing market, this alleged truism operated in conjunction with the less considered but no less consequential belief that whites' unquenchable hunger to own would endlessly propel property value, from the yeoman farms of the past to the new residential plots of the twentieth century.

But laying the groundwork for Hoover's proposition that the "wide distinction between homes and mere housing" was one of racial design were the theorizations and discursive experiments of realtors, land economists, and residential developers. This chapter contextualizes Hoover's assignment of homeownership as a racialized desire as the capstone of nearly two decades of arguments crafted by real estate professionals about the relative racial capacities for desiring, maintaining, and holding on to residential property—assertions that were themselves by-products of older claims positing the racialized predisposition for property and its attendant rights as best cultivated within white-majority nations. In engineering a coming "nation of home owners," realtors and policy makers alike aimed to marshal the allegedly innate racial longing for home ascribed to the country's white citizenry to create housing markets capable of shoring up the state, keeping workers rooted in one place, and promoting healthy families integral to the propagation of what one land economist termed "good population." The research, speeches, sales tips, and stories circulated within early real estate writing reveal how the "market gospel" of black devaluation was propelled by aesthetic judgements, racial philosophy, and theories of feeling forming the subjective core of residential value.

Scholars have studied the restrictive covenants, zoning ordinances, and neighborhood violence used to maintain residential segregation as law for decades and as practice for much longer. But less well examined is the degree to which the philosophical, scientific, and affective arguments made by the first generation of professional realtors for mass homeownership were racialized from their earliest conceptualization, combining the rhetoric of scientific racism and the study of innate traits with vaguer platitudes about the health of civilization, the family, and the state. In other words, mass homeownership did not merely become a vehicle for residential segregation in the midcentury—rather, realtors conceived of modern American homeownership as a racial enterprise from the start, catering to Anglo-Americans deemed innately built for it.[7]

This chapter explores how a shared belief in property as a principally white capacity helped to unite the real estate industry as a national profession at the turn of the twentieth century, a profession that would go on to play a consequential role in shaping state housing policy into the present. Focusing on the first two decades of the *National Real Estate Journal*, the house publication of the National Association of Real Estate Boards and the country's most prominent real estate guild, this chapter begins by recovering the foundational function of race in the affective, social, and scientific cases realtors built in support of homeownership's necessity for maintaining the nation's white-settler identity newly engined by residential expansion. Even after the Russian Revolution of 1917, when the explicit arguments used to promote homeownership in the U.S. began to rely less on race and more on patriotism, the structure of these arguments built upon earlier notions of ownership as a racial capacity even as the language of race began to disappear from realtors' public rationales. Although direct appeals to the Anglo-Saxon capacity for property diminished in realtor literature by the 1930s, it was in this same period that realtors began treating blackness as an absolute and uncontestable threat to the hard-won property values that whites were alleged to have instinctively cultivated through ownership. By the 1930s, the argument about the Anglo-Saxon's superior capacity for homeownership so deeply shaped the structure of residential property in the U.S. that it could be taken for granted as a norm alongside the alleged truism that the presence of black life inherently devalued a home's worth.

The last part of this chapter considers "sentiment for homeownership" as taken up by two of the era's most prominent literary works capturing the changing contours of the relationship between race, the senses, and homeownership—Sinclair Lewis's *Babbitt* and F. Scott Fitzgerald's *The Great Gatsby*. Both texts chart the increasing intertwinement of racial perception, residential property, and the value of whiteness. Refracting the rhetoric of homeownership emerging from the professionalizing field of real estate—and in *Babbitt*'s case, almost parroting this discourse word for word—these texts reverse President Hoover's theory of cultural causality. Rather than taking "poetry and song" as evidence of a timeless racial longing for property, these literary works suggest how aesthetic and discursive practices of seeing, assessing, and valuing race emerging from real estate's perceptual mandates shaped how people learned to look, see, and assign worth to bodies and buildings in growing concert.

Racial Longing in Hoover's Homeownership Songbook

Before turning to the writings of the first generation of professional realtors, taking a closer look at the songs Hoover selected as the most evidential "expressions of racial longing" for homeownership can help us more precisely locate the coordinates of this alleged desire. Hoover turns to three of the most canonical entries in the American songbook—"Home, Sweet Home," "My Old Kentucky Home," and "Little Grey Home in the West"—to frame the owned home as the eternal subject of racial longing. But while these songs were certainly beloved standards, each proves to be a poor representative of the case for homeownership. To start, while Hoover is right that these songs were not written about "tenements or apartments," they were not necessarily written about owned homes, either. Their popularity reflects a longing for home in times when people were moving far beyond their birthplaces; but none posit ownership as a significant amplifier of this longing, nor do they depict ownership as a decidedly American virtue. But if the songs Hoover selected weakly substantiate homeownership's seductiveness, considering their creation and circulation clarify his investment in claiming homeownership as an index of extranational white racial longing—a position eventually substantiated by the state's eventual subsidization of homeownership along largely racial lines.

"Home, Sweet Home," the oldest and most venerated song on Hoover's list, was one of the most popular songs of the nineteenth century.[8] It first appeared in the opera *Clari*, staged in London in 1823. Centered on a Milanese maiden's struggle to escape capture by a nefarious duke and return to her country home, *Clari* featured music by an English composer and lyrics by an American expatriate. While the opera was itself only a middling hit, "Home, Sweet Home" found popularity in England before finding an even larger audience in the U.S.[9] For the next century, "Home, Sweet Home" circulated among a wide and diverse public. It was a favorite of Union and Confederate soldiers alike during the Civil War and could be heard in both private parlors and dance halls. As music historian Richard Crawford notes, "'Home, Sweet Home' lies close to the heart of musical experience as most Americans of the

1800's understood it."¹⁰ But contra Hoover, nothing in the song suggests that the difference between "home" and "mere housing" depends upon ownership. Its lyrics speak more generally to the pain of being exiled from "the pleasures of home," indexing not just a physical place but the social relations the home contains. The singer progressively refers to her lost home in the song as "my lowly thatched cottage," "our own cottage door," and "that cottage," with the pronouns associated with her home becoming increasingly weaker arbiters of possession as the song marches on.¹¹

"Home, Sweet Home" is, by consequence, an awkward fit on a list of ownership anthems.¹² Yet, even while the song fails to offer strong evidence of an enduring American preference for homeownership, it does help us decipher Hoover's interpretation of the song as an "expression of racial longing." That "Home, Sweet Home" could just as strongly be claimed as an English song as an American one suggests that Hoover's generic phrase of "racial longing" did not refer to a conception of race organized by national origin or an even narrower understanding of Anglo-American identity wielded by erstwhile frontier historian Theodore Roosevelt. Rather, the transnational origins of and affection for "Home, Sweet Home" suggest Hoover's notion of "racial longing" indexed a vision of transnational white identity gaining traction in the nineteenth century that remained popular into the next.

The idea of a superior race of "Anglo-Saxons"—a racial category distinct to the nineteenth century—increasingly dispersed across the globe through colonial settlements circulated in texts propagating scientific racism and imperial expansion.¹³ The belief that Anglo-Saxons possessed a privileged capacity for ownership and an inherent respect for property rights anchored justifications for ongoing colonization projects pursued by white-majority republics. Proponents of these theories in the American context wielded them to justify Indian dispossession, continued African enslavement, and westward and hemispheric expansions. As sociologist George Fitzhugh argued of the Anglo-Saxon as part of his larger defense of slavery in 1854, "no people on earth love property more, will go greater lengths, so far as danger is concerned, to obtain it, or take better care of it after it is obtained."¹⁴ Similar sentiments buttressed colonization efforts by the English in Australia, Rhodesia, and South Africa. As legal scholar Brenna Bhandar writes, "the evolution of modern property laws and justifications for private property ownership were articulated through the attribution of value to the lives of those defined as having the capacity, will, and technology to appropriate, which in turn was contingent on prevailing concepts of race and racial difference."[15] Bhandar goes on to identify what she calls "a racial regime of ownership" persisting into the present that was produced through and used to justify colonial expansion.

Hoover possessed firsthand knowledge of this regime himself, spending nearly fifteen years managing mines around the world before entering political life. Hoover's formative time working in various global frontiers likely colored his later approach to domestic ownership. He spent his early adulthood administering and advising mining sites in Western Australia, China (where he and his family survived a siege during the Boxer Rebellion), Russia, Burma, and South Africa.[16] Following his extractive efforts across these lucrative frontiers, Hoover espoused the importance of managing mines in accordance with set racial hierarchies in his 1909 book, *Principles of Mining*. After "much observation and experience in working Asiatics and negroes as well as Americans and Australians in mines," he concludes that "one white man equals two or three of the colored races" in "the simplest forms of mine work," while for more skilled tasks, "the average ratio is as one to seven, or in extreme cases even eleven."[17] Boiling down racial difference into two base dichotomies—whites and coloreds—allowed Hoover's advice to be made operational in mines almost anywhere in the world.[18]

Placing Hoover's earlier theorizations about the physical, affective, and organizational capacities of races around the world alongside the transnational legacy of "Home, Sweet Home" helps situate his racialized understanding of homeownership within the broader global framework of white supremacy and differential evolution through which Hoover first articulated racial difference some twenty years earlier. The technocratic Hoover of 1909 couched his theories about differential racial capacities in the language of scientific racism and labor efficiency, while President Hoover of 1931 turned to the sentimental songbook to enforce a notion of racial capacity rooted in feeling. But both modes of argument emerged out of global frameworks melding race, feeling, and capacity circulating in the nineteenth century. The sentiments and science used to justify settler colonialism and imperial expansion in the nineteenth century also prop up early cases for mass homeownership in the twentieth, repackaging settled land as the horizon of the good life as the era of alleged endless open frontiers available for white conquest was coming to an end.[19]

The property feelings of white-settler diaspora shadow another of Hoover's songs, "Little Grey Home in the West" from 1911—this time amplified by World War I.[20] Whereas "Home, Sweet Home" could claim some modicum of American parentage through its American-born lyricist, both the lyrics and music to "Little Grey Home in the West" were penned by English writers. "Little Grey Home," moreover, makes an even weaker lyrical case for ownership. Whereas "Home, Sweet Home" at least invokes Clari's long-lost cottage as a physical referent of home, "Little Grey Home" does away with even that. Its lyrics dwell on the "contentment and rest" as well as with the "hands," "lips," and "eyes" the singer associates with a faraway "tumble-down nest" in an unspecified western somewhere. "Little Grey Home" further lacks lyrical specificity in regard to nationality, easing the way for the song's ready adoption in both world wars by a number of armies involved in the conflict. Unsurprisingly, given its English-language lyrics, the song was sung primarily by soldiers from nations with histories of white settler colonialism—the U.S., Canada, and Australia.[21] The song's adoption as an anthem by majority-white republics during and after World War I endorses Hoover's investment in home as capacity of white civilizations more broadly.

But it is the second song Hoover mentions in his 1931 speech that has the most to teach us about the connection between ownership, race, and home as advanced not only by the president but the broader public-private partnership being constructed for homeownership. "My Old Kentucky Home," a minstrel song penned by Stephen Foster in 1853, is the most American of Hoover's three songs in both provenance and popularity. While minstrel songs were generally written for raucous public performances, Foster's melodies made the jump from the stage to the parlor by combining the sentimentality and slower tempo of the home song with the Southern imagery and dialect associated with the minstrel tune.[22] As one of his biographer notes, Foster's songs "were refined enough to be welcomed in the middle-class home and even into the lady's parlor by virtue of their powerful sentimentality, which created a much desired emotional response that antebellum Americans relished in the listener."[23]

For maximum sentimental impact, Foster wrote "My Old Kentucky Home" with characters from Harriet Beecher Stowe's novel *Uncle Tom's Cabin* in mind. The song's enslaved singer mourns that "'twill never be light" for him again upon his sale further south to toil under even crueler conditions. But Foster's original verses explicitly identify this singer as "poor Uncle Tom, Good Night" before being changed to the more generic "My Old Kentucky home, goodnight." While all the songs Hoover selected to testify to ownership's virtues ultimately fail to do so, the inclusion of "My Old Kentucky Home" evokes a more vexed set of questions about the source and nature of Hoover's affective theory of ownership. The singer of "My Old Kentucky Home" does not own his home or himself; the "home" he pines for is not a "tenement or an apartment," but a plantation where he is owned. So why include this song as evidence of the racial drive to own a home in 1931? One might hazard that the "racial longing" to own that Hoover locates in "My Old Kentucky Home" is not that of the enslaved lyric subject but of Foster's, who, as the song's composer, could be said to be the source of song's possessive longing extending to both homes and people. It is Foster's possessive logic, as the scribe of this home song, rather than the enslaved lyric speaker, that the song most indexes. But it is also true that with the inclusion of "My Old Kentucky Home" in Hoover's songbook, references to the ownership of people in this set outnumber that of land or homes—a fact pointing to the reliance of the emerging affective case for mass homeownership on nostalgia for past sentimental possessions taking both real and chattel forms. Yet, given that Uncle Tom's cabin quarters inspired Foster's song—a space tended to by its "home-loving" occupant possessing a "gentle, domestic heart," as Stowe described Tom—as well as the fact of the relative spatial proximity of white and black dwelling space featured in Stowe's nineteenth century novel in contrast to the segregated districts becoming the norm by the 1930s, the specter of Uncle Tom as both a model of domestic affect and residential care and a reminder of the prior intimacies once common to living arrangements across the color line punctures the status of both ownership and segregation as transhistorical racial longings.

Together, all the songs Hoover referenced in his 1931 housing speech point to the place of recent notions of global white supremacy as well as of older antebellum investments in the value of blackness in imagining the project of mass homeownership. Whereas "Home, Sweet Home" and "Little Grey Home in the West" mark a global understanding of white capacity for ownership, Foster's "My Old Kentucky Home" underscores the distinctive role blackness would continue to play within the American residential imaginary. While Hoover's cited songs fail to offer solid evidence of an innate desire for homeownership, they succeed in pointing to race's key role in the modern case for homeownership. Within this sentimental assemblage, whiteness does not appear as a spatialized amenity whose preservation ensures the ongoing value of property but is wielded here instead as an enduring fount of distinctive property feelings justifying ownership from the frontier past to the residential present. But realtors would hone arguments supporting both approaches to whiteness—as the source of property and as a quality of property to be defended—as they experimented with a range of affective, aesthetic, and scientific strategies for turning the U.S. into a nation of mostly white homeowners.[24] It is to these writings shaping Hoover's sentiments that we turn next.

The *National Real Estate Journal* and the Acquisitive Anglo-Saxon Disposition

The craving for land seems to be an inborn instinct in the Anglo-Saxon race.
  —*National Real Estate Journal*, November 15, 1914

The priorities for the 1931 President's Conference on Home Building and Home Ownership were largely set by the real estate industry. The National Association of Real Estate Boards (NAREB), founded in 1908 and known today as the National Association of Realtors, most powerfully represented these private interests. The NAREB first partnered with the state in 1915 to shape housing policy. Hoover began working closely with the association in 1921 as Commerce Secretary while promoting the Better Homes in America program designed to "educate the American people to the higher standards of home life."[25] The federal government hired NAREB affiliates during World War I to help coordinate wartime housing for workers and its members would continue to shape housing policy following the mass foreclosures exacerbating the Great Depression and through the New Deal.

The NAREB was well represented at the 1931 White House conference, steering the meeting's agenda towards strengthening the private market and away from supplementing its shortcomings through public housing programs.[26] These priorities would go on to shape the state's more full-throated subsidization of the private housing market in the years to come while impeding a more comprehensive commitment to public housing. Hoover's business background as well as his dedication to what he termed "cooperative individualism" predisposed him to such a path. But the pride of place homeownership held in his governmental agenda as well as the arguments and tropes he deployed when arguing for its necessity—including those relating to race—were positions honed by realtors decades prior. The foundations for Hoover's framing of ownership as a "racial longing" were solidified in the writing realtors produced for each other and the public to legitimate the project of real estate and encourage the expansion of homeownership to the white middle class.

The founding of the National Association of Real Estate Exchanges—the first national organization of its kind—took place in a YMCA auditorium in Chicago in 1908. (The group would change its name to the National Association of Real Estate Boards, or NAREB, in 1916, and to the National Association of Realtors, or NAR in 1972)[27] Merging nineteen local boards and 120 founding members, the association aimed to "unite the real estate men of America, for the purpose of exerting effectively a combined influence upon matters affecting real estate interests."[28] The organization disseminated its efforts in its journal, the *National Real Estate Journal*, launched in 1910 and circulated to each of its members. In addition to publicizing convention happenings, sharing information from local boards, and flagging key legal decisions related to property, the journal's articles—generally written by members or guests at its conventions—ranged in subject from technical treatises on appraisal and taxation to sales tips, comics, and poems praising the realtor and the homeowner.

As described by historian Jeffrey M. Hornstein in his history of the NAREB, the *National Real Estate Journal* facilitated "the creation of a common language and the rudiments of an occupational culture with which men scattered in local boards across the continent could imagine themselves as a community of interest."[29] The journal's earliest covers visualize this aspiration, combining the distinct images of cattle grazing on farmland, an urban apartment tower, and a suburban single-family home into one harmonious visual spread. To address the challenges of selling real estate across these varied landscapes, the *NREJ* featured articles catering to these distinct typographies while also foregrounding issues such as legitimation and professionalization that unified realtors across spatial typologies.[30]

FIGURE 2. The cover of the inaugural issue of the *National Real Estate Journal*, published March 1910.

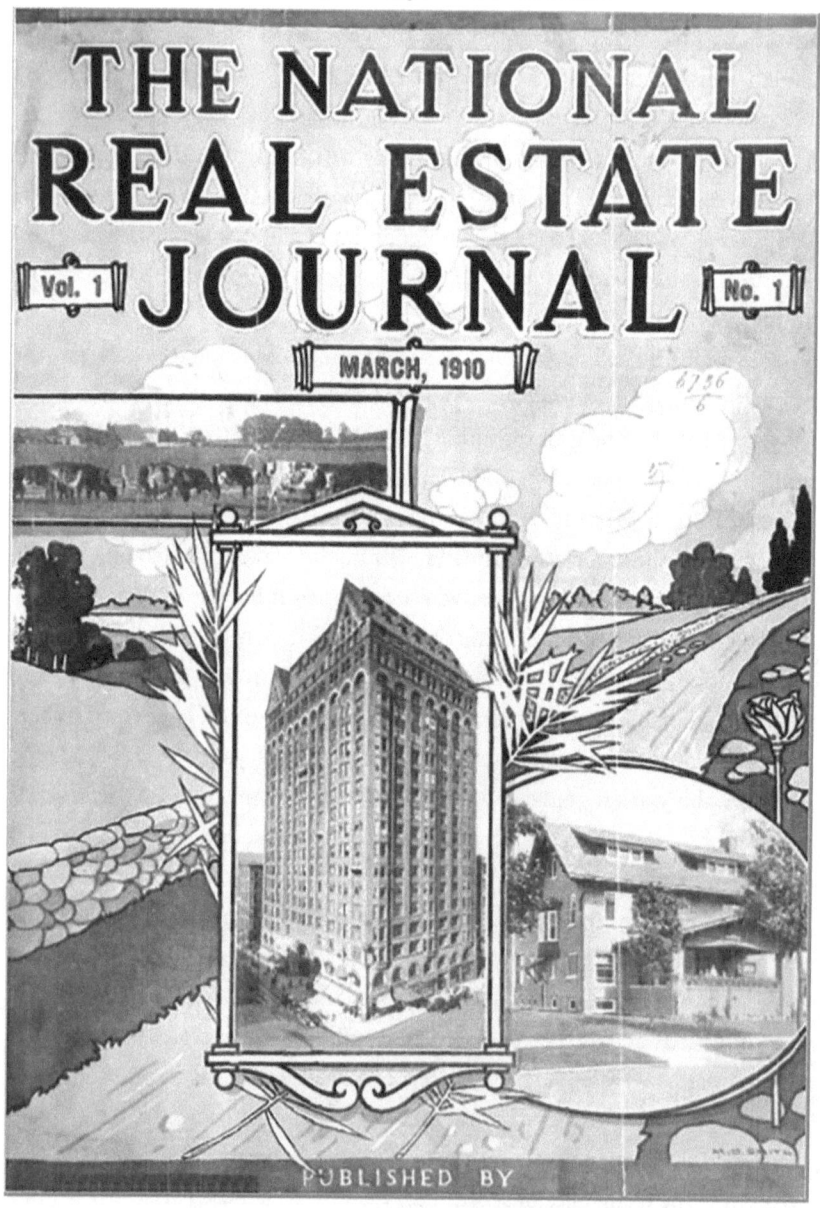

Source: National Association of Real Estate Exchanges, *National Real Estate Journal* 1, no. 1 (March 1910).

But racial ideology helped to further unify the association across the various regions it served. Hornstein recovers the efforts of realtors to render mass homeownership as "the universal and natural interests of '*the* middle class.'"[31] He pays particular attention to the association's incubation of a "national masculine vocational ethos" that unified realtors within the shared professional and moral project of property sales.[32] But whiteness proved just as crucial to the association's collective ethos, underwriting its vision of masculinity, patriotism, and moral virtue. "Members of the NAREB," as historian Paige Glotzer notes, "tended to have little in common during the organization's first decade aside from the fact that they were white men involved in real estate."[33] Not only were its members exclusively white men, but they rallied around the fundamental principle that whites possessed a privileged relationship to ownership.[34] White supremacy proved motile and adaptable across the varying regions to which the association catered, helping to unify realtors across urban, rural, and suburban areas.

The NAREB most infamously enshrined racial discrimination as a requirement for professionalization in 1924 when it adopted a code of ethics prohibiting realtors from selling homes to blacks in white neighborhoods, at the risk of expulsion. In 1927, Nathan William MacChesney, then general counsel to the NAREB, drafted a standard form for racial covenants barring anyone "having any appreciable admixture of negro blood and every person who is what is commonly known as colored" from renting or buying a covenanted property except as an employee.[35] But we find the rationale for such policies first emerging during the association's first decade, with NAREB members promoting the need for professionalization in its house journal alongside aspirational invocations of the Anglo-Saxon's innate capacity for all property—residential or otherwise. These efforts coexisted with the association's ambitions to promote mass homeownership as serving an increasingly urbanizing, wage-driven white American public. Over the course of its first three decades, the NAREB's publications provided its readers with rationales, pep talks, and sales pitches connecting ownership's general superiority as a way of life to its racial provenance. But we also find realtors remaking this argument over time for residential contexts, underscoring the specific sanctity of the owned home over a manifest destiny yoked to a specific vision of the land.

Before turning to these arguments, it is important to first understand the novelty of mass homeownership as a concept when the NAREB was first founded in 1908. The association's concentrated efforts to promote the ideology of homeownership reflects the sense of looming crisis that realtors either felt or opportunistically encouraged in response to falling homeownership rates at the turn of the twentieth century. The Jeffersonian vision of the U.S. as a nation largely made up of white yeoman farmers and further perpetuated by Western migration was interrupted in the 1890s by the mass movement of Americans and recent immigrants away from agricultural homesteads to industrial hubs where they labored increasingly outside the home. While governmental incentives such as the Preemption Act of 1841 and the Homestead Act of 1862 encouraged continued settler colonialism in the Western frontier, the industrializing economy of the late nineteenth century drove a growing number of Americans toward urban centers.

The changing use value of the home contributed to falling ownership rates. By the early 1900s, as historian Margaret Garb writes, "ownership of residential property, which was clearly distinguished from manufacturing sites, no longer provided families with the ability to generate income enough to sustain the household's independence."[36] For an increasing number of Americans, to own one's home was no longer to own the means of production, making residential ownership a luxury rather than a necessity or even a goal. As more Americans worked outside the home, the home came to symbolize a refuge from market relations rather than a site of value in and of itself. "Whether a resident owned or rented his or her home was a matter of indifference to many urban dwellers," as Garb writes. "The family home, in theory, stood outside market relations; its economic value was obscured by its sentimental functions."[37] As the home transformed from income generating to wage consuming, realtors increasingly framed homeownership in moral terms drawing on platitudes of race, family, and nation.

Even for the upper classes who could afford to own homes, apartment renting was promoted as the more chic and fashionable option. A 1931 article in *Architecture Record* notes that thirty years earlier, "every good Knickerbocker, with even the modest pretensions, considered it his duty to house his family within four walls wherein he would be the sole lord and master."[38] Yet "today," as this author declares, "New York is a city of apartments," before attesting to the virtues of renting: "In our busy city many New Yorkers who have tasted the sweets of apartment house life, with its freedom from many of the vexations of housekeeping, will never wish to return to the older method."³⁹ Writer Charlotte Perkins Gilman would push the argument for apartment living further in 1904. Noting that private homes were "no longer built in numbers worth mentioning compared with apartment-houses," Gilman posits the communal aspects of apartment living as the next evolution of dwelling, freeing up women in particular for work other than the domestic labor that homeownership required.⁴⁰

In the wake of these economic, spatial, and cultural shifts, homeownership rates in the U.S. stalled out between 1890 and 1920, hovering around 45 percent. The difficulty of home financing coupled with a plethora of new investment options other than the home further contributed to ownership's slow decline. For those with the means to buy, the home was one investment choice among many—including stocks, bonds, and commodity futures—rather than an inherently moral or noble pursuit.⁴¹ For those of lesser means, home financing was far more onerous at the turn of the century than it would become after the state interventions following the Great Depression. Lenders generally required down payments of as much as 50 percent and granted mortgages for the much shorter terms of five to ten years, making homeownership difficult for many working adults. Holding so much debt was not just onerous for many Americans but morally distasteful. "Fearful of the sin or stigma of indebtedness," as Thomas Sugrue writes, "many middle-class Americans, even those with a taste for single-family homes—rented or spent years saving money so they would not have to take on large amounts of debt to buy a home."⁴² Those most likely to own in this period were those who built their own homes, which allowed them to avoid a mortgage entirely; older Americans who could leverage a lifetime of savings for this purchase; or the wealthy who could afford to purchase outright.

Facing eroding ownership rates, the NAREB aggressively promoted real estate investments not just as a choice but as an instinct, a duty, and the noblest aspiration. One tactic of property boosterism featured in the *NREJ* involved connecting the real estate market of the present with nostalgia for the pioneering past. "The Realtor is the immediate successor to the pioneer," declared the president of the University of Wisconsin in a 1928 realtor convention speech. If the pioneer "cleared the forest to make farms," he charged, "the Realtor is clearing the farms to create cities."⁴³ A 1923 article in the *NREJ* forged similar connections to the frontier past, claiming the modern homeowner to be "the pioneer of today and of tomorrow standing on the doorstep of his own home who is going to safeguard and advance this Democracy of ours."[44]

But more often, the arguments made in the *NREJ* for ownership's virtues turned away from visions of pioneering to better cater to an urbanizing American population looking for homes with modern amenities more suited to cosmopolitan ways of life. W. W. Hannan, the association's first president, said as much in a 1911 speech delivered at its third national convention. While "the history of the race has been that of endless movement, of constant progress and always westward," Hannan insisted that "today there is no West—we have reached the end." He went on to triumphantly declare that "America is entering upon a new phase of national life; one whose problems are to be largely the problems of her cities, of life as it is lived en masse."[45] The modern realtor must be prepared to enter this new phase alongside his clients.

If the rhetoric of pioneering risked sounding too old-fashioned—potentially reminding Americans of the age and outdatedness of much of its housing stock—Anglo-Saxon heritage proved a more palatable rallying cry. Such invocations pushed beyond acknowledging the British roots of American property law to make broader claims about distinctively racial capacities for valuing and protecting private property undergirding the allegedly advanced Western civilizations. The notion of the white race's singular propensity for ownership has a long history, as detailed in this book's introduction, dating back to the Enlightenment justifications of private property that also rationalized the expropriation of land from those who failed to "improve" it, to cite John Locke, as well as chattel slavery. But while philosophers, states, and settlers have long invoked the allegedly inherent property capacity of whites to justify a slew of maneuvers and laws in specific national contexts, the conceit of a global Anglo-Saxon identity trumping national identity reached its peak popularity in the late nineteenth century. Conjuring an image of an international community united by the powerful bonds of race, the reclamation of Anglo-Saxon heritage in this period served to stabilize a transhistorical and transnational vision of global white supremacy. "This new racial consciousness," as political scientist Adom Getachew writes, "sought to forestall imperial loss and decline by consolidating a white world order, flattening racial distinctions between the 'darker races,' and reinforcing the global color line."[46] Drawing upon the racialized arguments used to justify land grabs in the name of empire, settler colonialism, and expansion across the globe, American realtors harnessed this language to convince white Americans that the stakes of investing in domestic residential property were just as immense as extraterritorial expansion.

The earliest invocation of Anglo-Saxon superiority in the *NREJ* appears in one of its inaugural issues from 1910. An article by a professor of real estate law at Northwestern University calling for a better system of land transfers cites the intensity of white feeling for property and its protection to underscore the necessity of land transfer reforms. "There is in the Anglo-Saxon heart a feeling inherited from ancestors of centuries ago, and amounting almost to an instinct that the ground upon which we live is entitled to a protection more careful, more perfect, than that given to any other form of property."[47] Rather than framing the drive for property as something transmitted through culture, the author describes an inherited *feeling* toward property manifesting itself in the "Anglo-Saxon heart," framing property and its alleged rights as a racialized sensitivity transmitted via blood rather than a learned orientation sown by law, education, or socialization. Such rhetoric echoes earlier arguments made by nineteenth-century British colonial settlers on behalf of land titling and transfers, as described by legal scholar Brenna Bhandar. British settlers invoked abstract qualities of racial superiority "rooted in expectation and the desire for security," as Bhandar writes, to justify their norms of ownership.[48] This 1910 *NREJ* article marks just how far this discourse had spread, no longer only used to justify land acquisition abroad but domestic forms of ownership, too. The global rhetoric of white supremacy energizing settler colonialism proved just as useful on the American home front.

Similar sentiments touting the instinctual love of property allegedly felt and exhibited by those of Anglo-Saxon descent continued to pepper the journal through the next decade. A 1912 article recounting the history of real estate law begins by claiming common law as a "distinctively an Anglo-Saxon institution" before insisting that it "probably never could have existed, and could not now exist, in all its fullness among any other people."[49] Here, the author's acknowledgment of institutional precedent quickly gives way to a claim about hierarchies among peoples based on innate capacities. Another *NREJ* article from 1912 concluded that Anglo-Americans have surpassed even their British brethren in property passion. Encouraging American investment in Canada, the author lauds "the Saskatchewan type" as an improved blend of "the Anglo-Saxon from the United States and from Great Britain."[50] Acknowledging rising immigration to Canada, he thankfully notes that with English immigrants now outnumbering "those of other tongues," the U.S. and Canada "will work together to advance the Anglo-Saxon civilization which seems destined to dominate the world."[51] In this author's vision of white North American solidarity, congenital fealty to property rights "made through type" means whites need only maintain majority rule to attain their destined imperial greatness.

Yoking racial supremacy to civilizational destiny was a widespread practice at the turn of the twentieth century. But the zealousness with which realtors put this discourse to use sits at odds not only with the broader notion of American democratic exceptionalism that realtors equally relished but also their aim to sell as much property as possible. Not all realtors could afford to be so racially selective given that non-whites also bought property during this period. But as a trade journal, the *NREJ* was not designed for wide circulation. The language realtors used to promote their profession to each other could diverge from their individual sales practices. One of the *NREJ*'s aims was to remake the image of real estate—tinged with the stain of disrepute for much of the nineteenth century—into something of civilizational import. Realtors were not mere salesmen in the journal's pages but "empire builders," "Scouts of Civilization," and "aiders and abettors in the creation of wealth." But even if the vision the industry sold of itself did not always line up with individual sales practices, the association's espousal of white supremacy had real implications for the practices of residential apartheid it would actively support.

The NAREB's racial discourse of property capacity would be adopted by the state with whom the association would first lobby and eventually partner. Take the presidential speech by Herbert Hoover that this chapter considered at its start. A 1912 convention speech delivered by journalist Allen D. Albert appearing in the *NREJ* matches Hoover's 1931 racial interpretation of the American songbook's property hymnals almost beat for beat. Albert begins his speech by citing an efficiency expert's claim that a yearning for home was common to all people. But Albert goes on to revise this expert's claim of universal longing, insisting "that strong as it is among the savages, strong as it is among the primitive people, in civilization no language other than our own contains a word for 'home' to which the word 'sweet' can be prefixed without incongruity." "We Anglo Saxons," he insists, "are the only people in all the world who would compose a poem or sing a hymn with those words, 'Home Sweet Home.'"[52] President Hoover's 1931 assertion that American "immortal ballads" touting the sweetness of home were "expressions of racial longing" flattens Albert's more pointed racial rhetoric of Anglo-triumphalism, but the fundamental structure of Albert's supremacist claims remains intact across the twenty years separating it from Hoover's. The racialized property propaganda first published in the *NREJ* traveled far beyond its professional audience.

Realtors and their fellow travelers flexibly deployed the language of Anglo-Saxon inheritance to serve a number of pro-property arguments. While one article writer insisted upon the superior feeling for home inherited by white Americans, underscoring their affective orientation toward ownership, another touted the race's superior organizational ability, producing enduring legal and state systems to protect property. In one instance, a realtor seemingly worried about the negative connotations of an innate insatiability for property attempts to positively spin this drive. His 1913 article cites Abraham's decision to seek the promised land of Canaan as evidence of an "acquisitive disposition" passed down generationally:

> That instinctive desire was developed, as you know, in Jacob, and also in his descendants, and that trait is possessed in a remarkable degree by the Anglo-Saxon people, which is used as one of the arguments whereby they say that the Anglo-Saxon race are descendants of the Test Ten Tribes of Israel. Their instinct to live comfortably and to acquire property may be called materialism but it means discovery, adventure and enterprise.[53]

In this convoluted biblical argument transmuting anti-Semitic claims of Jewish avarice into a laudable characteristic of the Anglo-Saxon race, the author makes a racialized "acquisitive disposition" the cornerstone of civilization. A year later in 1914, another contributor would abandon the language of racial instinct entirely to emphasize the advanced knowledge accrued by white civilizations. While "the craving for land seems to be an inborn instinct in the Anglo-Saxon race," this writer goes on to argue that this instinct has since evolved into a more sophisticated drive. "In recent years there has come to America a new feeling, not born of race instinct but the result of sound reasoning on the part of investors."[54] The racial logic of ownership perpetuated by realtors need not be coherent. Whether attributed to inherited feeling or learned reasoning, the rousing grandiosity of these varying racialized assertions about property capacity mattered most.

Contributors to the *NREJ* would occasionally diverge from these broader historical platitudes about racial hierarchies to proffer more pointedly eugenic arguments about race and population purportedly rooted in science. Though these articles tended to focus less on the particulars of residential space and homeownership to attend instead to the more civilizational link between property, racial purity, and white supremacy, they appeared in the *NREJ* immediately alongside articles more narrowly focused on homeownership and were read by realtors of all stripes. Whether selling homes in St. Louis, investing in homesteads in Nebraska, or studying land transfer systems in faraway frontiers, the broad swath of *NREJ* readers were continually reminded that the sale, circulation, and maintenance of property was first and foremost a racial duty that could also spur economic growth. The wedding of the language of racial duty with that of population management, differential birth rates, and racial genocide first appears in the *NREJ* in a republished 1915 convention address delivered by Thomas Forsyth Hunt, dean of the Agricultural Department of the University of California. Arguing that when whites moved to industrializing Southern cities, blacks acquire the lands they leave behind, Hunt warns, "God pity the southeastern part of the United States," for it is "only a question of time until the cities also will be inhabited by colored people."[55] Hunt specifically fears the effects of this demographic shifts on birth rates. "If families in the cities raise less than two children and families in the country raise three or more it does not require a profound mathematician to show what will happen." He further warns that following increases in black homesteading and foreign immigration, "unless conditions radically change in three generations or by 2015, the majority of its people will be descendants of peoples not now living in the United States." "We can see the buffaloes disappearing," Hunt concludes, "but we seem blind to our own fate."[56] Hunt underscores the crucial role realtors can play in mitigating this coming racial genocide—"the one thing I wish to drive home to this audience is, that after the land is occupied, you are not through with the problem."[57] Given his commitments to agriculture, Hunt's plea is for realtors to remain committed to securing and recapitalizing white rural homesteads, despite residentializing trends, for the good of the race if not their bottom line.

But the largest concentration of eugenic arguments appeared in the *NREJ* during the 1920s, coinciding with eugenics' peak national popularity. Whereas Hunt claimed that realtors played a key role in preventing future racial genocide in 1915, another convention speech demanded the reproductive vigilance of realtors in even cruder racial terms. In his 1921 NAREB address, S. S. McClure, editor of the popular *McClure's Magazine*, focused on "the ascendency and dominance of the white races, and the desire and need for colonization in other countries, especially by the Asiatic races, and dealing with the major phases of racial intermixtures."[58] Given that this speech is described rather than reprinted in full in the journal's pages suggests that its screed was perhaps too extreme even for the *NREJ*'s taste. The lines they do cite directly from McClure's address bluntly toe the eugenics line:

> America and England today own so much of the real estate of the globe that they are satisfied. Their fundamental problems are identical: first, to retain their great inheritance and as far as possible, in the newer lands, maintain the purity of race. All students of race problems agree with Agassiz who wrote: "Let anyone who doubts the evil of this mixture of races and is inclined from mistaken philanthropy to break down all barriers between them come to Brazil. He cannot deny the deterioration consequent upon the amalgamation of races, more widespread here than in any country in the world, and which is rapidly effacing the best qualities of the white man, the negro and the Indian, leaving a mongrel, nondescript type, deficient in physical and mental energy."[59]

McClure frames realtors as frontline workers in the mission to preserve a global white empire. Delivering this speech in the interwar period, he surmises the shift in American and British postwar priorities away from expansion and toward the careful racial management of conscripted lands and peoples. Louis Agassiz, professor of zoology at Harvard in the nineteenth century and once one of America's preeminent practitioners of scientific racism, needs no introduction in McClure's speech despite having been dead for nearly fifty years. McClure resurrects Agassiz's scientific racism to urge realtors that as overseers of the land in the postwar era, they must help ensure the endurance of the white race.[60]

The range of racial arguments appearing in the *NREJ* during its earliest decades at times reflects the long shadow cast by scientific racism and white supremacy at the turn of the twentieth century on the project of ownership more broadly. Even as the expanding residential spaces would reshape the sensorial and economic terms through which race was defined, mapped, and made legible, the rationale for redlining and residential segregation in some of the journal's earliest issues explicitly builds upon older claims about innate racial feelings for property dating back centuries. But the *NREJ*, privileging efficacy over consistency, featured articles that celebrated the white capacity for property alongside others underscoring the need to stimulate this alleged instinct to prevent its waning in a darkening world. Despite these differing logics, the articles published in the *NREJ* demonstrate the varying ways white supremacy preoccupied the professionalization of real estate from the start. Realtors sought to establish themselves as not only specialists but as empire builders dutifully promising to preserve the white right to property.

With this insight, we might build from Cheryl Harris's pivotal excavation of the American legal system's efforts to maintain "the valorization of whiteness as treasured property."[61] In uncovering the shared "conceptual nucleus" of whiteness and property based in the right to exclude, Harris demonstrates the various ways that "American law has a recognized property interest in whiteness."[62] These early *NREJ* articles buttressing real estate's professionalization suggest that the property-based interest in whiteness found recognition and cultivation far beyond the law. To extend Harris's argument, realtors not only wielded whiteness as a property to be valued—they approached whiteness as the genetic fount of property rights as well as the foundational desire for property itself. The project to stimulate mass homeownership in the twentieth century extended from this larger racial project as identified by Harris, a position openly articulated by early realtors who not only framed whiteness *as* property but rendered the capacity to own as an inherent property of whiteness itself.

Negro Exclusion and the Patriotic Turn

It must be remembered that the stimulation of home ownership is the problem of every citizen and institution that believes in and is desirous of perpetuating our present form of Government.

—"Home Ownership Assures Safe Government," *American Lumberman*, July 23, 1921

While realtors promoted a vision of global white diaspora united by a capacity for property during the field's earliest days of professionalization, the world events of 1917 and 1918 led realtors to adopt a more nationalist discourse of ownership. Articles in the *NREJ* continued to address the property moors of "we Anglo Saxons" well into the 1920s. But in the wake of World War I and the Russian Revolution, the journal's contributors more often articulated homeownership as a national project than as a racial one. Realtors increasingly turned to the language of citizenship, patriotism, and democracy to promote homeownership as a dampener of revolutionary animus and the foundation of social, political, and familial stability. But even as realtors increasingly peddled homeownership's necessity as a matter of state security, the journal's older framing of property passion as an index of racial supremacy continued to inform its vision for mass ownership, if more obliquely. Considering the *NREJ* along with its more public-facing educational materials in the early interwar period shows how earlier racial arguments about property capacity continued to shape the objective of mass homeownership even after the 1917 patriotic turn.

No amount of propaganda, however, could overcome the roadblock of affordability preventing much of the middle and working classes from buying homes in the 1920s. Realtors in this period advocated for measures to expand home financing's availability. But the expansion of home financing along class lines coincided with the increasing formalization of black exclusion from purchasing property in white residential areas, a decision treated by realtors not as a social preference but a financial necessity.[63] Contributions to the *NREJ* from this period also mark the surging support among realtors for racial covenants, separate housing tracts for blacks, and ethical codes forbidding licensed members from selling homes to blacks in white areas. This section charts how homeownership's new patriotic discourse linking political stability to the expansion of the white ownership class helped naturalize residential apartheid as a matter of both financial and state security.

To start, whether one sought to rent or own, most forms of dwelling became harder to attain upon America's entrance into World War I. The diversion of supplies, workers, and financial resources from the construction industry to the war effort led to a decline in both housing construction and available home financing. Manufacturing centers recruiting thousands of laborers to wartime industries experienced the most severe housing crunches.[64] These shortages led to the government's first foray into state housing to shelter war workers, paving the way for later public housing initiatives.

The NAREB largely supported state-built wartime housing, betting correctly that it would lead to broader state subsidies for the housing market rather than become a slippery slope to mass public housing.[65] Perhaps the greatest insurance against this outcome was the Russian Revolution. In response to the Bolshevist coup, the American state alongside private industry aggressively promoted strategies for preventing the spread of class insurrection. Articles in the *NREJ* after 1917 claimed homeownership could inoculate the nation against the arrival of Bolshevism on its shores, asserting that citizens financially invested in their homes were less likely to revolt.[66] "When our citizens are called upon to defend their country," as one author wrote in 1919, "the man who owns his own home is inspired to fight much harder for his flag."[67] Another contributor blamed the Russian Army's collapse on the unpropertied peasants composing its ranks who "refused to fight longer for a land of which they owned no part."[68] Pieces in the *NREJ* consistently cast homeownership as the most effective prophylactic against mass revolt and the boosting of home sales as not merely a financial imperative but a matter of national security. As historian LeeAnn Lands writes, "World War I, the Red Scare, and Russia's political turmoil provided ample fodder for the NAREB's drive to load homeowner and homeownership with status and cultural power."[69]

Realtors framed homeownership as a fix-all for radicalism of all stripes. Contributors to the *NREJ* preached that the homeowner was more likely to participate in elections ("He makes it his business to see that candidates are fit before election and not unfit afterwards"), become a more reliable worker ("It gives a man something to work for. It keeps him from aimlessly shifting around from job to job"), secure the well-being of future generations ("And children, what of the little waifs who have no stable abiding place?"), encourage thrift ("A husband and wife who own their own are more apt to save"), and even cultivate a more finely tuned appreciation for aesthetics ("it cultivates your eye for beauty—and teaches you to be economical").[70] Whereas earlier odes to real estate in the *NREJ* touted ownership as "the foundation on which have been reared the civilizations of all ages," realtor rhetoric after 1917 became snugly focused on the home front.

Though the emphasis on distinguishing between property-loving republicans and those untethered from both home and state intensified in the *NREJ* after the Russian Revolution, the rhetoric of these newer arguments built upon the journal's earlier civilizational discourse touting the fealty to property as a racial trait. These echoes appear most pronouncedly in *NREJ* articles disparaging the Industrial Workers of the World (IWW), associated with itinerants and migrant farmworkers portrayed as vehement non-owners. "A good home makes for good citizenship," as one 1920 *NREJ* piece insists, "and I doubt very much if you will find many among the I.W.W.'s who have a family and own their own home."[71] Another piece from 1918 more bluntly identifies those drawn to such a platform. "The dangerous, disintegrating doctrines that inspire the I.W.W. never originated around a home fireside," this author warns "but were hatched about the campfire of wandering hoboes" recruited not from "American homes" but "the landless and the homeless."[72] The difference between those from American homes who maintain a commitment to property and "the landless and homeless" constituting the IWW is not legal citizenship, it seems, but land of origin. The piece frames those arriving to the U.S. from nations (and peoples) with frailer attachments to property as the source of anarchic ideas unnatural to its shores and, by extension, its people—those whose "craving for land," as per the *NREJ* four years earlier, comes from "an inborn instinct" distinctive to "the Anglo-Saxon race."[73]

Analogues between *NREJ* attacks on radicals post-1917 and its earlier reverence for white capacity for property continue to accrue in its pages. Take, for instance, an official communication to NAREB members published in the *NREJ* in 1919 claiming that wherever mass homeownership takes hold "will be found a contented, law-abiding, constructive citizenship." These upstanding citizen-owners, he alleges, stand in sharp contrast to

> those who group themselves under leaders who stand for destruction of every existing order of Government, to whom the sacred word "home" has no meaning, who delight to parade under the names of Bolshevists, Anarchists, Nihilists, Reds, Radicals, etc., who, without home or country, drift from continent to continent, country to country, leaving a trail of misery and vice and destruction wherever you go.[74]

This memo conjures a mirror image of the propertied transnational Anglo-Saxons the organization had previously deployed to unite the field in noble racial service. Whereas earlier contributors to the *NREJ* evoked the transhistorical superiority of the property-respecting white race to encourage contemporary homeownership, this communiqué evokes its chaotic opposite for similar ends as a vision of international marauders refusing fealty to either state or race now rallied the profession. Even though this memo does not explicitly cite Anglo-Saxon supremacy, such invocations in previous issues of the *NREJ* shadow its vision of perilous radicalism imperiling any state founded on the sanctity of home—identified as the defining characteristic of white-majority states for much of the association's young history.

Saving Americans attracted to the IWW's form of radicalism, *NREJ* writers insisted, required widening the path to homeownership. "Inspire a man to procure a home of his own," as one *NREJ* contributor wrote, "and he may be safely trusted to be proof against the poison virus of the I.W.W."[75] But if homeownership inoculated the vulnerable worker from forms of radicalism, realtors recognized the limits of their propaganda to secure this vaccination alone. This is not for lack of trying, however. One *NREJ* article urged realtors to stimulate a desire to own so intense that class difference would be usurped by the "division of our people into those social classes of 'those who own real estate and those who do not.'"[76] But without the widespread construction of affordable housing as well as home financing to put it within reach of the working classes, the dream of achieving a nation of homeowners was doomed. The editorial page of a 1931 *NREJ* issue suggests as much. After a decade of efforts to encourage the desire to own, the journal's editors conclude that "at least among the poorer classes, the desire for a home is about as strong as it could be. What is needed, we feel, is not to encourage people to own their homes, but to show them how to go about it, to help them go about it. The desire is there."[77] Several New Deal programs would soon intervene on this front, making homes more affordable through mechanisms such as state-backed mortgage insurance promoting the thirty-year mortgage and the GI Bill. The NAREB's agitation helped set the stage for this later legislation.

While realtors rallied around a vision of mass homeownership premised on class inclusivity in the 1920s, the question of homeownership's racial inclusivity elicited a more muted response in the NAREB's journal if not its practices. Though the *NREJ* regularly touted the Anglo-Saxon's privileged relationship to ownership in the journal's first decade, references to African Americans remained much scarcer in its pages. The first reference to African Americans in the *NREJ* appears in a 1912 short article reporting on the resolutions passed by the "reputable real estate men in Roanoke," Virginia, renouncing the recent sale of homes to blacks in white neighborhoods. In addition to pledging to prohibit such sales in the future, this local coalition of realty firms collectively resolved to stand "in favor of the segregation law."[78] Such impersonal reporting on local boards and developers endorsing segregation and its strategies accounts for the majority of the journal's coverage of black residents through the 1920s. These offhanded acknowledgments of segregation's hardening infrastructure in the *NREJ* in this period belies the NAREB's active role in its buttressing, from the association's adoption of a race-based code of ethics in 1924 to the growing number of its members writing, adopting, and endorsing racial covenants en masse. Yet such efforts found little debate or even discussion in the *NREJ*. This dearth could be chalked up to the fact that most NAREB members already believed that the presence of blacks lowered property values in white neighborhoods, or to the intensifying housing activism of groups like the National Association for the Advancement of Colored People (NAACP) disincentivizing discussions of segregation in the association's publicly circulating materials. But the question of where and how to house blacks if not in proximity to whites—a source of potential revenue for realtors—also drew surprisingly little attention in the journal's first decades. The earliest indicator of the organization's approach to black property owners, present and future, appears in one of the *NREJ*'s first issues from 1910 in an article titled "Uncle Sam's New Empire" and consisting of a three-page spread touting the opportunities awaiting real estate brokers in the "New South."[79] In describing the South's "millions of acres of rich, fertile farm land" ripe for investment, the article makes no reference to the black population that largely worked and sometimes owned these acres.[80] This article's absenting of this substantial black population from its vision of the New South is in line with the journal's explicit celebration of property as an index of whiteness.

When black homeownership wasn't being either ignored or feared in the pages of the *NREJ*, it was breezily invoked as blight or as a joke. For instance, a 1918 piece urging the outlawing of unsightly billboards from residential areas made the comparison that billboards "contaminate a landscape in about the same degree that a negro family contaminates a white neighborhood."[81] Realtors had so internalized the logic of black residential exclusion and of blackness as illiquid asset by 1918 that it became the logic through which other forms of restrictions could be understood. Another article from the same year frames Negro interest in homeownership as an odd curiosity. In the piece, a realtor recounts the time when a black man stopped by his local "Own Your Home" campaign headquarters, reproducing the man's speech in dialect: "Ah wants to buy a home—and I got the money in mah pocket to pay for it wid."[82] After making fun of this man's incredulity at his inability to get a deed on the spot, the author marvels that this was "the one time that money won on the races was put to a good use," treating the concept of black homeownership as a humorous anomaly.[83] In light of the journal's broader emphasis on the Anglo-Saxon capacity for property as well as the ability for homeownership to save white Americans from radical influence, this piece suggests black incapacity for thrift and, by extension, ownership. Property could not save African Americans given the seeming acceptance by *NREJ* contributors that they could never truly or deeply desire it.[84]

But this article's staging of blackness's materialization through speech and, presumably, sight is just as crucial to the emergent parsing of the residential sensorium, since the work of reading and adjudicating blackness was central to the realtor's job. Given the entrenchment of the belief that detectable black presence was a universal threat to property values, the realtor's role was to be a skillful barometer of blackness as perceived by other white buyers—the ultimate source of residential property's value. Legal scholar Carol Rose, in tracing the centrality of sight to the history of property, underscores how "sight, both real and metaphoric, dominates the persuasive and rhetorical aspects of property."[85] Early realtors promoting mass homeownership reoriented what Rose describes as a general focus on *sight* within property rubrics to privilege acts of *racial perception*—the act of reading and interpreting race's affective and sensory evidence—increasingly dominating the persuasive and rhetorical aspects of residential property in the twentieth century. Compared to the earliest articles in the *NREJ* focused on whiteness's intrinsic fealty to property, the journal's approach to blackness involved foregrounding its sensorial discernment through legible racial signs so as to most efficiently exclude it from residential space. Realtors attended to whiteness's composition *through* property, touting the owned home's capacity to cause white Americans to both feel and be better, while relegating blackness to a detectable externality. As the real estate industry marketed mass homeownership's ability to remake the hearts and souls of white Americans, they insisted that this civic and spiritual makeover could only be achieved through the creation of systems securing black exclusion. This would have ramifications not just for the racial geography of the U.S. but also for the operation of racial perception and racial definition itself, as this book will continue to trace.

But for now, it's enough to note that the *NREJ* was largely uninterested in black tenants or owners (or their souls and feelings) and more interested in tracking the evolving mechanisms for surveilling and regulating the appearance of blackness in residential neighborhoods. A realtor would occasionally urge their fellow salesmen to target Negroes as potential customers, as the president of the Louisiana Real Estate Association did in his 1920 convention speech.[86] But the majority of *NREJ* articles about Negroes either reported on local board decisions to prohibit sales to blacks in white districts or publicized the decisions of various legal challenges to racial ordinances, zoning, covenants, and restrictions designed to bar their presence from white space. Contributors to the journal did pay some scant attention to the necessity of housing the growing number of blacks in Northern cities. An article about the 1919 Chicago race riots, for instance, optimistically posited that "this racial phase of land occupation in urban communities can be satisfactorily handled."[87] Reporting that "the influx of colored people into the Second Ward, Chicago, has reduced the value of real estate from one-third to two-fifths," the author ascribes this automatic devaluation as a "sentimental effect" unreflective of the personal feelings of whites toward blacks. This "sentimentality," the realtor argues "has to be reckoned with as one of the plain, matter-of-fact potentialities in real estate."[88]

But this author's call for realtors to help diffuse white "sentimentality" that framed black occupation as a financial threat would largely go unheeded.[89] Realtors did not spend much time debating the issue of Negro housing in the *NREJ*. The need for their exclusion from white space was largely treated as a truism requiring no further evidence or deliberation.[90] Readers were most likely to find the Negro referred to in the journal through the 1920s in articles about new subdivisions referring offhandedly to racial covenants excluding Negroes (and sometimes also Jews and Orientals) as an obvious necessity. For homeownership to do its alleged patriotic work of dampening the revolutionary inclinations of the white working class, home values needed to be seen as stable long-term investments capable of buoying their owners. The construction of homeownership as a civic, moral, and racial duty becomes crystallized in the *NREJ* during the 1920s, coinciding with the quieter acceptance that such a project depended on the exclusion of blacks from the residential neighborhoods being built and remade in this period.

Babbitt, Gatsby, and Residential Sight

In this final section I turn to two novels refracting the crystallizing racial logic of mass homeownership through fictional characters for whom residential ownership colors the ways they perceive, understand, and locate race. Placing these two types of real estate literatures—fictional and programmatic, professional and novelistic—in conversation reveals their shared interest in recalibrating racial perception relative to the nation's increasing investments—economic, affective, political, and aesthetic—in homeownership. To see race as a realtor—and, eventually, as a state given the increasing interdependence of these spheres—required attending to racial signs to ensure its proper spatial dispersal. To see blackness, moreover, entailed honing one's senses to its perception to secure its residential erasure. In contrast to the primitivist fantasia embraced by white modernist writers and artists who sought to harness a bit of black feeling while maintaining whiteness's biological integrity, the striver-centered novels of *Babbitt* and *The Great Gatsby* capture the changing terrain of homeownership actively remaking the work of racial perception and discernment itself.

It would be hard to talk about import of the modern realtor without considering the profession's most infamous cultural ambassador—the titular conformist of Sinclair Lewis's 1922 novel, *Babbitt*. Centering on the life of real estate agent George F. Babbitt in the fictional midsize town of Zenith, Lewis's novel viciously satirizes the hypocrisy, inanity, and self-loathing undergirding his middle-class lifestyle while also seeking to humanize its fallible protagonist. Babbitt's professional success, resulting from his "nimble[ness] in the calling of selling houses for more than people could afford to pay," is accompanied by his fine-enough home life in a modern residential development.[91] But restlessness—which literary critic Catherine Jurca understands in terms of a racialized feeling of spiritual dispossession—plagues him as well, a feeling accelerated by the stifling conditions required to maintain his success.[92]

Babbitt proceeds to blow up his life in a series of dalliances with Bohemianism and socialism before returning to his former conservative lifestyle by novel's end, reanchored by his owned home.

Despite accusations that the novel had no plot—as H. L. Mencken noted, "Babbitt simply grows two years older as the tale unfolds"—*Babbitt* was a bestseller whose protagonist quickly became a symbol of all that plagued contemporary middle-class living.[93] But the importance of Babbitt's status as not just as a businessman but as a realtor to his cultural iconicity has received little examination. On the one hand, George Babbitt came to be understood by the American public as an archetype of the white-collar businessman at large grappling with his middle-class status during this category's rapid expansion—a take Lewis himself encouraged. In a letter to publisher Alfred Harcourt, Lewis described his character as "the typical T.B.M."—short for tired businessman—designed to conjure "all of us Americans at 46, prosperous but worried, wanting—passionately—to seize something more than motor cars and a house before it's too late."[94] Babbitt stood in for salesmen, dealmakers, and speculators of all sorts coming to terms with the spiritual decay accompanying their new professional statuses, from the discontented commuter up to President Hoover himself. A 1930 article from the *Nation* titled "Our Super-Babbitt" invoked the character to demonstrate the disappointments of Hoover's first year in office, revealing the president to be "merely another capable American business with a knack for large affairs and a gift for publicity" in the vein of the fictional Babbitt and his middling ilk.[95]

But while the term *babbitt* became a shorthand in American culture for any kind of white-collar conformist obsessed with his self-image and standing, Lewis's novel also attends with great specificity to the quandaries of the professional realtor—a term the NAREB coined for its membership in 1916 and copyrighted in 1949. Babbitt's outward devotion to his local real estate board and his fixation on his reputation are in keeping with the NAREB's plight to replace the real estate broker's previous image as a slick huckster with a portrait of a duty-driven professional who is a pillar of his community. In a speech that could have been ripped from the pages of the *NREJ*, Babbitt attests to "the realtor's function as a seer of the future development of the community and as a prophetic engineer clearing the pathway for inevitable changes."[96] As the novel undercuttingly reveals in the next sentence, however, this figure's prophetic sight "meant that real estate broker could make money by guessing which way the town would grow. This guessing he called vision."[97] Babbitt's earnest-sounding realtor rhetoric, the fodder for Lewis's sharpest satire, was a product of extensive research. As his editor later described, Lewis put "as much study into the subject matter as a graduate student preparing," ultimately compiling a 193-page notebook of character bios, field studies, and plans.[98] Of this compiled research, as Lewis scholar James Hutchisson notes, "the most detailed—certainly the most technical—material in the notebook concerns real estate."[99] Lewis noted the average cost of an apartment in Cincinnati, one of the models for Zenith, the estimated costs of running a real estate agency the size of Babbitt's, a physical description of a real estate office he visited in Wilmette, Illinois, and partial conversations Lewis overheard there that he ultimately incorporated into the novel.

Lewis's real estate research informed what literary critic James Miller describes as the novel's "brokerist imaginary."[100] Miller identifies the brokerist imaginary, inherently contradictory in nature, as being organized by a commitment to civic values grounded in professional duty on the one hand, and the economic values of the free market rewarding extraction and exploitation on the other. The broker must sell a comforting and appealing vision of rootedness, responsibility, and honor unsullied by the commercial sphere while also maintaining, as Miller describes, "a belief in the alienability of all land" and "its capacity to be freely detached and marketed as a commodity."[101] While real estate was not the only professional sphere remaking itself in more genteel terms in the period while remaining ruthlessly speculatory in its practices, it was on the cutting edge of managing this contradiction, taking it up explicitly and self-consciously as an ideological tension to be corralled and steered. Real estate was not exceptional in the degree to which its imaginary was contradictory, but it was exemplary in the pervasiveness and efficacy of this rhetoric as plotted in the pages of the *NREJ*.

Despite the contradictions inherent to the brokerist imaginary, one commonality bridged its dueling imperatives of civic duty and economic rapaciousness: perceptions of black illiquidity. In the age of Jim Crow, African Americans were already largely barred from uniform civic participation, helping to render their expulsion from large swaths of residential space in the U.S. not only judicially sound until 1948—when restrictive covenants were ruled illegal—but civically tolerable and even keenly desirably to many white Americans for far longer. While residential restrictions against other minorities eased as the century progress, fear of blackness's specific powers of depreciation ossified. It was the realtor's civic duty—over and above his profit margin, in fact—that obligated him to uphold the sanctity of white neighborhoods as the NAREB ratified in its 1924 Code of Ethics, two years after *Babbitt*'s publication. According to this document, the realtor's historic role as "the instrumentality through which the land resource of the nation reaches its highest use and through which land ownership attains its widest distribution" imposed "obligations beyond those of ordinary commerce; they impose grave social responsibility and a patriotic duty to which the Realtor should dedicate himself."[102] These obligations, as stated in article 34 of the Code, required that "a realtor should never be instrumental in introducing into a neighborhood a character of property or occupancy, members of any race or nationality, or any individuals whose presence will clearly be detrimental to property values in that area."[103] Upholding his pledge to act "with integrity and honor" required forgoing such sales for the alleged greater good of existing white home values.

But black residential exclusion, it turns out, was also good for the bottom lines of realtors and many others given the amount money to be made from this residentially captive population. Racial covenants, realtors' codes of ethics, and unequal lending practices all intensified black ghettoes and enclaves where residents generally paid far higher rents and interest rates for far worse housing, generating immense income for an interracial cohort of realtors, landlords, and speculators.[104] When blacks were able to purchase homes, they paid higher down payments, interest rates, and closing costs. So while at the NAREB's behest, realtors forwent sales to potential black homebuyers in white neighborhoods who were often willing to pay far more for their homes than white buyers out of necessity, the money to be made from segregation's maintenance eased this temporary loss of income. In these ways, a belief in black illiquidity proved foundational to both sides of the brokerist imaginary, allowing realtors to frame acts of discrimination as a civic duty *and* a profit generator under the workings of racial capitalism.

Babbitt thus reflects the growing civic and financial pressure to eliminate blackness from the representational frame of white residential life entirely, with the realtor being at the vanguard of this perceptual feat. Unlike Southern landscapes featuring blacks and whites living in relative spatial proximity if under radically unequal terms, or the multiracial commercial and industrial districts of the North engined by cheap black and foreign labor represented in works of urban realism, emergent and revitalized residential districts and developments featured in a growing body of middlebrow literature in the twentieth century presented a new typology of space rejecting black presence all together. As modernized homes became less reliant on black domestic labor and residential enclaves become further isolated from commercial and industrial districts, the goal of much residential space in the early twentieth century—across urban, rural, or suburban locales—was not to manage blackness but exile it from its borders completely to a residential elsewhere out of sight. To revise the famous Du Bois quote, the project of twentieth-century mass housing was to *export* the color line so whiteness could become invisible and unremarkable in its residential steadiness, operating as the only game in town.

It follows, then, that, as in the *NREJ*, blackness in *Babbitt* does not occupy much of the novel's direct attention. The realtor's role as professional "seer" in relation to blackness was to maintain its exclusion. To *not* see blackness—or to see blackness so one's clients didn't have to—was the realtor's aim, a sign he had done his job. As in the *NREJ*, the discourse of real estate boosterism takes up an enormity of room in *Babbitt* relative to the minor space that explicit references to race and racial perception occupy. But unlike in Lewis's 1947 novel, *Kingsblood Royal*, openly satirizing the relationship between racial perception and residential value, in Lewis's 1922 depiction of the real estate market, racial myopia is the more effective and more mimetic approach. Babbitt's job as a realtor is to be more generally concerned with how things *appear*. In a passage marking the shallowness of Babbitt's knowledge of Zenith, while we are told it is "the duty and the privilege of the realtor to know everything about his own city and its environs" and to "know his city, inch by inch, and all its faults and virtues," the narrator informs us just how spurious his knowledge is.[105] Babbitt can faithfully recite market prices and fire insurance rates but does not know the size of the police or fire department, their levels of training, or their wages; he can speak eloquently about the proximity of schools to neighborhoods but can say nothing of the functioning of these schools.

The same can be said about Babbitt's relationship to race in the novel. Deep or engaged knowledge of race is unnecessary; the only time he sees or makes note of racial others is when they are in service to him in commercial areas. We see the "Lettish-Croat" maid who works for the Babbitts exactly once, ringing the dinner gong in Americana parody. Babbitt goes on to encounter a few nameless black porters, one while traveling in a Pullman car and another at a hotel where his hair and nails are trimmed. Blacks exist in and around the town of Zenith—and around the edges of the narrative itself—as lubricants for Babbitt's professional life. But where they live after the workday is done, however, remains unmarked within the novel; no black enclaves register on any of Babbitt's descriptive or physical maps of Zenith. Despite his job as prophetic "seer," the novel makes clear that black dwelling is not within his purview. To properly "see" as a realtor required cultivating a cribbed form of sight enabling him to only see within a specific umbra and to a certain scale in order to sell that partial sight to others.[106] His cultivated unknowingness is what makes him good at his job. The *NREJ* offered Babbitt and his fellow realtors keen instruction in this form of occluded sight.

If the avoidance of racial sight is the name of the game in *Babbitt*, in F. Scott Fitzgerald's *The Great Gatsby*, "ways of seeing people and property together," as Paige Glotzer describes the practiced perception of early realtors, is put to dynamic and frequent practice.[107] But before examining *Gatsby*'s racial perception as filtered through residential sight, let's briefly turn to another publication from the NAREB that cannily echoes some of the passions and performances of this novel's titular character. When the NAREB began publishing homeownership promotional material for the general masses in 1922, it drew from the ideology that had circulated in its in-house journal for over a decade prior to appeal to buyers as well as sellers. *A Home of Your Own and What It Means to You*, written by NAREB member M. W. Folsom, is a thirty-two-page book filled with bright pictures and easily digested prose making the case to the public for homeownership in moral, civic, health, and financial terms. The book is divided into discrete sections focusing on how ownership can better men, women, children, grandparents, workers, and bosses.[108] Although Folsom never explicitly refers to race in the book, all of its images feature white-appearing men, women, and children reaping the benefits of ownership's bounty.

But one image in Folsom's book captures the *NREJ*'s previous racial ideology while also hinting at the future relationship of whiteness and ownership.

This image appears in the first section of *A Home of Your Own* making the book's most forceful sales pitch. Emphasizing the connection between homeownership and manhood, this section's central image features a white man facing a picturesque single-family home complete with a blond child playing in its prettily landscaped front yard. Dreamily hovering above this crisply colored vision of domestic bliss appears an English medieval castle. Though he is turned away from us, the man's gaze tracks up as he stares at this chimera breaking through the pictorial frame of the American residential halcyon right in front of him. The caption below it presented on a scrolled banner labels this scene "His Castle," followed by the declaration that "Home Owning Breeds *Real* Men." The three scenes appearing before this figure—the floating castle in the background, the contemporary home of the middle ground, and the white child in the foreground—collectively offer him and us a fantasy of white genealogy made possible through homeownership. The single-family home in the middle ground physically links the mythic Anglo-Saxon past conjured by the castle to the child, representative of an ongoing white future. The home fuses past and future fantasies of white heritage.

In visualizing the idea that homeownership secures one's connection to a transhistorical Anglo-Saxon diaspora as well as its ongoing reproduction, this image condenses many of the racial claims appearing throughout the *NREJ* during its first two decades. The accompanying caption declaring homeownership's capacity to "breed *real* men" further underscores this messaging. The *real* in the caption indexes not only masculinity but race, given the continual insistence in the domains of American science, law, and real estate that only white men were real men.[109] Identifying the home as the agent bestowing masculinity, the caption reinforces the genealogical argument presented in the image. In breeding real men, the image and text both suggest, homeownership ensures the ongoingness of whiteness.

But in figuring homeownership as the source of this breeding, this caption's grammar also manages to flip on its head the racial logic most frequently appearing in the *NREJ*. While early contributors regularly presented homeownership as an innate white capacity strengthened with each new generation, Folsom's claim that "home owning breeds *real* men" presents ownership as the *agent* of whiteness's continuation rather than its *index*. Rather than reflecting the previous decades of racial real estate discourse, this sentence

FIGURE 3. Illustration from M. W. Folsom, *A Home of Your Own—and What It Means to You* (1922).

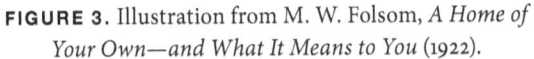

Source: M. W. Folsom, *A Home of Your Own—and What It Means to You* (Chicago: National Association of Real Estate Boards, 1922), 2.

anticipates the next phase of housing ideology in the midcentury that would figure ownership as the engine of a newly consolidated whiteness rather than claiming whiteness itself to be the perpetually self-sustaining source of the drive to own.

In its depiction of residential gazing that potentially doubles as a mode of racial formation, Folsom's image reverberates with the multiple moments of home-gazing that punctuate *The Great Gatsby*—moments that often telegraph the desires for and the limits of the owned home to fully vouch for racial identity in this period. The shifting ontology of whiteness depicted in

Folsom's guidebook rhymes almost literally with Jay Gatsby's vision for his extravagant castle-like West Egg, Long Island, home featured in Fitzgerald's novel in 1925. Fitzgerald describes Gatsby's West Egg mansion as having a distinctively "feudal silhouette." The home's previous owners were so committed to achieving this feudal fantasy that they offered to pay their neighbors' taxes if they would thatch their roofs with straw.[110] Gatsby's overzealous investment in the Anglo-looking appearance of his house, buying a home that not only chimerically invokes Anglo-Saxon heritage but that materially mimics it as well, is one of several signs to his pedigreed neighbors that he lacks racialized tact that ownership was supposed to mark. His house doth protest too much, serving as one more flag that forever underneath Jay Gatsby lies the un-Anglo James Gatz.

The Great Gatsby takes place in 1922, the same year Folsom published his promotional book. It's not hard to imagine either a young James Gatz or his decidedly Anglo creator, F. Scott Fitzgerald, perusing *A Home of Your Own* in his local realtor's office, absorbing its racialized message that "home ownership breeds *real* men." The illustration of this faceless man's raised gaze trained upon the dream of ownership in *A Home of Your Own* mirrors Gatsby's own penchant for gazing into the horizon from his dock. Read through the lens of Folsom's illustration, Gatsby's acts of residential gazing conjure his similar wish for homeownership to buy him breeding, making him white enough to be seen as an eligible partner for Daisy. In addition to his new surname and invented Oxford education, Gatsby's modern medieval mansion marks the unsubtlety of his attempts to both excessively perform and lavishly purchase his way into whiteness. Unlike his ally Nick Carraway, who is, it turns out, rightfully skeptical of homeownership's capacity to secure Gatsby's assimilation into the Anglo moneyed class, Gatsby believes deeply in the transformative power of property to trump his lesser origins.

Gatsby is enamored with homeownership long before he achieves it himself. Before he even meets Daisy, Gatsby is described as first falling for her family home in Louisville, Kentucky. "It amazed him—he had never been in such a beautiful house before."[111] Gatsby marvels at her home's coolly beautiful bedrooms, its busy corridors, and even the imagined presence of Daisy's previous suitors whose presence he felt "all about the house." His later curation of his Normandy mansion in West Egg is an attempt to ensconce Daisy within his own version of an ancestral estate. But for all its bells and whistles, what Gatsby seems to love most about his West Egg mansion is the fact that he owns it. He inadvertently admits with pride to Nick, for instance, that it took him three years to accrue the capital needed to purchase his home, undermining his own origin story as a moneyed inheritor. Upon Gatsby's death, his father proudly shows Nick the photograph his son sent of his home, presenting him with a beat-up picture "cracked in the corners and dirty with many hands" that belies the value both father and son placed in its possession.[112] Gatsby's desperate hunger for homeownership marks him not as a white yeoman but as a striver newly on the make, seeking to secure his breeding through ownership.

But to return to one of the home-loving ballads Hoover cited in his 1931 address, Gatsby's passion for home also recalls the occluded figure at the heart of Stephen Foster's minstrel song "My Old Kentucky Home." Gatsby's love of home and his relentless need to stage and care for it cause him to appear to the Tom Buchanans of the world as more akin to the "home-loving" Uncle Tom equipped with a "gentle, domestic heart" than the pedigreed Anglo-Americans Gatsby aches to impress. Whereas the wealthier and overtly pedigreed Buchanans and Carraways can live anywhere and in any way without their whiteness being called into question—Nick, after all, rents a cottage "squeezed between two huge places," while the Buchanans flit from residence to residence—Gatsby née Gatz needs every sign he can fashion and every gesture he can muster to attest to the lineage he has manufactured to distinguish himself from the Uncle Toms and Tomases of the world. But in his desperation for his owned home to secure his whiteness, Gatsby overplays his hand. His desire for such a literal representation of white roots ironically amplifies his unverified family history, as most of the characters in the novel remain more interested in his last name than the legitimacy of his deed or the pitch of his roof. When Tom attends his first party at Gatsby's, he sneers that its host "must have strained himself to get this menagerie together" before proclaiming "I'd like to know who he is and what he does," insinuating that Gatsby's house is not enough to vouch for his character or, as other critics have argued, his race.[113] Homeownership in *The Great Gatsby* is yoked to the specter of racial passing, America's other great literary obsession. Despite the *NREJ*'s efforts, in *Gatsby*, racial value is not yet fully yoked to residential value. Known heredity trumps residential occupation as the more valued site of racial identification and information.

Despite the promises held out by the image featured in Folsom's *A Home of Your Own*, homeownership could not yet breed whiteness in the 1920s, as Gatsby tragically discovers. His castle-like home fails to secure his racial belonging, as the discovery of his non-Anglo heritage contributes to his eventual rejection by Daisy followed by his own death. Gatsby's home fails to inaugurate him into the metaphysical whiteness Folsom sublimely depicted. It would take a few more years for homeownership to become capable of bestowing whiteness onto someone like James Gatz, as the later chapters in this book will illustrate. Homeownership would finally deliver on its promise to bequeath whiteness to those who could play this constructed part only after many years of remaking whiteness's definition and perception in residential terms.

2 Scoring Housing's Modern Jazzy Sound at the Rent Party

WHILE PRESIDENT HERBERT HOOVER TURNED to the "immortal ballads" of the American songbook to claim Americans "never sing songs about a pile of rent receipts," as discussed in Chapter 1, the youngest Hoovers had other types of "home songs" on the brain. When the Hoovers moved from Palo Alto, California, to Washington, D.C., in 1922 to accommodate his entry into politics as commerce secretary, Hoover Sr.'s technology-obsessed teenage sons brought their passion for sound recordings with them. Upon their arrival east, the Hoover boys purchased the latest phonographic equipment to outfit their new mid-Atlantic home. Allan, the youngest of the sons and described by his biographer as "grown up at fourteen in his first long trousers" at the time of the move, put their new machines to frequent use. His mother's secretary reported in 1922 that Allan preferred "records of the most modern jazzy kind."[1]

Given the newness of jazz as a genre and the small number of circulating recordings at the time, we can make some educated guesses as to what those "modern jazzy" sounds emanating from Allan's record player might have been. Most likely, Allan owned records by white jazz bands like Paul Whiteman or the Ray Miller Orchestra, the first jazz band to play at the White House in 1924. Perhaps he managed to acquire one of the earliest recordings by Fats Waller—the young Harlem stride pianist famous for his prolific songwriting, comedic performances, and wide physique—released by Okeh records in late 1922.[2] But even if the youngest Hoover was not yet hip to Fats Waller, the work of more mainstream artists like Whiteman and George Gershwin was heavily influenced by Waller and his Harlem peers on the rent party circuit remaking jazz through innovations in endurance, flexibility, and tempo. The jazz musicians driving the rent party scene, in concert with the dancers, merrymakers, voyeurs, and journalists attending and representing these parties, led Americans like the younger Hoovers to inadvertently attend to the sounds, if not the state, of black housing.

This chapter follows the "modern jazzy" sounds emanating from Hoover's D.C. home to trace the contrapuntal story about the value of ownership forged at rent parties—sites absented from Hoover's national soundtrack of home feeling. As examined in the previous chapter, Hoover, along with several contributors to the *National Real Estate Journal*, called upon a nineteenth-century archive of song as evidence of a distinctly racialized longing for housing. But the new music coming out of Harlem, Bronzeville, U Street, and maybe even Hoover's own state residence point to other ideologies of housing from the period refusing to understand ownership in racially supremacist terms. Rent parties—sometimes improvisatory, sometimes preplanned fetes thrown by residents of America's urban black belts to forestall eviction another month—were jumbles of people, sounds, and smells crammed into tight, dark, and damp spaces where social, physical, and sensory boundaries often blurred. The residential sensorium honed at the rent party was not built around assessing bodies and buildings to determine the long-term value of home investment as per the norms being constructed by realtors, lenders, and the state. Rather, these functions might best be described in terms of the sensory disorientation they induced where what it meant to belong to a body was open for questioning and possible re-formation into new unpossessable collectives and assemblages, if only for a moment.

Though these parties were designed to keep people housed, they kindled pleasurable sensations of *dispossession*, fueling new dreams of residential living beyond the horizon of ownership. Against negative definitions of blackness as the disinclination to own or value ownership, apathy toward possession emerges within the rent party as a virtue making for better music, more harmonious social conditions, and more inventive conceptualizations of how one might dwell. Neighborhood formation at the rent party was a matter of racial *deformation* as what it means to see, full stop, let alone see race or feel raced, appears in representations of these gatherings as under continual challenge. In this chapter, the work of the racial sign in the 1920s and 1930s also appears up for grabs as African Americans of various political orientations and class status weighed what mass homeownership might portend for the meaning, value, experience, and endurance of blackness. This chapter reclaims a range of rent party figures—from Fats Waller and writers Wallace Thurman and Ira D. Reid to black women who largely hosted and attended rent parties— to resituate them within the cultural archive of American housing. In rent party representations, we find an approach to housing not as a moral or civic duty but as a necessity around which social relations in excess of ownership could emerge. The rent party became the site for theorizing modes of dwelling beyond the racialized arguments for mass ownership emerging from the nascent public-private partnership constructing the modern housing market.

The Problem of Negro Housing

[W]e must seek not simply home ownership, small landholding and savings accounts, but also all forms of cooperation. . . .
 —W. E. B. DU BOIS, "The Immediate Program of the American Negro," *The Crisis,* (April 1915): 310–12

While the rent party has its roots in Southern church socials and fish fries, it took on its most iconic form in the Northern cities to which blacks migrated en masse in the early twentieth century.[3] Peaking in popularity in the 1920s and 1930s, rent parties helped working-class residents afford the inflated rents in crowded black enclaves where renters generally paid as much as 50 percent more for housing than their white urban counterparts. Tenants advertised gatherings on printed cards inviting locals and passersby to house parties where a small entry fee would go toward the occupants' rent. Known for good music, hearty food, bad liquor, low lights, close dancing, late nights, and the occasional violent outburst, rent parties were places for attendees to let loose while assisting their neighbors in avoiding dispossession for another month.

Rent parties were products of the conditions constricting black dwelling in the urban North. While realtors and bureaucrats deemed the shortages affecting the housing market after World War I a temporary crisis, blacks largely experienced crises of housing as an ongoing norm. Crowded quarters, aging housing, and the impending threat of dispossession characterized not only the living conditions of blacks who migrated north at the turn of the century, but African Americans more broadly post-Emancipation.[4] Although blacks owned significant property in both the North and the South before and after slavery, their sovereignty over that property faced continual dispute. For black landowners in the South, the Jim Crow regime and the state-sanctioned terrorism it endorsed weakened the enforcement of black property rights. The profits whites incurred from sharecropping further incentivized black peonage, necessitating their landlessness, conditions that made Northern migration for African Americans all the more appealing.

The dwelling conditions migrants found in the North, however, were not that much better materially than what they had endured in the South. Sometimes they were far worse. Before the nineteenth century, the relatively small number of blacks residing in the urban North settled in a number of residential patterns. While some lived in exclusively black neighborhoods, others resided alongside whites and immigrants in mixed neighborhoods. This trend changed drastically with the onset of the Great Migration in the 1910s, causing black populations to nearly double in metropolitan areas between 1915 and 1920. As the earlier wave of Eastern and Southern European immigrants who had arrived in the U.S. in the late nineteenth century began to be assimilated into whiteness in the early twentieth, their rates of residential segregation declined. The inverse proved true for African Americans, however, whose rates of segregation in cities steeply increased after 1910, when the creation of the black ghetto began in earnest, restricting blacks to dwelling in districts whites had largely abandoned. While whites treated black and immigrant dwellers similarly in the late nineteenth century, "the very consciousness of whites in the North," one critic notes, "seemed to change during the few years from 1917 to 1920 from an 'ethnic' view of urban diversity to one more centered on race."[5] Whites in this period increasingly feared blackness as an absolute threat to residential order and, most significantly, to residential value.

Municipal governments and private realtors deployed several tactics to consolidate and contain the rising number of blacks moving to Northern cities. When the use of public zoning to bar blacks from residential areas failed to pass legal muster, several extralegal tactics emerged to enforce black containment. These tactics included the adoption of ethics pledges by realtors barring them from actively integrating neighborhoods, the refusal of many banks to loan to blacks at fair rates, the emergence of neighborhood improvement associations seeking to maintain residential color lines, and the normalization of racial covenants in housing deeds. These efforts amounted to a fairly comprehensive system of private zoning intervening where state-mandated forms of racial segregation had not succeeded.[6]

Except for some concerned reformers and members of the slumming white avant-garde who viewed black housing as a lurid site of fascination, black housing in the North received little sustained attention in the white public sphere.[7] Efforts to prevent blacks from living in white residential spaces largely overshadowed charges for decent black housing. But the housing conditions of African Americans were taken up by Hoover's 1931 President's Conference on Home Building and Home Ownership. Although Hoover ignored this issue in his official remarks to the conference, one of the conference's eleven subcommittees was dedicated to studying Negro Housing. This committee, headed by educator and civil rights activist Nannie Burroughs, issued a report detailing the specific housing issues facing African Americans before formulating some solutions.

Though the housing industry largely ignored its findings, the Negro Housing Committee's report offered a clear-eyed assessment of the racism and inequality they insisted was largely responsible for the poor state and limited availability of Negro housing. "The racial factors in the problem of housing," the report asserted, "are very largely those prompted by whites in an attempt to limit the areas in which Negroes may live."[8] Despite their condemnation of the municipal and private policies facilitating residential segregation, the committee largely agreed with bureaucrats and realtors on one crucial point: homeownership was key to solving the housing problems of all Americans across the color line. Repeating the concerns of reformers and realtors, Burroughs's committee warned against the dangers of overcrowded apartments and tenements for black residents. "The extent to which morals and health are jeopardized by the promiscuous taking in of roomers has been well established by many studies," the report decreed, claiming boarders to be "one of the principal evils in Negro housing."[9] The antidote to this residential promiscuity according to the committee was to make homeownership—described as an "index to social stability and good citizenship"—more accessible to all.[10]

The report's insistence that the dangers posed by tenements to both tenants' morals and health were best remedied by replacing these structures with single-family housing reflects the sentiments of reformers across the color line.

But the indexical language deployed by the committee framing ownership as a sign of good citizenship and social belonging is particularly noteworthy given race's own indexical status. Like the *NREJ* article from 1920 predicting that ownership status would one day replace class difference, the committee similarly imbues ownership with the capacity to remake the legibility of the social order. But in this instance, they anticipate ownership replacing race rather than class as a sign of proper civic and social belonging. The report's insistence a few pages later that "the influence of home ownership is readily observed in the care and attractiveness of property, its state of repair, site, and gradually increasing value" similarly claims the owned home's appearance as a "readily observable" index of the homeowner's virtue.[11] The shadow of the racial sign's pernicious interpretation hovers over the committee's investment in ownership as an alternative semiotics of citizenship, potentially replacing racial difference. The committee prepared its readers for a world where neighborhood formation centered on homeownership across the color line could devalue the use value of the racial sign. Rather than reading bodies to assess the worth of a home or a neighborhood, the committee suggests that signs of upkeep and repair would be enough to discern between the dwellings of good citizens and lesser ones, stable neighborhoods and more socially volatile ones. Residential risk assessment would not rely on evidence perceived from the racial body but, instead, on what homes revealed about their occupants' emotional and economic capacity to own.[12]

The Negro Housing Committee's decision to render the road to civil rights as coterminous with the path to homeownership would find ongoing support in the decades to come. But the committee's embrace of ownership as an index of social stability and superior citizenship also implies their tacit acceptance of an understanding of citizenship increasingly yoked to homeownership as the *NREJ* was also positing.[13] In advocating for increased black access to homeownership, the committee could not consider whether the vision of citizenship that homeownership was alleged to beget was worth seeking or whether black homeownership was an assured path to equal treatment either on the market, in social life, or within the civic sphere. Given the ongoing devaluation of property held by black owners, the stubborn endurance of residential segregation, and the limited impact of decades of fair housing legislation, the committee's faith in black homeownership's transformative potential has still not been fulfilled. If homeownership was to index "social stability and good citizenship," as the Negro Housing Committee insists, they ultimately misjudged property's equalizing capacity within the strictures of capitalism, racial or otherwise. The ongoing belief in the contagious illiquidity of black property still orienting residential markets to this day speaks to how neighborhood formation centered on homeownership intensified both racial formation and racism alike rather than dampening or replacing race's utility. But while the largely middle-class black and white members of the Negro Housing Committee placed their faith in homeownership's promises to pave a path to full social, civic, and economic citizenship, rent party revelers across town were experimenting with other modes of dwelling and being at home.[14]

Diagnosing the Rent Party

There are no extant recordings of the rent party's sounds and sights. What we know about these functions largely derives from the writings and recordings of the jazz greats who forged their styles and personas there, a handful of renderings of these events in literature and art, belated autobiographical recollections written by their attendees, and salacious headlines appearing in the press reporting on the occasional stabbing or murder that took place there. Although "rent parties every night were the special passion of the community," as historian David Levering Lewis notes, "their very existence was avoided or barely acknowledged by most Harlem writers."[15] Lewis frames this representational schism as a matter of respectability politics, noting that "with the exception of Langston Hughes and Wallace Thurman, almost no one—at least no one who recited poetry and conversed in French at Jessie Fauset's—admitted attending a rent party."[16] But the rent party's inherent ephemerality and crowded, dark settings also contributed to the difficulty of its documentation. Even rent party devotees Wallace Thurman and Langston Hughes struggled to find a singular coherent representational schema for capturing its improvisatory movements and sounds that fostered its dense intimacies.

Take Hughes's collection of rent party invitation cards. When describing the rent party in his 1940 autobiography, *The Big Sea*, Hughes provides his readers with two paragraphs of description tracing the party's basic contours—its economic function, its typical musical setup featuring a piano and drum, the "awful bootleg whiskey and good fried fish or steaming chitterlings" sold for cheap, and the dancing, singing, and "impromptu entertaining" stretching until dawn.[17] While Hughes claims to have attended these parties every Saturday night during his Harlem years, he recounts their highlights in a few short declarative sentences: "I wrote lots of poems about house-rent parties, and ate thereat many a fried fish and pig's foot" and "I met ladies' maids and truck drivers, laundry workers and shoe shine boys, seamstresses and porters."[18]

Hughes acknowledges these parties in *The Big Sea* but doesn't put much work into trying to make his readers actually *feel* them. In the place of lyrical description, Hughes apportions three of the five pages devoted to rent parties in his memoir to reproductions of seven rent party cards he collected over the years—the only visual reproductions to appear in the entire book. Hughes's documentary ethos in relation to the rent party echoes James Agee's acknowledgment of the inadequacy of words to do his rural white subjects justice in *Let Us Now Praise Famous Men* a year later. "If I could do it," Agee writes in 1941, "I'd do no writing at all here. It would be photographs; the rest would be fragments of cloth, bits of cotton, lumps of earth, records of speech, pieces of wood and iron, phials of odors, plates of food and of excrement."[19] Hughes's rent party cards in *The Big Sea* similarly evoke the failure of words—particularly his own as the rent party's poet laureate—to adequately capture his experience of them, despite this being the ostensible aim of his memoir. He offers us instead these card-sized aesthetic works created by the party throwers themselves in the place of his own deep description of the rent party, allowing us to glimpse the flavor of these functions in the differing fonts, witticisms, and boasts hosts deployed to hype their parties.

Despite Hughes's boast of having written "lots of poems about house-rent parties," when we turn to his poetry from this period, the rent party finds even scanter representation. Hughes explicitly references this setting in just one published poem: "Rent Party Shout for a Lady Dancer," published in the *New York Amsterdam News* in August 1930, which was likely solicited by Wallace Thurman.[20] Compared to the numerous other Hughes poems set in cabarets and nightclubs or the odes he penned in this period evoking jazz, dance, and gin without specific situation, the rent party garners little particular attention in Hughes's poetry as a distinctive space or social form.[21] In his lone identifiable rent party poem, Hughes moves between stock descriptions of violence and dance—prominent tropes of the rent party that first found wide reportage in the pages of the *Amsterdam News*. Following the general incitement to "whip it to a jelly" common to the rent party, Hughes conjures an aggrieved rent party attendee who'd rather kill her man than lose him to another woman. Urging the piano player to keep playing, the speaker moves seamlessly between calls to "shake it slow" and the woman's plans to shoot or cut her beau. Unlike the sensory thickness Hughes hints at in his description of the rent party in his memoir, his poetic rent party shout distills this manifold energy into a singular figure moved by desire, rage, and jazz. The poem seems to be more inspired by songs one might hear at rent parties—hence its title of "Rent Party Shout"—than a representation of the rent party itself.

Hughes's limited poetic representation of the rent party may be more symptomatic of the representational quandaries of the rent party more broadly than his own lack of interest in depicting its tempos and dispositions. The ephemeral archive of the rent party befits not only the condition of economic precarity necessitating its invention but its material and perceptual conditions. Its dark and crowded spaces, rowdy live music, and intermingled smells of home cooking and sweat created a set of dynamic and blurry tableaus exceeding not only the recording capacity of cameras and phonographs but realist or lyrical representation at large.[22] The difficulty of providing images of these dark and disorderly scenes reflects the rent party's broader ethos of cultivating scenes of psychic and physiologic dispossession that also allowed tenants to maintain physical possession of rented space for one more month.

The meager archive left behind by the rent party has not stopped critics from assessing its value. Over the past thirty years, scholars of black performance have interrogated the rent party's significance while attending to the sensuousness foregrounded in its early representations. One of the rent party's starkest assessments comes from dance scholar Katrina Hazzard-Gordon. Despite describing rent parties in her 1992 book, *Jookin': The Rise of Social Dance Formations in African-American Culture*, as "the product of cooperation," she ultimately insists these parties "remained essentially an individual response to a large-scale problem" that "could not galvanize the community into a political unit."[23] "Had a political organization or strong tenants' movement addressed housing needs," she concludes, "the rent party might not have developed such support."[24] For Hazzard-Gordon, the rent party was the result of a political vacuum, marking the absence of black organization rather than its expression.

Hazzard-Gordon frames the rent strike and the rent party as oppositional forms. Yet both of these forms simultaneously punctuated Harlem's residential scene in the 1920s and 1930s, suggesting that one did not negate the possibility of the other. Women led the first rent strike of black tenants in Harlem in 1916, an action followed by further local tenant organizing in ensuing years. The best known of these was the Harlem Tenants League, led by communist Richard B. Moore between 1928 and 1930.[25] But most rent strikes, including those led by the Harlem Tenants League, elicited few concessions from landlords. These actions did not fail because rent parties distracted tenants from "real" politics. Rather, as historian Mark Naison notes, rent strikes proved challenging for Harlem's most vulnerable residents to execute due to the saturated housing market for blacks barred from residing beyond Harlem's heaving borders.[26] Given the difficulty of acquiring housing of any type in Harlem, black tenants risked ending up in worse accommodations or homelessness should strikes fail. Black tenants were largely at the mercy of landlords who knew they had nowhere else to go, inhibiting the efficaciousness of even the best-organized rent strike in Harlem without mass participation beyond its borders and across the color line.

It follows, then, that the period's most successful black rent strikes took place in Harlem's wealthy enclave of Sugar Hill. The Sugar Hill strikes began in 1934 when black professionals residing at 281 Edgecombe Avenue learned they were paying nearly double what its previous white tenants had paid in rent. In response, the residents collectively withheld rent and hired lawyers to fight their landlords in municipal court.[27] In contrast to the earlier efforts of working-class Harlem strikers, Sugar Hill tenants could afford both the money and the time it took to pursue their claims in court.

But other housing actions took hold among Harlemites who could not afford such tactics. The rent party, in fact, shares key similarities with perhaps the most successful tactic for combatting rental exploitation—eviction resistance. These actions, captured in literary works like Ralph Ellison's *Invisible Man* and Theodore Ward's *Big White Fog*, involved masses congregating at sites of eviction to move furniture back into the dispossessed units and obstruct police efforts to see evictions through, buying evicted tenants precious time to regroup. As with rent parties, eviction actions coalesced with little notice or planning and relied on strangers joining in to help resist.

Participants in eviction actions rarely knew the dispossessed personally.[28] The spontaneous and temporary collectivities nurtured by the rent party align most strongly not with the strike, but with the riot—a form that, like the rent party, is often "understood to have no politics at all, a spasmodic irruption to be read symptomatically and perhaps granted a paternalistic dollop of sympathy," as Joshua Clover writes.[29] "The riot, as is broadly agreed even among its partisans," Clover continues, "is a great disorder," a diagnosis often assigned to the rent party as well.[30]

The rent party's social and political contours have garnered more sympathetic examination in more recent work by James Wilson, Martin Summers, Stephen Robertson, Fred Moten, and Shane Vogel focusing on the sensuous forms the rent party sustained and encouraged.[31] Moten and Vogel most explicitly challenge Hazzard-Gordon's insistence on the rent party's apoliticism, if in different ways. Vogel does so by claiming rent parties as sites for rethinking the very terrain of the political itself. He considers the Harlem Renaissance at large and the rent party in particular as manifestations of a "different kind of politics: a sensate politics that figured prominently in the Harlem Renaissance's cultures of sexual dissidence."[32] To recapture the "radical experimentations with sexual subjectivity and dissident form" he finds the recent scholarly acceptance of the Harlem Renaissance's queerness to flatten, Vogel turns to descriptions of the rent party performing what he terms "critical sensuousness," where the senses provide "material for expanding the boundaries of the known world."[33] Vogel recovers the ways writers "advanced a critical sensuousness in their many depictions of the rent party, where the intimate contact and the transformation of domestic space queered proprioception, or the sense and calibration of the body in its spatial orientation."[34]

Fred Moten is similarly interested in how the rent party's dispossessive disorientations brought together the "open field" of the "everybody" with "those abstract equivalences we call anybody" and the "the nones who are, in their constantly novitiate, base communitarian devotion, no-bodies."[35] While Vogel claims the rent party to incubate a "sensate politics," even while marking its divergence from politics as commonly thought, Moten sees the rent party as political, extra-political, and apolitical simultaneously. Sitting in the slippages between the manifold meanings of *party*, Moten insists of the rent party that "this new political party is not a political party," before redescribing it as "the old-new, extrapolitical party of the ones who are none" and "the violent birth or birth announcement of the last political party."[36] It is the indeterminability of the party that makes it hard to cleanly demarcate it from the riot. Creating not quite a genealogy between the rent party and the riot, Moten instead posits the multiple relational possibilities between the two as synonymous, yoked, and coeval.

How the rent party causes one to feel in their body—disrupting whether one has *a* body at all but an everybody, anybody, and a nobody all at once—is critical to both Vogel's and Moten's conception of the rent party's political potential. This potential becomes even crisper when juxtaposed with homeownership discourse from the period promoting the singular affective charge of ownership rendered synonymous with the racialized capacity to *feel* and *be* singularly possessive of property ascribed to Anglo-American subjectivity. Realtor discourse alleged homeownership could transform revolutionaries into patriots, fold some immigrants into whiteness, and turn men into *real* men, primarily through property's capacity to allow one to feel, and thus be, more sovereign. The rent party's disruptive sensorium, by contrast, muddled subjects' perception of both each other and of themselves *as* selves as they attach to the scene rather than the space. What Moten and Vogel seem to be naming in the rent party's political possibility is its refusal of a politics organized around Herbert Hoover's vision of American individualism, a concept increasingly anchored after the 1917 Russian Revolution in the U.S. by homeownership. If homeownership was touted as the ideal apparatus for reproducing the social and racial status quo, tenants at the rent party extended their residence in the short term without pledging any long-term allegiance to the physical and economic structures buttressing their continued exploitation.

This is not to deny that those living in the crowded and crumbling conditions of many Harlem tenants would have likely leaped at the opportunity to buy or rent elsewhere. Joshua Clover's observation that while the riot "makes structured and improvisational use of the given terrain," "it is a terrain they have neither made nor chosen" also applies to the rent party.[37] But in the course of fulfilling the base economic need of staying sheltered, rent parties made space for hosts and attendees to treat housing as *merely* a necessity rather than fetishize ownership as a calling, a civic duty, or a "universal yearning" as promoted by both the private housing industry and the state. The state envisioned mass homeownership as a practice that could protect the bodies of its citizens from the sexual, sensory, and sanitary dangers of living too closely and without permanent financial investment. But the rent party was an economic necessity that also suggested the vital sociality and even plural forms of subjectivity to be found outside of ownership.[38] Whereas ownership ideology sought to define whiteness in terms of the desire to be sovereign over property, rent partygoers' indifference to ownership, if not good housing, registers their resistance to engaging property as a capacity of any sort. Many of these attendees already suspected or knew that property would never make them sovereign citizens. Some of them were recent migrants familiar with practices of unjust dispossession in the South. Others were finding their exploitation on the Northern housing market to be just as brutal. The racialization of homeownership solidly under way by the 1930s was an extension of the larger cycle of racialized dispossession with which many migrants were already intimately familiar. Unlike those involved in rent strikes, rent party attendees sought no bargain with the state or the economy. Disinvesting from ownership ideology that viewed them as instruments of depreciation and contagious illiquidity, we find these partygoers pursuing other strategies of investment.

All We Want Is Everything: The Rent Party's Dispossessing Women

The most romantic accounts of the rent party come from the jazz musicians whose rhythms fueled it reveries. Figures such as Willie "The Lion" Smith, Thomas "Fats" Waller, and James P. Johnson—the titans of Harlem stride piano—all honed their craft on the circuit. Their rent party accounts provide us with a sense of their scale, scope, and sounds. Although the audiences at an average rent party were smaller than those found at larger Harlem nightclubs, they still drew robust numbers. "They would crowd a hundred or more people into a seven room railroad flat, and the walls would bulge," recounted Smith, with some parties spreading out to the hallways throughout a particular building.[39]

Rent parties were often also interracial affairs. George Gershwin was known to sit on the floor at parties where he observed with awe the stride piano greats in action.[40] Writer Bruce Nugent's account of the rent party in his unpublished novel *Gentleman Jigger*, written during the late 1920s and early

1930s, depicts the broad spectrum of figures across the color line patronizing these functions. While jazz musicians and historians tend to foreground the interracial boys club of musicians that held court at the rent party, Nugent underscores the queerer constituencies drawn to these parties welcoming various social and sexual crossings. From "slightly colored debutantes of sepia society" and intellectuals to "producers, number-runners, chorus-girls, gangsters, schoolboys, sailors, motion-picture stars, prizefighters, athletes, bartenders, dope-peddlers, parents, schoolteachers, authors, gigolos, artists, whores, pickpockets, millionaires, reporters, communists, laborers," Nugent concludes his breathless list by noting that "all colors from white through to black" could be found at a rent party.[41] Unlike the segregated clubs in Harlem, these places were known for welcoming all who could pay the entry fee across lines of, class, sexuality, and race.

Accompanying the compressed space and mixed company of the rent party was the unceasing tempo and extended duration of its soundscape. As Fats Waller's son, Maurice, recalled, "people came to have a good time and they didn't want to hear the blues."[42] Except for the occasional risqué up-tempo blues number, rent party attendees generally preferred jazz to the blues they associated with a slower-paced Southern melancholy.[43] Not only did the music need to be quick but it needed to last. Willie Smith noted the stamina required of rent party pianists charged with playing "all day long and half of the night." "We would wake up on the piano, and then we went to bed on the piano."[44] The long duration of these events coupled with the continuous improvisation demanded of musicians made rent parties excellent incubators for jazz pianists. The need to keep everyone entertained, moreover, fostered a competitive spirit among musicians. Jazz historian Paul Machlin describes the cutting contests between the multiple pianists working a party: "Each pianist would try to outdo ('cut') his predecessors in the complexity and sophistication of his tricks, and each developed, as a result, an individual, unmistakable style. The greater the difficulty of the music performed, the greater the stature accorded the pianist."[45] Jazz historians credit these competitions with gestating the personas and distinctive styles of the stride pianists shaping the next generation of jazz music.[46]

Most of the celebrated stride pianists credited with emerging from the rent party scene were men. Given the alleged unsuitability of blues for the atmosphere of the rent party, the blues women vocalists who reached their peak popularity in the early 1920s were largely shut out of the circuit. The lone exception is Gladys Bentley, the queer tuxedo-wearing blues pianist who eventually skyrocketed to fame entertaining patrons in New York and California with her risqué songs.[47] Though she, too, got her start on the rent party circuit, if one only read the masculinist accounts of rent parties by male jazz musicians and historians, one might think there were no women at all at these functions except for those romantically pursued by jazzmen.

But women played a major role in the life of the rent party as hosts, entertainers, and attendees. Parties were most often held on Thursday and Saturday nights, the nights that black domestics most regularly had off. In Langston Hughes's collection of rent party cards, the majority of them list women as hosts. Women also helped to invent and refine the social dances popularized at rent parties, including the Charleston, Black Bottom, Bump, Mess Around, and the Fish Tail, co-opted by Broadway and the cabaret scene.[48]

The ephemerality of the rent party's archive mirrors the scantiness of the archive of the working-class black women whom these parties both catered to and supported. But the traces of these women within the rent party's archive suggest their embodied refutation of the homeownership ideology crafted and circulated by both the housing industry and the state in this same period. Given the frequent correlation within the literature circulated by the National Association of Real Estate Boards between homeownership and the yoked virtues of masculinity and whiteness, black women would seem by default to possess the weakest drive to ownership according to such a capacity matrix. But it was the economic conditions that working-class black women faced in the North rather than an innate resistance to owning that led to their reliance on the rental market. Saidiya Hartman has described the limited economic opportunities and the exacting legal and social regimes of discipline and punishment these women faced upon migrating north while also attending to these women's experiments in daring to pursue their desires despite these conditions. Echoing Shane Vogel's focus on the "radical experimentations with sexual subjectivity and dissident form" undertaken by black and queer Harlemites, Hartman reclaims the innovative radicalism of the young black women whose "transformations of sexuality, intimacy, affiliation and kinship taking place in the black quarter of northern cities," she writes, "might be labeled the revolution before Gatsby."⁴⁹ Despite being largely written out of the histories of both the rent party and residential property, the domestics and wayward girls around whom the rent party scene revolved had firsthand knowledge of the racialized contours of both of these spheres. Employed by the white families the NAREB most sought to target while being themselves subject to the exploitative rental economy absorbing most of their hard-earned wages, these women were perhaps best equipped to assess the limitations of the racialized rhetoric of ownership while seeking other ways of claiming space.

Following Hartman's "aesthetical and riotous history of colored girls and their experiments with freedom," I posit that the efforts by black women to resist, decenter, and queer the homeownership ideology promoted by private housing industry and reproduced by the interracial state is an experiment we are still learning to sense.⁵⁰ The very women Nannie Burroughs hoped to save from the jeopardized health and morals bred by the "promiscuous taking in of roomers" through homeownership embraced rent parties as a chance to escape the various scales of containment fostered by the laboring and housing conditions of the North. Renting, despite being a racially exploitative force in Harlem, proved most amenable to the careful avoidance of being trapped, possessed, and contained for many of these women. The two female protagonists of two Harlem Renaissance works—Ira Reid's "Mrs. Bailey Pays the Rent" and Wallace Thurman's *Harlem*—use the rent party to pursue projects in excess of ownership and its affiliated virtues. Though written by men, these pieces center women as the rent party's driving forces and spiritual centers who have the least to lose by rejecting ownership and the limited prospects of citizenship it was alleged to beget.

Mrs. Bailey's Dispossessive Futurities

In addition to going unseen by jazz musicians and historians' affectionate accounts of the rent party in the period, black women proved of little concern to many of the reformers ringing alarm bells about the dangers of such seedy scenes. A 1935 article published in the *New York Amsterdam News* underscores this invisibility. The piece's sarcastic headline—"Socialist Uncovers Something New in Harlem: The House Rent Party"—mocks the belatedness of one political figure's discovery of the form. The socialist in question was

Louis Waldman, chairman of New York State's Socialist Party. Referring to him as "the crusading Christopher Columbus of the 'renting parties,'" the piece skewers Waldman's recent efforts to pressure the district attorney into more forcefully policing these gatherings on the grounds that they perpetuated mixed-race interactions particularly damaging to white women.[51]

The article counters Waldman's outrage on behalf of young white naïfs by declaring "the exploitation of Negroes by greedy landlords" to be the rent party's true scandal, indicting both Waldman's racist myopia as well as his surprisingly deficient economic analysis of the rent party. To counter the seductive power of the rent party, Waldman called for the construction of social centers to alleviate the conditions of "poverty and squalor" driving troubled white girls to these soirées. In his focus on protecting white womanhood, he demonstrates his disinterest in the fate of black women attending these same functions. The article caustically concludes by reporting that when Waldman was "asked whether the social centers he recommended should be segregated, he declined to make a direct answer and left the problem to the 'good people of Harlem.'"

Whereas Waldman concerned himself with white women's well-being within the rent party circuit, black journalist Ira D. Reid squarely centers his 1927 account, "Mrs. Bailey Pays the Rent," around a black woman. Reid's title derives from the piece's lyrical epigraph, the jazz standard "Bill Bailey, Won't You Please Come Home," in which the fictional Mrs. Bailey implores that she'll "do the cooking" and "pay the rent" if her husband would only return home.[52] Although he was employed by the National Urban League, Reid's account eschews empirical evidence such as interviews, economic data, or even realist description.[53] Forgoing sociological dissection, his piece reads more like a lyrical sketch than gritty urban reportage.[54]

Anticipating Hughes's memoir by thirteen years, Reid reprints a set of rent party cards as the article's lone illustrations. As with Hughes, a good deal of Reid's collected cards list women as hosts. Reid focuses his account on a party given by a composite of these women whom he names Mrs. Bailey after the article's lyrical epigraph. In his description of Mrs. Bailey's party, Reid grants us little access to her interiority or that of her guests. Whereas the Mrs. Bailey of song offers to pay the rent as a way of enticing her husband to come home, Reid leaves the motivations of her textual namesake beyond paying the rent unmarked. Whether this Mrs. Bailey is married or wants her husband to come home is unknown. While the home of the eponymous Mrs. Bailey of song is defined by traditional virtues such as marriage and her cooking, Reid's host seems uninterested in this vision of home. This other Mrs. Bailey is too busy choreographing the complex movement of bodies temporarily occupying her space. She doesn't yearn for the attributes that realtor discourse in this period persistently yoked to homeownership—marriage, children, democracy, a strictly defined sense of moral virtue. Maybe she wants these things, maybe she doesn't; maybe she is too busy or too overworked to entertain these desires; perhaps she would abandon her current space and company in a heartbeat to own a home elsewhere; or maybe the burden of an owned home makes her shudder. All we know is that Mrs. Bailey wants to pay her rent this month and that throwing a good party is integral to that mission.

Reid inundates us with the flurry of tasks required at the party's start, from renting chairs to setting up the live band. We are briefly introduced to the party's saxophonist, whom Reid explains had recently "quit the stage to play for the parties because he wanted to stay in New York."[55] The rent party not only enables rent party hosts and musicians to afford to stay put—this quote suggests that these functions were part of what made staying in Harlem worthwhile in the first place. For this saxophonist, New York at large rather than privately owned domestic space accrues the status of home and the rent party is what allows him to inhabit his version of the homestead. From the start of Reid's narration of this party, a different teleology of home emerges that frames the rent party as both a financial necessity for enduring Harlem's harsh conditions and what made Harlem worth enduring at all. Ownership is not the catalyst for belonging here. Rather, the apartment merely frames the vibrancy it briefly collects.

Whereas realtors promoted ownership as the most significant event in a person's life—instigating an end of history of sorts for owners depicted as living in perpetual comfort and security forever and ever after buying—Reid presents the rent party as a churning mixture of subjects and events that seem to add up to everything and nothing simultaneously. A nameless woman deals poker in a back room, while the music in the front starts to pick up and, consequently, quickens the dancers. A girl remarks that "this party's getting right" before Mrs. Bailey proceeds to announce the evening's menu of pig feet and chili, inciting a fevered rush to the kitchen. The muscle the hostess has hired to keep the peace intervenes when a fight breaks out on the dance floor between two men over a woman. The musicians "exhort" to fifteen or twenty dancing couples while "bedlam reigned." The party encourages temporary forms of sociality that reach great crescendos before dissipating just as quickly. Reid's narration has a blasé quality, capturing the everydayness of the rent party undermining the broader public's fascination with Harlem as both a site of primitivist fantasy and moral deviance. By narrating the rent party as a genre with certain conventions, including violence, he disturbs its reputation as a purely chaotic space. The specific kind of social and sensorial disorientation one seeks at the rent party on its dance floor or in its kitchen or backrooms, Reid suggests, is carefully cultivated by the Mrs. Baileys who make it possible.

The function finally wraps at two o'clock in the morning when the woman who lives upstairs comes down to complain. Although Mrs. Bailey "laughed in her face and slammed the door," the party winds down anyway as "Mrs. Bailey calmly surveyed a disarranged apartment, and counted her proceeds."[56] While the sketch details all the rent party's notable customs—its rich food, sultry sounds, fervent dancing, backroom gambling, and envy-inspired violence—Reid refuses to offer a verdict regarding the rent party's value as he surveys alongside Mrs. Bailey its lingering residues and profits. Unlike in ownership ideology, there's no moral story to tell here about this financial and social form keeping Mrs. Bailey sheltered one more month.

Juxtapose Mrs. Bailey's cool intake of her rented space and her profits to the effervescent feelings realtors, reforms, and state officials ascribed to women living in an owned home. Though much realtor discourse tethered ownership to visions of white masculinity, the industry also recognized the power of promoting ownership to white women who managed the household. One woman-authored piece appearing in the *NREJ* in 1924 made the case for ownership to women by exhorting that "next to possessing a new husband or a new baby, owning a house is the most wonderful and thrilling thing in the world!"[57] "You trip up and down the stairs with your heart singing, 'Mine, mine, mine!'" the author narrates to her readers. The woman who owns her home is overcome "with that sweet, delicious feeling of possession that makes your spine tingle and your throat ache." The delicious feeling of owning is so satisfying, this author writes, "you cheerfully plan to do without that fur coat" or "decide to give you your trip to the Riviera," willingly sacrificing lesser consumer goods for the richer pleasure of improving their home. Recognizing that consumer goods posed the greatest competition for a woman's dollar, realtors emphasized the joy to be found in investing in the home, packaged as the most satisfying purchase a family could make.

But just as Mrs. Bailey does not pine for a lost husband, she also does not long for furs, trips, or homes. Consumption in the article takes place in relation to appetites rather than things. Whereas Louis Waldman in 1935 called for "social centers" to provide refuge for poor white women otherwise drawn to the rent party, Reid depicts Mrs. Bailey's party as a social center in its own right, providing an opportunity for individual financial gain (rent, wages for the musicians, gambling) alongside the collective pursuit of "bedlam," enabling attendees to endure the financial and racial inequities shaping their circumstances for one more night. Reid avoids adjudicating the rent party's "by-products both legal or otherwise" as either virtues or vices. He instead floats along the surface of its various vignettes, privileging the limning of its atmosphere over ascribing its content a value. Refusing to collapse domestic space into interior subjectivity, Reid adopts a kinetic form of narration that sketches events and movements within the rent party to depict this scene that is domestic yet public, contained yet overflowing, circumscribed but porous.

"And so the rent party goes on," Reid remarks, going on to note its evolution within and beyond Harlem. He notes the rise of "Harlem copyists of Greenwich Village" throwing parties not out of need but "for the lark of it" as well as the increasing presence of professional gambling and outright crooks at these functions displacing the joyfully chaotic intimacy of its more amateur forms.[58] "Not always is it a safe and sane affair," he laments, since "you are seldom certain of your patrons." Given such risks, Reid notes, "there may be tragedies." He reprints an article from the *New York Age* reporting on an incident at a rent party where "one jealous woman cut the throat of another, because the two were rivals for the affections of a third woman."[59] The *Age* sensationalizes this violence by comparing it to a "recent Broadway play" before decrying the rent party as being "dangerous to the health of all concerned."

But Reid provides no further commentary on this anecdote beyond introducing it as tragedy. He does not deny the rent party's occasional violence but neither does he dwell on it nor the queer desire that fueled its unfolding. Just like the outburst at Mrs. Bailey's party, the violence emerges from someone's efforts to possess the object of their affection when challenged by a rival. No matter the source of the desire, the attempt to seek possession within the rent party's rhythms produces its greatest tragedy.[60] Unlike realtor discourse's celebration of the Anglo-Saxon's "acquisitive disposition" begetting spiritual and physical security, it is the eruption of the desire to possess during the party that causes the most explicit harm.

While Reid stops short of vesting the rent party with a specific political valence, he does hint at its capacities as an organizing form. Reid notes the increasing difficulty of determining "whether or not one is attending a bonafide rent party" given the growing number of conglomerates throwing them under the guise of the individual. "The party today may be fostered by the Tenants Protective Association, or the Imperial Scale of Itinerant Musicians, or the Society for the Relief of Ostracized Bootleggers."[61] Rather than condemning this co-option, however, Reid acknowledges that "musicians and bootleggers have to live as well as the average tenant, and if they can combine their efforts on a business proposition, the status of both may be improved."[62] He frames the rent party as a vehicle for any number of social and political configurations, from noble collectivists to the lumpenproletariat of smugglers. Whereas the *NREJ* warns against the "dangerous, disintegrating doctrines" that recruit "the landless and the homeless," the rent party seems primed to not just attract a similar demographic but unite them. It is here where Reid's political imagination for the rent party crests as he imagines various collectives uniting to make shared use of the form for mutual benefit.

Yet Reid offers up one last anecdote that returns us to the ambivalent position he most readily occupies in the piece. His final words underscore what he describes as the "very close margin both socially and economically" under which rent parties operated. Reid describes a nine-year-old boy gazing up from the street to his apartment in the middle of the night. When the music dies down for a moment, the boy seizes the opportunity to shout up to his mother that he's tired and wants to come home. A man sticks his head out of the window to relay the following message concluding the article: "Your ma says to go to the Midnight Show, and she'll come after you. Here's four bits. She says the party's just got going good."[63] Reid neither laments nor celebrates this young boy's plight. As with the *New York Age* excerpt, he presents this occurrence without commentary, treating it as a self-explanatory illustration of the rent party's complex demands. The mother is absent from this scene, her wishes ventriloquized by this nameless man who may or may not speak for her. Reid could be said to occupy a similar position—acknowledging the women who drive the rent party while underscoring his inability to access or fully represent their subjectivity.

Whereas the lyric epigraph opening Reid's piece is about a husband and wife, he leaves us to wonder about the fate of this different dyad of mother and son. Given the boy's expulsion from one rented space to take up refuge in another, it's hard to know if his exile is one of salvation or neglect or whether the collectivity he might find at the midnight show is markedly better or worse than what might be found at the party. But there is no third option granting him his wish of protected rest. The boy must leave home to have a home to return to. This ending foregrounds several competing futurities, with the boy's immediate future and perhaps his longer-term prospects placed next to the potential futurity of a party that "just got going good." There is no prescribed ending for the various entities and relations the rent party both unites and displaces. Reid does not express nostalgia for a lost Southern mutualism as some rent party critics did; nor does he offer up ownership as the solution to the black housing crisis in the North. Reid merely frames the divergent desires of this young boy who wants to stop and his mother who needs to keep going. The rent party cannot reconcile their aims—only set them in relation to one another. Whereas reformers of the day would have us hear the boy's cries as a moral shame, Reid, Vogel, and Hartman urge us to attend to his mother's utterances just as closely. What might the party that is "just getting good" make possible for the one and the many? What modes of dwelling and living can she glimpse therein?

"In constantly telling us that there's a party going on," critic Fred Moten writes, "the party is constantly showing us that there's a riot going on, which is how it gets itself smiling, like an antinuclear family affair."[64] Reid's disinterest in rebutting or reining in the rent party's more riotous aspects seems to anticipate Moten's appraisal. "Mrs. Bailey Pays the Rent" continually probes the rent party's potential for creative destruction, weighing whether this phenomenon is merely a regrettable symptom of capitalist exploitation or a seed leading to its disruption if not destruction. In collecting tenants, musicians, bootleggers, and the various unassociated into relation and fostering an atmosphere where possessiveness is the ultimate agent of tragedy, Reid's vision of the rent party helmed by the stoic Mrs. Bailey mirrors the social scene of the eviction riot fomenting across Harlem at this time. Both formations challenged the dichotomies of inside and outside, stranger and kin, owning and dwelling. In Reid's nameless mother, we find an older iteration of Jennifer Nash's more recent question: "what might it mean for black feminism to argue for a vision of itself that is about black women ceding a desire for ownership in the name of a different way of relating to knowledge?"[65] Whereas Reid's story opens with the Mrs. Bailey of song repeatedly crooning for her husband to please come home, we close with this unrelenting figure biding her time, waiting for the good times to start with the strangers with whom she is in the moment making home.

Cordelia's Nonproprietary Appetites

Like Ira Reid, Harlem Renaissance writer Wallace Thurman approached the rent party with studied ambivalence. As the rent party's most dedicated scribe, Thurman wrote numerous articles about these functions and incorporated them into at least three works of fiction. At times, he harshly critiqued the rent party. As Thurman wrote in an unpublished piece likely from the late 1920s, "Harlem house rent parties are more an institution of necessity than one of pleasure." "Despite the freedom and frenzy of these parties," he continues, "they are seldom joyous affairs. On the contrary they are rather sad and depressing. A tragic undercurrent runs through the music and is reflected in the eyes and faces of the dancers. Their frankly sensual movements become writhings of despair."[66] Writing at the height of the rent party's romanticization, Thurman insisted that the public's fascination with its revelries not overshadow the conditions of inequality that necessitated them in the first place. "Thurman's rent party," as Shane Vogel writes, "was not a fantasy of abandon invented for white spectators but a struggle to claim a few moments of pleasure in the interstices of a pitiless and discriminatory renter economy."[67]

Yet Thurman's repeated engagement with the rent party suggests his unfinished business with the form. He best sums up his own undecidability as such: "House rent parties have their evils," describing them as "an economic evil and a social evil that makes them necessary, but they also have their virtues." But "[l]ike all other institutions of man," Thurman reasons, "it depends upon what perspective you view them from."⁶⁸ His most ambitious effort to represent these multiple perspectives in a single work is the play *Harlem*, which Thurman cowrote with William J. Rapp. Opening in February 1929, *Harlem* ran for ninety-three performances on Broadway and played in Detroit, Chicago, Toronto, and Los Angeles before abruptly closing for good in June after a series of financial disputes between the show's largely black cast and its producer.

Despite its short run, the play attracted notoriety for its depiction of the rent party's kinetic dance floor in the first and third acts. These scenes proved particularly popular with white downtown audiences and were credited with putting the rent party on the radar of a much broader demographic. As theater critic Theophilus Lewis noted in the *Inter-State Tattler*, the play's theatrical introduction of the rent party "to the white light district" made it "the subject of a great deal of comment."⁶⁹ The play's success led Lewis to wonder, "now that the rent party has been introduced to the white world, the question is, What will the ofays do with it." Lewis, echoing Reid's concern about the "Harlem copyists of Greenwich Village," leaves this question unanswered. Precisely because of the rent party's inherent adaptability, it could be imported far beyond the specific economic, cultural, and racial conditions from which it first emerged.⁷⁰

The capacity for adaptation is a theme in *Harlem* itself, which follows a family of Southern migrants attempting to adapt to black life in the urban North with varying degrees of success. The play was also itself an adaptation of Thurman's 1926 short story "Cordelia the Crude." Focused on the sexual hunger of its titular sixteen-year-old protagonist, described as the "undisciplined, half literate product of rustic South Carolina," the original short story centers on Cordelia's life in New York after migrating there with her family against her wishes.⁷¹ Thurman blames Cordelia's relocation for stoking her rebellious nature. She refuses to work or go to school, wearing down her parents with her intransigence. The story's male narrator encounters Cordelia in a movie theater cruising for sexual partners as she selects him to accompany her home. Before he enters her apartment for what we assume to be an intimate encounter, he thrusts a few dollars into her hands and flees. The story ends with the narrator meeting Cordelia again six months later in a Harlem whorehouse, where she refers to him as her first paying customer.

The play *Harlem* retains the story's basic contours of Cordelia's personality and family life. The theatrical Cordelia is also willfully unemployed, preferring to seek pleasure any way possible while her family disparages her choices. But unlike the short story's conclusion that prostitution inevitably awaits a girl of Cordelia's appetites, Thurman and Rapp do not reproduce this conclusion onstage. Instead, the theatrical Cordelia ultimately leaves her family for good at the end of the last act to make her fortune as a performer. As Amritjit Singh and Daniel Scott note, Thurman's controversial decision to "resist moralizing about Cordelia's choices" drew the ire of many in the black press.[72] R. Dana Skinner, for instance, expressed his outrage in *Commonweal* that the play reveled in showcasing "as the law permits—gambling, drunkenness, sordid dancing, shooting and amours of Cordelia."[73] "Anyone given to prejudice or haphazard judgements," Skinner continued, "would come away from this play with the impression that Harlem is a den of black filth where animal passions run riot and where the few Negroes with higher ideas or ideals are hopelessly snowed under by black flakes from a sodden sky." The play's unwillingness to punish Cordelia for her excessive desires, this critic suggested, induced a sense of fatalism stranding blacks of "higher ideals" alongside careless thrill-seekers.

But Cordelia's indefatigable restlessness—her perpetual weariness of either owning or being possessed by another—allows her to avoid either a resigning fatalism or ongoing disturbance. Her longing to be sovereign over her relations with others overrides her investment in property. If property discourse in the period categorized whiteness in terms of the desire to own, Cordelia is propelled by an anarchic mode of desire repulsed by ownership— an affective reaction the play's critics were quick to reject lest it be seen as a property of blackness writ large. The outrage that critics expressed regarding the play's unwillingness to punish Cordelia for her nonpossessive desires suggests the danger she posed to property-centric strategies of civic inclusion that required black subjects to appear eager for and capable of ownership. But while critics of *Harlem* feared Cordelia's nonpossessive hungers might become synonymous with black capacity, I wish to consider what her lack of attachment to ownership makes bearable. What other modalities of occupying space does she wrench open within the constraining circumstances of the exploitative rental and labor markets she maneuvers, set on keeping her in a circumscribed set of temporary spaces?

The play opens as the recently migrated Williams family prepare to throw a rent party whose profits they desperately need. The Williams household—consisting of Father and Mother Williams and five of their six children—share their tiny five-room railroad flat with two sets of roomers: Basil and Jenks, a pair of young male roommates, and the unmarried couple, Effie and Jimmie. Most of the first act involves members of the household expressing their disapproval of eighteen-year-old Cordelia, the oldest Williams daughter. The stage directions introduce Cordelia by her desires and temperament, noting she is "inspired to activity or joy only when some erotic adventure confronts her or a good time is in view. She has no feeling for her parents or for her brothers and sisters. Considering herself a woman of the world, she holds their opinions and advice in contempt."[74] The stage directions then transition to Cordelia's physicality: "She is extremely sensual and has an abundance of sex appeal. Her body is softly rounded and graceful. Her every movement and gesture is calculated to arouse a man's eroticism."[75] Thurman and Rapp juxtapose Cordelia's lack of feeling with the riot of feeling she can produce. This imbalance drives much of the play's turmoil.

The Williamses generally regret their decision to migrate north. As Cordelia's sister Mazie declares, "Nobody here but Delia has betta times. Ma and Pa both workin' all de time. We nevah gets out to play! All de beds in de house rented out! And den dese Saturday night parties! Pa gets drunk; Ma cries all day Sunday; Basil and Delia fights."[76] Cordelia's mother, who keeps the family financially afloat by taking in washing, is a God-fearing woman whom the stage directions note "all of the children save Cordelia depend upon" for "her strength and judgement." Her father, by contrast, a "surly, overworked Southerner," has been "rendered helpless" by the North, where he is unable to find steady work. Thurman and Rapp explain that "his blustering exterior conceals a profound sense of inadequacy in his new environment."[77]

But Cordelia displays neither pity for nor fealty to her family and their predicament. When they express dismay at her behavior, she asserts that she does not need their room and board and can leave at any time to make her own life. As her sister snarkily quips when Cordelia insists she'll eat at the restaurant on the corner if her family refuses to feed her, "An' course they'll feed you for nothin'. Delia Williams don' need no money, she don't." "Dat's all right what I need, hot mamma," Cordelia replies, insisting that "what

Delia ain't got, someone else has."[78] Cordelia rejects all that immediately surrounds her as well as the expectations for what she should desire and how she should get it. She perpetually sets her sights on things beyond her reach and what she's supposed to want, including Basil, the West Indian college student suitor desperate for her affection and her family's choice of partner for her.

Cordelia also actively rejects the shame that others attach to her appetites. When Basil expresses his feeling of embarrassment that he's been courting Cordelia without being engaged, she proclaims, "I don't see what you gotta be shamed of. I'm not, an' I thinks I'm de one to judge de shame."[79] When openly confronted about her pursuit of Roy, a slick number runner, Cordelia unflinchingly articulates her longing. After Basil demands she leave Roy alone, she responds, "I don' see why I should. Seems to me, you expects too damn much."[80] She refuses to be bossed unless she desires bossing. "I'll do as I please," she declares, "an' I'm goin' to keep on doin' so."[81] All she wants is for her family to "leave me be." In the short story, a good deal of Cordelia's resentment for her family stems from her opposition to their choice to migrate north. In the play, her oldest brother and the first of the family to migrate exhorts that "since you're here, I guess we has to make the best of it." But Cordelia seems cannily aware of the trap into which her family has fallen into by leaving behind the South—whose evils they knew and could face with the help of a community—for a North in which they know no one and find little refuge from its economic inequities. Imbued with the knowledge of the impossibility for black advancement in both the North and South, Cordelia acts like a person with nothing to lose. While the people around her remain either cruelly optimistic about their prospects or broken by their sense of overwhelming defeat, Cordelia refuses these extremes by refusing to check her sensual and material desires, openly pursuing them outside respectable norms.

Cordelia's openness about her desires and her disdain for her kin's cautious striving unnerves her family. Unlike Mrs. Bailey, whose motivations Reid leaves undescribed, Cordelia articulates exactly what she wants at all times. "I got all I needs but freedom," Cordelia attempts to explain to her mother. "Jes' cause I don' wanna tend to babies, slave, cook an' wash for Pa, or for some white woman don' mean I don't know what's bes' for me. I ain't cut out for dat. I'm cut out for something big, something more excitin' and beautiful dan bein' a washwoman or a lady's maid."[82] After Cordelia declares her intention to seek this beauty by "goin' on de stage," her mother protests that she'd rather Cordelia be dead, to which she responds with disgust, "Well, I ain't gonna die! I'm gonna live, see! And by God, I'm gonna live high!"[83] What Cordelia wants is in excess of romantic or parental love. Pointing to her own parents' seeming unhappiness together, Cordelia proclaims, "I ain't fixin' to marry nobody, nevah! Life's too short."[84] She openly rejects the exploitations of both wage labor and the marriage contract, taking her greatest pleasure in the play during the raucous scene of the rent party and her private intimacy with Roy, allowing her to lose herself to another without subjugation.

In Act I, Cordelia's family members debate Harlem's status as a "city of refuge," as her eldest brother asserts, or a "city of refuse," as proclaimed by her mother, who describes Harlem as a series of "dark houses made out of de devil's brick, piled up high an' crowding' one another an' smellin' worse dan deh pig pen did back home in summer."[85] Mrs. Williams finds nothing in the city worth salvaging while her son clings to his belief in the black man's freedom to make something of himself there. The elder Mr. Williams harbors the darkest take on their situation of all three. Hinting at the destruction of their home in the South, Mr. Williams recognizes they cannot return there while also rejecting Harlem as a place of liberation. The only freedom he has so far found there, he asserts, is the freedom to "slave in some dingy hell hole like dis. Dey ain't nothin' for a nigger nowhere."[86]

But whereas her father insists there is "nothin' nowhere" for black life, Cordelia chooses to claim all available space for her version of living. Uninterested in either her brother's bourgeois optimism, her mother's righteous sense of damnation, or her father's nihilism, Cordelia sees things worth wanting all around her in the place she currently lives. In making a refuge out of refuse, she refutes the very terms of her family's debate about Harlem's value. Despite being denied so much given her status as a poor, black woman, Cordelia nonetheless still wants it all. She longs for the freedom to own but also the freedom to be dispossessed, valuing neither as inherently superior. She doesn't long to "trip up and down the stairs with your heart singing, 'Mine, mine, mine!'" as the NREJ prescribes, nor does she have the religious faith or seek the virtues her family insists she pursue. She mostly wants to be "left be" to desire in an unadulterated fashion. The act of desiring for Cordelia does not denote absence or unfulfillment but rather a hunger for a something else, since the world that exists is not the world she believes she deserves. The kind of freedom she wants, we sense, does not yet exist.

Cordelia's unencumbered desires situate her within the anarchic demographic that realtors alleged ownership could contain and transform. Recall the *NREJ* piece from 1919 that contrasted the noble citizenship embodied by those who own homes with "those who group themselves under leaders who stand for destruction of every existing order of Government, to whom the sacred word 'home' has no meaning, who delight to parade under the names of Bolshevists, Anarchists, Nihilists, Reds, Radicals, etc., who, without home or country, drift from continent to continent, country to country, leaving a trail of misery and vice and destruction wherever you go."[87] Cordelia's lack of allegiance and her refusal to stay home seemingly earns her a spot on this open-ended list. Following the *NREJ*'s frequent tethering of whiteness to the capacity for ownership, Cordelia's blackness makes her even more susceptible, according to such logic, to destructive transience. As Saidiya Hartman writes of another black woman in Harlem whose desires similarly render her an anarchic force in the eyes of her own community as well as the state, "To wander through the streets of Harlem, to want better than what she had, and to be propelled by her whims and desires was to be ungovernable."[88] "Her way of living was nothing short of anarchy," Hartman insists of such girls, even if "only a misreading of the key texts of anarchism could ever imagine a place for wayward colored girls."[89]

Cordelia's role as the beating heart of the rent party underscores her particularly anarchic relation to private property. Despite her harsh treatment by other characters, the play encourages spectators to become most arrested by Cordelia's willful presence and unwavering principles of desire within the matrix of the rent party. Whereas the rest of her family views the function as a requirement if they are to afford their rent, the intense pleasure Cordelia takes from the rent party suggests that the value she finds there is in excess of financial profits. Two short dance scenes appear in Act I. The first consists of a more private moment between Cordelia and Ippy, the party's hired pianist. Prior to the party, Ippy plays a tune as Cordelia dances. The stage directions note that "Cordelia abandons herself to the song and dance. She is radiant."

Her dancing so overwhelms Ippy that he stops playing to passionately implore Cordelia to team up with him and perform professionally. Cordelia, "quickly putting up her defenses," rebukes his suggestion: "When I pulls a wagon, I pulls it alone. I don't want no excess baggage."[90] Their moment of private revelry allows her to abandon herself to the moment; but once Ippy suggests he financialize this feeling, Cordelia recoils. She seeks the right to abandon herself and to reclaim herself when ready. Given the economic and sexual exploitation threatening working-class black women in Harlem at every turn, Cordelia's refusal might also reflect her weariness of the inequity likely to manifest itself in their partnership—played out by the writing out of women in jazz histories more broadly. While Cordelia recognizes the sociality necessary to her self-abandonment, she holds out for a financial situation in which she can go it alone.

The infamous first act rent party scene begins soon after. Rather than marking out the party's motion in detail, Thurman and Rapp instead evoke its atmosphere in lyrical terms. The stage directions begin by describing the mounting tension induced by the music. "Liquor has lit the fire," the authors note, while "Ippy's music is fanning it to a flame." The dimly lit room suddenly "surges with strange insinuating, slow rhythms, as the dancers revel in the movements of their bodies. A few dancers shout encouragements to one another before moving into the mess-around."[91] A long description of this scene's frenzied crescendo follows:

> (. . . Ippy bends his long, slick haired head until it hangs low over his chest, then he lifts his hands high in the air and as quickly lets them descend on the keyboard. There is a moment of cacophonous chaos, followed by a tantalizing melody, beginning slowly and easily. Body calls to body. They cement themselves together with limbs lewdly intertwined. A couple is kissing. Another couple is dipping to the floor and slowly shimmying belly to belly as they come back to an upright position. A slender, dark girl with wild eyes and wilder hair stands in the center of the room supported by the strong lithe arms of a longshoreman. Her eyes are closed. Her teeth bite into her lower lip. Her trunk is bent backward until her head hangs below her waist and all the while the lower portion of her body is quivering like so much agitated Jell-O. **Ippy begins singing.**)
>
> IPPY: She whips it to a jelly!

(He bangs on the keys with renewed might. Everybody is deadly serious. Desire is sad. The music finally slows down. The dancers are hardly moving. They are just rhythmically hugging. . . .)[92]

Although Cordelia is front and center in every other scene in which she appears, here we lose her as Ippy conducts these individuals into a blending mass. Ippy controls the motion of this scene, causing it to erupt into "cacophonous chaos" before tamping it back down. As Shane Vogel argues, Thurman's depiction of the rent party's fluid intimacies "emphasizes how the sensory attunement to something beyond the ordinary organization of the senses can displace the self and bring a new self into being, even momentarily."[93] From the stage directions, this scene not only marks the reorganized senses of the dancers but of us as spectators as well, glimpsing bits of eyes, teeth, trunk, waist, limbs, bellies, and hair as the stage directions describe. Ippy's music attunes the dancers to each other so they can become fragments moving in sync, forming a collective body whose agency is hard to attribute. If "vision is an essential part of the rhetorical and persuasive equipment of property," as legal scholar Carol Rose has argued, touch and sound persuade here in the name of some other regime as visible boundaries prove hard to stabilize.[94]

Performance scholar James Wilson has recovered white theater critics' particular interest in this scene as beautifully primitivist, ruling it exemplary, in Wilson's words, of "a presumed historical and biological primitiveness and barbarism associated with black bodies."[95] As critic Richard Lockridge asserted at the time, the actors in this scene "forget they are acting" and "give themselves over to rhythms which the [N]egro has brought to the white man and which the white man, however he may try, is always a little too self-conscious to accept."[96] Turning a blind eye to the complicity of urban white theatergoers in the exploitation necessitating the rent party's existence, Lockridge limns this scene as a gift offered up and refused across the color line. Thurman and Rapp's stage directions, however, avoid the language of giving and getting entirely. Couples kiss and dip and support one another, but the directions do not deploy the language of exchange to frame these acts. The white man cannot refuse this "gift" because it isn't anyone on the floor's to give, perhaps except for Ippy. And even though Ippy controls the tempo, the stage directions inform us that "the dancers revel in the movements of their bodies" and, eventually, just pieces of bodies. The ensemble, like the exemplary female dancer, are like "so much agitated Jell-O," gelatinously sliding up against another.

But as Thurman also insists in another piece about the rent party, the overarching affective atmosphere of this scene is one of sadness. The tempo ultimately slows, leaving us to stew in the "deadly seriousness" of desire's melancholia as the dancers can do nothing but buttress one another to prevent their collapse. This note was missed, however, by critics like Lockridge who reveled in this scene as a primitivist gift of manic movement. Thurman (who most likely penned this scene, given the appearance of this sentiment elsewhere in his work) ultimately envisions this scene invoking not just a sadness but futility, finally evoking the containment, immobility, and exhaustion that the rent party also indexes. Although Cordelia gleefully desires at will throughout the play, here the desire provoked and released by the rent party's other revelers gives way to collective ennui.[97]

But for Cordelia, this sadness will not be remedied by property, marriage, faith, or the forms of exploitative wage labor she's expected to accept. She longs not for a home of her own, but for a stage she can command. After her own romantic pursuits spectacularly combust, causing her family a good deal of pain in the process, Cordelia moves to leave for good in the play's final scene. With her last words before walking out the door, she challenges her family to "jes' try an' stop me. I'm goin', see! An' when you hears from me again, I'm gona be livin' high, standin' in de lights above deir heads, makin' de whole world look up at me."[98] There is a meta quality to this line given that the actress delivering them is, in fact, inhabiting Cordelia's dream of making it on the stage even as the plays us leaves us unsure as to whether the fictional Cordelia will ever do so. The audience watches Cordelia precisely from the vantage point she describes in her last words, commanding the theater to look up at her. Her final words underscore her wish to command space rather than own it, seeking to move from stage to stage, from relational scene to another, preferring to arrest the fictional and impermanent spaces she occupies rather than possess them.

Neither Mrs. Bailey nor Cordelia is your typical communitarian subject. Whether Mrs. Bailey has any investment in the rent party beyond the rent itself is unclear, while Cordelia firmly articulates her disinvestment from the collective of her family or a larger sense of black community at every turn.

These women host the masses that seek release from themselves alongside and amid each other if not precisely *with* one another.[99] The only solidarity its attendees seek is to temporarily occupy space with one together. Yet homeownership is not packaged or privileged as the end goal for these antiheroines. In fact, ownership is an explicit obstacle for Cordelia, who recoils from any attempt to fix her body or her desires into one form that her family can possess and support. This is not to deny the often-dilapidated conditions black Harlemites occupied in the segregated and exploitative city, nor to claim the rent party as a utopian space of relief or solidarity. Thurman and Reid both mark these spaces in terms of tragedy and sadness, a move made necessary by the intense fetishization of the rent party as a primitivist fantasia by white spectators. Mrs. Bailey and Cordelia represent black subjects enduring the racialized property system built upon black exploitation that reached maturation in the urban North in the 1920s and 1930s without positing ownership as the key to neither their personal nor political fulfillment.

Duke Ellington's Bungalows

We find echoes of the sentiments, strategies, and imaginaries ascribed to Mrs. Bailey and Cordelia in the words of jazz legend Duke Ellington, who frequented the rent party scene after moving to Harlem from Washington, D.C., in the early 1920s. Ellington is one of the figures who have dominated the historiography of the rent party at the expense of its female organizers and patrons. But his musings on the rent party take on a different timbre when encountered in the wake of these fictional women. Like these predecessors, Ellington imagines a vision of residential living that isn't centered on the right to exclude—the foundational tenet of private property—but on fostering different forms of adjacencies that do not rely on possession.

In a section of the 1944 multi-issue feature on Ellington in the *New Yorker*, the musician conversationally moves from a description of the sonic landscape of Harlem apartments to a memory of the rent parties at which he performed and, finally, to inventing a grand vision for urban dwelling. In the most famous part of this interview, Ellington describes the Harlem air shaft as capturing the "full essence" of the neighborhood before offering a dynamic description of its sensory richness he tried to capture compositionally. Air shafts—slender openings mandated in New York City buildings constructed after 1879 to ensure all rooms would have an exterior window—were known for intensifying the sensory experience of dense living rather than substantially improving ventilation and circulation. Ellington's description of the communal experience shared through the air shaft echoes some of the qualities of the rent party. Ostensibly functioning as "one great big loudspeaker," Ellington narrates the sounds (the radio, the janitor's dogs, gossip, folks "praying, fighting, snoring"), sights (the neighbor's laundry), smells (coffee, dried fish with rice, a "great big turkey"), and physical intrusions ("the man's upstairs' aerial falls down and breaks your window") circulating via the air shaft.[100]

But whereas the air shaft gives tenement dwellers intimate sensory access to the lives of their neighbors, this intimacy is largely experienced from a space of remove. The air shaft circulates, muddles, and distributes the sensory outputs of individual households that nonetheless remain discrete units even as the evidence of their living proliferates through the channel of the air shaft. But the rent party requires even more of its participants—bodies and their outputs alike mix while discerning the source of sensory outputs is not always easy to do in the dark, damp quarters crammed full of people, food, and music. Whereas Ellington claims to have been able to represent the air shaft compositionally in his song "Harlem Air Shaft," first recorded in 1940, when he begins to recount his experiences of the rent party in the next part of the interview, Ellington is less interested in finding a representational language for these functions. Rather, he seems more interested in finding the appropriate residential imaginary for prolonging its best qualities. Reminiscing about music produced during "the old rent party days," Ellington describes his escapades with Harlem pianists and rent party regulars Raymond "Lippy" Boyette and James P. Johnson:

> "I can still hear Lippy coming into a tenement at four in the morning and shouting, 'it's Lippy, and James P. is with me!' We'd be in bed and hear that ole click, clack, click of those triple locks and when they'd open up, Lippy would shout, 'Wake up everybody and dust off that piano so James P. can play!' Everybody would crowd around and James P. would milk 'em around, kind of teasing 'em when they asked for a piece, saying 'Is this what you mean?' And 'Or is this the number?' And then finally bang into it. That's real dramatic timing.
>
> "James P. was an artist and the people wanted to hear him at any hour. Now everybody wants to know your pedigree. I think I'll build a city like that.

A guy has a new painting or a poem that he wants people to enjoy at four in the morning, and it's all right. I'll have nothing but bungalows, so we can always knock on windows and walk in and sit down and start playing on a man's piano without offending anybody." He was silent for a moment and then said, "I like that city idea." He thought awhile. "I really like that city idea. I think I'll call it Peaceful Heaven."[101]

The improvisatory setting of "the old rent-party days" lubricates Ellington's envisioning of a city enabling endless rent parties while negating their financial necessity. James P. stumbles in from a late night out in Harlem—very likely at a rent party—to continue the party on a smaller scale if with the same playful intensity. On a continuum with the rent party, the musical scene conjured by Ellington features revelers similarly unrestricted by the conventions of either private property or business hours. The sound of the tenement's triple locks opening provides the sonic preface to the orchestration to come as "everybody," now awake, eagerly anticipates finding release when James P. finally gives up the musical goods. Ellington's transition resonates with Fred Moten's observation that "the rent party is a study group, where the theory of life is the theory of style, which emerges in a style of theory in which convolution, in the interest of revolution, is mobilized as the celebratory echo of the plain, the contrapuntal, the fungal, the fantastic."[102] To borrow Moten's phrasing, the rent party (or rent party afterparty) appears here as a study group of sorts readying Ellington's entrée into urban planning. The open circulation of the arts he imagines at the end of this passage is facilitated by his vision of residential architecture necessary to bring such a scenario into view. The tenement Ellington once occupied, gleefully invaded in the middle of the night by James P. and Lippy, becomes the basis for his utopian vision of the city that replaces tenements with bungalows but remains open to multiple forms of occupancy. Single-family homes as propagated by the National Association of Real Estate Boards these bungalows are not. Ellington's bungalows welcome the "we" to "walk in and sit down and start playing on a man's piano without offending anybody." They essentially allow rent parties to happen at any time, framing a form of occupation built on a principle of compulsive *inclusion* rather than the right to exclude at the heart of property's theoretical "bundle." Blackness appears fundamentally liquid in this scenario, as black bodies are free to move through and across residential space since their value is not predicated on a form of market perception taking their contagious devaluation as a foundational truth. Rather than a matter of assessable "pedigree," value in Ellington's utopia is instead based on shareable contributions. The residential sensorium envisioned here is organized around communal aesthetic experience that may reorganize perception versus individual acts of detection meant to stabilize value. It is not a room of one's own but a room of anybody's that most excites Ellington.

Ellington, like Cordelia and Mrs. Bailey before him, diverges from the reformist vision of the Negro Housing Committee to posit a vision of residential living superseding the limited horizon of private property. The vision Ellington articulates in 1948 is not that far from what we might imagine Cordelia forwarding as she, too, finds peace in the improvisational scene of the social that precludes ownership. Like the woman at the end of Reid's piece who proclaims that the party is just getting good while her son just wants to rest, Ellington imagines a space where both their desires can be accommodated "without offending anybody." "Peaceful Heaven" comes from the capacity to host and hold space without exclusion or boundary.

To conclude, I end with a photograph of Duke Ellington taken outside the White House in October 1931, only a few months before Hoover's presidential conference on housing. Despite publicly agreeing to meet with Ellington, President Hoover refused to do so when the day came. An inveterate improviser, Ellington showed up to the White House anyway and posed for a few photographs outside of it.[103] His physical exile from the center of executive power symbolically conjures the congealing tenets of black exclusion that would anchor the public-private housing partnership in the U.S. for the next several decades. Unlike the gazing illustrated figure in 1922's *A Home of Your Own* appearing at the end of the previous chapter, Ellington does not longingly look toward this civic palace as if to measure his own sovereignty against it or signal his possessive desire. Ellington faces away from the White House, turning it into his background, as a man looms behind him in a doorway as if to ensure that he remains outside.

But Ellington had designs for a different vision of architecture and social relations than those being hatched in the White House in consultation with the real estate industry over the next few months. Although Hoover omitted Ellington's contributions from his catalog of songs about home, Ellington

FIGURE 4. Duke Ellington outside the White House in October 1931.

Source: Bettmann via Getty Images.

inserts himself into Hoover's presidential record not once but twice—in this image capturing both Ellington's presence and Hoover's absence but also as the architect of the "jazzy sounds" Hoover's sons played through their residence, bringing a trace of the rent party into the sonic life of state power. But Ellington is guilty of his own occlusions; his rent party reminiscences focused on the exploits of Lippy and James P. leave out the black women hosting, choreographing, and enabling these functions. The Cordelias and Mrs. Reids of the rent party scene have left even fewer traces behind, failing to find mention in either the archives of Ellington or the state. We turn instead to performance scripts and sketches—improvisatory genres in their own right—to catch glimpses of the women looking to dance their way into some other residential form.

 # Making Ownership Feel Good Again
Rewriting the Land Man after
the Great Depression

WITH THE ONSET OF THE Great Depression, rent party revelers were joined by many more Americans learning to live with dispossession. While homeownership made sturdy cultural and economic inroads with the American public during the 1920s, the Depression laid ownership's ongoing volatilities starkly bare. As credit dried up and unemployment surged into the early 1930s, small property owners struggled to make payments or secure second mortgages, leading to mass foreclosures where owners lost their substantial down payments and their homes. During the first few years of the Depression, a third of farmers lost their land to foreclosure, nearly half of all residential loans were delinquent, and home values declined 30 percent between 1928 and 1933. No matter what kind of property you owned or where, most Americans experienced the precarity of ownership in some form.[1]

The housing reforms of the New Deal brought about by the Home Owners' Loan Corporation (HOLC) and the Federal Housing Administration (FHA) would eventually soothe the property scars of white Americans who were either burnt by foreclosure and devaluation during the Great Depression or unable to afford ownership in the first place. By the 1950s, state efforts to subsidize the private lending market for an expanding category of white Americans would turn the owned home into an affordable and stable asset for accruing wealth and passing it down. But from the vantage point of the 1930s, widespread homeownership for even the white middle class seemed far from assured. In fact, a number of social critics in the period insisted that the nation's future depended upon destroying sentimental myths of ownership's absolute virtue once and for all so an expanded conception of good housing for all might take hold. In articles published in the *New Republic*, *Survey Graphic*, and in standalone monographs, economists, journalists, and local officials insisted that the only way to keep all Americans decently sheltered was for the government to stop reifying *ownership* and to start investing in *housing* of all forms.[2]

But such an overhaul in housing policy would fail, these critics acknowledged, if the structures of good feeling yoked to ownership weren't also dismantled. Following centuries of proclamations about the special depth of white property feeling and the real estate industry's more recent efforts to further incite this longing, a number of commentators in the 1930s sought to sever American's emotional dependence on ownership for good. As journalist Rose M. Stein wrote in 1932, "every prospective home buyer should be immunized with an antitoxin against the blah-blah of own-your-own-home campaigns."[3] Economist Stuart Chase echoed her sentiments in 1938, describing the desire for homeownership as a "cultural lag" "based more on sentiment and emotion than on facts." While realtors deployed melodramatic tropes of "home and mother, the misty eye, the silent tear" to cast homeownership as "one of those immortal 'principles,'" Chase warned that owning in actuality is "often disastrous for you and me and Adam."[4] "A lot of us feel better if we own," he acknowledges, but asks readers to "let us try, however, to detach the desire from mere possession and transfer it to the sense of *living*."[5] The chairman of the New York City Housing Authority, Langdon Post, similarly bemoaned what he deemed "the wicked exploitation of the natural desire to own a home which had swept the country during the 1920's."[6] Yet, given that "land is something which can be seen and felt and lived on," Post, too, admits that the materiality of its possession "gives a feeling of security."[7] To dismantle such feelings promoted through sentimental propaganda but also the physical sensorium of ownership grounded in land you can walk and walls you can touch, these critics suggested, would require systematic deprogramming.[8] Creating new housing regimes beyond homeownership would entail reorienting the residential sensorium away from property's emotional *and* material attractions.

But how were Americans to develop an immunity to ownership's "toxic" feeling, overcome this cultural lag of sentimentality, dispel the false security of owning land they could see and feel, and lose their faith in property? Moreover, given the historical racialization of property longing as something that could render one white or make one more proximate to its attendant rights, what would loosening one's feel for property mean for the interpretation, value, and legibility of race? Such questions shadowed cultural production from the 1930s grappling with how property's broken promises also threatened to "break" understandings of race constituted through property. The pain of property lost and denied anchored a range of reformed epics, reparative melodramas, and didactic satires confronting the trauma of dispossession. Some of these works—operating in the mold of the nineteenth-century theatrical genre of mortgage melodrama—imagined a family's life-altering experience of dispossession to only deepen their hunger for the ownership's stability, ultimately reifying property as the horizon of American aspiration. Others actively combatted the "misty eye" and "silent tear" long associated with the owned hearth by satirizing these tropes or experimenting with new forms reorienting readers toward other ways of conceiving security and respite. But no matter whether a work glorified property's pursuit or narrated the process of becoming disillusioned with its promises for good, narratives of the 1930s regularly centered property as a problem that was both economic *and* affective in nature with ramifications for the value and meaning of race.

These dynamics animate two of the decade's biggest bestsellers—Margaret Mitchell's 1936 novel, *Gone with the Wind*, and John Steinbeck's *The Grapes of Wrath*, from 1939. Whereas Steinbeck wrote several works in the 1930s exploring the racial sanctity of property feeling amid contemporary mass dispossessions—an oeuvre I'll discuss later—Mitchell's historical epic transported Depression readers to a prior moment of property insecurity similarly prompting ownership's affective and racial recalibration: the Reconstruction Era. Emancipation and the lost ownership of chattel slaves intensifies the desire of white characters like Scarlett O'Hara to hold on to the land and, by extension, the sense of racialized sovereignty ownership begets. Love of property—in excess of the land's actual value—becomes Scarlett's saving attachment, nourishing her when her relationships with husbands, children, or community fail. Scarlett takes refuge in owning the land after the Civil War while the previously enslaved of Tara transform into her dependents who lack her property drive. Her hunger to own endures, distinguishing her from the newly freed whom she supports even as her dominion over the land ebbs and flows—a tale rhyming with much of Mitchell's reading public in the 1930s, primed for a heroic story of white resilience through property, as well as one of black dependency via spatial containment.

If Mitchell depicted ownership's power to restabilize white sovereignty, Nathaniel West suggests the horrors awaiting white subjects who continue to mindlessly believe in property's promises. *A Cool Million: The Dismantling of Lemuel Pitkin* (1934) darkly parodies Algeresque fantasies of class mobility by foregrounding the physical and psychic injury experienced by a true believer expecting his property to guarantee his security. Protagonist Lemuel Pitkin's efforts to forestall foreclosure on his mother's New England ancestral property fail horrendously, leading to the further losses of his eyes, scalp, limbs, and eventually his life. The inequities of property also ground Richard Wright's *Native Son* (1940), in which the racist exploitation of residential real estate organizes the worlds of the black Thomas family and the wealthy white Daltons. Bigger's confusion when asked by the police for his thoughts on private property following Mary's disappearance contributes to his being written off as too dumb to be a suspect, while his omnipresent interpolation as a threat to white property values, no matter his thoughts or deeds, rationalizes his ongoing subjugation.[9] Whereas the depth of Scarlett's property feeling in *Gone with the Wind* resecures her whiteness, the protagonists of West's and Wright's novels are destroyed by racialized property systems in which the depth of property feeling alleged to distinguish and shield worthy white citizens turns out to be a cruel exploitative scam, as in *A Cool Million*, or a weak firewall easily penetrated by *Native Son*'s Bigger Thomas, whose treatment as surplus to be contained and extracted from seeds his murderous nihilism.

The travails of property traveled widely across the cultural sphere during the 1930s—from the home-threatening tornado in the 1939 film *The Wizard of Oz*, to the period's two Betty Boop cartoons about foreclosure and Laura Ingalls Wilder's Little House on the Prairie books turning housing insecurity into an admirable adventure, through the five Broadway plays staged between 1927 and 1935 featuring mortgage debt as a plot device and the 1935 publication of the first novel to include the HOLC as a plot point.[10] As with the work of Mitchell, West, and Wright, cultural production from this period representing the traumas of dispossession generally sought to either restore the privileged relationship between whiteness and property by doubling down on the distinctive intensity of white property feelings or debunking the value of property feeling across the color line in alignment with political projects from socialism to libertarianism.

Yet, despite a decade of films, novels, plays, and cartoons underscoring property's depressive nature, faith in the power of property not only survived across the color line after the Great Depression but came back stronger than ever on the other side of it. In contextualizing homeownership's resurgence in the midcentury following the traumas of the Great Depression, historians and social scientists have mainly focused on the housing reforms of the New Deal making homeownership both cheaper for white Americans and more easily segregated through the subsidized construction of homogeneous suburbs. Yet, if we return to the warnings issued by Stein, Chase, and Post that the affective attachment to ownership was just as important as its financial stability, we should also look to fiction of the 1930s as it encouraged white reconciliation with ownership as a stable asset that could also secure one's racial belonging. Although the Great Depression damaged the allegedly privileged relationship between whiteness and property, I recover the role that narrative played in not only resecuring but thickening these tethers in this period as writers across the political and aesthetic spectrum in the 1930s explored the role that race might continue to play in Americans' conception of property.

This chapter recovers the range of this racial reckoning with property while demonstrating how narrative in the period not only encouraged white Americans to keep the faith when it came to property but insisted that this faith was, in fact, the best litmus test of whiteness itself. First recovering John Steinbeck's anxieties about his privileged status as a property owner while writing about the chronically dispossessed during the Depression, I map his enduring investment in the idea of the white "land man" defined not by the fact of owning but by the undying desire to own. In emphasizing yearning for the land as the cornerstone of whiteness, Steinbeck charts a path toward a resolidified racial identity held together not by title to the land but by tenderness for it. Steinbeck's exploration of the racialized feeling of the "land man" culminates in *The Grapes of Wrath*, in which the characters most capable of transitioning from "land men" to "house men" in a residentializing West are most likely to survive their yoked racial and domestic precarity. While the whiteness of Dust Bowl migrants is challenged, Steinbeck foreshadows their eventual reincorporation into whiteness buoyed by their perceived capacity as potential homeowners. I then turn from Steinbeck's "land men" to work by W. E .B. Du Bois and Richard Wright, who, in the Depression's aftermath, considered whether it was more optimal to fight for the Negro's access to "land man" status by proving his hunger for the land or to cede this ground to construct other orientations toward dwelling. In revisiting the lost cause of forty acres and a mule in the wake of both the Great Depression and the Great Migration, in which blacks were leaving the land in droves, Wright and Du Bois highlight the differing roles property might play in antiracist struggle organized through increasingly residential terms.

Ma Joad's Little White House: John Steinbeck's Residential Imaginary

What the Okies and, one suspects, what Steinbeck wants for them—a little white house and a piece of land of their own—sounds more like the old formula of forty acres and a mule than "bolshevik collectives."

—MARGARET MARSHALL, "Writers in the Wilderness,"
The Nation, November 25, 1939

Are the Joads of the 1939 novel *The Grapes of Wrath* white? They had unquestionably been read as such prior to the Dust Bowl and Depression.[11] The novel, moreover, never doubts their Northern European ancestry, with Steinbeck underscoring the family's derivation from the heartiest of "American" stock. But the swiftness of the Joads' dispossession from the land, the brutal conditions of their exodus, and the high demand for new exploitable labor in the West raised questions about the sanctity of Dust Bowl migrants' whiteness as evergreen, immutable, and license to "the ownership of the earth forever and ever, Amen!" as W. E. B. Du Bois defined whiteness fifteen years prior.[12] Before the Dust Bowl, the Joads' whiteness had not only been secure but was viewed as foundational to the nation, given the centrality of such families to prior visions of Jeffersonian agrarianism and frontier expansion. But as historian Walter Stein notes, "the future unfolding of the migrant problem hinged upon whether the Okie's whiteness or his role as field worker took priority."[13] Steinbeck depicts the Joads in the midst of this unfolding, as they and those around them work to get a handle on the durability and utility of their whiteness within the changing regional, national, and economic scene of property.

The status of the Joads' whiteness as it reflects Steinbeck's own racial thinking in this period has been an ongoing topic of debate. Since Michael Denning's provocation in 1996's *The Cultural Front* that the popularity of *The Grapes of Wrath* derived from Steinbeck's decision to foreground "the story of white Protestant 'plain people'" at the expense of Mexican and Filipino farmworkers preceding the Joads in the fields, critics have attempted to complicate Denning's pejorative assessment.[14] Such responses frame Steinbeck's whitewashing of farm labor in the novel and his more open flirtation with eugenics in its pamphlet precursor, *Their Blood Is Strong*, as a testament to his savvy manipulation of white supremacy to illustrate its limits rather than its validity.[15] In such a vein, critic Charlie Cunningham insists upon the novel's refusal of "simple racial nationalism" to deliver its decisive message that the Joads' whiteness "will not save them" from exploitation, since "it is only through collective action that they prevail."[16]

The Joads' whiteness, however, is what *did* eventually save them if we look to their historical counterparts in the years following the Depression. The whiteness of migrants like the Joads and their descendants would not only endure; it would help to broker their midcentury transition from exploited farmworkers to citizen homeowners. This transition, though glimpsed in Steinbeck's prose, is not fully captured within the novel itself. But the real-world models for the Joads would bear out such a trajectory by the late 1940s, when, as Bryan Yazell writes, "the white migrant figure had moved from the fringes of society to the center of the security state."[17] The end of *Grapes of Wrath* famously leaves the Joads stranded, scattered, and at their most precarious, even as they achieve a new horizon of solidarity symbolized by Rose of Sharon's selfless act of breastfeeding a starving stranger. But history suggests that the Joads' hard-earned ethos of solidarity would soon become re-racialized in light of the exclusionary demands associated with homeownership after World War II. Folded into the booming defense industry in California, white migrants were increasingly integrated into civic enterprises as a matter of national security. Steinbeck's novel keenly anticipates their reassimilation by using the Joads to exemplify their usefulness as productive state assets—demonstrated by their embrace of hard work and traditional family structures as Yazell notes, but also through their commitment to whiteness's distinctiveness, which would prove key to their residential assimilation to come.

To know the end of this historical story is not to refute the wobbliness of the Dust Bowl migrants' whiteness in the 1930s before their acceptance by the state as productive laborers and, as I'll emphasize, viable homeowners capable of earning wages outside the home to fund their new residential lives. Rather than read *Grapes* as a reflection of Steinbeck's personal racial ethos, good or bad, I take Steinbeck's equivocations regarding the meaning and status of whiteness of the Joads at face value and as a genuine impasse. The ambivalences, equivocations, and contradictions in Steinbeck's approach to whiteness not just in *Grapes* but in his work across the 1930s reflects the broader crisis around whiteness's representation and meaning during the depths of the Depression, straining the sanctity of its privileged relationship to ownership. While the migrant crisis served as the immediate catalyst for *Grapes of Wrath*, the entwined relationship of race, fantasy, and property haunts Steinbeck's work across the decade. These early works ask what form the privileged relationship between whiteness and property—once deemed pivotal to the founding mythos of the nation—might take after mass dispossession.

Steinbeck is largely remembered as a novelist of agricultural life whose fictions tend to unfold in rural settings. And this is for the most part true. But the residential imaginaries Steinbeck bestowed upon the Joads and others in agricultural settings undergoing massive spatial and economic reorganization offer us insight into how whiteness as a racial category not only survived the Great Depression but was made stronger and more expansive by this crisis. The ability to ascribe a residential imaginary organized around the single-family home to Dust Bowl migrants pointed to their long-term fitness for whiteness. Following work by Colleen Lye and Bryan Yazell expanding how we account for the contingencies of whiteness in the 1930s largely through labor, I argue that another key front for this work was in the capacity for Okies to be understood—and to understand themselves—as residential subjects capable of homeownership, where the future of whiteness would lie in the decades to come.

"The Right to Have So Much": Steinbeck and the Sublime Pain of Homeownership

Of the hundred fastidious journal entries John Steinbeck recorded while drafting *The Grapes of Wrath*, nearly a third reference the wonders and miseries of homeownership. In the early stages of the novel's composition, Steinbeck bemoaned the intensifying residential development around his small Los Gatos, California, home, the first he had ever owned himself. "This place is getting built up," he complained in a July 1938 letter to his editor, "and we have to move."[18] With the help of his realtor father-in-law, Steinbeck and his wife began searching for a roomier and more remote home. Their hearts were soon set on a forty-seven-acre homestead known as the Biddle Ranch in the Santa Cruz Mountains. Steinbeck's journal describes how his longing for this property threatened to distract him from his work. "We're hipped on this ranch. Can think of little else. But I must," he notes in one entry, while confessing in another that "if we could get this ranch I'd feel better. Certainly it is the most beautiful place I ever saw."[19]

But dreaming about this new expansive residential property while simultaneously writing about the plight of the dispossessed perhaps began to take its toll.[20] Steinbeck describes his guilt in his journal, noting that "there is a great weight on my heart. I guess it comes from having property. More and more. It is such a beautiful place. I hope we can sell everything else and just have that one thing."[21] He worried most fiercely about the corrupting status of selling property, noting his resentment at being "in the position of seller."[22] His fear of ownership's effects continued after their move to the Biddle Ranch acres: "I grew frightened of this property. It is so much. One person or two have not the right to have so much."[23]

While the overwhelming sublimity of his ownership angst shadowed the writing of Steinbeck's most famous novel, the function of property and its attendant feelings had been on his mind for far longer. Although Steinbeck is most known for his tales of migrant farmers and embattled farmland, he grew up in a household headed by a civil servant who owned a two-story gabled home that, as Steinbeck's biographer insists "radiated a solid, almost stolid aura of respectability and privilege."[24] Before he could make a living from writing in the 1930s, Steinbeck rarely held a regular job and lived in his parents' Pacific Grove cottage or places he and his wife cheaply rented. The Pacific Grove cottage was an especially important lifeline for the writer. "The Depression was no financial shock to me," he would recall in 1960. "My father owned a tiny three-room cottage in Pacific Grove and he let me live in it without rent," a fallback he described as an "asset" allowing him "safety" in difficult times.[25] In addition to buttressing Steinbeck's literary plots, property played a central role in his material life as well.

Given how much property both plagued and saved Steinbeck, it follows that much of his fiction grapples with the affects and ethics of property more broadly and residential property more particularly reshaping the American landscape in this period. "Man's longing for land," as one Steinbeck scholar notes, "appears in some form in nearly every novel."[26] More precisely, at least sixteen of Steinbeck's fictional works between 1932 and 1962 showcase what another critic has deemed his "conspicuous" interest in property.[27] Whether Steinbeck "definitively advocates for private ownership of property" or "thinks in terms of the dispossessed" remains a matter of critical dispute.[28] But it's clear that Steinbeck remained committed to describing not only the seductiveness of ownership but the feelings of shame, guilt, and suspicion that accompany and complicate this longing, even as this longing was itself being radically refashioned in the middle of the twentieth century as more Americans left farmsteading behind to reside in new and reformed residential spaces across urban, suburban, and rural settings.

It is telling, then, that Steinbeck most directly stages his ambivalences about homeownership in his only work primarily about non-white characters. Nineteen thirty-five's *Tortilla Flat* revolves around the scheming antics, lingering melancholies, and hedonistic ethics binding a group of Monterey, California, paisanos—a term used to describe Northern Californians of mixed Spanish, indigenous, and "assorted Caucasian" ancestry.[29] In this episodic work, Steinbeck follows this idle assemblage of mestizo comrades as one of them—the charismatic Danny—inherits a pair of residential homes that he and his friends quickly and spectacularly lose in an effort to live with as few bourgeois attachments (and as much alcohol) as possible. Given how much *Tortilla Flat* focuses on homeownership's failure to bring satisfaction or index virtue, there is a certain irony to the fact that the novel's unexpected commercial success enabled the Steinbecks to become homeowners for the first time. But in light of Steinbeck's racialization of dispossession's alleged freedoms in this novella, we can also read *Tortilla Flat* as a useful fiction allowing Steinbeck to indulge in a racial fantasy about the crude nobility of unpropertied life as a prelude to his own inevitable march toward ownership. Satirizing residential norms eased his own inevitable entrée into this updated version of the white man's burden he creatively learned to endure.

Tortilla Flat is a strange book that appears even stranger—and darker— when we consider the historical context surrounding its publication. For one, its treatment of dispossession as a quasi-noble adventure during the Great Depression did not go without notice. The novel's romanticization of being unhoused left the book open to charges of escapism at best and tone-deafness at worst.[30] Moreover, Steinbeck set his escapist tale of paisano property indifference at the same time as Mexicans and Mexican Americans were being forced off their land and out of the country en masse. During the early 1930s, hundreds of thousands of Mexican Americans—of whom an estimated 60 percent were American citizens—were forcibly relocated to Mexico in nationwide repatriation drives as part of white nationalist panics about resources during the Depression.[31] While Steinbeck entertained his largely white bourgeois readership with his paisano characters who yearned to shed their property attachments, the state was targeting Mexicans for compulsory removal. It is easy to imagine how Steinbeck's portrayal of paisanos as naturally uninterested in property and defiantly untethered from the state or the market may have eased minds potentially troubled by the racialized terror of unlawful deportation.[32]

Given the mixture of Spanish, European, and indigenous ancestry comprising paisano identity, we might also read *Tortilla Flat* in relation to the radical changes to Indian sovereignty also taking place in the 1930s. As literary critic Louis Owens notes, Steinbeck generally "chose to deal with flesh-and-blood 'Indian-ness' in the form of the Mexican or Mexican American," using native ancestry to lend his paisanos an air of mysticism, while ignoring the tens of thousands of North American Indians also residing in California.[33] North American Indians rarely feature in Steinbeck's fiction as people, Owens writes, appearing instead as a shadowy "index to the American myth."[34] Steinbeck's approach to Indianness in his fiction from the 1930s emerged against the backdrop of the 1934 passage of the Indian Reorganization Act (IRA), also known as the Indian New Deal. Like Steinbeck, the commissioner of the Bureau of Indian Affairs, John Collier, approached "mystical" native cultures as valuable alternatives from which white Americans should learn and preserve. To this end, the IRA encouraged a return to native sovereignty by phasing out allotment policies that had resulted in the selling off massive amounts of native land.[35] Like many on the left in the period, Steinbeck and Collier romanticized the more "natural" communal cultures of native peoples they believed lacked a deep history of private property.

Tortilla Flat embraces mythos of native collectivity, even as Steinbeck himself took increasing refuge in private property during the throes of the Depression. At the start of the novella, Danny inherits two homes in the Tortilla Flat district just north of Monterey. While Danny's new status as property owner raises his standing in the community, his friends ultimately destroy his holdings through their rough occupancy. But despite these property breaches, the bond between Danny his friends only deepens as their collective disinterest in possession grows, incrementally freeing themselves from what they call "the weight of property," a phrase Steinbeck repeated in his own account of his property feelings in his *Grapes of Wrath* journal entries.[36] When Danny dies at the novel's end, his friends honor him by burning his lone remaining home to the ground. Rather than leaving the home to be resold, "better that this symbol of holy friendship, this good house of parties and fights, of love and comfort should die as Danny died," Steinbeck writes.[37] Following through on the novel's opening claim that the value of Danny's house derived from "the parts that are men," Steinbeck conceives of the home as a site for collecting meaningful social ties, if temporary, rather than as an inherently valuable asset in its own right. There is no equity to extract or accrued value to cash out from the home upon Danny's death. When the men disperse, so, too, must the house return to the earth. The paisanos ensure that no one's future security will depend on this unevenly dispersed resource.

While Steinbeck talked openly about his desire for the novel to deflate "the mystic quality of owning a house," why he needed a Hispanic cast of characters to carry out this task is less clear.[38] One answer is that Steinbeck could only envision collective forms of dwelling untethered from property through non-white characters. The idea that whiteness was distinctly defined by an inherent and indefatigable drive to own would shape much of Steinbeck's work in the 1930s, including his later portrayal of the Joads' land hunger. To that end, Michael Denning explicitly contrasts Steinbeck's depiction of "the noble white Americans of *The Grapes of Wrath*" with the "minstrel show Mexican Americans of *Tortilla Flat*," while critic Arthur Pettit reads the novella even more extensively as primitivist fantasy.[39] While I subscribe to Denning's and Pettit's assessment, I want to speculate on another role this fantasy might have served for Steinbeck and his readers during the Depression, dispossessing huge swaths of Americans across the color line. Even as dispossession disproportionately affected non-white communities, the Great Depression laid bare the fact that whites were not immune to such catastrophe, no matter the depth of their longing for property or the skill of their management of it. Given that the long-standing racialization of ownership capacity, the nationwide upheaval of the property system in which one's desire for property failed to prevent their dispossession necessarily placed pressure on the meaning of Anglo-American identity routed through property. Put differently, if whiteness was alleged to be constituted by a distinctive yearning for private property and aptitude for its conservation, the mass dispossessions of the Depression pointed to whiteness's potential depreciation. In this context, Steinbeck's fictional paisanos appear less as attractive alternatives to a white middle-class readership and more like sage tutors in disavowing the "mystic quality of owning a home" before whiteness's own mystic quality dissipates.

Perhaps, then, the most alluring fantasy of *Tortilla Flat* for Steinbeck's white readers lay not in losing themselves in a world of racial others so as to reveal the "corroded Anglo soul" but in recognizing—and even headily relishing—the possibility of their own racial precarity in a moment when private property's buttressing of whiteness seemed susceptible to collapse. The charm and the thrill of *Tortilla Flat* for white readers lay, potentially, in studying the paisanos' open ambivalence about property in a world where dispossession may not only be understood as evidence of racial failing but as an orientation one could learn to embrace. *Tortilla Flat* offers a shadow space for its white readers to try on ambivalences about property and possession, to imagine feeling otherwise toward ownership and, by extension, the "stuff" of whiteness itself.

A key context for understanding the affective function of *Tortilla Flat* in this period is the amount of shame, guilt, and personal responsibility accompanying dispossession for many white Americans during the Great Depression. Studs Terkel captures this affective turmoil in his oral history *Hard Times* when, as he writes, "suddenly idle hands blamed themselves, rather than society" for their downward mobility.[40] "The millions experienced a private kind of shame" in the wake of pink slips, foreclosures, and evictions. As noted by a psychiatrist in Terkel's history who marveled at the relatively low incidents of social disturbance during the Depression, "everybody, more or less, blamed himself for his delinquency or lack of talent or bad luck. There was an acceptance that it was your own fault, your own indolence, your lack of ability. You took it and kept quiet. A kind of shame about your own personal failure."⁴¹ Following centuries of conviction that whiteness imparted an innate respect for property and its maintenance, many dispossessed white Americans believed they had failed whiteness in losing their property rather than believing that whiteness's promises and mythos had failed them. With *Tortilla Flat*, Steinbeck's readers could inhabit an ethos of intentional dispossession, making the shame around property loss as a personal and racial failure more manageable. It might be better to learn to let go of property, and, by extension one's attachment to whiteness defined by a desire for property, than to be rudely stripped of property and potentially one's whiteness—the situation in which the fictional Joads find themselves a year later.

But this exercise in feeling also ends up disappearing the structural origins of dispossession. This is where the danger of *Tortilla Flat* ultimately lies. By making dispossession a mere matter of feeling differently and learning to want elsewise rather than a symptom of racial capitalism predicated upon the uneven dispersion of dispossession, Steinbeck fails to anticipate how the home's mystic quality would only grow stronger in lockstep with the further mystification of whiteness. Steinbeck's experimentation with fetishizing the paisano's "natural" antipathy for homeownership would eventually give way to his dalliance with eugenics in 1938's *Their Blood Is Strong*, where he heralds the distinctive property pedigree of white migrants. The sublimity of dispossession—which ultimately drives Danny to his death in *Tortilla Flat*—would remain a racialized relic of paisano living in Steinbeck's corpus. As Steinbeck himself came to experience the emotional intensities of ownership, a new racialized fantasy of possession would occupy him via the Dust Bowl migrants. With *The Grapes of Wrath*, Steinbeck described a vison of residential longing expansive enough to hold together both the striving Steinbecks and the dispossessed Joads—a vision that required eliding not just the paisanos but any non-white subjects as more than minor characters in his literary works, even as the spectral presence of minorities continued to prove necessary to this vision. This new dream of residential whiteness centered on the Steinbecks and the Joads of the world exiting the Depression together as shared investors in the strengthened racial project of residential homeownership.

The Blood of the Land Man

Exit the paisano and enter the Dust Bowl migrant. If the Dust Bowl migrant posed a new "racial puzzle" for Americans in the 1930s, to cite Colleen Lye,

John Steinbeck made several attempts at this figure's decoding.[42] Prior to his novelistic uptake of this enigma for a national audience in 1939's *The Grapes of Wrath*, Steinbeck took a more regional and journalistic approach to this figure in a series of articles titled "The Harvest Gypsies," commissioned by the *San Francisco News* in the fall of 1936. Two years after the series' publication, the Simon J. Lubin Society republished an expanded version of these pieces as the pamphlet *Their Blood Is Strong*. Across all three iterations of his Dust Bowl writing, Steinbeck yokes the migrants' whiteness to their historical relationship with the land. But he most explicitly racializes this tether in his articles, which more persistently frame the white migrant's distinctive longing for the land as an inherited predilection biological in nature rather than as a cultural preference learned and passed down over time, the explanation Steinbeck came to favor in *Grapes*.

The titles alone of these works allude to this ontological difference. In "The Harvest Gypsies," Steinbeck's use of a descriptor for another racial group—the Romani—as a modified analogue for white Dust Bowl migrants creates an atmosphere of racialization that pervades his approach in the articles that follow.[43] The pamphlet version's title even more directly indexes the centrality of race to Steinbeck's approach, identifying the Okies' blood—a common shorthand for race—as the source of their distinctive strength. Compared with the biblical origins of "the grapes of wrath," describing God's vengeance on all evil reaped from the undifferentiated "vine of the earth," the titles of his preceding Dust Bowl pieces mark Steinbeck's heightened dependence on race in his earliest attempts at demystifying the white migrant. While there is no doubt that eugenics more strongly shades Steinbeck's approach to the Dust Bowl migrants prior to *The Grapes of Wrath*, attending to these earlier efforts to center this figure's innate desire for land and fitness for ownership will help us trace the afterlife of this logic in *Grapes*.

The articles in "Harvest Gypsies" and "Their Blood Is Strong" forge an early distinction between the "earlier foreign migrants" of Chinese, Mexican, and Filipino descent working the California fields and more recent migrants from the Midwest. While this earlier group of foreign laborers had "invariably been drawn from a peon class," Steinbeck contrastingly situates the new migrants as "small farmers who have lost their farms" but also "farm hands who lived with the family in the old American way."[44] These men had, he writes, worked their "own farms" and "felt the pride of possessing and living in close touch with the land."⁴⁵ Referring to these new migrants as "resourceful and intelligent Americans," Steinbeck acknowledges the hardships they faced during their westward journey before he locates their cleverness in the face of this adversity as "the ingenuity of the land man."⁴⁶ The "land man" in Steinbeck's expansive understanding of this term is not limited to describing one who has owned land in the past but marks any typology of person with a history of valuing ownership. In his usage, the title of land man encompasses farmers and farmhands alike, figures united not by their history of ownership but by their shared derivation of pride from "possessing and living in close touch with the land."⁴⁷ The land man, whether he be a former owner or a sharecropper like the Joads, is distinguished for Steinbeck by his feeling for the land and a sensorium organized around the aspirational horizon of ownership. What separates the foreign "peon" from the native "the land man," then, is not any actual material relationship to the land but a feeling for its worth and a desire for its ownership.⁴⁸

This sensational definition of the "land man" grows more biological in nature across the series. While the earliest language about the "land man" is couched in a rhetoric of nationalism, this vocabulary soon shifts to focus on the specific capacity of white migrants to "weather much more for their blood is strong."⁴⁹ Steinbeck described the Dust Bowl migrants as the "descendants of men who crossed into the middle west, who won their lands by fighting" and who, because of "their tradition and their training, they are not migrants by nature."⁵⁰ In this description, we hear echoes of another prosaic naturalist, Theodore Roosevelt, who, prior to becoming president, theorized the creation of a new Anglo-American race whose experience of conquest facilitated their evolution into a heartier form. Steinbeck follows other theorists of race in the late nineteenth and early twentieth centuries in the ease with which he transposes "tradition and training" into "nature."⁵¹ He solidifies this transition when, after reflecting once more on their "overwhelming need to acquire a little land again," he ultimately identifies the Dust Bowl migrants as heralding a "new race" that he notes is "here to stay and that heed must be taken of."⁵²

But if the Dust Bowl migrants constitute a new race following their recent dispossession and exploitation, what is the relationship between the whiteness of the middle-class Californian Steinbeck and his readers and this "new race" whose claim to whiteness was no longer so solid? Does this "new race" of the

Dust Bowl migrants relinquish all claims to whiteness, or is this new status merely a novel modulation of it? Steinbeck comes closest to answering these questions when emphasizing the distance between the "we" of his presumably white Californian readers and the Dust Bowl migrants. After stressing that this "new race" of migrants remain "American people," Steinbeck contends that "we must meet them with understanding and attempt to work out the problem to their benefit as well as ours."[53] While there is a clear distinction here between the "we" and the "them," it is hard to precisely locate where this readerly "we" sits in relation to the new race or to parse the exact nature or age of their division.[54]

Although Steinbeck provides no further details about the nature of this shift, the rhetorical work of this announcement is clearer. Theatrically staging the chasm between the Dust Bowl migrants and more established white Californians early in the series sets Steinbeck up to deploy his expansive definition of the "land man" to secure the eventual racial reconciliation of the "them" and "us" in the articles that follow. In engineering this reconciliation, Steinbeck insists that the economic need for the Dust Bowl migrant's exploitation in the West has artificially stifled his ability to prove his status as a "land man." Farming conglomerates depended upon Okies to remain landless to ensure their long-term dependency on low wages, a dependency further ensured by union-busting laws. For Steinbeck, the tragedy of the Dust Bowl migrants lay in the lack of opportunities for them to prove their property mettle and, by extension, their fitness for whiteness.[55] In the absence of opportunities to own homes or farms in the West, Steinbeck seeks other ways to recover and make legible their historical "land man" status. In contrast to the allegedly innate disinterest in property characterizing foreign "peons," which enables Steinbeck to frame them as "natural" migrants, or the property apathy he assigned to the paisanos of *Tortilla Flat*, Steinbeck establishes the Dust Bowl migrant's enduring instincts for ownership. The categorization of these migrants' "new race" ultimately appears as a temporary setback that can be reversed by public and private interventions rescuing this populace from the exploitative conditions hastening their deracination.

In staging the Dust Bowl migrants' worthiness of whiteness, Steinbeck dwells on their past racial pedigree while also presenting evidence of their ongoing capability as owners. We find Steinbeck leaning on the former strategy in a section titled "Good Old Names," where he notes "the names of the new migrants indicate that they are English, German and Scandinavian descent," before listing a few of their monikers: "They are Munns, Holbrooks, Hansens, Schmidts."[56] That Steinbeck's own Germanic name would not have been out of place on this list seems to be its point.[57] While the Dust Bowl migrants might appear racially distinct to their beholders after their experiences of starvation and poor housing, Steinbeck turns to their names as signs of their pedigree where their poverty-stricken bodies in the present might fail to offer such evidence.[58] Names were one way to remind readers of the new migrants' derivation from the stock of "old Americans," as Colleen Lye has argued, which their starved bodies and destitute living conditions may no longer trigger.[59]

If names remind readers of the Okies' pedigree, Steinbeck's depiction of their ongoing desire for decent dwellings points to their continued fitness for whiteness. Steinbeck's attention to the Dust Bowl migrants' desire for clean shelter is contraposed in *Their Blood Is Strong* to his earlier description of foreign "peons" whose alleged disinterest in ownership or decent dwelling writ large naturalizes their suitability for exploitation. Once more, Colleen Lye proves exceedingly insightful on this front. Investigations of the lives of foreign migrants who worked the Californian fields, she notes, "usually concluded that a low standard of living was natural to the numerous foreigners among them."[60] Lye cites a 1920 commission report using the dwelling practices of Japanese farm laborers, described as living in shacks "not fit for human habitation," to attest not to the depths of their exploitation but to their tolerance for such living. Arguments like these were used to justify the renewal of the California Alien Land Law, prohibiting Asian noncitizens from owning land. Against such a backdrop, Lye argues, Steinbeck's representation of the Okies re-racialized the "customary labor form" of Asian labor in the West. "The Okie," she concludes, "is simply the name for the Asiatic who won't go away."[61]

Lye's excavation of the Asiatic form lying just below the surface of the Dust Bowl migrant's representation allows us to better see the dual excavations Steinbeck continually performs upon this figure in these articles—staging the Dust Bowl migrant's potential for permanent Asiatic degeneration while continuing to point to the remnants of this figure's lingering white instincts as a "land man" suggesting his status as white could be rekindled and rescued.

Steinbeck warns that the Dust Bowl migrant will increasingly morph into the foreign "peon" without the reader's immediate help in stanching his exploitation to preserve his status as a "land man"—qualities that can still be glimpsed in flickers and flashes for now, but whose steady erosion makes his immediate salvation all the more urgent. Housing is the terrain where Steinbeck most firmly stages the imminent threat of the migrant's degeneration.

In the absence of opportunities to demonstrate their capacities as "land men," the Dust Bowl migrants' ability to care for their homes—their capacity as "house men"—becomes the next-best indicator of the Okie's fitness for whiteness. It is to this end that Steinbeck brings readers to a squatter's camp to witness the well-tended home of a Dust Bowl family recently arriving in the West. Spying a ten-by-ten-foot house made of corrugated paper, Steinbeck observes "here is a house built by a family who have tried to maintain a neatness."[62] Neatness indexes their proximity to their previous lives as land men both in spirit and fact. "Five years ago this family had fifty acres of land and a thousand dollars in the bank," Steinbeck notes before recounting their prior participation in community life as an outgrowth of their settled status.[63] In the wake of this family's dispossession and migration, "now they have nothing." Despite this hardship, Steinbeck underscores that "there is still pride in this family," as "his spirit and his decency and his own sense of dignity have not been quite wiped out."[64]

Yet, Steinbeck goes on to note, this "spirit" can only last so long before it is obliterated for good, as a neighboring home in the camp forebodes. Steinbeck contrasts the fine paper home of the first family with a nearby family's rotted and tattered canvas tent held together by wire and containing a single bed that all six family members share, foul clothes, and—most damning—an open privy in the nearby willows. This family's loss of dignity is visible not only in the status of their shelter but in the "dullness" and "sullenness" of their faces. The externalized signs of their degeneration are now written onto the surfaces of their bodies. They, too, were once land men. Prior to their migration, the father owned a grocery store that housed the family in the back. Yet, Steinbeck warns, there is even farther for this family to fall, turning to yet another neighboring family who has turned to constructing a home out of branches, weeds, paper, and carpet strips. They no longer even bother with the privy, relieving themselves wherever proves most convenient. "This is what the man in the tent will be in six months; what the man in the paper house with its peaked roof will be in a year, after his house has washed down and his children have sickened or died, after the loss of dignity and spirit have cut him down to a kind of sub-humanity."[65] Whereas the similar living conditions associated with Japanese farmworkers were wielded by the 1920 commission as evidence of their innate primitivism, Steinbeck inverts the causality for the Dust Bowl migrant to insist that poor living conditions eroded the "dignity and spirit" innate to the white "land man." The housing conditions of the Dust Bowl migrant serve as both the evidence of his ongoing, if waning, fitness for whiteness and as one of the precipitating causes of his racial degeneration.

This emphasis on capacity helps explain why Steinbeck embraces government camps not as a solution to California's broader *labor* crisis—which would encompass Mexican and Filipino laborers who also worked the fields—but as a way of alleviating the *migrant* crisis specific to the Okies. Echoing his logic of the "land man," government camps are meant to solve not a structural problem of exploitation in Steinbeck's oeuvre but an affective problem of "dignity." Their purpose is to help the Okies to remember, recall, and act upon the instincts instilled upon them as "land men" by granting them the resources to care for their dwellings. As Steinbeck admiringly insists of the camps, "from the first, the intent of the management has been to restore the dignity and decency that had been kicked out of the migrants by their intolerable mode of life."[66] Given his brand of leftism at the time, Steinbeck is careful to note that this inherent dignity is not an index of "self-importance" but "a register of a man's responsibility to the community"—reflective of the collectivism he would underscore in *Grapes*.[67] But Steinbeck takes pains to locate the source of this communal responsibility in the biological predilections of the "land man," denoting the limits of whom this collectivism can properly serve.

Steinbeck reaffirms this logic by stressing in the series' penultimate article the ineligibility of the foreign peon to participate in this collective vision. While calling the state's treatment of foreign labor "a disgraceful picture of greed and cruelty," Steinbeck quickly redirects part of the blame for that treatment to the predilections of the Chinese themselves.[68] "The traditional standard of living of the Chinese," he writes, "was so low that white labor could not compete with it."[69] In his phrasing, the problem is not the low wages paid to the Chinese or the draconian legal apparatuses dictating how and where they lived. Rather, the exploitation of the Chinese is due in part to their "traditional standard of living"—with "traditional" accommodating both a cultural and a racial understanding of this deficit. Steinbeck goes on to note that despite their "low" standard of living, Chinese "family organizations allowed them to procure land and to make it produce far more than could the white men," inciting "white labor" to begin "a savage warfare on the coolies."[70] Even here, where Steinbeck directly acknowledges the amassing of property by Chinese families, he avoids the aspirational and romanticized language he uses earlier to describe the land longings held by those of "old American stock." When it comes to the Chinese, Steinbeck uses more transactional language—family "organizations" "procuring land to make it produce"—as opposed to the more spiritual connection he ascribes to the Dust Bowl migrant "living in close touch with the land."[71]

Steinbeck deals similarly with consequent waves of Mexican and Filipino farm labor. But he also notes, with a sense of relief, their declining numbers. "The receding waves of foreign people labor," he concludes, "are leaving California agriculture to the mercies of our own people."[72] Steinbeck clarifies who this "our" refers to in the next sentence, insisting that "the old methods of intimidation and starvation perfected against the foreign peons are being used against the new white migrant workers."[73] Whereas earlier in the series, Steinbeck distinguished between the "we" of the readers and the "they" of the Dust Bowl migrants, the two are now fully reconciled as an "our" before he reclaims the migrant workers as "white" at the end of the sentence. Cast earlier in the series as a "new race," Steinbeck now repositions the "white migrant worker" as merely a new type of laborer whose recovered racial status demands Californians to intervene to temper their exploitation. The word *white* goes on to appear in this final section a total of six distinct times—describing "the new white migrant workers," "white labor," "white American labor," and the future of farm labor as "white and American." If Steinbeck staged the precarity of the Dust Bowl migrant's racial status early in the series, he eagerly enacts their racial reinstatement by its end.

Steinbeck ultimately claims that "farm labor in California will be white labor, it will be American labor, and it will insist on a standard of living much higher than which was accorded the foreign 'cheap labor.'"[74] The specter of the "land man" enables this proclamation; the white migrants' refusal to live "low" proves key to reconstituting their whiteness and, by extension, ending their exploitation. With the Dust Bowl migrant's whiteness now reconfirmed, Steinbeck can rousingly conclude the following in the series' penultimate lines: "The new migrants of California from the dust bowl are here to stay. They are of the best American stock, intelligent, resourceful; and, if given a chance, socially responsible."[75] With their whiteness now safely secured, Steinbeck can ask his reading public to extend a chance to this figure whose "blood" has gifted him with the intellectual and affective resources to be allowed reentrance into the "our" of "our own people." But Steinbeck's work was not yet done. He would soon turn to the fictional Joads to better articulate the residential nature of the chance the Dust Bowl migrant should be extended. The land man's ability to transition into a homeowner would become the new terrain not just for the Joads' survival but for whiteness in the twentieth century at large.

Visualizing the Residential Future in The Grapes of Wrath

In his closing speech to the President's Conference on Home Building and Home Ownership in 1931, Secretary of the Interior Ray Lyman Wilbur emphasized housing's importance not just to the civic and social life of the nation but to its biological future. Like most attendees, Wilbur attested to housing's importance to "wholesome living" and "the success of our democracy."[76] "Health, happiness, and good citizenship are furthered by proper housing," he asserted, while "unhappiness, delinquency, and crime are furthered by bad housing."[77] But Wilbur's remarks eventually moved to more distinctively evolutionary terrain. "We still have to determine the effect of our methods of housing upon our primary biological needs," he insisted, before hypothesizing that "we can be sure that we can not change materially the essentials of human habitation without reacting biologically."[78] In this, he continued, "we can learn from the birds." "The shiftless, careless robins who pick poor places for their nests and build poor nests, raise but few young who become full-fledged, successful robins."[79]

Given the systemic failure of the economic system after the 1929 crash, Wilbur's focus on the individual negligence of "shiftless, careless robins" reflects his investment in the individualism touted by the Hoover administration and dictating its limited response to the Great Depression. But Wilbur's reference to the potential biological implications of altering the "materially essential" forms of "human habitation" speaks to the eugenic undertow also structuring his thought. Although Wilbur insists earlier in his speech that homeownership should be promoted "for all families irrespective of income, race, occupation, or other factors," his concluding suspicion that not all people had the capacity to make wise housing decisions reflects his long-standing interest in biological determinism.[80]

Before being appointed secretary of the interior in 1929 by Hoover—an old college pal—Wilbur taught medicine at Stanford before serving as its president for nearly three decades. While at Stanford, Wilbur was actively involved in the American Eugenics Society and the Eugenics Research Association and incorporated eugenics into Stanford's medical curriculum.[81] He also chaired the 1925 Survey of Race Relations, studying Asian labor on the West Coast. Recognizing the economic necessity of Asian immigration, the survey group insisted on the importance of limiting their mixing through interracial marriage and reproduction. Such findings reiterated the claims of other Californians, including Steinbeck, positing the Asian immigrant's tolerance for poor dwellings as an obstacle for white workers. "Living conditions on the ranch or farm are in many cases unsuited to most white labor," the group insisted in 1925, making "the supplanting of Mexican and much of the Oriental labor" in the West unforeseeable.[82]

Of course, the unforeseeable was just around the corner. In a few years' time, the Dust Bowl would push destitute white migrants west, where they, too, would come to accept the standards of living of their predecessors. As we've already seen, the question of how to reconcile the whiteness of the Dust Bowl migrants, becoming increasingly "suited" to the living conditions once ascribed to the distinct tolerances of foreign laborers, proved particularly urgent in the West. But Secretary Wilbur's 1931 remarks suggest the national stakes for maintaining housing standards. Whereas housing already served as an index of a people's standard of living—itself a proxy for their level of civilization—Wilbur's bird analogy suggests housing's power to *remake* dwelling capacities rather than just reflect them. As Wilbur says elsewhere in his speech, "We are endeavoring within a few decades to remold the mass through individual changes brought to us in an almost overwhelming manner by science and invention."[83] Housing was one such area where the masses might be scientifically—and biologically—remade for generations to come.

Like Wilbur, Steinbeck's transition from the regional arena of the West to the national stage also took place in the midst of the Depression. After the surprise embrace of *Tortilla Flat* and the even splashier success of 1937's *Of Mice and Men*, Steinbeck was hungry for further acclaim, making the drafting of *The Grapes of Wrath* particularly pressure-filled. He had already tackled the Dust Bowl crisis in a more propagandistic manner in *Their Blood Is Strong*, where he openly wielded the rhetoric of eugenics to reconcile the migrants with whiteness to render them worthy of state and philanthropic intervention. Writing for this regional audience for whom the language of blood and standards of living was commonly used to distinguish between white and foreign labor, Steinbeck tactically redeployed this rhetoric to argue for the Dust Bowl migrants' enduring status as "land men" and, by extension, white. But Steinbeck intuited that he would need to find another way to racialize the Dust Bowl migrants for a national audience less familiar with the racial terrain of the West.

Accordingly, *The Grapes of Wrath* would need to first situate the Okies against the backdrop of blackness, the lingua franca of both American racialization and aesthetics. The specter of blackness, of course, was already shaping the Western reception of the Okies. A Bakersfield, California, movie theater hung a sign reading "Niggers and Okies Upstairs," while childhood taunts of the Okies often insisted on their status as "worse than niggers."[84] Steinbeck himself incorporated this discourse into *Grapes* in the form of a hostile Californian proclaiming Okies "as dangerous as niggers in the South!"[85] But these allusions to blackness were generally abstract, wielding blackness to racialize the Okies without any direct references to actual black people. The waves of Asian and Mexican labor in California preceding the Okies in the fields more immediately shaped the economic terrain of racialization of the West. But prior to their westward migration, Steinbeck first establishes the Joads' status as "land men" and, by extension, as white, through Tom Joad's articulation of his non-blackness.[86]

Let's begin with the revelation that the Joads are sharecroppers. Within Steinbeck's larger oeuvre, the fact that the Joads do not own their land is not particularly telling. As Steinbeck established in *Their Blood Is Strong*, whether one owned or merely "felt the pride of possessing and living in close touch with the land" qualified one equally for "land man" status. This same logic extends to the ragtag farm laborers in 1937's *Of Mice and Men* whose fantasies of the good life rooted in the land inform the novella's sympathetic core. Even Crooks, the story's disabled black "stable buck," is granted a distinctive Western lineage, making him briefly, if fleetingly, eligible for "land man" status. Loudly insisting he is no "southern negro" but born "right here in California" to a father who owned a ten-acre chicken ranch, Crooks stakes his claim to land man status on his proximity to ownership and his distance from the Southern enslavement.[87] But while Crooks briefly indulges in a fantasy of co-ownership with his fellow white farmhands, the threat of racial violence causes him to quickly withdraw from this scene of property aspiration. Although all the men's land fantasies are eventually dashed, Crooks more swiftly recognizes the limits his race places on even fantasizing about land within the anti-black atmosphere of the West. We never learn what happened to his father's land, but the fact of Crooks's non-inheritance of it suggests the fragility of black title to the land in a system in which "land man" status is synonymous not with ownership, in fact, but with whiteness.

Given the centuries-old opposition between blackness—defined in part as the incapacity for possession—and "land man" status, it tracks that when Tom admits to the driver who picks him up in Chapter 2 that his father is "a cropper, but we been there a long time," he attempts to distance himself from blackness soon after.[88] Though white tenancy was common in Oklahoma, Steinbeck's scripting of Tom's hesitancy around this admission—quickly qualifying the Joads' tenant status by insisting on their "long time" occupancy of the land—suggests the racial vulnerability his confession provokes.[89] In addition to their sharecropping status, the specific amount of land the Joads work—forty acres—as well as Tom's status as an ex-con introduces just enough of an atmosphere of blackness that Steinbeck must clarify their racial identity. This clarification comes one conversational turn later when, in a moment that feels like a non sequitur, the driver recites a "piece of poetry" he invented to pass the time. Failing to remember all the words, the driver recites the portion he can recall: "An' there we spied a nigger, with a trigger that was bigger than a elephant's proboscis or the whanger of a whale."[90]

For such a tightly plotted novel without a lot of extraneous material despite its size, this moment in *Grapes* puzzles. The first direct reference to race in the novel, this poem doesn't seem to tell us much about the Joads or anything else. But while it has the feel of an aside, there is an epistemological logic at play here that becomes central to the Joads' framing. Coming right after the driver has clocked Tom as an ex-convict based on his clothes and gestures, the driver's poetic fragment uses physiognomic difference to locate the otherness of the "nigger." Whereas Tom's difference as both an ex-convict and a sharecropper can be rectified—in line with the possibilities for the Dust Bowl migrant's reincorporation into whiteness Steinbeck describes in *Their Blood Is Strong*—the difference of the "nigger" appears to go deeper than clothes and gestures. Blackness is easily "spied" and made apprehensible here without even a process for its observation. The sharing of this aesthetic experience of blackness between Tom and the driver, moreover, allows them to reconsolidate their whiteness as a collective unit.

This poetic aside catches, with Tom repeating it a few pages later. After the driver drops him off, Tom returns to this refrain in partial form as he continues his journey home: "He said experimentally, 'there we spied a nigger—' and that was all he could remember."[91] In this version of the poem Tom recalls, the reference to genitalia has been excised. The phrase now attests to the more generic experiencing of seeing blackness. As a mantra, the poetic fragment conjures the idea of a racial other whose otherness is never in doubt or in question. The poetic figure's blackness remains easily "spied" even without the evidence lying under his clothes. Tom utters this phrase "experimentally"—testifying perhaps to the tentativeness of his speech act allowing him to not only believe in this difference but to embrace it as a defining factor of his own white racial identity. But the experiment also seems to lie in the collective act of vision the poem also encodes—"we spied a nigger"—a grammatical echo of his earlier articulation of his relationship to the land—"we been there a long time." Both of these *we*'s—the *we* of being on the land a long time and the *we* of spying a "nigger"—prove central to the articulation of the Joads' claim to whiteness within the context of the Midwest.

But the terrain of racialization will soon change for the Joads—not only because their move westward will set their racialization against the specters of Asiatic and Hispanic form, to echo Colleen Lye, but because the construct of the "land man" was itself in flux. In moving off the land and away from their ancestral farmstead—self-owned or not—the Joads joined the growing number of Americans across the color line leaving behind Jeffersonian agrarianism to earn their living through wage work. Wilbur and Steinbeck variously forewarn that changes to how Americans occupied their homes would fundamentally alter the character and capacities of Americans themselves. If "shiftlessness," the trait Wilbur ascribes to careless robins who make poor nests—and a descriptor long associated with blacks and, increasingly, with Okies—threatened the integrity of the nation, both Wilbur and Steinbeck underscore the nation's interest in aiding the transition of the ancestral "land man" to more stable forms of residential occupancy.

When representing the Joads' Oklahoma farmstead, the novel does little to differentiate between the broader forty acres they farm and the physical home located on this acreage. Tom Joad arrives "home" twice. Upon finding his parents' property vacant, he walks to his uncle John's homestead, where the entire family is preparing to travel west. The time readers spend on the Joads' land is brief, amounting to about half a day, little of which is spent inside the home itself. Tom reunites with his mother in a dramatic domestic scene of delayed recognition, but the deliberations about the family's imminent westward migration take place outside around the fire as the family moves porously between interiors and exteriors in their preparations. Some sleep in the house while others like Grampa and Granma Joad sleep in the barn, further marking the decentralized position of the home.[92] The farm and the house in Oklahoma sections of the novel are thought and used in tandem as coextensive spaces. When homes are bulldozed in the novel, it is to cement a family's expulsion from the land at large.

If the Joads' home is largely coextensive with the land, the materials used to mark Pa Joad's forty acres tell a different story about the utility of borders. The boundaries around the Joads' land are generally porous, made up of crooked poles holding up drooping wires. Tom describes the function of this physical perimeter as largely affective rather than practical. "We didn't really need no fence there," Tom tells Jim Casy. "Pa kinda liked her there," he continues, because "it give him a feelin' that forty was forty."[93] Pa's savoring of the feeling of possessing forty acres—whether he owned them outright or not—recalls Steinbeck's earlier portrait of the land man in *Their Blood Is Strong* whose desire to own outweighs in importance his ability to do so. But the Midwestern sections of the novel also mark the racialization integral to the origins of the "land man," a status built on settler colonialism and in contradistinction to blackness routed through slavery. If "spying a nigger" enshrines Tom's whiteness in the present following his post-incarceration precarity, killing Indians first inaugurated the Joads as "land men."

Steinbeck most fully narrates this history in one of the interchapters describing dispossession's generic beats. Standard to such a scene, as Steinbeck writes, is the dispossessed's recitation of the origin and evolution of their land claim. Such a tale typically begins with the original theft of the land: "Grampa took up the land, and he had to kill the Indians and drive them away."[94] The originating act of theft inaugurating a settler's possession is both passive—the land is "took up"—and murderously active, involving the killing of Indians and the theft of their land. This "taking up" is inherited by a second generation of occupants whose clearance of the land is framed in more pastoral terms. "Pa was born here, and he killed weeds and snakes."[95] But debt soon intercedes, with one bad year leading Pa to "borrow a little money," followed by more bad years and more debt until "the bank owned the land then," leaving the family to sharecrop.

When the sheriff arrives to take the land for good, the tenants announce their intentions to resist. "We'll get our guns, like Grampa when the Indians came. What then?"[96] But while murdering Indians is how tenants ancestrally earned their status as "land men," the sheriff is quick to remind them that killing white men to save their land would make them murderers and thieves. Slaughtering Native peoples for their land validated the white settler's racialized capacity as a "land man," but this status ultimately fails to protect the next generation of settlers subject to a new capitalist regime in which the land no longer requires such intimate occupation to extract a profit. In this context, whiteness no longer serves as a resource for the land's valuation, which threatens in turn to devalue whiteness. Part of the pain of dispossession experienced by the Joads and their peers derives from their realization that whiteness will not protect them from an increasingly abstracting form of capitalism wherein the fate of their land is determined by the bureaucratic "monsters" of banks and companies whom Steinbeck describes as breathing profits rather than air. "When the monster stops growing, it dies. It can't stay one size."[97] The dream of the Joads, shared by many of Steinbeck's protagonists from the 1930s, remains anchored in a model of Jeffersonian agrarianism centered on small farms and intimate living where whiteness separated the "land men" from exploitable migrants and Native peoples deemed to lack instincts for settlement. The Great Depression accelerated the dismantlement of this white agrarian fantasy, if only to relocate the value of whiteness into more residential terrain.

The Joads' transition to the West, then, marks not only their physical migration but also the larger transformation of the relationship between property and racialization in a residentializing world. With the increasing dismantlement of the sharecropping system and the movement away from farmsteading in the 1930s, Steinbeck casts the category of the white settler in the Midwest as on the verge of extinction.[98] What will come of the "land man," the novel asks, given the uprooting of not only his way of life but his entire sensorium oriented around the aspirational possession of the land? The narrator of one of the early interchapters most directly approaches this dilemma when he wonders in the wake of dispossession "how'll it be not to know what land's outside the door?"[99] This question extends a claim made by another tenant in an earlier interchapter that "if a man owns a little property, that property is him, it's part of him, and it's like him."[100] Being a "land man" means being oriented by and in the land as an extension of one's own person, a mode of being Steinbeck infuses with an inherent grace even as he eventually works to capture and reorient these affects for more collectivist purposes.

The novel treats the fusion of the tenant's self with the "land outside the door" as a laudable and even noble form of personhood allowing property and man to exist symbiotically via a mutual ontology. When this corporeal connection to the land is lost through evictions and corporate management, when "a man gets property he doesn't see," as Steinbeck puts it, "the property is the man, stronger than he is," until, eventually, the man becomes "the servant of his property."[101] The language of servitude is revealing, gesturing toward the racialization that has always underwritten the intimate agrarianism Steinbeck treats so tenderly. The hunger for self-sovereignty, theorized across the nineteenth century into the twentieth century as a catalytic desire for white subjects, is entangled with an intimate vision of ownership where the boundaries of the self might be porous with the land, but this land/person subject is ultimately bounded by a perimeter establishing the right to exclude others from this space that is also the self. When Steinbeck and others invoke the poor "standard of living" ascribed to foreigners, they do not merely mean a tolerance for the unhygienic or the meager but also a more sensuous incapacity to feel or desire this more transcendental vision of propertied personhood in which "property is the man."

As the Joads hit the road, it is the adaptability of their "land man" instincts and affects that will come to determine their various aptitudes for making the transition not just to migratory living and wage labor in the short term but also their eventual, if altered, return to propertied (or property-adjacent) living in the long term. Steinbeck depicts the Joads and their fellow migrants hitting the road as sharing the same histories but also the same aspirations and orientations. But as their travels continue, their collective vision of "land man" living starts to splinter as each family member hazards different answers to the question of "how'll it be not to know what land's outside the door." The Joads' differing abilities to translate that knowing into residential terms will determine their varying success at transitioning from exploitable migrants back into a more solid form of whiteness retoggled for residential life.

While all of the Joads desire a place to call their own, their exodus from Oklahoma brings the differing contours of these desires into increasing relief. The death of Grampa Joad coming soon after the family's departure signals the terminal point for Jeffersonian agrarianism in its oldest form—a death the novel marks as an inevitable necessity.[102] Describing Grampa as "vicious and cruel and impatient" and his wife as surviving for so long "only because she was as mean as her husband," the novel extends little sympathy to this first generation of Midwestern white settlers who die or become burdens in quick succession.[103] Grampa not only "earned" his land in Oklahoma through the brutal slaughter of indigenous peoples, but deeply enjoyed its brutality. "Time Grampa an' another fella whanged into a bunch a Navajo in the night," Tom notes, "they was havin' the time a their life."[104] While Steinbeck takes pains to illustrate the similarities between the eldest Joad's brutal conquest of Oklahoman land and the violence inaugurating California's settlement, Grampa and Granma Joad's steep declines nonetheless mark their unfitness for a Western future. Steinbeck's critical portrait of these figures further underscores his own lack of sentimentality about this era's necessary end.

With Grampa's death, Connie and Ma Joad emerge to fill the ideological vacuum of how the Joads should live now, with each envisioning the family's future unfolding in versions of little white houses. The explicitly residential imaginaries of these two characters—soon spreading to most members of the family—also make them the most resilient adult members of the extended Joad clan. Though Connie survives by running off to follow his suburban dreams while Ma endures by seeding hope for collective life in others, their shared capacity to adapt to the residential conditions of the West leaves this unlikely pair in the best position to navigate the coming future organized around wage work and residential collectivity.

Before focusing on the twinned residential imaginaries of Connie and Ma Joad, let's first trace agrarianism's last gasp in the novel, most fully personified by Pa Joad. Like his father, Pa continues to desire land upon which he can own and work—a predilection threatening to doom him to obsolesce in a residentializing West.[105] As Ma Joad becomes the family's moral compass and tactical leader, Pa Joad has increasingly less and less to do in both the family and the novel.[106] His earliest description of his vision for living centers not on the physical home but on the prospect of possessing land, with Pa Joad announcing his hopes that "we'll get out west an we'll get work an' we'll get a growin' land with water."[107] This seemingly modest aspiration—employing the same obfuscating possessive language of "getting" that the Joads generally favor—quickly proves futile as the realities of their structural exploitation in the West come into focus.[108] Pa expresses his land-oriented dream of dwelling just once more in *Grapes*, within the relative comfort of the government camp around trusted men. "I jus' thought," Pa Joad tentatively utters, "if a fella had a acre. Well, my woman she could raise a little truck an' a couple pigs an' some chickens. An' us men could get out an' find work, an' then go back."[109] By this point in the novel, Pa's land-centered vision of the good life has markedly narrowed. Rather than desiring "growin' land" upon which he and his family could make their living, Pa's fantasies now revolve around acquiring land on which his wife and children could labor for sustenance while the men pursue wages elsewhere to support this pastoral life. But even this more modest dream proves unattainable, as the Joads find themselves homeless once more and with little money. Bemoaning his uselessness to the family near the novel's close, Pa confesses to spending "all my time thinkin' of home, an' I ain't never gonna see it no more."[110] Lacking any future-oriented imaginary for dwelling by this point, Pa sinks into a melancholic relation to an unrecoverable home inseparable from the land.[111]

Ma Joad's response to Pa's despair—that women can "change better'n a man"—reflects the mix of idealism and practicality coloring her orientation toward a reconfigured residential way of life.[112] Ma Joad's dream of dwelling comes to take pride of place in the novel, receiving the most repeated elaboration of all the Joads' good-life aspirations. She first describes this vision soon after they leave Oklahoma. Taking pleasure in imagining "how nice it's gonna be, maybe, in California," Ma Joad visualizes "people just bein in the nicest places, little white houses in among the orange trees." Ma continues to speculate, "I wonder—that is, if we all get jobs an' all work—maybe we can get one of them little white houses."[113] Unlike her fictional predecessors George and Lennie in *Of Mice and Men*, whose dream of "livin off the fatta the land" becomes a tragic refrain, Ma Joad's vision is not centered on easy and total sustenance but the attainment of wage work to support their family life clustered around a "little white house," a house presumably owned by the ranch where they might one day live and work. Like other migrants in the novel, Ma Joad talks about "getting" a home, a verb obfuscating both the specific method of its possession and the mode of occupation, be it through ownership or tenancy. But no matter whether the home is owned, rented, or loaned, Ma desires a single-family home as the centralized location to which her family can consistently return.[114]

The Joads' previous lives as sharecroppers has primed Ma Joad's vision for residential living prioritizing stability, dignity, and community over ownership status. The family's time in the government camp deepens these priorities, but the seeds for this orientation are first sown during their transition from owners to croppers half a generation prior. The Dust Bowl migrants serve as Steinbeck's ideal revolutionary subjects, in part because they have already learned to value long-term intimacy with the land and a broader social that does not depend on exclusive title to the land. These preexisting investments both ready the Joads for more formally political modes of collective action as well as demonstrate the homegrown nature of this orientation produced not only by international agitators but their own local experience of dispossession. In other words, Steinbeck demonstrates how the slow dispossession of the Midwestern "land man" over decades enabled the transference of his commitments from ownership to other forms of occupation. But the racialized roots of this emerging collectivism—built on the theft of the land from Native peoples and the ongoing exclusion of blacks—become increasingly occluded in *Grapes*, if no less important, as Ma Joad's residential vision becomes its anchoring refrain.

Ma Joad's dream of *living* in a white house rather than owning one eventually colonizes the dreams of her kin. Unlike Pa Joad, whose imaginary for dwelling diminishes in scale across the novel until he reverts to longing only for the past, Ma's residential imaginary increasingly infects the speech of others. Tom translates Ma's vision to Rose of Sharon, assuming that like her mother, she, too, dreams of bearing her child "in one a them white houses with orange trees all aroun'."[115] Pa also reiterates his wife's vision, explaining that "Ma favors a white house with oranges growin' around," identifying the origins of this vision as emerging from "a big pitcher on a calendar she seen."[116] Such "pitchers" have also informed Tom's dwelling imaginary, noting "I seen pitchers of a country flat an' green, an' with little houses like Ma says, white."[117] Whereas the rest of the Joads continually readjust their dreams of the good life relative to their conditions, Ma remains steadfast in this singular want that spreads to many of her relatives.[118]

But Ma also recognizes how their recent history of dispossession has altered her residential imaginary. In a passage that begins with the rallying cry that "we're Joads" and "don't look up to nobody," Ma acknowledges the difficulty of holding on to their dignity given not just their recent exodus but their longer trajectory of foreclosure and tenancy. "We was farm people till the debt," she notes, until the arrival of "them people"—referring to the bankers who pushed them off the land. "They done somepin to us. Ever'time they come seemed like they was a w-whippin' me—all of us."[119] But Ma holds on to her will to not just live but thrive due to the fellowship she finds with her peers on the road and in the camps. "These folks is our folks—is our folks. . . . Why I feel like people again."[120] The painful training the Joads undergo in transitioning from "farm people" to croppers to migrants has taught them to value their relationships with their family, the social, and the land in excess of their ability to own it. While not all the Joads are able to fully embrace this lesson, Ma Joad is an example of how the capacities of the "land man" could be rerouted toward more collective means.

And yet, while Steinbeck highlights the burgeoning collectivism shaping Ma Joad's orientation, one can't help but also see the ways this dream also resembles the coming mass suburbs where home values would be derived from another form of collectively dependent occupancy through the unit of the homogeneous neighborhood. In ways resembling Steinbeck's portrait of the emerging solidarity between Dust Bowl migrants, social interdependency between suburban neighbors would also dictate processes of home valuation dependent upon the characteristics of the surrounding neighborhood—most keenly, white exclusivity. Unlike farmland that was valued according to its ability to produce, the value of residential homes depended upon the perceived value of its surrounds. While residential protectionism is certainly not the collectivism Steinbeck had in mind when imagining the radical potential of white migrant solidarity, migrant solidarity and mass residential investment both entailed expansive forms of cross-class and transregional collectivity premised on the exclusion of racial others who threaten to depreciate the whiteness that fragilely binds these collectives. In using Ma Joad's faith in her migrant peers to reorient the instincts of the "land man" to serve the greater collective good of "land people," Steinbeck fails to anticipate how her collectivist energy would prove just as useful to the ethos of residential valuation. While the Joads are violently barred from making homes in residential Californian communities within *Grapes*, by midcentury Dust Bowl migrants would be welcomed into these communities as part of the expanding class of white Americans newly pegged as good investments. The future of suburban California would be premised on the Joads and the Steinbecks coming together to exclude black and brown others whose devaluing presence threatened to disrupt the collective value of their newly consolidated whiteness—framed as a neighborhood's greatest amenity.[121]

Such a reading of the future co-optability of Ma Joad's residential imaginary requires reading against the grain of the novel, especially in light of Steinbeck's efforts to separate Ma Joad's "pitcher" of a little white house in an orange grove from the residential imaginaries originating with Connie and spreading to several of her children more fully seduced by dreams of bourgeois living organized around conspicuous consumption. Connie, Rose of Sharon, and Al all have designs on lives funded not by farming or farm wages but through more industrial, commercial, and professional forms of labor. They dream not of land but of living "in town," envisioning themselves as the owners of homes, refrigerators, and non-utilitarian cars made possible by gaining a foothold within the middle class. Most of Connie and Rose of Sharon's conversations on the road revolve around their dreams of bourgeois living to come. Rose of Sharon later shares these visions with her mother, which feature Connie working "in a store or maybe a fact'ry" before eventually owning his own store so the couple can acquire "a place, a little bit of a place" to live.[122] Sharon admits she hopes the whole family will eventually join them in "town life." While Rose of Sharon mourns these lost residential dreams after Connie's abandonment, Al breathes life into them once more upon his own engagement at the novel's end, describing his intentions to "get a job in a garage" and live in a "rent' house for a while," presumably with the intention to eventually own "in town" as well.[123]

While Connie's ur-suburban residential imaginary—later imparted to Rose of Sharon and Al but originating with him—shares some contours with Ma Joad's vision of acquiring a little white house, their base similarities bely their deeper differences. Connie aspires to middle-class homeownership, seeking to join the ranks of the Californians who have abetted the migrants' exploitation and abject treatment. It is not surprising, then, that Connie, too, abandons the Joads, recognizing that his more immediate advancement into the middle class requires him to forsake the Joads and any solidarity with the migrants. Whereas Ma Joad adapts the drives of the "land man" to more residential ends not necessarily predicated on ownership, Connie fetishizes a narrower form of homeownership predicated on the exclusion of those like the Joads or their quiet assimilation. But the residential Californians whom Connie is eager to join garner Steinbeck's direct ire in the interchapters. While "the Californians" seek "accumulation, social success, amusement, luxury, and a curious banking security," he writes, "the new barbarians wanted only two things—land and food; and to them the two were one."[124] This aspirational schism between middle-class Californians—described as "men of the towns and of the soft suburban country" who were "terrified for their property"—and the agricultural (and literal) hunger of the migrants takes on a racial tint, with the perceived barbarism of the migrants echoing Steinbeck's insistence in *Their Blood Is Strong* that they constituted a "new race" who are "here to stay."[125]

But unlike earlier groups of migrants from Asia and Mexico, the Dust Bowl migrants would be reconciled back into whiteness by way of the very structure necessitating their initial exclusion—property. Although Steinbeck never tells us what becomes of Connie after he leaves the Joads, it is not hard to imagine him following the path of precursors like Gatsby and predecessors like Tom Roth in Sloan Wilson's *The Man in the Gray Flannel Suit*, John Cheever's suburban protagonists, and *Mad Men's* Don Draper, who managed to triumph over their entwined racial and economic precarity to varying degrees through homeownership. The second part of this book will focus more on the alchemy of racial valuation in relation to the homebuying market, but for now all we need to note is that Connie's wager that his quickest path to the middle class required obtaining a firmer footing in whiteness likely paid off.

The irony, however, is that so, too, will Ma Joad's wager pay financial and racial dividends in the long run. While we're unsure where Tom's awakening will lead him, Connie and Ma Joad are the adult family members most likely to thrive in their new Western environs due to their varying forms of residential adaptability. If Steinbeck spied in Ma Joad's dream of living with dignity the potential for a nascent socialism, realtors and crafters of state policy also harnessed the potential indexed by Ma's hunger for a little white house, constructing in the years following the novel a subsidized housing market premised on the erection of a million new little white houses, wage labor, and an expansion of whiteness capable of comfortably assimilating the Joads into the "soft suburban country" that Steinbeck himself occupied. In Chapter 14, Steinbeck famously notes that "the quality of owning freezes you forever into 'I,' and cuts you off forever from the 'we.'"[126] But this turns out to be not quite true given that that the value of homeownership increasingly depends on the "we" of the neighborhood dictating a home's worth. While Steinbeck valorizes the government camp, the state's most fulsome intervention in the residential lives of its citizens would come not in the form of public housing but through the subsidization of the residential housing market for a newly expansive category of white Americans for whom ownership would soon become even cheaper than renting.

But more than even Ma Joad or Connie, it is Ruthie and Winfield—the youngest Joads—who are most primed to reap the benefits of the residential world to come. In one of his most prophetic moments, Tom describes the new sensorium Ruthie and Winfield will come to inhabit as the first generation of Joads to come of age in the West. Tom reflects that even if his grandparents had survived the trip, their age meant "they wouldn't of saw nothin' that's here." Rather than taking in the West on its own terms, Tom notes, "Grampa would a been a-seein' the Injuns an' the prairie country when he was a young fella" while Granma would have viewed the West through the lens of "the first home she lived in" back in Oklahoma. But, as Tom then declares, "who's really seein' it is Ruthie an Winfiel."[127]

Ruthie and Winfield—the youngest inheritors of the "land man" mantle and the least unencumbered by the agrarian sensorium of the past—exceed even Connie and Ma Joad in their chances of adapting to the economic, affective, and racial landscape of the residentializing West. The post-Depression trajectory of the real Dust Bowl migrants suggests the potential outcomes awaiting them. Ruthie and Winfield—twelve and ten years old, respectively, during the tenure covered in *Grapes*—would be teenagers when the war industry boomed in California in the early 1940s and young adults when America became a nation of homeowners in the early 1950s.[128] As *Grapes* demonstrates, Californians at first largely supported Dust Bowl migrants' exclusion from their residential communities, imploring state officials to "not put these vile people at my door to depreciate my property and to loot my ranch," to cite one frenzied resident. But residential Californians proved far more willing to accommodate the growing class of wartime laborers into which many of the Dust Bowl migrants would be absorbed.[129] During World War II, industry in California grew a staggering 96 percent.[130] Sprawling subdivisions quickly rose up around defense centers in the West to provide affordable housing in these newly dense areas.[131] As Becky Nicolaides has shown, Californians greatly benefited from federal housing subsidies derived from the New Deal promoting white homeownership, particularly in working-class areas.[132] By 1950, 31.1 percent of Californians lived in the suburbs, far ahead of the 13.9 percent national average of suburban dwellers.[133] Most of these suburbs were segregated. By 1946, for instance, 80 percent of Los Angeles residential property had racial covenants written into their deeds—a requirement for most state-backed mortgages.[134] It is easy to imagine Ruthie and Winfield joining other Dust Bowl migrants whose contributions to the war efforts enabled them to purchase homes in the largely white residential communities dotting their peripheries.

A 1952 article reporting on where the Okies were now expressed wonder at their newfound social and economic mobility. Describing their transformation from "the pariahs, outcasts and social lepers of yesterday" into "worthy and respected members of the communities in which they settled," the piece notes that Dust Bowl migrants and their descendants now enjoyed "better homes, better jobs, and greater economic security than ever before"—a fact best evidenced by the "modern but modest frame cottages" in which they dwelled and a far cry from the "tar-paper shacks, tents, and trailers" of yore.[135] As Steinbeck critic Milton Cohen points out, "if the Joads finally did buy their white cottage, it would probably have been in a big city, near an aircraft plant or shipyard." While Japanese migrants who once worked the same fields as the Dust Bowl migrants faced internment and the theft of their property in the 1940s, migrants like Winfield found employment in defense factories and put down payments on homes likely to have racial covenants written into their deeds. Others enlisted or married enlisted men, as Ruthie may have done, enabling such families to benefit from the GI Bill's low-cost loans most readily available to white veterans. The collectivism Steinbeck nurtured in the Joads easily translated into the white solidarity holding new mass suburbs together via racial covenants, residential steering, and campaigns against affordable housing. The ability for Ruthie and Winfield to "really see" California in the long run, as Tom predicted, involved their learning to see it in increasingly residential terms—terms largely predicated on maintaining white occupancy as a neighborhood's most valuable amenity.

In tracing the Joads' transition from nineteenth-century "land men" to twentieth-century "house men," I recover Steinbeck's commitment to staging the Joads' future potential not only as laborers but as *homeowners*, setting the stage for the Dust Bowl migrants' broader incorporation into the residential spaces through which the nation's new civic fabric was increasingly being knit. If the whiteness of the Joads was in doubt during the 1930s, their eventual assimilation into the residential housing market in the years after the Depression speaks to the enduring power of their whiteness, which, despite being severely tested, ultimately maintained its value via the expanding residential market that re-enshrined its worth. If title to the land in Grampa Joad's era was tethered to the murder of Indians and the theft of their land, Ruthie and Winfield are poised to settle the country's new residential frontier—a process forgoing the outward violence joyfully relished by Grampa Joad to instead deploy the quieter and more banal tools of financing, subsidies, and the pastoral image of the home. In this understanding of Ma Joad's little white house, whiteness is more than a cosmetic detail; it also indexes the foundational exclusions making this "pitcher" desirable and, even more importantly, stable in value.

Competing Reconstructions: Reappraising Forty Acres and a Mule During the Depression

For a poor people, [colored people] buy and build the best homes in the world. Compared with poor Italians, Slovaks, Jews and Irish people, they sacrifice far more for a home than any—they overspend on homes; they will have them; they fight and bleed and die for them.
—W. E. B. DU BOIS, "Hopkinsville, Chicago and Idlewild,"
The Crisis, August 1921[136]

While Steinbeck sought to reclaim the Joads' whiteness in the wake of their sudden dispossession by reminding readers of their ancestral status as "land men," black thinkers during the Great Depression debated the usefulness of fighting for inclusion into this racially mediated category. Given the even starker rates of rural dispossession for blacks and the further sedimentation of urban ghettoes insulating white neighborhoods from the illiquid effects yoked to black-held or black-adjacent property, what forms of residential life were they to rally around? While the Depression newly underscored the precarity of ownership for a swath of white Americans, how did this period's mass dispossessions register to black Americans already well versed in this lesson? While this chapter has so far focused on how John Steinbeck imagined a residentializing form of whiteness that could weather the property storms of the Depression, I end by attending to how two black writers—W. E. B. Du Bois and Richard Wright—turned back to the broken promises of land during Reconstruction to interrogate the ongoing importance of ownership in a nation built on the premise that its "land men" are inherently white.

Du Bois insisted in 1968 that "the story of the Depression as it affected American Negroes has not been adequately attempted."[137] While several historians have since helped tell this story, the cultural memory of the Depression remains overdetermined by the portraits of white migrants created by John Steinbeck and Dorothea Lange and images of downtrodden white men in soup lines. One reason for the continued underrepresentation of the black experience of the Depression, as historian Cheryl Lynn Greenberg notes, is that "Black Americans lived in a depression long before Wall Street's collapse in 1929 gave the economic catastrophe a name."[138] The story of black property relations before and after the Depression helps illustrate this. At the Depression's start, a quarter of black families owned their homes, compared to half of all white families. Black farmers, however, most immediately experienced the Depression's effects, losing almost 10 percent of their total acreage by the end of its first year and a third of the value of their land. By the Depression's end, the number of black farmers owning or managing farms fell to less than 15 percent of all black agricultural workers, even as the proportion of white farm owners and managers rose.[139] In Georgia, white sharecroppers at the end of the Depression earned more than black farmers who owned their land.[140] The insistence of white Southerners that "it is not good for a Negro to own property," as sociologist Guy B. Johnson observed in 1934, abetted the continued loss of black land in the South as legislators explicitly designed New Deal legislation to prevent black agricultural workers from reaping its benefits.[141]

The story of black occupancy in the North was similarly austere. Although rents fell across the board in the 1930s, rents in black areas remained significantly higher than those in white areas during the Depression. In New York in the early 1930s, the average Harlem tenant paid almost double what equally poor Italians paid to rent in East Harlem, even as black family earnings were nearly cut in half. While poor whites paid roughly a quarter of their income in rent, black families spent more than half of their earnings on rent.[142] Despite the discriminatory living conditions in the North, black southerners continued to move to Northern cities during the 1930s, if at slower rates than before given the collapse of industrial work. But despite the lack of jobs in the North, the enduring reign of Jim Crow in the South, the lack of federal aid for black farmers and farmworkers, and the overall decline of farmsteading continued to make migration northward worthwhile for black southerners.[143] While Steinbeck glimpsed a brighter residential future for the white "land man" on the other side of the Depression, black residential futures in this period seemed to portend a further intensification of the dispossession and exploitation shaping black dwelling in Southern hamlets and Northern ghettoes alike.

In the midst of these two "Great" events—the Great Depression and the Great Migration—hope for black mobility through landownership in the

South seemed to be at an all-time low.¹⁴⁴ It is in this context that we find black writers returning to the broken promise of forty acres and a mule from the prior century to variously redeploy and interrogate its utility within a residentializing United States. W. E. B. Du Bois in 1935's *Black Reconstruction* and Richard Wright in 1941's *12 Million Black Voices* contrastingly evoke Reconstruction to make sense of the residential landscape of the present. What sort of resource was the lost pledge of landownership for these writers as blacks continued to give up on the idea of agrarian self-sufficiency, often under duress, to rent within the discriminatory markets of the North? In the varying ways they frame freedmen's desire for property, Wright and Du Bois stage different lessons about the efficacy of using property and its attendant rights as the central terrain for antiracist struggles. Their work suggests the discordant reverberations of forty acres and a mule in the 1930s as a rallying cry for reparations, a cautionary tale, and a bad object that must be shed.

Let's begin with Du Bois's mammoth 1935 chronicle, *Black Reconstruction in America: 1860–1880*, which he penned during a period of ideological transition. In the early 1930s, Du Bois sharply broke with his antisegregation stance to abruptly support a strategic economic black separatism. The Great Depression has been credited with hastening his disillusionment with "interracial unity, either with working class New Deal Liberals or with Communist party radicals," as James O. Young puts it, as the economic downtown disproportionately left black Americans dispossessed, out of work, and excluded from many of the benefits inaugurated by the New Deal.¹⁴⁵ While Du Bois pragmatically promoted black economic self-sufficiency in the 1930s, he immersed himself across *Black Reconstruction*'s seven hundred pages in charting the failed development of an interracial working-class coalition during Reconstruction. Then, as now, Du Bois suggests, the financial incentives for both Northern and Southern white elites to maintain black subjugation proved too lucrative to overcome. Du Bois charts how the ruling classes effectively limited black landownership to profit from ongoing black servitude through peonage.

Throughout *Black Reconstruction*, Du Bois mourns the lost opportunity after the Civil War to massively redistribute Southern land to the freedpersons who had worked it. "If the basic problem of Reconstruction in the South was economic," he argues, "the kernel of the economic situation was the land."¹⁴⁶ Du Bois asserts that whereas those in the industrial North were slow to realize the importance of land to the South's economic, civic, and social development, "the Negro unerringly and insistently led the way" in understanding the centrality of land to their sovereignty. "The main question to which the Negroes returned again and again," Du Bois insists, "was the problem of owning land," as "Negroes expressed their right to the land and the deep importance of this right."[147]

The idea that possession of the land is crucial to sovereignty is an old one. But Du Bois's insistence on the Negro's specific *understanding* of this bond driving his desire for land is noteworthy. In Du Bois's emphasis on the Negro's "expression" of their right to the land as well as the "deep importance of this right," we hear the echo of the construct of the "land man" from the previous section, defined not by this figure's actual ownership of the land but by the *desire* to own. The centrality of land longing to the right to own shadows Du Bois's continual underscoring of black hunger for the land in *Black Reconstruction*. His repeated emphasis on the Negro's feeling for the land allows him to reclaim Negroes of the past as "land men" while also disrupting the afterlife of land man ideology forwarded by contemporary realtors and land economists: that blacks—specifically new migrants from the South—were bad owners due to a mixture of inexperience, apathy, and an inherent predisposition for degeneration spreading to all they touched. These more recent theories about black incapacity for homeownership underwriting residential valuation in the twentieth century were built upon theories of settler-colonial agrarianism initially constructing the white "land man" long central to the national mythos.

The residential afterlife of "land man" thinking appears, in fact, in one of the most influential documents shaping theories of residential investment: Homer Hoyt's 1933 dissertation, *One Hundred Years of Land Values in Chicago*, which would go on to be one of the most cited dissertations of all time. In the thesis he penned while studying land economics at the University of Chicago, Hoyt reproduced a list from a local real estate broker listing Negroes and Mexicans as "exerting the most detrimental effect" on land values due to having "standards of living below those to which most Americans are accustomed."[148] Hoyt, whose dissertation led to his hiring by the Federal Housing Administration in 1934, would go on to turn this local broker's list into federal policy, helping enshrine segregation as the norm of residential investment in the U.S. Hoyt's reference to racialized "standards of living" rhymes with this phrase's deployment in reports on California described previously that documented the poor living conditions non-whites were alleged to more innately tolerate.[149] As the U.S. continued its march toward residentialization, the phrase "standard of living" attached to the arena of housing helped to obscure the biological determinism underwriting theories linking race, property, and value. "Standard of living" refers to the perception of how others lived—a judgment directly tied to an area's valuation. Whether this "standard" was caused by the innate racial traits of occupants, their cultural predilections, or as the consequences of structural discrimination is of no consequence to the term's functioning; it only seeks to capture the perception of how one lives rather than its reality or cause. The explosion in usage of the term during the 1930s dovetails with the creation of new state policies making residential segregation the subsidized status quo.

I pause on the racialized uptake of "standards of living" in the 1930s order to suggest how more contemporary conversations about race, capacity, and property may also have shaped Du Bois's emphasis on naturalizing black historical yearning for possession across *Black Reconstruction*. Writing freedmen back into the story of "land men," Du Bois marks their hunger for "land which they could own and work" as being "the natural outcome of slavery."[150] "The Negroes were willing to work and did work," Du Bois insists, "but they wanted land to work, and they wanted to see and own the results of their toil."[151] Even as he writes the Negro back into the category of the "land man," Du Bois simultaneously dismantles the idea that this category is reliant on biological inheritance at all. Unlike the blood-originating hunger for landownership Steinbeck ascribed to white settlers, Du Bois frames the origins of black land hunger as a direct reaction to theft of their labor rather than as an innate orientation to ownership itself. Freedmen wanted the land not because their nature drove them to demand it but because they were owed it.

Despite the differing origins of their land pangs, Du Bois—like Steinbeck—focuses on the desire of freedpersons to both "*see* and *own* the results of their toil." Echoing Pa Joad's need for a fence to "give him a feelin' that forty was forty," Du Bois suggests that seeing the evidence of one's ownership was just as important as the title to the land itself, reinforcing the notion that "land man" subjectivity must be tended to in affective and perceptual terms.

Foregrounding freedmen's hunger for land ultimately allows Du Bois to valorize redistribution of private property as the most effective strategy for folding the newly freed into capitalist systems of production, both then and now. As Du Bois writes, "to have given each one of the million Negro free families a forty-acre freehold would have made a basis of real democracy in the United States that might easily have transformed the modern world."[152] For Du Bois, remaking not just the nation but the world after the evils of slavery depended upon expanding access to private property. Reconstruction's best outcome, he suggests, would have been the instantiation of a more just and perfect multiracial liberalism buttressed by the equal right to own.[153]

But Du Bois was not the only black thinker in this period to reevaluate the Reconstruction Era. Six years after *Black Reconstruction*, novelist Richard Writer made a very different case for the period's possessive legacy. Wright's 1941 photo-text, *12 Million Black Voices*, offers a poetic counterpoint to Du Bois's chronicle. Unlike Du Bois's vision of Reconstruction featuring freed men and women working to remake themselves through the land, Wright focuses on blacks after Emancipation who strategically rejected the land that had incentivized their theft and enslavement for so long. He depicts Reconstruction as a time when blacks could finally be free from the land rather than more deeply tethered to it.

In *12 Million Black Voices*, Wright paired images he selected from the Farm Security Administration's photographic archive with his lyrical narrative of black life in America from colonial encounter in Africa to the present. His book was one of a number of photo-texts published during the Great Depression focusing on American folk populations. But Wright's innovation in this genre was to narrate the story of black life using a univocal "we" to speak for the 12 million Africans shipped to the New World and their descendants. Accusing the reader of "tak[ing] us for granted," Wright sets out to demonstrate on behalf of the working-class black folk that "our history is far stranger than you suspect, and we are not what we seem."[154]

While Du Bois understood Reconstruction as history's tragic denouement, Wright treats this era as a slight picaresque within the black experience, granting it only a few paragraphs of description. Describing the "4,000,000 of us black folk stranded and bewildered upon the land" after Emancipation, Wright details in just a few scant pages the limited options available to the newly freed. "Some of us turned back to the same Lords of the Land who had helped us as slaves and begged for work," he writes, while others began "a new kind of bondage: sharecropping."[155] But Wright devotes most of his attention to those who charted a third path. "Glad to be free," he writes, "some of us drifted and gave way to every vagary of impulse that swept through us."

> Confined for centuries to the life of the cotton field, many of us possessed no feelings of family, home, community, race, church, or progress. We could scarcely believe that we were free, and our restlessness and incessant mobility were our naïve way of testing that freedom. Just as a kitten stretches and yawns after a long sleep, so thousands of us tramped form place to place for the sheer sake of moving, looking, wondering, landless upon the land.[156]

Whereas Du Bois detailed a Reconstruction ethos organized by black hunger for the land—demonstrating the Negro's affective history as a "land man"— Wright presents this period as one where blacks tested out what it might look like to be free of the land. Not only did the Negro lack possessions but she "possessed no feelings" for possession or progress in the terms most associated with the "land man." The freedman merely wanted to keep testing his freedom, moving without purpose or desire but for movement's sake, Wright insists, forsaking any of the affective hallmarks of land man status in his narration. While Du Bois's vision of Reconstruction rested upon black hunger for landownership, for Wright the most meaningful way for freedmen to reconstruct was by turning their backs—and their feelings—away from the land for good.

Wright never uses the term *reconstruction* to describe the historical moment after Emancipation. His refusal of this proper periodizing name is in keeping with his broader investment in capturing folk experience often left out of formal histories of the period. But Wright's avoidance of the term also reflects his unwillingness to render this specific period as one concerned with rebuilding—hopeful or otherwise. Wright instead renders the newly emancipated as seeking to lose attachments—including to property—after the shackles of slavery. If the sovereign possession of property is not the endgame for black liberation, Wright suggests, a vision of Reconstruction organized around the broken promise of forty acres and a mule becomes less pivotal— just one more iteration of black injury during the long regime of racial capitalism rather than an event of any particular or useful value as Du Bois frames it.

Wright ultimately posits a positive vision for ongoing reconstruction in *12 Million Black Voices* rooted not in ownership or the family unit but in collectivization:

> After having been pulverized by slavery and purged of our cultural heritage . . . we are unable to establish our family groups upon a basis of property ownership. For the most part our delicate families are held together by love, sympathy, pity and the goading knowledge that we must work together to make a crop.[157]

The Moynihan Report of 1965 would later declare the divergence of some black family structures from traditional bourgeois norms a handicap to be overcome.[158] But Wright claims divergent black family organizations, purposefully un-optimized for capitalist reproduction, as a strength. In the wake of the slavery's alleged "pulverization" of black culture as well as ongoing black exclusion from avenues of advancement after Emancipation, Wright casts the black folk as revolutionaries ripe to reconstruct the world for a radically different order. It is not the property hunger of the "land man" that drives Wright's black subaltern, but their relationships with each other that propel their survival with and upon the land. While Steinbeck sought to reorient the land hunger of the Joads for more communal purposes, Wright suggests Steinbeck was looking in the wrong place for such revolutionary animus.

In proper Marxist fashion, Wright goes on to use his reading of this collectivist economic base of black life to understand its cultural superstructure. He credits the collectivist roots of the black family for incubating specific forms of black joy: "that is why we black folk laugh and sing when we are alone together. There is nothing—no ownership or lust for power—that stands between us and our kin." "Because our eyes are not blinded by the hunger for possessions," he continues, "we are a tolerant folk." Wright ultimately argues that "our scale of values differs from that of the world from which we have been excluded; our shame is not its shame, and our love is not its love."[159] Less interested in a properly historical account of the past, Wright instead seeks to capture the beauty of black survival in spite of enslavement and racial capitalism. Rather than seeking entrance to the category of the "land man," Wright embraces black exclusion from this status as the origin of another kind of subjectivity and sensorium seeking a form of liberation in excess of land-based sovereignty.

As blacks in the early twentieth century continued to give up on Southern landownership to move into redlined Northern cities with few avenues for ownership, and as the Great Depression's long shadow continued to lay bare ownership's vulnerabilities, the utility of Reconstruction's lost property promises remained an open question. Du Bois's emphasis on African American desire for land possession during the post-Emancipation era stages ownership as the ongoing and most fertile terrain for black enfranchisement. Wright, on the other hand, mines Reconstruction for its latent revolutionary animus rooted in black rejection of owned land begetting new social collectives and forms of feeling. For both of these thinkers, the historical question of black orientation to the ownership had direct consequences for defining its meaningfulness in the present. The dream of forty acres and a mule emerges for them not so much as the given terrain for reparations but as a cipher for debating ownership itself as the social, economic, affective, and political animus for black living, past and present.

PART II

A Nation of Homeowners

IN 1945, THE HOMEOWNERSHIP RATE in the U.S. surpassed 50 percent for the first time.[1] Americans bounded this milestone in a leap rather than a crawl, moreover, as the homeownership rate rose 18 percent between 1940 and 1960—a significant hike compared not only to the ebb of the Great Depression but to homeownership's slow decline during the first two decades of the twentieth century. Not only had the dream of mass homeownership envisioned by the first generation of professional realtors largely materialized by the midcentury, but, as they also envisioned, it was largely and most profitably realized by white Americans. The housing reforms of the New Deal—particularly the establishment of the Federal Housing Administration (FHA) and the insurance it provided for amortized thirty-year mortgages—made homeownership newly affordable primarily for a broadening category of white American that assimilated Italians, Eastern Europeans, and some Jews into propertied residential life.

The power of the real estate industry also consolidated by the midcentury, with the National Association of Real Estate Boards (NAREB) shaping federal housing policy at almost every turn. Kenneth Jackson notes that "no agency of the United States government has had a more pervasive and powerful impact on the American people over the past half-century than the FHA."[2] But considering that the FHA, in both its philosophy and methods, was essentially co-managed by the NAREB, we might push this further to say that no private organization has had a more pervasive impact on the state and, by extension, its citizens, than the NAREB.[3] While "the organized real estate industry was one of several institutions which created and maintained the racial ghettoes in America" as Robert Weaver observed in 1967, "by the mid-1960's it was *the* principal institution."[4]

The importance of the NAREB-shadowed FHA to the racialization of residential life in the U.S. cannot be overstated. While "FHA operations began to racialize whites' vision of housing economics during the 1930s," as David Freund writes, by midcentury "the agency's story about race, property, and housing was rapidly inscribed in a very powerful state apparatus, whose representatives insisted that it was economics and the market, not individuals and their prejudices, that were setting the rules."[5] Whereas realtors in the first few decades of the twentieth century created their own workarounds to steward residential segregation when state enforcement failed—adopting racial covenants and codes of ethics—the creation of the FHA enabled residential apartheid to expand to a new scale. "What realtors had previously been able to do themselves," as Gene Slater writes, "they now accomplished far more thoroughly through the federal government."[6] The strengthened partnership between the state, realtors, and lenders allowed them to collectively perform the work of racial discernment and dispersal more efficiently and under even greater cover than individuals could alone, making these practices bureaucratically commonplace. The midcentury gave rise to an incredibly effectual discrimination machine operating across public and private systems of buying and lending that facilitated disinvestment from sites of black life while making residential discrimination the compulsory norm whether residents across the color line desired this outcome or not. This lack of agency was part of the point, transforming residential apartheid from a matter of personal choice to a structural financial necessity for the state, lenders, and residents hewing to the alleged "truth" of the market, no matter how lamentable its racism.[7]

Unlike the burgeoning residential sensorium of the early twentieth century built upon an understanding of whiteness as the distinctive feel for property, the vast public-private partnership managing the midcentury housing market increasingly required the *disavowal* of racial feeling, preferring to package residential segregation as an impersonal effect of the market. The systemic construction of residential apartheid, managed behind the closed doors of government agencies and financial institutions, aligned with the racial liberalism of the period in which biological definitions of racial hierarchies or explicit expressions of racial hatred became less acceptable in public life even as racial inequality became further embedded in the bureaucratic structures of residential life. The burden of maintaining residential segregation shifted away from local homeowners and neighborhood associations soliciting realtors' assistance at the turn of the century and more toward a nationwide network of midcentury bureaucrats directing forms of racial surveillance and financialization through back channels far from the block. By the 1950s, residential segregation was less frequently described as the will of specific people—or a by-product of their blood, to cite John Steinbeck—and more commonly ascribed to market logic deemed impossible to change. The NAREB's journal no longer touted the Anglo-Saxon's distinctive capacity for ownership; it didn't have to—a coordinated residential network, already convinced of black illiquidity, maintained segregation as a matter of financial law rather than eugenic principle. Violence and intimidation, though far from obsolete, became less crucial to segregation's maintenance as housing operators sought to more quietly steer the "inharmonious"—a category increasingly synonymous with black residents. In a word, the housing industry invested in segregation without segregationists.[8] The midcentury residential sensorium was no less anti-black, but the housing industry's bureaucratic innovations made black containment appear more seamless, efficient, and agentless, but also more necessary.

Black homeownership rose, too, in this period. But the extraction of black wealth through housing also intensified: in black belts where home improvement loans were scarce, housing stock was aging, and rents remained disproportionately high; through exploitative contract loans estimated to have extracted between three and four billion dollars from black consumers; and for black homeowners who, when they did manage to secure loans, paid exorbitant interest rates to move into neighborhoods likely to be disinvested from upon their arrival.[9] In contrast to realtors at the turn of the century framing blackness as an incapacity for property and its care, their midcentury successors naturalized the housing market's aversion to black presence as an impersonal financial truth that must be upheld, if with rueful liberal reluctance. But unlike attention-getting images of snarling dogs and unleashed fire hoses associated with white supremacy in the civic arenas of the Jim Crow South, the more banal mechanisms used to maintain residential segregation's solid state—nonpublic maps, standardized forms, apologetic shrugs—proved harder to represent, sensationalize, and mobilize against.

By midcentury, the question no longer seemed to be, to cite Du Bois at the turn of the century, how it *felt* to be a problem. For those overseeing the midcentury housing market, the priority was how to see, surveil, and neutrally manage the fact of black devaluation, removing feelings from the allegedly empirical work of racial detection as much as possible. Residential segregation wasn't personal, these officials insisted, hoping to avoid the representational regime forged by Southern resistance to civil rights actions using direct violence to uphold unabashed white supremacy. The "market imperative" for segregation bolstered by housing professionals, as David Freund writes, "provided a ready vocabulary for men and women fearful of what black occupancy would do to their neighborhoods, their families, and their investments" while still allowing them to see themselves as good Cold War citizens.[10]

But the changing emotional and market logic of residential segregation was not merely a matter of updated vocabularies. The midcentury inaugurated deep changes to the overall residential sensorium as the number of Americans both financially and affectively invested in residential space—and, by extension, in whiteness as its most valuable amenity—swiftly emerged as a new majority. Real estate developers, with the assistance of state subsidies, built new mass suburbs far from black or black-adjacent residential districts, while older urban residential spaces became battlegrounds where blockbusters colluded to incite fear about the inevitability of Negro invasion. These changing physical, economic, and affective conditions of mass homeownership at midcentury remade not just who counted as white but the very measures of whiteness itself, moving away from blood and ancestry and toward performance, appearance, and location. Likewise, the perceivability of blackness as something describable on a standardized form took priority over anthropological or genealogical racial knowledge driving its measurement decades prior. In contrast to the passing panic about "secret Negroes" whose undetectable blackness increased the threat they posed to whiteness in the late nineteenth and early twentieth centuries, midcentury residential regimes fetishized the *appearance* of race over mining for its alleged biological reality beneath unstable surfaces. Market value relied upon the *sense* of a place as glimpsed by potential homebuyers on the sidewalk rather than deep knowledge of residents' backgrounds—information proving harder to come by in new mass suburbs occupied by recent arrivals. Mass homeownership transformed what it meant to both sense race and be sensed as race, deemphasizing rules of heredity like the one-drop rule to usher in much more fungible—if no less inflexible—understandings of race more acutely distributed across appearance, and, increasingly, place.

The second half of this book tracks these evolving norms of residential perception and racial knowledge, the changing nature of neighborhood observation and valuation, and the lingering ambivalences about homeownership despite its growing sedimentation as a normative site of emotional, financial, and racial attachment. The chapters that follow chart the changing practices of racial description tethered to residential space in a newly majority-homeowning U.S.—a task tackled by appraisers, lenders, and government bureaucrats as well as poets, writers, and painters collectively attending to the neighborhood as an ever-more-consolidated racial unit. And yet, despite the heightened observational scrutiny bestowed upon neighborhoods, these chapters also chart the strategic racialized postures of unseeing, impersonality, and invisibility becoming endemic to the residential sensorium. For writers like Jane Jacobs and John Cheever, the broadening of whiteness achieved via mass homeownership—created through the demotion of what were once considered racial differences to assimilable ethnic differences—changed how whiteness looked, felt, and could be read. These writers descriptively recalibrated property's racial *feel*, updating its changing norms, protocols, and experiential qualities for a new generation of homeowners. For black writers at midcentury, the raucous experiments in letting go of property's promises once encapsulated by the rent party gave way to a dispiriting sense of apathy for some and a renewed investment in property's saving graces for others. As the black residential imaginary adjusted to the demoralizing realities of discrimination at midcentury—either by becoming more inured to its harms or by reattaching to property even harder—writers including Gwendolyn Brooks, Lorraine Hansberry, and Kristin Hunter worked to varyingly depict and, at times, puncture the limiting horizons for black dwelling enclosed by ownership.

Appraisal Manuals
Looking at Residential Looking on the Midcentury Block

AS RESIDENTIAL SEGREGATION FURTHER STABILIZED at midcentury, representations of neighborhood integration prevailed. Novels, short stories, and plays written about the travails of families and communities when blacks moved onto white blocks were a continual part of the cultural landscape between the end of World War II and the 1968 passage of the Fair Housing Act. Focusing on individual efforts at integration, this thematic became more commonplace following the 1948 Supreme Court ruling *Shelley v. Kraemer* invalidating racial covenants.¹ Of these works, Lorraine Hansberry's *A Raisin in the Sun* is the most known today. But her play belongs to a broader cohort of work by blacks and whites attempting to turn residential integration into a story for mass consumption. Starting with Maxine Wood's 1946 Broadway play, *On Whitman Avenue*, residential integration was taken up in naturalist novels by Millen Brand (*Albert Sears*, 1947), William Manchester (*The City of Anger*, 1953), and Frank London Brown (*Trumbull Park*, 1959), in Sinclair Lewis's 1948 satire, *Kingsblood Royal*, and in suburban integration melodramas such as *First Family* (1960), *Peaceable Lane* (1960), and *No Down Payment* (1957).

Much—if not all—of this work could be classified as social issue fiction, kin to what James Baldwin pejoratively called protest fiction—works whose "power as a corrective of social force," as Baldwin writes, were insufficient to "override its deficiencies as literature."² Residential integration even served as one of protest fiction's ur-subjects for Baldwin given that his first effort at defining its qualities occurred in a 1947 book review essay panning two novels on the topic.³ Protest fiction is characterized by wooden characters navigating social conflict—usually racial in nature—to either work up the nerve to do the right thing or tragically martyr themselves while trying. Such works failed to move audiences, Baldwin insists, because they standardized the experience of both race and racism, causing readers to tune out rather than attend more meaningfully to these phenomena. "The very frequency and sameness of the reports," as Baldwin negatively refers to protest fiction, "operate on the public mind as a bludgeon, numbing the hypothetical response; it may, indeed, be insisted that unless the report has the urgency of a revelation, the report is worthless."[4] Readers of protest fiction, he insists, are ultimately "shown nothing, we feel nothing, nothing is illuminated."[5]

Feeling nothing, however, was also proving increasingly central to the changing residential sensorium of the midcentury. If property was cast as a matter of racial *feel* and *feeling* earlier in the century, by the 1950s, when open expressions of racist hatred or biological rankings of racial difference were becoming less tolerated within the public sphere, the housing market became the impersonal scapegoat used to enforce residential segregation as an economic necessity rather than a personal preference or civilizational imperative. Whereas Baldwin critiqued protest fiction for its failures to provoke new, deep, or memorable feelings in readers, the housing industry's embrace of market rhetoric to justify segregation suggested stoicism's usefulness to its bureaucratic maintenance. In fact, the flood of cultural works bemoaning the wrongs of integration may have even *eased* segregation's more covert and impassive enforcement, drawing attention away from its systemic consolidation through appraisal forms and noncirculating redlined maps to focus instead on its louder, if increasingly rarer, manifestation through interpersonal encounters and openly hateful refusals.

But draining the feeling from segregation's maintenance also necessitated placing more faith in acts of observation and surveillance necessary to its bureaucratic enforcement. Baldwin critiques protest fiction not only for failing to elicit deep feeling from its readers, but for the shallowness of its powers to "show" and "illuminate." Yet surface-level illumination and selective appearance were precisely in line with home appraisal's observational practices of race, as we will see. We get a sense of the kind of shallow racial looking valued by appraisers from one of the era's most iconic cultural works about residential integration: Norman Rockwell's 1967 illustration, *New Kids in*

FIGURE 5. Norman Rockwell, *New Kids in the Neighborhood*, 1967

Source: Printed by permission of the Norman Rockwell Family Agency, Copyright ©1967 the Norman Rockwell Family Entities.

the Neighborhood. Despite its pictorial status, this work shares many of the aesthetic predilections Baldwin ascribed to literary "reports." Rockwell created *New Kids* for the cover of *Look* magazine in 1967 to accompany an article about black families moving to the largely white neighborhoods of Park Forest, Illinois. As the magazine's name proposed, *Look* was an image-centric publication competing with *Life* magazine for a broad readership. The magazine's invocation to look—and its employment of Norman Rockwell as its looker-in-chief following his frustrated departure from the more conservative *Saturday Evening Post*—resonate with the general ethos of protest aesthetics as diagnosed by James Baldwin. Such works bank on the possibility of an intimate story to unlock a well of common feeling capable of changing people and, by extension, society to arrive at a more equitable future. Rockwell's late career marks his increasing interest in using illustration to this end.

Painted a year before the passage of the 1968 Fair Housing Act, *New Kids in the Neighborhood* shares many of the hallmarks of residential protest literature—a focus on children whose natural instincts for friendship are distorted by the bugaboo of segregation, a tightly framed focus on individual encounters, and an overall ethos of liberal humanism.⁶ Set in a residential setting, likely a suburb, Rockwell's illustration revolves around the gazes exchanged between a pair of black children moving into the neighborhood and the block's young old guard of three white children who stare right back. Despite the physical gulf separating these groups as they size each other up, Rockwell includes details pointing to their similarities. Both girls sport pink hairbows while each of the boys carries a baseball glove, if hidden guardedly from view. In a particularly on-the-nose nod to the color line, the black girl carries a white cat ready to spring from her hands while the petite black dog at the feet of the white children looks just as eager to joyfully pounce—perhaps a rebuttal to images of snarling dogs enforcing segregation in the South. The homes appearing behind the children are modest and largely indistinct, as if marking the architectural uniformity soon to override the children's racial differences. A mover heaving a trunk in the midground is turned away from this foreground scene, engrossed in his own labor as a temporary member of this community. It takes some effort to spot the only other figure in the frame—an adult also beholding this scene behind slightly parted curtains in the background.

Rockwell's provocation in *New Kids* derives from whether *Look*'s audience will view this scene in the same way as the spatially distant, if financially more intimate, background homeowner in the painting also witnessing this exchange. Whereas the viewer of *New Kids* is primed to notice the details connecting the children, the housing market has conditioned the neighbor in the window to privilege perceivable racial difference given race's allegedly outsize importance to property values. While at first glance we might assume this voyeur, like us, keenly watches both sets of children, closer attention to the painting reveals the moving van to largely obstruct this figure's view of the white children. What this lurker spies from the window, then, is not a scene of integration but, rather, a scene of black invasion as integration was commonly described by those seeking to stanch its spread. While the black children cautiously peer out at their young white beholders, this duo is ultimately outnumbered by the four neighbors whose gazes are trained solely on them, appraising their presence according to a system of value interested only in the perceivability of the racial detail.

Readers of this image have latched on to its muted optimism, pointing to the parallel details Rockwell embeds across the two groups and their mutually interested leaning in as evidence of the children's flowering friendship to come.⁷ But while the surveying adult's place in the background may suggest their ultimate insignificance relative to the power of innocence to overcome racial antagonism, it also reads as an ominous reminder of the forces likely to emerge from out of the painting's background to obstruct any further acquaintance. Whether these new kids will have the opportunity to become old residents is ultimately left hanging in the balance, leaving us unsure if this is an illustration of nascent integration or a rendering of the moment before segregation's inevitable retrenchment caused by white neighbors either forcibly driving out these new black residents or fleeing for greener and whiter pastures.

The evidence from the period points strongly toward the latter. Though residential integration harbored ready-made intrigue for novelists, painters, and playwrights, its occurrence was a blip within the relatively steady state of segregation characterizing most midcentury U.S. neighborhoods.⁸ Many of the blocks that blacks "pioneered" into quickly "changed over" into all-black ones—a process encouraged by lenders deeming interracial neighborhoods losing bets, state agencies refusing to insure mortgages in changing areas, and speculators making massive profits from buying homes cheaply from whites and reselling them to desperate black homebuyers at a premium. Efforts to maintain residential segregation, of course, failed constantly. Despite the best efforts of the NAREB's code of ethics, the money to be made from predatory blockbusting was too great. But when neighborhoods integrated, the FHA incentivized their quick return to a steady state of segregation by subsidizing white flight to areas deemed less likely to "tip." Since lending maps ranked integrated neighborhoods nearly as low as all-black ones, segregation tended to follow hotly on integration's tail. Despite frequent representations of showdowns between white neighborhoods and new black residents, tense encounters between such families was not the only, or even the most common, story of race and housing at midcentury. Despite the aesthetic shortcomings of such works, their voluminous production at midcentury suggests the extent to which residential integration has overdetermined residential representation.

As this chapter will suggest, no matter how closely viewers looked at Rockwell's children or how intensely his illustrated children might look at each other, the form of revelatory looking embraced by protest fiction to change hearts and minds proved a grave mismatch for the bureaucratic forces designed to override personal feeling or subjective looking to enshrine the rule of black devaluation and maintain residential segregation as a stable norm. Although undoubtedly bolstered by individual acts of racial discrimination, segregation's maintenance at midcentury increasingly depended upon a matrix of financing decisions, government interventions, and professional codes enforced by a multiracial alliance working to depersonalize, rationalize, and streamline the profitable business of segregation.[9] These bureaucratic efforts toward impersonality, secrecy, and obfuscation effectively blunted the development of a representational mode for residential segregation at large. How does one effectively represent not just a few sour-hearted apples intolerant of black neighbors, but an expansive system designed to promote racism as quietly as possible and with an apologetic smile? In juxtaposition to the psychodramas and select emotional breakthroughs comprising the literary hallmarks of residential integration, representing the systemic creation and collection of racial data designed to quickly weed out black buyers and mixed neighborhoods without as much as an in-person meeting proved a harder story to apprehend, let alone satisfyingly tell to others.[10]

But while fiction about residential integration describes what happens when mechanisms of residential segregation fail, a range of comparatively unspectacular works from the period capture the more impersonal and allegedly objective processes of neighborhood observation used to uphold segregation. More precisely, it is within the expanded category of the report that Baldwin dismisses in his critiques of protest fiction where we find writers attempting to account for race on the residential block rather than lament the fact of racism. Such texts, rarely urgent or dramatically revelatory, focus on the mechanics of how race was seen, appraised, and categorized, dwelling in the more nebulous moment of racial sight, measurement, and recording rather than the dramatic scene of encounter following the crystallization of racial knowledge. Reports are useful precisely because of their investments in observation and description, which can lay bare the thinness of the line separating objective assessment from subjective supposition. Such lines proved particularly blurry when it came to neighborhood appraisal, entailing aesthetic and functional valuations of buildings, racial assessments of residents, and social estimates of local harmony. As one of the fathers of real estate appraisal, Frederick Babcock, noted, "so the habits, the character, the race, the movement, and the very moods of people are the ultimate factors of real estate value."[11] Appraisers charged with learning to see and value qualities like mood, habit, character, and race alongside roof slopes and sewer lines were responsible for becoming experts in observing as racist markets might. Understanding the midcentury residential sensorium requires approaching appraisers as perceptual workers measuring the residential according to a very specific sensorial blueprint while also limning the tactics writers invented to measure this measuring—to look at residential looking.

Reports are revelatory, contra Baldwin, not only for what they divulge about their subject matter but for their disclosures of their maker's fantasies of and for empiricism, particularly regarding race. As Nicole Fleetwood notes, "seeing race is not a transparent act; it is itself a doing"—a fact appraisal makes extraordinarily visible.[12] The act of producing racial assessments, be they of bodies or temperaments, is always simultaneously an empirical judgment and a practiced intuition, a documentation and a fictionalization, a beholding and a making. The expanded genre of residential reportage considered in this chapter acknowledges racial observation's key role in organizing the U.S. housing market while demonstrating this project's instability as an empirical practice despite its effectiveness as a mechanism for segregation. Residential reportage encompasses professional appraisal materials, but also broader modes of residential observation exploring methods for and the utility of looking closely. When writers such as Thomas Pynchon, Gwendolyn Brooks, Richard Wright, Ralph Ellison, and James Baldwin set aside fiction to take up modes of urban reportage to look more closely at real undervalued neighborhoods, what they imagined acts of looking to accomplish must be situated in relation to the professionalization of residential description but also its broader saturation of "common sense" in a majority-homeowning U.S. Inversely, professional appraisers posited themselves as trafficking not in subjective assessment reducible to the "merely" literary but as producing empirical facts about race and its market effects. Understanding how speculative acts of racial appraisal shaped the speculative system of residential real estate is a story not only of political economy and policy, but of perception and aesthetics.

In what follows I compare subgenres of appraisal narratives that variously describe and obscure procedures for perceiving and assessing race as a means of valuation. Beginning with the emergence of appraisal as a professional field, I consider how manuals and textbooks designed to train burgeoning property valuators differently managed the task of racial appraisal from the 1920s to the 1960s. I then turn to midcentury texts by Jane Jacobs and Gwendolyn Brooks that at times reify and at others revise tactics for racial appraisal circulating within real estate and planning fields. Jacobs in her urban planning intervention *The Death and Life of Great American Cities* (1961) and Brooks in her 1951 piece of reportage "They Call it Bronzeville" conduct differing trials in seeing and, consequently, valuing bodies and buildings in concert with one another. I close this chapter by turning to a pair of works by Thomas Pynchon featuring residential segregation published within a two-year burst—the 1964 short story "The Secret Integration" and Pynchon's lone piece of reportage, "A Journey into the Mind of Watts," from 1966. Influenced by Jane Jacobs but also James Baldwin's residential essays, Pynchon experiments in these works with the utility of urban looking. But Pynchon's fiction is where he's most able to produce the most agile "reports" on segregation, helping him to avoid some of the empirical traps plaguing his most direct works of urban observation.

The Specter of Appraisal

Midcentury literary experiments in neighborhood observation emerged against the backdrop of residential looking's professionalization. While this book's first chapter focused on the wide-ranging affective and aesthetic theories and approaches that real estate professionals deployed to bolster homeownership's racial provenance, here I trace the racial vision of the real estate industry's empirically minded sibling, appraisal. Whereas realtors were willing to use any tactic—from race science to sentimental songs—to sell homes, appraisal was positioned as a stoic check on the emotional logic of property. Property appraisal became a discrete discipline in the U.S. at the turn of the twentieth century and concretized as a profession in the 1920s. The American Institute of Real Estate Appraisers (AIREA), founded in 1932, has been referred to as "the intellectual wing of the NAREB."[13] Influenced by the actuarial research emerging from insurance fields—which also relied heavily on race science—real estate appraisal fashioned itself as a science reliant on the impartial collection and study of data.[14] Unlike the realtor selling a vision of the good life resonant with current buyers, the appraiser sought to hone himself into an objective instrument for assessing present and future property value, impervious to aesthetic trends or affective whims.

When it comes to race-based appraisal, redlining maps most readily come to the minds of most as this work's hallmark form. But maps were only one iteration of racial appraisal, which involved the creation of standardized forms, manuals, formulas, and curricula designed to survey, study, and ultimately steer decisions about where to invest in and insure properties and where to deny resources—decisions enshrining racial inequities for generations.[15] Appraisers, the beating heart of redlining, pioneered not only the "informatics of race," as Colin Koopman refers to the technologies used to turn racial difference into meaningfully distinct data, but also the pose of objectivity abetting redlining's mass uptake by private lenders and the state.[16] Because of appraisal's veneer of objectivity, the field's endorsement of the principle of black devaluation eased its adoption by federal agencies who, too, claimed to be impersonal stewards of the market in which they were helpless to interfere or refute. Accepting racism as a respectable and unchanging truth, appraisers constructed an effectual informational system organized around an understanding of certain minorities as inherent threats to white residential stability, enshrining their alleged contagious illiquidity into the fabric of residential financing itself. The algorithmic systems they crafted to privilege segregation codified this practice as an inalienable truth resistant to persuasion, change, or disruption, rebuking the emphasis on reforming feeling that had been central to antiracist strategy from the nineteenth century forward. Redlining, then, entailed constructing structures of discernment designed to reproduce racism *in spite of* the idiosyncrasies of individual racial perception and feeling. Such practices were designed to be immune to the moral, emotional, and subjective revelations that protest aesthetics sought to induce.

Appraisers emphasized the importance of race to home value from quite early in the discipline's formation.[17] Frederick Babcock, who would write the first underwriting manual for the Federal Housing Administration (FHA) in the 1930s norming previously localized assessment practices, was the first to suggest in print that appraisers attend to "social influences" when valuing a property. He penned the 1924 manual *The Appraisal of Real Estate*, credited as the first document to formalize race's function in valuation. Babcock brought these methods with him to the FHA, instructing valuators appraising homes for federally insured mortgages to investigate areas surrounding the location to determine whether or not incompatible racial and social groups are present, to the end that an intelligent prediction may be made regarding the possibility or probability of the location being invaded by such groups. If a neighborhood is to retain stability it is necessary that properties shall continue to be occupied by the same social and racial classes. A change in social or racial occupation generally leads to instability and reductions in values.[18]

If "the challenge for any forecaster was to separate the genuinely predictive data from that which was simply noise," as historian Benjamin Wiggins insists, "for Babcock, race was a clear signal in a noisy mass of statistics."[19] Babcock would go on to enshrine the importance of the racial signal during his time at the FHA.

Homer Hoyt joined Babcock at the FHA in 1934 as the agency's chief land economist. In his economics dissertation, *One Hundred Years of Land Values in Chicago*, published by the University of Chicago Press in 1933, Hoyt affirmed Babcock's insistence that race affected property value. As already noted in my introduction, Hoyt's book includes a list he claims to have obtained from a West Side broker ranking sixteen "racial and national groups" according to their influence on land values. Ordered from "most favorable" to "those exerting the most detrimental effect," the list places English, Germans, Scotch, Irish, and Scandinavians at its top, followed by North Italians and then Bohemians and Czechoslovakians. Rounding out the bottom are South Italians, Negroes, and Mexicans.[20] While noting that "the ranking given below may be scientifically wrong from the standpoint of inherent racial characteristics," Hoyt insists that this list—received secondhand from a broker and reprinted without any supporting evidence—"registers an opinion or prejudice that is reflected in land values."[21] With this explanation, Hoyt admits appraisal's privileging of "opinion" and "prejudice" in assessing land values, even when those opinions have been discredited or opposed, making appraisal a science of belief no matter how faulty, an empirics for measuring and reinforcing perception alone. Babcock and Hoyt's theories of race's effects on property valuation, backed by the NAREB, would directly shape the appraisal procedures and loan decisions of the FHA for its first decade and indirectly steer these practices in the public and private sector for far longer—transforming the residential sensorium in the process.

Appraisers were tasked with reporting on the neighborhood's "racial and social" makeup and finding out whether racial restrictions were written into local deeds. These guidelines enabled the agency to selectively stabilize and expand homeownership in the U.S., insuring nearly a quarter of single-family home loans between 1937 and 1939 and 45 percent of homes during World War II.[22] To reduce the appraisal labor needed to process such large numbers of applications, the FHA recruited appraisers to collect information about neighborhoods in order to produce studies of roughly 140 metropolitan areas for employees to consult during lending decisions. As Carl Nightingale writes in *Segregation: A Global History of Divided Cities*, the FHA "engaged in enormous projects to map all the urban neighborhoods of the United States with the goal of identifying the most promising areas for future residential investment."[23] These maps, organized largely by data about racial occupancy, functioned primarily as labor-saving tools, as historian Jennifer Light has shown, allowing application readers to reject applicants seeking homes more quickly in "grade D" areas—the grade given to areas with an "intermixture of races."[24] Saving appraisers time in the field, the maps helped the FHA turn around applications in less than two weeks.[25]

The data for these mapping studies was largely collected by realtors affiliated with the NAREB. Hoyt preferred this labor to be carried out by prominent men in each region "between 50 to 75 years old, who have resided in the community for the past 35 years," signaling his confidence in long familiarity over learned methodology as a means of appraisal.[26] But realtors were also the target audience for these findings, since they, too, used knowledge of racial occupancy to steer residents to "stabilized" properties qualifying for mortgage insurance. Nightingale describes the federal government as setting up a "nationwide network of exchange" where local data was ushered up to these federal agencies before making its way back down to the local realtor. "Thus the mapping studies," Nightingale writes, "became a kind of proprietary forum for the national dissemination of local information about property values."[27]

Nightingale, along with historians David Freund, Kenneth Jackson, Jennifer Light, and others, has marked the importance of forms and classificatory documents produced by the FHA and its predecessor, the Home Owner's Loan Corporation (HOLC), for the collection of racial data.[28] But while we know for certain that appraisers for public and private financial institutions collected and used data about racial occupancy of neighborhoods to decide which loans to approve or insure, we know relatively little about the actual procedures appraisers undertook when doing this racial accounting.[29] Although Babcock used the vague vocabulary of "inharmonious groups" while Hoyt named sixteen property-impacting "racial and national groups," both insisted on the necessity of racial appraisal while providing little to no instruction as to how appraisers were to draw these distinctions. How was one to carry out an investigation predicting the likelihood of "invasion," to borrow Babcock's language? Or distinguish not only between black and white occupancy but Polish versus Lithuanian residents, to deploy Hoyt's?

The lack of observational direction regarding racial appraisal's specific survey methods was also a hallmark of the field's commonplace forms. The "Report of Valuator" form issued by the FHA asked appraisers to mark, in addition to details about a home's physical properties, the presence of "inharmonious racial and social groups" in the neighborhood, whether there was danger of their future "infiltration," and if there were racial restrictions listed in the deeds. Yet the form provides no instruction as to what counts as "inharmonious" or how to measure its presence, leaving this determination up to the valuator's discretion. In order for the FHA's maps to be of applicable use, the individual valuators collecting the neighborhood data informing these area maps deployed some sort of process for identifying the "inharmonious"—a classification playing the largest role in determining an area's grade. Yet it can be easy to forget when looking at a totalizing color-coded map that it was composed through the aggregation of multiple individual and subjective acts of observation. By requesting that appraisers measure race without describing any best practices for doing so, lenders and insurers take for granted that a) identifying these groups was so obvious a task it didn't need explicit direction, b) it was more generative to let appraisers define these categories as they saw fit, and c) only the perception of "inharmonious" groups and their classifications mattered, since this "sense" of things was the most important factor in predicting a property's future value.

The point of residential appraisal forms, it seems, was not necessarily to provide an empirically accurate reading of a block's social and racial demographics, but to successfully speculate how bodies would "commonly" be read and reacted to by the average white homebuyer, the figure around which real estate markets in the U.S. were designed to serve. In directing appraisers to report on difference without indicating any best procedures for surveying or determining it, housing agencies and banks indicated they valued the perception of race as either locally or commonly defined over allegedly empirical accounts of how one might come to identify it. So while appraising a building's physical properties might be straightforwardly described as a series of actions designed to reveal the "truth" of a building's condition, evaluating a neighborhood involved inhabiting and reproducing local practices for making largely racial judgments that were not based on a practice of "deep" excavation rooted in genealogy or meaningful contact but on what could be glimpsed and tolerated by one's current or future neighbors.[30] Racial appraisal was described in ways more akin to the task of assessing a home's "visual appeal"— recognized by most manuals as a somewhat subjective judgment anchored by regional norms rather than as an empirically available fact.

The task of converting the amorphous factor of "social influence" into a financial assessment introduces a tension within the field's own sense of scientific mission and method. Was appraisal to be a science of property observation? Or was the appraiser's aim to become a well-tuned social barometer for white middle-class perceptual practices—more Howellsian social broker than empiricist of property? Further complicating appraisal's mission was that practices for perceiving and claiming to know race were far from settled across this period. Systems like the one-drop rule privileging hidden genealogical knowledge over bodily observation at the turn of the century were proving less and less useful in a world of urbanization, migration, and social anonymity. What distinguished a racial difference from an ethnic or national one, moreover, was far from systemized in the first half of the twentieth century.[31] The practices of looking that were scripted by appraisal materials reflect some of the logics undergirding broader national efforts to stabilize racial perception and definitions in the first half of the twentieth century, from the passage of Jim Crow laws to Supreme Court rulings in citizenship cases barring Indians and East Asians from claiming whiteness.[32] In all of these instances, we find the desire to mark and classify race coexisting with ambiguities as to how exactly such an adjudication should be done.

Given the FHA's insistence that "inharmonious groups" impacted home value, manuals training burgeoning realtors and appraisers needed to address this crucial step of assessment. But appraisal literature generally obscures the matter of *how* exactly this assessment of the inharmonious was to be carried out. Appraisal manuals belong to the broader canon of neighborhood description at midcentury revealing how mass homeownership not only produced a new demand for racial observation but shaped its unfolding. Charting how appraisal manuals described the work of racial appraisal between the 1920s and 1960s will allow us to put them in conversation with other forms of neighborhood observation that both reacted to and reshaped the midcentury racial imaginary increasingly attached to place and possession.

In early appraisal manuals attempting to demonstrate the field's legitimacy as a profession, the task of identifying race for the purposes of valuation belongs to a broader imperative to package appraisal as an empirically oriented science. In Frederick Babcock's 1924 manual *The Appraisal of Real Estate*, the first to insist that race should be factored into valuation, he strongly advocates for real estate appraisal becoming like a science. The appraiser, in his words, must avoid being one "who looks at the property immediately and applies his judgment as to value" and should rather carry himself like "a research investigator occupied solely with the gathering of data and their orderly classification."[33] He suggests that the appraiser go outside of himself and dis-embed himself from the scene of the local in order to judge a property based on the "facts" on the ground. In fact, this is what ends up being so important about the later FHA manuals—they replace the language of explicit discrimination based in racial animosity with the language of data, classification, and value, proving to be more concerned with race's influence on market prices than its intrinsic definitions or characteristics. Appraisers were to understand themselves as apolitical observers, helpless to change the circumstances leading them to literally devalue black life. Historian David Freund charts this discursive change in residential segregation in *Colored Property: State Policy and White Racial Politics in Suburban America*. To his assertion, I simply add that the seeds of this shift are first planted in this discourse of empiricism preceding and ultimately shaping discussions of race.

But discrepancies in the field about how much standardization was too much remained. Whereas Babcock remains insistent that "data" and "classification" can fully supplant personal "judgment," Robert Thorley and William

H. Stickney in their 1926 text, *Real Estate Forms*, echo Homer Hoyt's less public assertions that personal judgment can never be completely excised from the process of valuation—in fact, they suggest that personal judgment may be the appraiser's most valuable asset when balanced with data:

> Appraising requires a thorough knowledge of the principles and practices of real estate in all its branches. There are no set forms in this branch of the profession. Here the personal equation enters to a great degree, as the integrity, ability, knowledge, and sound reasoning powers of the appraiser, coupled with the use of all information compiled and long experience in dealing with sales, rentals, leases, mortgages, finance, and property management, are his aids.[34]

For Thorley and Stickney, good appraisal judgment accrues through "long experience" coupled with empirically based "information." Whereas Babcock's 1924 method, invested in norming a national standard of classification, would become publicly adopted at the federal level, Thorley and Stickney have no such national aim. They are writing for local appraisers whose knowledge of local idiosyncrasies is what makes them good at their jobs. Only in this process of "accrued judgment," balanced by "information," can one anticipate what the local "common man" will want or fear. Babcock and the FHA manual created under his tutelage obscures this process of experience to make appraisal sound as universally "scientific" as possible.

In Stanley L. McMichael's *Appraising Manual*, published in 1937, we find Babcock's earlier language of empirical appraisal more explicitly meeting the language of racial adjudication. In a section on "blighted areas," McMichael advocates that the appraiser "approach the problem with an open mind and effectively combat any preconceived notions, blind prejudice, or snap judgment he may have formed."[35] He asserts that "appraisal should be made with the head and not with the heart, and he must base his conclusions on facts and not fancies, bearing in mind at all times that he is judging the future and not the past."[36] The idea that appraisers should focus on a property's future value over its present was one of the field's key interventions, gaining steam first in the 1920s.[37] But the vague task of "judging the future and not the past" with "the head and not with the heart" is a directive toward a frame of mind and away from any actual tactics of interpretation. This insistent language of rational observation feels increasingly performative—a way for appraisal to claim the authority of a science while masking its inability to hone racial perception into a fine-grade instrument.

Other manuals used the language of observation to argue that certain races were less fit to own property. In Harry Atkinson's *Fundamentals of Real Estate*, published in 1939 and 1946, the author points to the "tendency of certain racial and cultural groups to stick together, making it almost impossible to assimilate them in the normal social organism."[38] Noting that Germans "take pride in keeping their property clean and in good condition," Atkinson insists that "unfortunately this cannot be said of all the other nations which have sent immigrants to our country." Such populations, he argues, "have brought standards and custom far below our own levels" and "like termites, they undermine the structure of any neighborhood into which they creep."[39] Atkinson's emphasis on "standards and customs" echoes the rhetoric found in the work of John Steinbeck as well as more explicit eugenicists in the period making racialized arguments about inherent incapacities for ownership. And yet despite the urgency with which Atkinson endorses racial appraisal's necessity, he, too, fails to provide directions for how one goes about deciding which people are "like termites" and incapable of ownership. He merely notes that "in different cities their origin varies," leaving readers with a vague warning that those that "*stay* foreign" remain "a definite thorn in the side of the real estate specialist and property owner."[40]

While appraisal manuals by the 1950s had largely excised language correlating race with one's fitness for ownership, they prove just as unforthcoming regarding any actual practices of racial appraisal. Earl Teckemeyer's *How to Value Real Estate: The Foremost Factor in Selling* (1956) includes a section titled "Infiltration of Foreign or Racial Groups." Teckemeyer writes that "the danger of deflated values from such sources is so self-evident that it does not require heated debate or lengthy discussion."[41] "It is not difficult to ascertain the areas where such changes are taking place," he continues, "and not difficult at all to determine, by comparing recent sale prices of properties on the market, what the normal percentage of devaluation must be to bring the value in line."[42] What is striking about Teckemeyer's manual is that references to the need to closely survey neighborhoods prominent in previous manuals are now gone. The "dangers" of infiltration are "so self-evident" and "not difficult" to either determine or ascertain that he omits both the intellectual pose of empiricism and the "what" of interpretation. The passage is not geared toward a mode or framework of assessment, but rather a defense of what has already become "self-evident," pointing to an assessment that has seemingly already taken place in the past. He manages to reify racial accounting's centrality to property valuation while uttering few words explicitly referencing *race*. If Babcock's appraiser was the ultimate Enlightenment hero, boldly empirical in his observational work, then Teckemeyer's appraiser is merely a number cruncher, conveniently beholden to the market.

In Alfred A. Ring's *The Valuation of Real Estate*, from 1963, the language of empiricism becomes integrated with a liberal apologetic. He writes that "despite educational and legal efforts to bring about the acceptance of true democratic doctrines, enforced—even when inadvertent—mixing of residents with diverse historical backgrounds within a neighborhood has immediate and depressing influences on value." "Often," he continues, "just the threat of infiltration—such as rumors within a stock market—causes market values of real properties in the area to be adversely affected."[43] Upon citing a statistic by another real estate manual about "Negro occupancy" lowering property values by 25 percent, Ring concludes that

> the necessity and importance of inventorying and reporting the background characteristics of neighborhood residents appears obvious. It must be kept in mind, however, that it is not the opinion or personal preferences of the appraiser that are to be reflected, but rather an objective prediction of the anticipated action or reaction of typical buyers.[44]

The language of Babcock's scientific appraiser returns, but defensively, as a shield for the appraiser to wield in the face of accusations of "personal preference." Ring laments that "true democratic doctrines" based in equality do not yet line up with market desires. But the valuator's job is to bury his opinion and be the eyes for the "typical buyer." Again, how one hazards an "objective prediction" of the typical buyer's reaction is not detailed, providing a defense of method without supplying the method itself. But even as Ring remains as procedurally opaque as previous manual writers, his choice of test case marks how the object of racial appraisal had changed. His focus on Negro occupancy reflects the diminishing importance of nationality to valuation as well as the further normalization of black illiquidity as the foremost threat to property values. Yet, even as the "what" of appraisal shifted, its practice remains necessary, important, and obvious to Ring as something rooted in both rumor and fact. Appraisal is simultaneously the science of observation, the speculative art of prediction, and the formal act of narrativizing the actual presence of racial others as well as the specter of their potential manifestation.

What remains consistent across these manuals is that none explicitly address the process for determining and inventorying the presence of the "intrusive." They treat racial observation as imperative even as they absent its mechanisms. Appraisers mark a need for flexibility in assessing these categories. But this flexibility suggests the tractability underlying practices of racial appraisal despite appraisers' attempts to anchor them in scientific empiricism. The presence of blockbusters or real estate speculators actively manipulating the vulnerable empiricism of appraisers and homeowners to make a quick profit suggests just how unsteady this science actually was. Blockbusters of all races staged scenes of racial invasion designed to scare white homeowners into underselling their properties to speculators who would resell them to blacks at inflated prices. Speculators choreographed stunts such as hiring black women to walk baby carriages through white neighborhoods and orchestrating phone calls to homes where the caller asked "for such people as 'Johnnie Mae.'"[45] "Sometimes calls," one speculator describes, "would consist only of a whisper, a drunken laugh or a warning—such as 'They're coming!'"[46]

Where appraisal manuals fail to tell us how the "inharmonious," real or imagined, become known and read on a block, blockbusting practices start to provide us these details in their strategies for staging the presence of the "invasive" minority body. These self-consciously performative enactments of blackness on the level of the block suggest just how little observation was required to appraise race in the context of property, a context in which the appearance of the racial sign proved far more important than any pretense of attaching this sign to a set of characteristics as scientists had propagated only a few decades prior. Given the manipulability of the racial sensoriums of appraisers, realtors, and homeowners, we might understand these various constituencies less as scientists counting race with ontological certainty and more like astute students of the financial value of the racial trace. Unlike the American obsession at the turn of the twentieth century with racial percentages and the science of physiognomy, the housing market encouraged Americans to traffic in more fungible and approximate fictions of race, sloughing off the veneer of exhaustive precision undergirding earlier tenets of racial detection for what could be gathered in glimpses out the window or deciphered from telephoned whispers.

Appraising with Jane Jacobs and Gwendolyn Brooks

Though appraisal manuals were written for a specialized audience, most Americans at midcentury lived in neighborhoods shaped by their mandates. The imperative to approach neighborhoods as observable sites of value correlated to their racial demographics extended beyond professional appraisal, finding its way into midcentury discourses of urban planning, long-form reportage, and literature. While appraisal manuals insisted on the necessity of racial accounting to the endeavor of neighborhood observation even as appraisers remained mum on methods for doing so, other narratives describing people in the process of perceiving neighborhoods give us insight into how writers differently understood the efficacy of looking as a strategy not only for documenting residential segregation but for redressing it.

In what follows, I examine the efforts of two such midcentury writers— Jane Jacobs and Gwendolyn Brooks—as they imagined the relationship between residential looking and racial looking in ways that diverged from professional appraisal's market obligations. Though Jacobs and Brooks might seem like an odd pairing—Brooks being best known as a poet and Jacobs as an urban theorist—both were perpetual genre-crossers interested in the work of residential observation in spaces not traditionally considered models for living. In light of appraisal's interest in racial observation as a financial instrument, these writers raise questions about whether the command to "look closely" embraced by appraisers upholding residential segregation could ever be made to serve other means.

In her now-classic 1961 book, *The Death and Life of Great American Cities*, Jane Jacobs argues that the legacy of urban planning in the twentieth century was, for all of its utopian intentions, largely one of dispiriting displacement and destruction. Describing planners and mortgage brokers as the entrenched practitioners of "pseudo-science" akin to bloodletting, Jacobs accuses these figures of misguidedly applying abstract theories to cities. She proposes instead that those seeking to improve urban life should directly observe it to learn what makes for a vibrant place where people actually want to live. Jacobs so strongly believed in the power of observation that she forwent including illustrations in her book entirely, urging her audience to instead "please look closely at real cities" and "listen, linger and think about what you see" to see successful cities in action.[47] Whereas appraisers were tasked with impartially observing neighborhoods for the purposes of assessment, Jacobs implored her readers to develop a more muscular observational practice to first learn from cities before intervening in them.[48]

The first prolonged example Jacobs provides of her brand of urban close-looking comes on page 9 of *Death and Life* when she describes observing Boston's North End. Though the two experts she consults about this neighborhood, a planner and a banker, both consider it a slum, Jacobs contrarily declares this district "the healthiest place in the city."[49] She first recalls her impressions of this neighborhood in 1940 when it was "badly overcrowded," playing host to "the flood of immigrants first from Ireland, then from Eastern Europe and finally from Sicily." But revisiting the neighborhood in 1960, she now marvels at the North End's streets "alive with children playing, people shopping, people strolling, people talking."[50] Taking stock of the improved building exteriors and the street's mingled usages, Jacobs finds herself so stimulated by the "infectious" nature of "the general street atmosphere of buoyance, friendliness and good health" that she "began asking directions of people just for the fun of getting in some talk."[51]

For all of her antagonism toward her institutional forebears in the field of urban assessment, Jacobs's pedagogy of observation largely ignores its own conditionality—something appraisers had been intensely, if imperfectly, considering for decades prior. She critiques the banker and the planner for not looking often or closely enough at the North End to correctly assess its "health." But her own looking is not without idiosyncrasies, leading her to privilege certain diagnoses over others. If we take Jacobs's description of the North End as a model of her observational method, this practice largely centers on what the eye can take in from and of the street. She never enters a home in this neighborhood. Instead her sense of their interiors comes from the "Venetian blinds and glimpses of fresh paint" she spies through windows. The only time she directly engages anyone in the neighborhood is to ask for directions she doesn't need "for the fun of getting in some talk." This remark emphasizes the performance of something like local color over content, or her own pleasant experience of exoticism over residents' own experience of the health of their surrounds. This is not to romanticize the depth of knowledge local informants may or may not have divulged to her had she asked—only to demonstrate how Jacobs naturalizes her particular observational procedures. She takes as a given, furthermore, that it is the North End rather than her own perception that is the moving part in this scene. But it is unclear if what Jacobs offers us here is new knowledge about the changes to the North End in the twenty years since her first visit or of the changes to her own appraisal criteria and residential sensorium in this time.

Like the professional observers shaping appraisal science, Jacobs is particularly oblique about her own mechanisms of racial observation. The lack of racial markers in Jacobs's account of her second visit to the North End is particularly noteworthy in this regard. While she accounts for the immigration history central to her experience of the neighborhood in 1940, charting the "flood of immigrants first from Ireland, then from Eastern Europe and finally from Sicily" that called the North End home, no references to race or ethnicity appear in her later account of the neighborhood in 1960. The North End continues to retain its identity as an Italian neighborhood even today, but how one saw and racially assessed Italians *had* substantially shifted in the decades separating Jacobs's two visits. By the time of her second visit, some of the Italian immigrants who had lived there in the 1940s had secured mortgages in suburban neighborhoods where their ability to secure mortgages rested upon being seen as "harmonious" enough not to trouble the property values of their neighbors.[52] As for the Italians who remained in the North End, despite retaining the legibility of this identity through their contextual association with this neighborhood, these residents had taken on many of the privileges as well as the prejudices of whiteness. North Enders largely opposed the presence of African Americans in their neighborhood, which became a seat of antibusing sentiment in a few short years.[53] Whether Jacobs's elision of racial markers in her more recent observations of the North End tells us more about the racial status of Italians or Jacobs's own racial vision is hard to say. But her directive to "please look closely" proves less straightforward in relation to racial reading.

Jacobs's elision of both the race of others as well as her own position as observer matters to the shape her diagnosis of the North End ultimately takes. The elements Jacobs admires of the North End—the "general street atmosphere of buoyance, friendliness and good health"—could be read as symptoms of its homogeneity facilitating this easy ambience. One wonders if Jacobs would have experienced the street with the same jubilance had she herself not been appraised by the residents of the street as a white woman whose racial presence did not threaten their "good health." Although critics have taken Jacobs to task for not attending more fully to race's effects on neighborhood outcomes in *Death and Life*, she does take up this matter later in the book when she addresses the larger structural forces shaping cities. She acknowledges that "planning and design" fail to "automatically overcome segregation and discrimination" since "too many efforts are also required to fight these injustices."[54] Jacobs also focuses on the power of credit-blacklist maps, another name for redlining, to decimate vulnerable neighborhoods. She describes this mapping as an "impersonal" act operating "not against the residents or businessmen, as persons, but against their neighborhoods," a reading that reverberates with the rationale found in many appraisal manuals.[55]

Yet, despite acknowledging the structural and impersonal forces incentivizing residential apartheid, Jacobs notes that while good urban design alone can't fix segregation, bad urban design "*can* make it *much harder* for American cities to overcome discrimination."[56] She goes on to argue that tolerance for racial others, framed as the by-product of "intensely urban life," becomes "possible and normal only when streets of great cities have built-in equipment allowing strangers to dwell in peace together."[57] Jacobs's belief that the physical re-equipment of urban streets could bring Americans many steps closer to "overcoming" racial discrimination seems just as utopian a premise as those promoted by the urban planners she so fiercely critiques.[58] Despite acknowledging redlining's "impersonal" functioning, Jacobs ultimately underplays residential apartheid's foundational role within the housing market in order to assert her faith in the transformative power of street-level encounters.[59] Jacobs frames such encounters not only as a sign of healthy cities but a pillar of antiracism. Given the fetishization of token levels of diversity undergirding today's gentrification processes, Jacobs's devotion to streets that *look* and *feel* diverse over other measures of equity and stability suggests the limits of individual encounter to ameliorate inequity.

Jacobs overlooks the nonneutrality of her own racial perception as well as the extent to which accumulated practices of assessing race shaped how professionals and residents alike came to value certain neighborhoods over others and informing the broader residential sensorium. Faith in observation, we should remember, also guided the activities of blockbusters who manipulated homeowners primed to defensively scour their neighborhoods for "inharmonious" racial signs. In her appreciation of neighborhoods with lively street culture, Jacobs at times misses just how quickly a "good" neighborhood might reveal its less virtuous qualities in the presence of someone deemed to threaten its worth.

Juxtapose Jane Jacobs's mode of urban empiricism with Gwendolyn Brooks's experiments in the genre a few years before. Though regional works of place have long been integral to American literature, Brooks joins a slew of fiction writers turning to nonfiction at midcentury to reflect on metropolitan life amid intensifying urban crises. Such works include Richard Wright's *12 Million Black Voices* (1941) and parts of "How Bigger Was Born" (1940); Ralph Ellison's "Harlem Is Nowhere," written in 1948 but published in 1964; Nelson Algren's *Chicago: City on the Make* (1951); James Baldwin's "Fifth Avenue, Uptown: A Letter from Harlem" (1960); and Thomas Pynchon's "A Journey into the Mind of Watts" (1966, more on this later). These writings have largely been understood as companion pieces to the more studied fiction of these authors. But when we read them together as constituting a genre of writing interested in appraisal, observation, and valuation at midcentury, they appear less like supplements to the fiction and more like narrative experiments forsaking traditional fictionality to address the systemic injustices underlying residential apartheid that don't easily lend themselves to plot or lyric. We might understand these neighborhood-oriented works of reportage by fiction writers as not only reckoning with the limits of fiction but as attempting to make visible the imaginative work underlying broader modes of racial perception, whether such texts were self-consciously fictional or not.

While Gwendolyn Brooks's most extended explorations in seeing within undervalued urban environments take place in her fiction, we find her working with similar themes in her October 1951 article for *Holiday*, a cosmopolitan travel magazine featuring heavily illustrated pieces by the period's most famous writers. Brooks's one and only piece for *Holiday*, titled "They Call It Bronzeville," remains something of an anomaly within her oeuvre. Though critic Robert Farnsworth describes Brooks as a "poet-reporter," unlike fellow Chicagoans Richard Wright, Nelson Algren, and her friend Frank London Brown, she had little experience with reportage.[60] Her decision to produce a more journalistic piece of writing a year after *Annie Allen* won the Pulitzer Prize for poetry before abandoning this genre for good is a curious one worth interrogating. Why take up urban reportage—if a highly imaginative iteration of it—at the peak of her fame as a poet? And why put this genre down again so quickly? The answer lies, I argue, in Brooks's ultimate skepticism of empirical observation's capacity to produce new knowledge about the fact of racism.

Brooks's skepticism of empirical observation in her piece for *Holiday* was catalyzed by another work of urban reportage haughtily flaunting its faith in urban looking to dubious ends. In December 1950, *Harper's* published the latest entry in journalist John Barlow Martin's "series of social studies" focused on Brooks's hometown. In "The Strangest Place in Chicago," Martin details the decline of the Mecca Flats, located on the city's South Side. Once a "showplace for Chicago" following its 1891 construction in advance of the World's Columbian Exposition, the building had since deteriorated and was on the verge of being razed by the nearby Illinois Institute of Technology to build their new Mies van der Rohe–designed architecture school, permanently displacing the Mecca's largely black residents. In his description of the Mecca, Martin embraces his position as an excavating outsider, leading his readers from the sunlight-filled city center into the building's ancient dark depths. Seeking to illustrate "one of the most remarkable Negro slum exhibits in the world," Martin invites his readers to "see what the Mecca looks like inside, see who the people in it are and how they live, whence they came and why they stay."[61] His desire to turn the Mecca into an "exhibit," premised on the notion that "seeing" and "looking" at the building and its residents during one brief visit could meaningfully and totally address "whence they came and why they stay," would be challenged by Brooks in her own take on urban reportage the following year.[62]

In contrast to Martin's invocation of the "shabby" neighborhoods shadowing Chicago's sunny downtown Loop ten months earlier, "They Call It Bronzeville" opens with a blunt description of its title South Side neighborhood as "something that should not exist—an area set aside for the halting use of a single race."[63] From the outset, Brooks discourages her reader from a romantic, folksy, or exoticizing reading of Bronzeville by underscoring its origins in discriminatory processes. Unlike Jacobs's exuberant account of the North End and Martin's voyeuristic detailing of the Mecca's degeneration, Brooks is less interested in detailing the physical properties of South Side buildings and streets and more intent on establishing the region's origins in racial inequality, a fact that no tally of vibrant corners, Venetian blinds, or unseemly ruins can ameliorate. "However, since Bronzeville does exist," Brooks continues, "it is satisfying to demonstrate that here resides essentially only what is ordinary: human struggle, human whimsicality, and human reach toward soul-settlement, toward peace if not happiness, sufficiency if not fortune."[64] The story of Bronzeville, Brooks warns, is fundamentally one of ordinary compromise. There are no lessons to be taken away about how cities work here, only examples of people enduring them. For Brooks it is precisely the lack of profundity to be derived from a study of this neighborhood that most strongly attests to the injustices its singular demographics mark.

While Jane Jacobs stages herself in *Death and Life* as heroically rebuking the common wisdom of the banker and planner who consider the North End a "slum," the figure we follow for most of "They Call It Bronzeville" is not Brooks but a hypothetical white "Stranger," spelled at all times with a capital S. Brooks's white Stranger both responds to Martin's voyeurism and anticipates Jacobs's future embrace of this role a decade later. But whereas Jacobs's object of observation is the neighborhood, and Martin takes Mecca Flats as his "slum exhibit," Brooks takes as her primary object of investigation this imagined observer. Her observation of the work of observation aligns Brooks more closely with the discourse of appraisal than Jacobs's brand of populist planning, which takes looking for granted as an obvious method for producing deeper knowledge of a place. Through a speculative form of third-person narration, Brooks describes the Stranger's perceptual and affective experiences of Bronzeville while denying the reader any direct access to his interior or those of the persons or buildings we glimpse through him. We are proximate to the

Stranger and to Bronzeville but intimate with neither, with Brooks providing brief details about what he "might" have experienced moving through the neighborhood while deferring any analysis of these details.

The Stranger, perhaps having absorbed the fictions of integration as well as a host of Martin-esque "social studies" suffusing the literary scene in this period, expects spectacular encounters and outrageous sights to dominate his visit to the South Side. But his visit is generally humdrum. "So up and down, up and down, and across and back our Stranger, seeing exquisite homes in one block and miserable homes in the next; seeing neat gardens, and painful alleys."[65] The languid ordinariness of such a scene suggests the unexceptional quality of Bronzeville's varied property landscape. We might ask why Brooks accepts the class inequality indexed by these "exquisite" and "miserable" homes as unexceptional while singling out Bronzeville's racial homogeneity as its constitutive wrong.[66] Answering this question would require placing Brooks's approach to visible signs of race and class in conversation with broader debates about how race and class were made empirical and their respective roles in determining who had access to property and its consequent valuation. With the 1944 GI Bill's expansion of mortgage loans to white working- and middle-class veterans—benefits generally denied to most black veterans—the federal government helped create a housing market that understood the expansion of mortgages to the white middle and working classes as a means of producing financial value for consumers and markets. But similar extensions to "inharmonious" racial and social groups of a similar class were assumed—and thus assured—to lower property values for white homeowners while also stabilizing rental markets dependent on segregation for their profits.[67] Given the empirical energy the FHA and home financiers put toward quantifying race on the block while trusting the market to sort white-enough-seeming homebuyers into neighborhoods by class and buying power, Brooks foregrounds the act of neighborhood observation as an inherently racialized act in this period.

The object of Brooks's observation in the article is not so much Bronzeville, which she describes in terms of an ordinariness bordering on boredom, as it is the Stranger, whose attempts to categorize it or produce a narrative about its meaning are continually stymied. "His tour of Bronzeville over," Brooks writes, "our friend from out of bounds is a little bewildered. He does not know quite how to feel. Perhaps he expected something different. He has not known many Negroes."⁶⁸ The article concludes with the Stranger's struggle to bring Bronzeville into description. "Back home, the Stranger wonders to himself. He shakes his head. He holds his chin. He plans to tell his friends where he has been. 'I have been—I have been—' He has been—in a place where People live."⁶⁹ Brooks proves less concerned with what the Stranger sees and more with his failure, marked both social and aesthetic by the off-rhyme of "live" in this poetic ending, to turn seeing into knowing. The Stranger's empirical account of Bronzeville does not ultimately allow him to say much about what this place *is*, denoting instead his failure to classify it as anything more than a generalized "place where People live."

In some ways, Brooks most fully inhabits the ethos of the scientifically oriented appraiser in "They Call It Bronzeville," continually working to get beyond her own perceptual embeddedness by staging the experience of Bronzeville through the perceptions of a white Stranger. Whereas Jane Jacobs figures herself in opposition to appraisers and planners whose versions of urban empiricism she undermines while leaving her own observational methods uninterrogated, Brooks toggles between dual empirical practices—hers and the Stranger's—refusing to settle on a perceptual anchor other than the one that she states up front: that an all-black Bronzeville shouldn't exist. The Stranger's concluding assessment of Bronzeville as "a place where people live" rather than where Negroes live might seem like a liberal triumph of color-blindness. But if we remember Brooks's warning at the article's start that Bronzeville be understood first and foremost as a product of segregation, the Stranger's decision to leave race unmarked suggests he has missed the point. Brooks enacts a delicate balance here, stripping racial reading of its powers of fixity by detailing the ordinariness of Bronzeville's streets while at the same insisting that its total blackness be appraised and accounted for as an index of inequality. The Stranger's account of Bronzeville—culminating with his anti-epiphany about its mundanity—presents its blackness to *Holiday*'s readership as an inescapable fact rather than something one must personally feel or experience. There are no dramatically revelatory encounters with racial others here teaching the Stranger, and thus the reader, something new about race, distinguishing it from fictions of residential integration. The article's most poignant realization comes, rather, from the Stranger's failure to make sense of Bronzeville's blackness, the reasons for which cannot be found by looking harder or better at its streets but originate somewhere beyond Bronzeville itself.

Brooks's insistence on the futility of close observation to address or reform residential segregation sits in contrast not only to the heroic empiricism touted by Jane Jacobs and appraisal discourse but also the emotional empiricism promoted by James Baldwin. At the end of "The Image of the Negro," after attesting to protest fiction's aesthetic and political shortcomings, Baldwin ultimately posits the development of what he deems a more "personal" literature as the antidote to this wanting fiction's deficiencies. Accused by Baldwin of rehearsing worn tropes of morality through canned emotional registers, protest fiction obscures "the fear and desire and hatred and shame . . . which have made the oppression of black by white a more complicated reality than these novels indicate." Literature dedicated to capturing these uglier and wilder feelings, he suggests, is more likely to communicate something novel about the operation of racism than literary "reports" compulsively restating its familiar effects.

But in "They Call It Bronzeville," published four years after Baldwin's essay, Brooks does not heed Baldwin's call for a more personal literature but questions the utility of either looking more closely at segregation's material manifestations or charting its affective provinces more precisely. The work of reportage as conceived of in Brooks's article is not to produce new descriptions of segregated spaces but to describe the failure of description to address the inequality already in plain sight. Given racial description's centrality to the explosive growth of the private housing market in the twentieth century dependent on black stagnation, Brooks's foray into urban reporting raises questions about the efficacy of neighborhood description when the only fact that matters—the fact of segregation—has already been established. Following Brooks, then, redressing residential segregation requires redirecting our attention away from the neighborhoods that segregation *produced* and toward the methods contrived to observe, record, and appraise racialized bodies in order to enforce their segregation.

Appraisal in the service of redlining was not merely a discriminatory practice—it was a perceptual schema that simultaneously reified race's significance and the necessity of its surveillance while evading what exactly one was to read or survey when doing this observational work. Appraisal discourses helped enshrine racism as an unchanging feature of the free market while treating race as something unfixable and contextual, a matter of local convention rather than universal law—except in the case of blackness, posited as an unchanging depressor of value in all situations and contagiously illiquid. This logic ultimately enabled certain groups to become assimilated into whiteness and, by extension, homeownership and its rewards while reinforcing blackness's status as an unchanging threat to value necessitating its exclusion. The literature of residential segregation reveals the performative role urban empiricism often played in projects of neighborhood valuation, suggesting that to see like a state at midcentury—or a banker or a planner, for that matter—was ostensibly reducible to seeing like a federation of white Strangers whose racial schemas and residential sensoriums came to serve as unassailable market truths.

Final Reports

I close this chapter with two final "reports" on residential segregation written by someone not usually connected to this topic—Thomas Pynchon. As literary critic Sarah Wasserman observes of his work, "for all the games that Pynchon plays with form and language, he continually reaches for a *literary form* that can adequately represent the painful mess of history" (emphasis mine).[70] And yet, like Gwendolyn Brooks before him, Pynchon inexplicably turns from literary form to reportage to bring one of history's most recent painful messes into view: the 1965 Watts riots. "A Journey into the Mind of Watts," published in the *New York Times Magazine* in June 1966, has largely been read by critics as a corollary to his novel *The Crying of Lot 49*, published just a few months before. In "Journey," Pynchon approaches black-occupied Watts as "a pocket of bitter reality" whose beholding has the power to deflate the fantasy-saturated world of nearby white Los Angeles. As Pynchon insists of white Angelenos, "somehow it occurs to very few of them to leave at the Imperial Highway exit for a change, go east instead of west only a few blocks, and take a look at Watts. A quick look. The simplest kind of beginning."[71] They fail to see Watts because, for them, "Watts is a country which lies, psychologically, uncounted miles further than most whites seem at present willing to travel."[72] Pynchon suggests that despite its physical proximity to nearby white suburbs, Watts limned through the lens of the white residential sensorium might as well be on Mars.

Critics have largely understood the observational ethos Pynchon takes up in "A Journey into the Mind of Watts" to be a remedy to the insularity afflicting white Californians in *The Crying of Lot 49*. As Sally Bachner notes, if that novel's protagonist, Oedipa, had only followed Pynchon's prescription to leave the white oases of Southern California to observe black residential space, she would have sooner discovered the truth of her existence via Watts's confirmation of the "real"—"a world in which you might be brutally attacked at any moment, either by the police or your desperately poor neighbors."[73] In Pynchon's journalistic account, Watts is like smelling salts to the beguiled white residential sensorium. Embodied observation of black residential life rocks the white Stranger to their core, stripping them of their residentially honed sensory defenses to initiate them into the cold, hard truth of an unequal world.

But, following Brooks, what happens when we trouble Pynchon's naturalization of looking and its capacity to enlighten Oedipa or any of the white Angelenos Pynchon wrote about and to in the 1960s, including himself? Pynchon likely first consulted Jane Jacobs's *The Death and Life of Great American Cities* while writing his earliest novel, 1963's *V*. But we see the ongoing influence of Jacobs's directive to "please look closely at real cities" in his continued investment across the 1960s in personal observation's power to counteract what Pynchon describes as the "Disneyfied landscaping" of Watts's white surrounds.[74] Though he was also reading James Baldwin in this period—a writer who similarly put aside fiction to describe segregated neighborhoods through direct witness—Pynchon seems to have hewed more strongly toward Jacobs's muscular and unself-conscious mode of observation rather than the interrogation in Baldwin's nonfiction, following Brooks's earlier work, of what it means to look in the first place.[75] More in keeping with Jacobs than Baldwin or Brooks, Pynchon's reportage presents readers with an uninterrogated practice of looking by his observing I's seemingly seamless universality—an erasure of positionality also increasingly common to the discursive life of whiteness at midcentury (more on this in the next chapter).

Before turning to the observational practices yoking Jacobs and Pynchon, I want to first pause on the mode of observation Pynchon was also encountering in the work of James Baldwin (it is less clear that he was reading Gwendolyn Brooks) to understand the more reflexive observational path not taken by

Pynchon. Despite Baldwin's critique of protest novels as "reports," his residential missives from the period underscore the powerful work of reportage. This is the case in his 1961 piece "A Negro Assays the Negro Mood," first published in the *New York Times Magazine* in 1961, five years before Pynchon's piece. At first glance, Baldwin, like Jacobs, seems to advocate for the transformative power of looking at black enclaves, inviting his white readers to "walk through Harlem and ask oneself two questions: Would I like to live here? And, Why don't those who now live here move out?"[76] Baldwin quickly answers his own queries, insisting that unless said observer believes in the inferiority of the black race, "the answer to both questions is immediately obvious"— no, they would not like to live in Harlem, and blacks remain there because racism prevents them from living elsewhere. Arriving at such a conclusion, however, is not a heroic act in and of itself but takes only "minimal effort," as Baldwin notes. Looking is literally the least one can do to acknowledge what is already obvious—that "the Negro's status in this country is a cruel injustice and a grave national liability." For Baldwin, as with Brooks, looking at black neighborhoods can only reinforce what one already knows about structures of racism responsible for the inequity easily visible within Harlem, Watts, or Bronzeville.

Baldwin more explicitly addresses the limits of looking in an essay in *Esquire* from 1960, "Fifth Avenue, Uptown: A Letter from Harlem." Though Baldwin concludes this essay by imploring white readers to "walk through the streets of Harlem and see what we, this nation, have become," he undercuts looking's effectiveness as a catalyst for revelation earlier in the piece when describing a white policeman who observes Harlem each day as part of his job.[77] During his routine surveillance of Harlem, the policeman "cannot avoid observing that some of the children, in spite of their color, remind him of children he has known and loved, perhaps even of his own children."[78] And yet, enlightenment fails to accompany his ongoing observation. In fact, experiencing this regular form of cross-racial recognition has the opposite effect on him. Rather than allowing the similarity of Harlem's children to his own to soften him, such exposure only hardens him: "He can retreat from his uneasiness in only one direction: into a callousness which very shortly becomes second nature."[79] White observation of black space does not breed tolerance, as Jacobs describes, or even the apathy noted by Brooks; in

Baldwin's account, observation further desensitizes the white viewer to black humanity. If witnessing Watts brutally awakens the white beholder in Pynchon's reportage, observing Harlem here only further inures white witnesses to racial revelation. It is only Baldwin, observing the white policeman observing black space—looking at residential looking—who understands something new about what looking can and cannot effect.

But not all hope for residential looking is lost, Baldwin concludes. Harlem has empirical lessons to share, but only if its white beholders reorient their vision and expectations. Returning to Baldwin's final provocation in "Fifth Avenue, Uptown" for his white readers to "walk through the streets of Harlem and see what we, this nation, have become," it is crucial that the perceptual point of this closing exercise is not to better see Harlem's *residents*. Rather, observing the unequal living conditions they endure is what teaches Harlem's beholders about what "we, this nation, have become." Unlike the appraiser's form of perception designed to quickly see signs of blackness and, by proxy, devaluation, Baldwin asks Harlem's beholders to see here the "we" responsible for its creation and exclusionary upkeep. Baldwin, like Brooks, prescribes a practice *of looking at looking* revealing looking's fallibilities while also amending what such looking evidences—not black incapacity or its inherent illiquidity as the market vision of appraisers would have it, but the structural nature of racism reproducing itself in black belts across the U.S.

There is not much looking at looking, however, in "A Journey into the Mind of Watts," or questioning of the limits of what looking can reveal. Unlike Gwendolyn Brooks's relentless attention to the preconceived generic expectations of the white Stranger in black space, Pynchon naturalizes his occupation of Watts, never doubting his own observational prowess within a neighborhood in which he does not reside.[80] His presence as a lone white observer in a predominantly black neighborhood appears to raise no eyebrows or produce any disturbance within the world on which he is reporting. He does all the looking and, oddly, no one seems to be looking back. Pynchon only occasionally employs direct quotes from Watts residents, as David Witzling notes, quotes that remain unattributed.[81] Pynchon is the sole synthesizer of the disparate and disembodied voices he proceeds to report out to his readers, our sole arbitrator of this "pocket of bitter reality." His comfortability with interpreting the world of Watts enables him to narrate even the interior experiences of Watts residents through the second person, taking up the perspective of a black resident to declare that "the history of this place and these times makes it impossible for the cop to come on any different or for you to hate him any less."[82] In this seeming nod to Baldwin's earlier efforts in "Fifth Avenue, Uptown" to describe the experience of a white policeman in Harlem, Pynchon conversely describes a black resident's experience of the police in Watts. But whereas Baldwin's speculation about the officer's sensorium allows him to posit observation's limits in ways this figure would never admit to Baldwin, Pynchon's reasons for leaving this quote unattributed or perhaps inventing it altogether is less clear. It most strongly testifies to Pynchon's mastery of Watts—he hears all and sees all with ease, delivering seamlessly the truths he extracts from Watts directly to his readers.

Throughout the article, Pynchon remains confident in his ability to parse the real from the illusory in Watts without any acknowledgment of how his own presence might affect his discernment. As soon as the essay's seventh paragraph, he appears to have fully penetrated Watts to see through to its inner depths when describing a recent murder. Pynchon writes here that while this recent act of violence "hasn't made it look any different" on the surface, "underneath the mood in Watts is about what you might expect." But exactly how Pynchon managed to move from looking at Watts to transcending its surfaces to access its underlying mood is left unstated. As Pynchon posits, "everything seems so out in the open" in Watts, "all of it real, no plastic faces, no transistors, no hidden Muzak, or Disneyfied landscaping or smiling chicks to show you around. Not in Raceriotland."[83] Pynchon's observational hubris here seems to only confirm the reality function of Watts that he wields as a tool to force white visitors to face the falseness of their own enclosed existence. Like the appraisers that precede him in acts of neighborhood observation, looking at Watts for Pynchon is primarily a means for assessing the value of whiteness—this time to puncture it rather than inflate it. Yet the method and aim of Pynchon's mode of observation and that of the appraiser's remain parallel—both pursue the studied observation of black neighborhoods to provide crucial information about the relative state of whiteness. Gone is Baldwin's "we" or Brooks's self-conscious inhabitation of the white Stranger, enacting a conversation about looking across the color line. Pynchon looks through Watts's blackness to better see whiteness alone.

If the form of the report allows Pynchon to style himself as an all-powerful observer, using Watts to rip through the white residential sensorium, it is in his fiction that he appears to interrogate looking's revelatory effectiveness with deeper skepticism. In "The Secret Integration," a short story he published two years before in a 1964 issue of the *Saturday Evening Post*—Norman Rockwell's old stomping ground—Pynchon approaches residential segregation in ways that more explicitly trouble the utility of empirical assessment and the ability to distinguish the white faux from the black real. Pynchon notes the semi-autobiographical roots of this story, transposing some of his own childhood experiences from Long Island onto a fictional town in the Berkshire Hills of western Massachusetts.[84] A pastiche of mythic tales of rambunctious and searching white youths, most notably Mark Twain's fictions about Huckleberry Finn and Tom Sawyer, "The Secret Integration" features a group of prank-loving boys seeking to disrupt the institutional norms anchoring their small-town life. While the fictional town of Mingeborough, which the boys call home, is homogeneously white, a new housing development on the edge of town has recently been integrated by the Barringtons, a black family.[85] Near the story's opening, Tim, our young narrator, walks in on his mother harassing the Barringtons through the telephone as she archly delivers the following message: "You niggers, dirty niggers, get out of this town, go back to Pittsfield. Get out before you get in real trouble."[86] Despite the racism of their parents, Tim, along with a small group of his white friends, have befriended the youngest Barrington, Carl, who joins his gang of merrymakers in carrying out pranks. As we learn more about Tim and his friends, including a detailed remembrance from the previous summer in which the children witness a black man's unjust treatment and his overall melancholic plight, we watch them grapple with integration as a novel concept. Though the boys sense there is something uncouth about their parents' racism, they also slowly begin to understand the limits of their own ability to fully break with the town and the safety it offers them. As Tim achingly realizes, "everybody on the school board, and the railroad and the PTA" complicit in the town's segregation was nonetheless "somebody's mother or father." "There was a point," Tim continues, "at which the reflex to their covering warmth, protection, effectiveness against bad dreams, bruised heads and simple loneliness took over and made worthwhile anger with them impossible."[87] In contrast to the impersonal bureaucratic racism honed by the housing market, Tim gives readers a bottom-up rendering of the personal ties and intimate feelings that make disrupting the segregated social world of those he cares for—no matter how ugly their behavior—ultimately too much for him to bear.

The tension between the children's desire to disrupt the town in which they live and their attraction to its comforts of kinship and community comes to a head when, upon passing by the Barringtons' home, they discover that a large amount of trash has been dumped on this black family's lawn. As the boys begin to clean up the mess, they discover the trash of their own households. Tim, stumbling upon "all the intimacy of the throwaway part, the shadow-half of his family's life for all the week preceding," takes stock of the "ten square yards of irrefutable evidence" pointing to his familial complicity in this racist act. Mrs. Barrington—one of the lone named black characters to speak in Pynchon's early fiction—yells at the children to go home. Though they protest, insisting "we're on your side," the woman responds, "we don't need you on our side. I thank our heavenly Father every day of my life that we don't have any children to be corrupted by the likes of you trash."[88] The boys slink toward home, glancing at Carl to see whether he'll stay with them or join his mother. While waiting for his decision, we get the story's big reveal: Carl is imaginary, a product of the white children's fancy designed to help them accomplish the story's titular feat—achieve a secret integration. As the narrator describes, "Carl had been put together out of phrases, images, possibilities that grownups had somehow turned away from, repudiated, left out at the edges of town, as if they were auto parts."[89] Carl, like the trash that instigates the revelation of his immateriality, is also amassed from Mingeborough's leftover scraps. These parallel iterations of racialized "waste," however, end up only reflecting the composition of the white racial imaginary rather than "real" knowledge of black people. Pynchon describes Carl as an amalgamation of "things they could or did not want to live with but which the kids, on the other hand, could spend endless hours with, piecing together, rearranging, feeding, programming, refining."[90] While Carl's invention at first has the veneer of innocent exploration, Pynchon's description of his utility soon turns more predatory. "He was entirely theirs, their friend and robot, to cherish, buy undrunk sodas for, or send into danger, or even, as now, at last, to banish from their sight."[91] In the story's final paragraphs, Carl disappears, seemingly for good, as the children make their way home, "each finally to his own house, hot shower, dry towel, before-bed television, good night kiss, and dreams that could never again be entirely safe."[92]

Unlike Pynchon's assuredness of his role as our guide to Watts in 1966, the boys of the "The Secret Integration" are far less certain of the difference between reality and unreality, fact and fiction. From the color-changing trick a doctor uses at the story's opening to fool Tim into willing his wart away and the boys' confusion about integration as both a mathematical technique and a social relation, to their enduring faith in myth including their own invention of Carl, the story remains committed to questioning the usefulness of observation and close study in disrupting what ultimately hails the boys the strongest—the sensation of safety they derive from their family and institutions, even if that safety relies upon ugly acts of racial exclusion that undergird their creature comforts. Whereas Pynchon looks at Watts to make a point about the failures of white America, "The Secret Integration" finds all the evidence it needs of the raw violence of American life right in the boys' own backyard, in their own discarded refuse. Even when confronted with their own complicity—facing a version of the "real" on the Barringtons' lawn that Pynchon later associates with Watts—this revelation fails to blunt their desire to return to the exclusionary safety they continue to enjoy, haunted as they may be by this choice. In "The Secret Integration," knowing better doesn't mean doing better, and seeing clearly only gives way to more fiercely clung-to illusion.

This chapter began by asking us to turn our attention away from the spectacular fictions depicting historically fleeting moments of integration to instead consider the utility of the report in documenting the observational forms used to maintain the relatively steady state of segregation. In the case of Pynchon's work from the 1960s, however, fiction proves to be the more flexible resource for observing residential observation than his lone effort at documentary reportage, which falls into the same old pitfalls of empiricisms prior. "A Journey into the Mind of Watts" ultimately takes Watts for granted as self-evident in its appearance, enabling its narrator's easy journey from Watts's surfaces to the interior lives of its thinly imagined residents before dramatically recentering white self-delusion. Although it seems like heresy, Pynchon's faith in the disillusioning capacity of the properly observed scene marking some of his work from the 1960s seems to have more in common with the melodramatic realism of protest fiction than we might expect. While Baldwin accuses the protest novel of "showing nothing" to its readers, Pynchon's efforts to not just see Watts but see *through* it ultimately direct us back to white illusions of insularity, another form of "nothing" in Pynchon's assessment. "Watts lies impacted in the heart of this white fantasy," Pynchon writes, a fantasy bookended by aerospace firms and Sunset Strip orienting the dream lives of white Angelenos.[93] But in observing Watts, he fails to question the instrumentality of his own approach to Watts, which is largely wielded by Pynchon to destabilize white perceptions of reality and, by extension, forms of feeling. But considering the impersonal, unfeeling infrastructure appraisers had been building for nearly half a century to reify their commitment to black devaluation as an unchanging fact, Pynchon's desire to teach white Angelenos to approach black space as a prism for shattering their own phenomenological coordinates seems naïve at best and predatory at worst.

The image Pynchon ultimately paints of Watts is, in fact, not that far from other media portrayals focusing on the scars left by violence and neglect. No amount of sympathetic looking by individuals seeking enlightenment by observing Watts, Harlem, or Bronzeville—be their gaze heroically muscular in its penetrative search or one that lazily browses nearby surfaces—can counteract the impersonal observational modes designed to override epiphantic forms of looking to preserve stoic racist market "truths." While Pynchon in "A Journey into the Mind of Watts" keenly mimics Jane Jacobs's energized practices of looking, the Pynchon of "The Secret Integration" seems wearier of observation's capacities to deliver anything except what one already knows. As this early story set in the Berkshires suggests, what we need to understand the creation of an all-black Watts can be found in the yards of the rehabbed homes and new builds within the midcentury's largely homogeneous white neighborhoods. As Pynchon later wrote of his approach in "The Secret Integration"— which he deemed "more of a journeyman than an apprentice effort" compared to his other early stories—"for the first time I believe I was also beginning to shut up and listen to the American voices around me, even to shift my eyes away from printed sources and take a look at American nonverbal reality."[94] Pynchon might have overestimated his capacity to serve as conduit for revealing the real of Watts. But his attentiveness to "nonverbal reality" in this earlier story, entailing a shifting of the gaze away from the straightforwardly empirical to the sonic and the gestural, seems most powerfully fulfilled in "The Secret Integration," where the white fantasy of Carl lives adjacent to the real racial assaults perpetrated against the Barringtons. The boys' efforts at an elaborately imagined secret integration ultimately dissolves, but it is the banality of the open secret of segregation—encompassing both its quiet acceptance by the children at the story's end as well as the impersonal and generic mechanisms of anonymous calls, classified maps and standardized forms used to efficiently maintain it—that calls for our ongoing formal attention.

Feeling Racial Attachments to Property with John Cheever and Lorraine Hansberry

FROM OBSERVING RESIDENTIAL OBSERVATION, WE now turn to two midcentury writers capturing less observable changes to racial feeling and definition shaped by mass homeownership. John Cheever and Lorraine Hansberry—two of the most prominent chroniclers of homeownership in the twentieth century—moved in tighter orbits than our literary canons disclose. Let's begin with their history as neighbors. In 1962, Hansberry decided to split her time between the Greenwich Village carriage house she had purchased three years before, fresh off the stage success of *A Raisin in the Sun*, and a newly bought split-level ranch in Croton-on-Hudson in Westchester County, New York, thirty miles north of Manhattan, funded by the film rights to *Raisin*. Upon moving into her Croton home, Hansberry coyly hung a sign christening it Chitterlin' Heights. In the tradition of A'Lelia Walker's Dark Tower salon and Wallace Thurman's Nigeratti Manor, Hansberry's tongue-in-cheek reference to a dish associated with Southern black foodways highlights the dissonance between tony, white Westchester County and a genealogy of black residential life purposefully excluded from such spaces for much of the previous century.

One of Hansberry's new neighbors in Westchester County was John Cheever. In 1961, Cheever bought his first—and last—home in the town of Ossining, immediately to the south of Croton-on-Hudson, after renting in the county for nearly a decade. Cheever reflected on his decision to permanently leave Manhattan, where he had lived since the 1930s, in a 1960 article for *Esquire* titled "Moving Out."[1] Although Cheever admits to occasionally returning to his old New York haunts "where the rents would make your head swim," he happily declares "the truth is that I'm crazy about the suburbs and I don't care who knows it."[2] James Baldwin, who was friendly with Cheever, nonetheless provided a sobering counterpoint to his joyous portrait of escape. In "Fifth Avenue, Uptown," directly following Cheever's essay in the *Esquire* issue, Baldwin paints a very different picture of the possibilities for spatial mobility.[3] "The people in Harlem know they are living there because white people do not think they are good enough to live anywhere else."[4] Baldwin focuses on Harlem's ongoing stagnation, while Cheever jubilantly frames himself as an urban "evacuee."

Although Hansberry's most famous work depicts the trials of black residential living in a fashion more in keeping with Baldwin, while Cheever's short stories chart the changing feeling and force of whiteness amid its intensifying relation to homeownership, these two writers nonetheless ended up living about an hour's walk from one another up until Hansberry's death in 1965. I have found no record that the two ever met or knew each other personally, though they shared at least one acquaintance in Baldwin. Given that both Cheever and Hansberry were dog owners, perhaps they crossed paths during evening walks with their pets along the Hudson River. Maybe they ran into each other at the grocery store or the dentist. Most likely, the proximity of their homes is trivia. After all, they weren't the first or last writers to move to Westchester from New York City.[5] At minimum, the residential proximity of Cheever and Hansberry suggests the two did not occupy utterly separate worlds. Their status as neighbors helps us, if nothing else, better locate them as peers. Despite their differences in genre, generation, race, and class (with Hansberry coming from the more pedigreed family), John Cheever and Lorraine Hansberry both detailed how mass homeownership remade the residential sensorium and, by extension, the contours of racial perception.

In considering Cheever's and Hansberry's portraits of mass homeownership's effects on racial formation and perception together, we get a new understanding of literature's role in not only representing but codifying these new conditions. Though the emergence of new suburban developments subsidized by the federal government designed to attract white families is a key turning point in U.S. residential history, suburbanization has overdetermined the story of homeownership. The iconography of the midcentury suburb has become such a powerful totem that it is difficult to envision the residential beyond either Levittown-esque banality or black enclaves like Harlem or Bronzeville posited as their heaving other. But not every white neighborhood was a suburb (take *Raisin*'s Clybourne Park), nor was every suburb exclusively white (take Croton-on-Hudson). And even in more homogeneous suburbs, what whiteness meant, how it was defined, and what it felt like, moreover, was no settled matter but was being actively reconfigured by homeownership's specific economic and social demands. When we take classic tropes of suburban living—conformity, quietism, safety—for granted, we forget that these tropes were being constructed and contested at midcentury as part of a complex feedback loop in which cultural representations of the suburbs were not just mirrors but scripts for suburban living being studied by its rookie occupants.[6]

In disrupting the image of the classic suburb, this chapter is indebted to the new suburban history, a phrase coined by Kevin Kruse and Thomas Sugrue in their 2006 volume of the same name.[7] The essays collected there seek to upend the image of sleepy suburban hamlets where both the houses and the people "all look just the same," to quote Malvina Reynolds's 1962 folk song "Little Boxes." But whereas the new suburban history overturned trite images of the suburbs by recovering its more tumultuous and diverse trajectories to better situate this typology's broader impact on everything from politics and religion to race, I suggest that attention to the suburbs of all orientations has helped to overwrite homeownership as a broader force remaking the meaning of the residential and its racialization within and beyond the suburbs. Focus on the suburbs versus the residential or homeownership continues to enable the fiction that they can be treated in isolation, untethered from other spatial typologies—the very image of the midcentury that suburban developers and regional planners sought to project.[8]

Literature is a useful tool for carrying out this reconfiguration, but only when we disturb literary studies' own unhelpful spatial canons. While the new suburban history has troubled clichéd understandings of these spaces, literary canons still largely take the category of suburban literature for granted. Despite critic Catherine Jurca's efforts to recover the changing formation and function of whiteness in early representations of suburban space, the ongoing power of a term like *white flight* applied to the midcentury suggests the flatness still attending its thinking.[9] As a descriptor, *suburban white flight* stills each of its constitutive terms—the suburbs, whiteness, and flight—to encourage their apprehension as static and self-evident categories, obscuring the ways each of these terms was being actively remade in collision with one another at midcentury. *Suburban white flight* suggests whiteness was merely consolidated rather than remade by mass homeownership, that people left older neighborhoods as a matter of individual choice alone, and that the suburbs were passive receptors of such movement. But the redlining that was endemic to the project of mass homeownership reshaped not only the suburbs, but urban and rural space as well, while the meaning and discursive life of whiteness was being revised in light of its new economic and spatial coordinates. And while the language of flight evokes individualist acts of relocation, movement to the suburbs was subsidized in coordination with the disinvestment from inner-city neighborhoods encouraged by the state, making incentives to relocate economically difficult to defy.

Black orientations to property were also in flux at midcentury as the question of whether property rights were to be the end goal of civil rights came to a head. Black writers explored whether it was still possible in this period to think progress beyond rubrics of property, which had animated black freedom struggles since Emancipation. As the Black Popular Front continued to ebb through the Cold War, despite some powerful holdouts, alternative paths to the good life not routed through property became harder to map within the black imaginary. The anarchic spirit of the rent party seemed long past. Even as public housing became a new frontier for antiracist struggles, dreams of ownership nonetheless reigned. If whiteness was historically defined as the capacity to own, blackness seemed defined at midcentury by an undeterred longing for ownership despite its endless deferrals and disappointments.

More than a passive chronicler of the changing relationship between race and property, literature gave form to its new social, perceptual, and emotional life within quickly transforming residential enclaves. Hansberry and Cheever did not just render the residential scene; rather their massively popular and widely circulated work gave original shape to new norms for navigating the race and space for those living in redlining's extended wake. These writers produced representations that became, in many ways, more ubiquitous than accounts of its direct experience. While at first glance, Hansberry's *Raisin in the Sun* and Cheever's Shady Hill stories seem to focus on different ends of the property spectrum, reading them together as anchor texts within the larger canon of homeownership literature gives us a more varied and entangled portrait of literary production than canons of suburban literature versus urban literature, theater versus literary fiction, American versus African American literature, or radical aesthetics versus more liberal ones have allowed us to see. Cheever's and Hansberry's paths to representing ownership's forms and feelings turn out to share canny similarities when resituated within a broader network of literary production foregrounding race, space, and homeownership. Cheever's literary tropes for representing the new constitution and presentation of suburban whiteness recall strategies developed by black writers to describe space's role in shaping new racial regimes. And although Hansberry chafed at dismissive attempts to read *Raisin* as a play that was merely "about real estate," embracing this frame as a dynamic rather than a deadening descriptor allows us to better attend to her complex treatment of black attachment to property. Focusing on her dynamic rendering of George Murchison, a character often flatly read by critics as a clown, allows us to see the varying forms that black attachments to property take in *Raisin*. Considering Cheever's and Hansberry's renderings of racial feeling's contortions, contradictions, and coalescences in the wake of mass homeownership's tantalizing promises and lingering burdens gives us a broader and more tumultuous picture of residential living that unsettles rather than rests on categories of race, the suburbs, or individualist flight.

We Wear the White Mask: John Cheever Writes Race

The world of John Updike . . . does not impinge on my world. On the other hand, the world of John Cheever did engage me.
 —JAMES BALDWIN, *Paris Review*, 1984

In a 1984 *New York Times* interview, a nearly sixty-year-old James Baldwin was asked whether there were any white writers of his generation he would describe as "witnesses," a term he often used to describe the desire to represent the American experience as structured by oppression but also endurance.[10] Baldwin responded by insisting that since "most white American writers seem to have cut off their heritage at Ellis Island," their "testimony" typically failed to "include enough." After naming Norman Mailer as a writer who fell short of the title, Baldwin addressed the work of John Cheever and John Updike.

Deeming their suburban subjects "roughly the same," Baldwin nonetheless claims Cheever an exception to the failure of most other white writers: "Somehow those lost suburbanites in Cheever's work are very moving. He engages your compassion. His people are not remote. The work of so many white writers is remote for me. I'm not trying to put them down. It's simply that they are not relevant to my experience."[11] Baldwin repeated a version of this claim in his 1984 *Paris Review* interview, using similar frames of engagement and impingement to describe Cheever's suburban canon.[12]

Baldwin had met Cheever on several occasions. Most notably, they shared a stage with Philip Roth twenty-five years earlier during a series of talks sponsored by *Esquire* called "Writing in America Today," held at the campuses of the University of California, Berkeley; Stanford University; and San Francisco State University over three nights in October 1960.[13] One might imagine that Cheever, whose darkest stories of suburban life entertained the notion of finding redemption in the suburbs' enrapturing summer light, was the odd man out next to the seemingly more provocative pair of Baldwin and Roth.[14] The *New York Times* circulated a version of this claim in the run-up to the talks, reporting on "the general hope" preceding them "that Cheever, Roth and Baldwin would disagree violently about practically everything."[15] But Cheever's remarks and the responses they elicited not only show him holding his own as a critic of American pieties but suggest that he was the most controversially received of the three. In his remarks, Cheever lamented the "abrasive and faulty surface of the United States in the last twenty-five years," insisted that the "nightmare symbols of our existence" meant that "life in the United States in 1960 is Hell," and concluded that "the only possible position for a writer now is negation." While Cheever's observations earned him a standing ovation from the Berkeley students, audience members "over 40 and some of them over 60," as reported by the *Times*, were provoked to "climb and totter to their feet" to accuse Cheever of "deliberate obscurity" and "anti-Americanism." Baldwin is described as having "rushed to Cheever's defense" before this hostile group of Berkeley elders to confirm Cheever's sense of the "unprecedented" state of their "insane and obscure civilization." But Baldwin's remarks failed to appease those who continued to harangue Cheever while the students who had applauded him earlier "clammed up." The atmosphere by then was so bitter that the moderator of the event concluded the evening by asking Cheever why, given his pessimism, he "even bothered to write at all."

Perhaps it is this critical and confrontational Cheever, along with his compassion-eliciting characters, whom Baldwin fondly remembered in 1984 for his talent to "engage." Given that Cheever's fiction has been largely relegated to the margins of American literary studies despite periodic lamentations of this fact, the rougher edges of his soft-eyed approach toward the new class of midcentury suburbanites that so disturbed his Berkeley audience in 1960 and warmed Baldwin in 1984 have gone overlooked.[16] Cheever remains trapped on the writing-workshop side of the literary divide—assigned to teach students how to write rather than how to read—validating the sense that his work is most usefully read as an example of timeless craft rather than as engaging with the world during the forty years during which he published.

I second Baldwin's insistence on Cheever's relevance but anchor this designation in Cheever's attention to the fluctuating definitions and experiences of whiteness shaped by mass homeownership. Resituating Cheever alongside Baldwin and Roth allows us to see the ways in which his work, like theirs, was deeply interested in the experience of race and, particularly, how whiteness newly felt and functioned in suburban spaces precipitating its remaking as a racial category. The entanglement of suburbanization and racial formation shadows the inhabitants of Cheever's most famous fictional enclave, Shady Hill, even when characters fail to articulate their experience in such terms, struggling as they do to perform their roles as members of a community whose financial and social value is predicated on racial exclusion. The protocols for being a homeowning subject in the postwar period were still being scripted when the Shady Hill stories were written in the 1950s. It was during this period that a majority of whites in the U.S. first became homeowners, aided by the relatively recent financial mechanism of the thirty-year mortgage.[17] I suggest that one reason Baldwin singled out Cheever's work as relevant to his experience was that his suburban stories depict whiteness not as an eternal construct written on the body but as an experiential and economic formation being reshaped by changing conventions of place, property, and financial valuation. Cheever describes the thoughts, feelings, and exploits of his white suburbanites without naturalizing their experience, never letting his readers forget the social and spatial conditions undergirding both their routines and its disturbances.

More than the other suburban writers with whom he is often lumped, Cheever captures the new alchemy of whiteness emerging from the nation's changing spatial landscapes.[18] In contrast to the previous chapter's attention to popular middlebrow melodramas of integration now long out of print, Cheever's stories do not cast tortured liberal white suburbanites against their openly racist neighbors in morality plays about the evils of discrimination.[19] And unlike canonical suburban fiction by writers John Updike, Sloan Wilson, and Richard Yates, the Shady Hill stories aren't ultimately about the struggles of one tortured man or family set into chaos by their choices or circumstances. Rather, Cheever's work privileges the formation of the neighborhood as the site of subjectivity, foregrounding neighborhood formation at midcentury as a process of racial formation.[20] His characters struggle with and within whiteness as a category undergoing both phenomenological and epistemological restructuring. It is Cheever's insistence on attending to whiteness as something requiring new descriptive attention following the expansion of suburban homeownership that distinguishes his fiction from his peers, often more willing to take whiteness for granted as something characters simply possessed rather than something characters constantly strived to maintain. Resituating Cheever next to Roth and Baldwin at the end of the 1950s as a canny student of race allows us to recognize him as one of the period's most preeminent witnesses of whiteness at a moment when this identity was becoming more difficult to bear witness to, given how the demographic expansion of whiteness was paradoxically contributing to its growing discursive invisibility.

Cheever was in his late forties and midcareer when he published his 1958 short story collection *The Housebreaker of Shady Hill*. Consisting of eight tales set in a fictional Westchester suburb—seven of which first appeared in the *New Yorker* between 1953 and 1957—each of *Housebreaker*'s stories focuses on a different Shady Hill family's quiet sorrows and secret treacheries. The collection is populated by assemblages of characters—the Beardens, the Farquarsons, the Rogers, the Parminters—who wander through the protagonists' homes and lives. Though each story centers on a specific family, the collection offers a group portrait of the performances, appearances, and deceptions that allow the neighborhood to endure. When Cheever penned them, he did not yet live in the one and only home he would own during his lifetime in Ossining, New York. Cheever was a newcomer to the suburbs, narrating its customs as recent convert rather than as an entrenched insider. It was a position he shared with many of his white middle-class readers and subjects, some of the earliest Americans to benefit from the thirty-year amortized mortgage and experience the yoked spatial and racial reorganization of metropolitan areas facilitated by this financial mechanism.

Referred to first as a suburb and later, with more irony, as a banlieue and a village, Shady Hill is best described as a redeveloped commuter town comprised of smaller neighborhoods containing residents of varying income levels. Shady Hill's richest residents (and a few broke pretenders) live in large Dutch Colonials located in the Blenhollow neighborhood, from which they steer the town's social and civic life. The more tattered Maple Dell area, consisting of older white-frame houses, is described as "more like a development than anything else in Shady Hill."[21] Across the tracks live "the near-poor," who reside in small houses with wooden lace trimmings.[22] A few Irish cooks and German gardeners also live in Shady Hill, typically with their employers. But beyond these marked figures, the stories make few direct references to race or ethnicity within or beyond its borders. Because of the enclave's racial homogeneity, difference is most explicitly defined in terms of those who deviate from its social norms: renters, proponents of public libraries, men who dress too brightly or wear their hair too long, and divorcées. Yet given that African Americans function as Shady Hill's ultimate outsiders, the specter of racial alterity shrouds social dissidents who, in challenging the town's norms, become viewed by their neighbors as symbolic gateways to the difference they most fear.

A generation prior, this imaginary town, like real suburban enclaves across the U.S., was "full of good farming people" living on acres of meadowland.[23] Mrs. Heinlein, one of the few remaining Shady Hill residents from this earlier era, distinguishes herself from the community's more recent suburbanized inhabitants in "The Sorrows of Gin" by insisting that, despite her present circumstances obliging her to babysit for her wealthier new neighbors, she descends from "patroons," landholders granted manorial privileges in the seventeenth century by the New England Dutch. Rather than solidifying her prestige, however, this old-timer's insistence on blood dates her, marking her as a holdover from an older spatial and racial system no longer influential here. While Mrs. Heinlein touts her invisible lineage over her present-day appearance or holdings—a hallmark of both hereditary, monarchal regimes and ante- and postbellum iterations of the one-drop rule—her newer neighbors, now making up the majority of Shady Hill's inhabitants, differently approach the notion of social standing. Heinlein's heritage means little to them since none of them originally hail from Shady Hill, reminding us that midcentury suburbs were largely outposts of migrants who had left their extended families and birthplaces behind. The familial pedigrees of Shady Hill's more recently arrived occupants are best left unknown or unsaid: their pasts, as Cheever's stories insinuate, best left uninspected. Whereas new spatial mobility and genealogical anonymity were hallmarks of racial passing a few decades earlier, Shady Hill's midcentury residents silently agree to look away from each other's pasts and origins as long as their neighbors look white enough and actively help to preserve the town's exclusivity. To be white in Shady Hill is not a matter of breeding, as Mrs. Heinlein's diminished status suggests, but of appearance and perceived assimilation.

That Mrs. Heinlein's traceable line of racial and spatial descent means little in Shady Hill attests to the ways mass homeownership was remaking the measures of whiteness. Whereas the one-drop rule was law in almost every state in the U.S. by 1925, mortgage lenders in the 1950s were less interested in a potential borrower's family tree than they were in their capacity to invest in, maintain, and perform whiteness as an exclusionary category. As David Roediger notes, the allegedly "white suburb" of the midcentury "could have been termed 'mixed' too, if the national heritage of those moving there were traced back far enough."[24] But, as the unfashionable Mrs. Heinlein bemoans, admittance into midcentury suburbs depended on a definition of whiteness rooted not in heritage—despite the nation's genealogical obsession with race only a few decades before—but appearance, performance, and, increasingly, how and where one resided. To borrow George Lipsitz's terminology, to buy a home in the segregated suburbs at midcentury was to "possessively invest in whiteness," a phrase highlighting the relationship between whiteness and asset accumulation.[25] If one phenotypically looked the part, whiteness was something in which one could invest and protect given its direct impact on a home's value, the largest financial investment most Americans would now make.

While there are many excellent studies by social scientists and historians about how the suburbs reified racial divides, these studies tend to overlook the role narrative played in not only mirroring the growing correlation between whiteness and homeownership but normalizing its emerging scripts of performance and collective investment. Suburban literature did not just record white residential life but helped to invent and solidify its protocols. What it meant to be white in the wake of mass homeownership, given the new financial incentives for those who could afford to throw their lot in with a more absorptive and accessible form of whiteness, was a descriptive problem as well as an empirical one. Instead of reading Cheever's stories as reflections of suburban life, we might instead consider them as experiments in representing whiteness's new idioms—favoring the Beardens of the world over the Heinleins—and what it felt like to live them.

One of these idioms, as Mrs. Heinlein's diminished social status marks, is that the past is no guarantor of the present. In fact, in Shady Hill, where most residents were recent arrivals, it is not just polite but imperative that the past stay past. Most of Shady Hill's occupants live there precisely because its physical and social histories have been largely wiped clean, allowing them to write this space and, by extension, themselves anew. As Cheever describes in "The Country Husband," "the people in the Farquarsons' living room seemed united in their tacit claim that there had been no past, no war—that there was no danger or trouble in the world."[26] This posture of communal forgetting was one Cheever himself relied upon to smooth his own entrance into the elite social circles he most sought. More Jay Gatsby than Nick Carraway, Cheever's personal path to the white moneyed suburbs was rocky. Bouncing in and out of the middle class for much of his early life, he disguised his precarious origins with prestigious flourishes designed to make him seem more the conventional WASP for which he was often mistaken.[27] "I have been a storyteller since the beginning of my life, rearranging facts in order to make them more interesting and sometimes more significant," as Cheever wrote his journals.[28] He refers to his family elsewhere as "unclean outcasts whose destiny, written in the stars, was to empty garbage pails and pump the shit out of septic tanks but who, through some cultural miscalculation, imagined themselves being carried off the shoulders of their teammates and then dancing with the prettiest girl in the world."[29] It follows that Cheever, like his characters, would find himself attracted to the midcentury suburbs, billed as virginal spaces where homeowners who could secure financing were able to remake themselves through a down payment and white-enough skin.

In addition to serving as a handy analogy for glossing Cheever's biography, *The Great Gatsby* proves useful for parsing some of the key differences between earlier modes of residential racial formation as described in F. Scott Fitzgerald's 1925 novel of the Long Island suburbs and midcentury Shady Hill. From Gatsby's mansion—a replica Normandy castle that announces a little too literally its occupant's designs on claiming a certain pedigree—to his disavowal of the name Jimmy Gatz for the more WASP-sounding moniker of Jay Gatsby, Gatsby's perceived status as a racially passing subject has been remarked upon by a generation of literary critics detailing Gatsby's reception within the novel as not quite white, making his courtship of Daisy not just socially undesirable but akin to a crime.[30] No matter how much property Gatsby acquires, the recentness of his assimilation—confirmed by his recently Anglicized last name—dooms his further integration.[31] Once Tom implies the taint in his bloodline, Gatsby's fate is sealed. Daisy relents to Tom's insistence they return to the more secure network of whiteness from which she cannot afford to fall while Gatsby is killed for a crime Daisy carelessly committed. Homeownership fails to afford Gatsby full admittance to whiteness nor its protections.

By the time we reach 1950s Shady Hill, property *is* a viable tool for producing and sustaining whiteness, capable of overwriting the uncertain origins of its residents if they look enough of the part. Whereas the recentness of Gatsby's assimilation dooms his project of social mobility—despite the suggestion within the novel, as James Smethurst notes, "that the 'old money' characters in *Gatsby* . . . are descended from earlier Gatsbys made good"— Cheever constantly gestures toward the indeterminate origins his Shady Hill protagonists have only recently shed and mostly kept hidden.[32] Johnny Hake "learned to chin" on "the framework of East Side apartment-house canopies," while the "dark-haired, dark-eyed" Marcie Flint, advocating for a public library that her neighbors fear would make the community vulnerable to outsiders, is retrospectively associated with racial otherness.[33] Donald Wryson never knew his father while Will Pym notes how a Baltimore settlement house helped him move from impoverishment to his comfortable life in Shady Hill.[34] Cheever repeatedly points toward the indeterminate origins of these characters as marked by their geographies, coloring, and parentage— qualities that only a few decades earlier were hallmarks of racial passing, including in *Gatsby*.³⁵ In Shady Hill, however, such pasts are the norm rather than the exception. Racial belonging is not a matter of the longevity of one's affiliation with whiteness but one's total commitment to it. There is no Tom Buchannan here to root around in one's past, fishing for proof of a sullied bloodline somewhere down the line. If you could get a mortgage to buy a house in Shady Hill, commit to the community's social codes, and look white enough, you could partake of its privileges. Since mostly everyone in Shady Hill hails from elsewhere, there is a shared social and economic commitment to leaving the pasts of one's neighbors unexcavated unless their present performance falters. *Housebreaker* captures whiteness's changing definition as it tilted away from blood and toward surface-level performances and financial investment.

Rather than proof of lineage, Shady Hill residents—following the assessment norms of the housing market—most value their neighbors' commitment to preserving the town's social norms, according to which men commute to the city for work while the women stay home and run the neighborhood's social life, with everyone converging at alcohol-fueled parties. Shady Hill's maintenance hinges on knowing when and where norms of behavior and performance were to be upheld (any public and/or sober site of surveillance) and when residents should strategically squint to maintain the town's social harmony in which they have literal investment as homeowners (generally at night or at any function with alcohol). Social norms can carry such weight in Shady Hill, in part, because the work of maintaining its racial exclusivity was largely outsourced to mortgage lenders and realtors elsewhere tasked with steering away the "inharmonious" before they could consider or fund a move there. Though white homeowners at midcentury were still willing to turn to violence to keep out alleged intruders when necessary, racial apartheid in the suburbs was increasingly enforced through quieter practices of exclusion implemented by bureaucrats rather than mobs.³⁶

Whiteness's new measures made it easier to surveil but also simpler to rhetorically avoid. Although homeownership binds the community of Shady Hill, the whiteness on which this ownership hinged is rarely acknowledged directly. Racial others are only obliquely marked by the stories' white characters in coded references to "slums" and their potential "victimization" by their othered occupants. Whiteness, moreover, is deployed in *Housebreaker* as a descriptor of race or skin tone exactly twice. But the stories' general silence regarding race is not a disavowal of its importance; rather, the lack of explicit references to race mirrors the ways in which whiteness was managed and maintained in midcentury suburbs. Due to the success of forms of racial exclusion rooted in differential access to residential property quietly managed by realtors and bureaucrats, whiteness could be approached in communities like Shady Hill as a matter of atmosphere rather than corporeal truth: pleasantly dematerialized as the normal state of things because its others have been either assimilated into whiteness or exiled from its spaces.[37]

By largely declining to name the whiteness organizing Shady Hill's social world, Cheever's stories seem to epitomize claims most notably forwarded by Ruth Frankenberg and Richard Dyer in the 1990s under the rubric of critical whiteness studies, which highlighted whiteness's discursive invisibility as a manifestation of its privilege.[38] The notion that "whiteness never has to speak its name, never has to acknowledge its role as an organizing principle in social and cultural relations," as George Lipsitz describes, animated much of the critical work aiming to make this invisibility legible.[39] Persuasive critiques of critical whiteness studies refute its genealogy, the radicalism of its politics, and, most forcefully, its key claim about whiteness's invisibility. As Sara Ahmed insists, "whiteness is only invisible for those who inhabit it," given its hypervisibility to those denied its privileges—an argument that, as Robyn Wiegman notes, James Baldwin helped initiate in the midcentury.[40]

But rather than exemplifying arguments about whiteness's discursive invisibility, I see Cheever's Shady Hill tales offering evidence that this invisibility is not a transhistorical truism but a product of specific historical and spatial contexts. A casual look back at U.S. history suggests that whiteness has not evaded naming or perception with much consistency, reappearing front and center in rallying cries and hierarchal schemas in any number of situations. Even if we limit ourselves to the past century, such instances abound. From Theodore Roosevelt's warnings about the threat of race suicide, the mass popularity of race science in the 1920s, and the white-supremacist protestors Martin Luther King Jr. faced in Chicago in the 1960s to the present efforts of the alt-right, history suggests that whiteness is not always aesthetically or rhetorically invisible but attains this status in specific times and places. It would be safer to say that it is whiteness's flexibility rather than its invisibility that makes it distinct, with its representation and definition shifting in accordance with how its dispensations might best be maintained.

The Shady Hill stories do not reflect the timeless invisibility of whiteness, then, but the specific iteration of its invisibility at midcentury when systems of redlining—most often enforced beyond its boundaries—made it possible to take for granted the homogeneity within them. The suburbs enabled whiteness to become, to quote Dyer, "everything and nothing" on a new scale, its ubiquity rendering its description redundant.[41] As Catherine Jurca notes in *White Diaspora*, "the suburb's racial composition is so unremarkable to most white novelists that in general it is indistinguishable from the suburb's middle-classness."[42] Whereas urban literature in the early twentieth century abounds with explicit efforts to measure, perceive, and maintain whiteness amid growing fears that this racial category was becoming less visible (and thus less viable) in expanding cities, suburban literature reflects the success of new housing developments in easing these accounting concerns. But Cheever's decision to not remark on the physical whiteness of most of his characters doesn't mean that whiteness remains unmarked. While there is a clear vocabulary in his stories for denoting class distinction, the more elliptical treatment of the enclave's whiteness does not suggest its unremarkability so much as its idiomatic particularity. Absence is a language, too, one Shady Hill's residents learn to speak fluently as part of inhabiting the whiteness that is both mandatory and unutterable within its borders.

Following critic Timothy Aubry, we might approach Cheever's representations of whiteness as a training manual of sorts. "Many readers at the fringe of middle-class affluence," as Aubry writes, "would have found Cheever's fiction immensely instructive, even when alienating."[43] "Learning to feel addressed by Cheever's fiction," he continues, "is a lesson in how to become a proper upper-middle-class suburbanite."[44] While Baldwin's remarks about Cheever put pressure on Aubry's assumptions that Cheever was primarily read by white suburbanites, we might nonetheless think of his various audiences as studying—if not exactly aspiring to replicate—the complicated performance of whiteness in Shady Hill that obliged residents to embrace and protect this status without ever articulating their identification with it. While Cheever's tone toward the suburbs has been a point of controversy since the 1950s—with readers and critics disagreeing about the degree to which Cheever valorized or critiqued these spaces—his efforts to "engage compassion" for his "lost suburbanites," as Baldwin notes, echoes Baldwin's own diagnosis of the harmful and painful repressions required of white Americans.[45] "Because they think they are white, they do not dare confront the ravage and the lie of their history," Baldwin insists, going on to note that this same population believes "as even no child believes, in the dream of safety"—an applicable gloss of Shady Hill of there ever was one.[46] If "part of the price of the white ticket" requires its holders to "delude themselves" into believing in their own whiteness, as Baldwin insists, then Cheever details the turmoil surrounding this payment while just as dutifully explicating the pleasurable experience of its returns.[47] It seems most accurate to say, then, that Cheever neither celebrates nor condemns his white suburbanites but seeks to describe how they negotiate the costs and rewards of their inhabitance, unfolding the pleasure and pain accompanying the possession of and by whiteness: sensations further heightened by whiteness's rhetorical incommunicability within their local worlds.

The "dream of safety" undergirding whiteness as described by Baldwin faces continual puncturing in the Shady Hill stories. For all the emphasis placed on the town's insular safety, its own residents often pose the greatest threat to its peace. A mother flips through issues of *Life* magazine to remove "scenes of mayhem, disaster and violent death that she felt might corrupt her children," while a father in another tale confiscates his daughter's copies of *True Romance* for similar reasons.[48] Town council members in "The Trouble with Marcie Flint" unite to resist a proposal for a public library they worry will "make this community attractive to a development" and eventually, as they agitatedly insist, murder sprees.[49] Yet we witness the residents of Shady Hill regularly doing damage to one another all on their own, slandering and even shooting their neighbors, poisoning their own children, and sleeping with each other's spouses. The collection's titular story, "The Housebreaker of Shady Hill," most powerfully highlights this contradiction. When the wife of one of Shady Hill's wealthier families openly laments at a party that her husband walks with large sums of money "through a terrible slum to get to the station" every night, leaving her "so afraid he'll be *victimized*"—with both her neighbors and Cheever's readers grasping the racialized fear underlying her language of space and persecution—her secretly broke and desperate neighbor Johnny Hake is inspired to rob the husband himself.[50]

But race is far more central to the workings of "Housebreaker" than its occluded racial language would suggest. This becomes evident when we compare it to a novel published fifteen years earlier that explicitly marks how space produces racialized subjects. In tone and setting, Richard Wright's bestselling novel *Native Son* could not be more different from "Housebreaker." *Native Son* charts the coming physical death and symbolic rise of Bigger Thomas, a black Chicago South Sider whose dire circumstances help facilitate his terrible crimes, while Cheever coyly describes the desperation and relatively frivolous circumstances leading the white Johnny Hake to a short-lived thieving streak. But for all their stark differences, these works' shared commitment to describing protagonists shaped by the entwined spaces of the black ghetto and the white enclave—spaces that actively haunt one another in both texts—suggests the utility of reading these spaces and their literatures in concert.[51] The extent to which "Housebreaker" is a story about whiteness's midcentury operation becomes most visible in relief, situated next to the story of someone "living outside of our lives," as Bigger's lawyer refers to him.[52]

If *Native Son* reveals "the extent to which the freedom of white people to exercise the right to live where and as they like, in city or in suburb, is enabled and underwritten by the constraint of others," as Catherine Jurca writes, "Housebreaker" underscores just how much freedom such spaces afford their white residents.[53] The only Shady Hill story narrated in the first person, "Housebreaker" immerses the reader in Hake's anxious rationalizations as he sneaks in and out of his neighbor's bedrooms, observing the intimate details of their lives while stealing their money. Hake's explanations of his criminal motivations are laughable compared with those that Wright makes on Bigger's behalf; instead of pointing to epic structural forces of race and poverty, Cheever's protagonist blames an unhappy weekend with his father for his compulsion to rob. In his reading of "Housebreaker," Keith Wilhite finds that the "sense of inevitability surrounding Hake's stroll into burglary speaks directly to the physical and social nature of suburban space," where to walk "is to be always on the verge of trespass" given the amorphous line between private and public space.[54] However, the more crucial inevitability is not Hake's trespass, it would seem, but the lack of consequences he experiences in its wake. Despite his secret financial woes, Hake's status as a known entity in the neighborhood—a status reliant on his race, if not solely reducible to it—ensures he will survive his misfortunes intact.

The ease with which Hake strolls between public and private spaces in Shady Hill differs markedly from Bigger's racialized containment within the South Side, inhibiting his movements long before he goes on the lam. Bigger's physical awkwardness as an employee within the Daltons' home only reinforces the division between their nicely outfitted home and his family's shabby apartment, owned by Mr. Dalton's real estate company and helping to finance the Dalton home's finery. But whereas *Native Son* propels both Bigger and the reader to become conscious of the spatial and economic connections between black stasis and white mobility, "Housebreaker" charts the benefits of keeping such knowledge tacit. Guilt and paranoia consume Hake in the wake of his thieving, but the social and geographic landscape of Shady Hill allows him to reverse his actions and soothe his conscience with relative ease. When his financial fortunes turn around, he simply breaks into his neighbors' homes to return their money. Hake suavely covers his tracks in the story's final scene when a friendly patrolman spots him exiting a neighbor's home he has illicitly entered. Asked why he is out at such a late hour, Hake tells the officer that he's walking his dog, confessing to the reader that "there was no dog in sight, but they didn't look."[55] After calling out for this invented pet, Hake describes himself in the story's closing line as "whistling merrily in the dark." As Wilhite writes of this ending, "the burglary has altered precisely nothing within the order of Shady Hill, moral or otherwise, not even a 'mote of sunlight.'"[56] Unlike the snowfall during Bigger's capture making his dark skin all the more trackable, Hake's envelopment into darkness at the story's end highlights the perceptual cover his whiteness grants him within Shady Hill, enabling his crimes to remain unseen. Whereas "Housebreaker" begins with Hake sitting naked in the dark and confessing his crimes to the reader, the character's final return to darkness is less a moment of vulnerability than it is an unnerving fade-out: there is nothing left for Hake to tell us about Shady Hill beyond his merry whistling, drowning out all of the darker notes sounded earlier in the story.

But unlike "Housebreaker," which comes closest to directly acknowledging Shady Hill's racialized landscape through a fearful reference to the "terrible slum" external to it, "The Worm in the Apple" openly names the whiteness central to Shady Hill's operation. In addition to its brevity and satire, "Worm" is distinct for being the only story in *Housebreaker* not to have first appeared in the *New Yorker*. Cheever biographer Blake Bailey understands its presence in the collection as the clumsy result of Cheever's final efforts to "tilt the thematic balance" of the collection from ambivalence to irony.[57] Cheever's embrace of satire in this singular story, dramatizing the distance between his authorial voice and that of his suburban protagonists, enables him to directly articulate whiteness's centrality to Shady Hill and the collection at large; this makes "Worm" less an anomaly and more a key to *Housebreaker*.

The stories surrounding "The Worm in the Apple" in *Housebreaker* are fairly uniform in style and construction, each trafficking in mild absurdities and angst-ridden self-delusions while bestowing its protagonists with at least one moment of grace that never lets the reader fully lose sight of the suburb's appeal. But "Worm," appearing at the collection's halfway point, disrupts many of these conventions. At just under two thousand words it is more sketch than story, interrogating the genre tropes of suburban literature as they were being solidified in the 1950s. "The Crutchmans were so very, very happy," the story opens, "and so temperate in all their habits and so pleased with everything that came their way that one was bound to suspect a worm in their rosy apple."[58] The first of several potential worms appears when the teenage son of Helen and Larry Crutchman dates Carrie Witchell from the lower-class neighborhood, Maple Dell. But rather than define Maple Dell by its residents' class difference, the narrator notes that Carrie "is really beautiful and everyone knows how her shrewd old parents are planning to climb out of Maple Dell on the strength of her white, white skin."[59] In achieving this, she would have joined the many residents of Shady Hill who, as other stories in the collection recount, similarly used their white-enough exteriors to better their circumstances. But Carrie tries passing too close to home. Her spatial and racial origins cannot be overlooked by the community because they mark boundaries still actively feared by Shady Hill as a threat to its value.

The reference to Carrie's whiteness becomes all the more impactful when we consider the story as self-reflexively reflecting on Cheever's own fictional propensities. The narrator directly addresses readers who expect the Crutchmans to "suffer the celebrated spiritual destitution of their age and their kind," after which point "the worm in the apple would at last be laid bare."[60] Cheever acknowledges his own penchant for representing the suburbs' secret miseries while marking the reader's complicity in desiring such revelations. But this self-reflexive tone also enables Cheever's narrator to dwell on Carrie's doubly white skin in ways his characters can't or won't, explicitly racializing Maple Dell's perceived inferiority, which is left unarticulated elsewhere in the collection. The direct reference to her physical whiteness, one of only two such moments in the entire book, comes at the midpoint of a story that is itself situated at the collection's midpoint. This neatly nested reference suggests that race, far from being a worm arriving from outside Shady Hill to sully its riches, is more accurately thought of as the core that structures and produces it.[61] As the rare Cheever story not to grace the *New Yorker*'s pages, "Worm" offers the collection's readers a different take on both Shady Hill and Cheever's construction of it than his periodical readers would have experienced. For readers expecting the kind of compassionate farce for which Cheever was known, this story offers a glimpse of the racial scaffolding propping up this sunny fictional world.

Despite the Crutchmans' close calls with calamity, "Worm" concludes with a perverse parody of a fairy-tale ending. "Through the prudence and shrewdness of Helen's broker," its final lines impart, the Crutchmans "got richer and richer and richer and lived happily, happily, happily, happily."[62] The worm's appearance is indefinitely forestalled, illustrating just how hard it is for any event or action to permanently disrupt the security that the enmeshed properties of whiteness, wealth, and real estate grant the Crutchmans. The story's hyperbolic flourishes—its repetition of words, knowing nods to the reader, and detached attitude toward its subjects—actually intensify the accuracy of the account. Their happiness approaches mania, with the five concluding "happilys" marking not the deepness of their feeling but its impenetrability.

"The Five-Forty Eight" ultimately makes good on "Worm's" titular promise of infiltration. Featuring the least sympathetic of the Shady Hill protagonists, the story centers on the singularly named Blake, who sleeps with his secretary Miss Dent before callously firing her. The story details Miss Dent's attempts at retribution as she, unwilling to be ignored any longer, follows Blake onto the train to Shady Hill and holds him hostage at gunpoint. Lynne Waldeland, one of Cheever's earliest scholarly critics, argues "The Five-Forty Eight" is out of sync with the other collection's stories, insisting that because "it features the only really despicable character from Shady Hill in the book," it therefore "adds no real insight into Shady Hill as a community."[63] I would counter, however, that the story's chief insights do not derive from the reader's encounter with the ignoble Blake but rather the beleaguered Miss Dent, a figure of literal darkness who eventually forces her antagonist's face into the dirt. This act of compulsory blackface marks race's meaningfulness in a visceral sense within Shady Hill, but it also gestures toward the limitations of recognition as a generative form of disruption. While her dark presence in Shady Hill, along with the agency she exercises within its borders, seems to suggest the promise of integration as a form of redress, Miss Dent's walking away from this suburb at the story's end may be the more significant gesture.

In a style more like that of Flannery O'Connor than of Sloan Wilson, the narrator of "The Five-Forty Eight" follows Blake's thoughts and feelings while leaving Miss Dent something of a cipher that we view mostly through Blake. Repeatedly referred to in the story in terms of her "dark" hair and eyes, Miss Dent reads like a classic passing character; from her deep melancholy to her nervous disposition, she is a tragic mulatta in type if not in name.[64] Her darkness is further concretized by her association urban space, with the narrator even informing us at one point that "the slums and the city reminded Blake vaguely of the woman who had followed him."[65] After Blake cruelly discards Miss Dent following their affair, firing her behind her back and then rebuffing all contact, she suddenly reappears months later in his workplace lobby. He attempts to slip away but soon spies her following behind him in the reflection of a store window: "He could have turned then and asked her what she wanted, but instead of recognizing her, he shied away abruptly from the reflection of her contorted face and went along the street. She might be meaning to do him harm—she might be meaning to kill him."[66] Blake's withholding of recognition as a defense mechanism follows the general pattern of behavior ascribed to Shady Hill's residents. If he can just make it home, Miss Dent and all the things she stands for—blackness, the city, his own ignoble actions—can remain unseen and sloughed off, compartmentalized to the urban center that Shady Hill is designed to stand apart from.

Unlike Johnny Hake in "Housebreaker," Blake does not escape his predicament unscathed. Miss Dent follows him onto the train and holds him hostage by discreetly pressing a gun into his ribs. The "NO TRESPASSING" signs glimpsed along the journeys signal the threat Dent seemingly poses to the world of Shady Hill.[67] The train is meant to grant its residents easy access to the city while discouraging the kind of blowback Dent's dark presence marks. Upon their arrival, however, it is not Miss Dent who seems out of place but Shady Hill that appears increasingly off-kilter. In a vignette describing the goings-on at the train station when they arrive, a woman late to pick up her husband weightily announces that "all our clocks are slow."[68] In concert with these details foregrounding Shady Hill's cultivated belatedness and antipastoral status, Miss Dent tells Blake—in one of the few descriptions of the suburb offered up by someone who doesn't live there—that "I thought it would look different. I didn't think it would look so shabby." Her desire at the beginning of the story to insinuate herself within Blake's world—by writing a letter to him addressed "dear husband," for instance—now fades.[69] Rather than longing to impose herself on Blake and his domain, Miss Dent now embraces her distinction from him and his surroundings, declaring herself to be "better than Blake" and refusing to "waste my life or spoil my life like this."[70] She instructs him to "put your face in the dirt" and, upon becoming "skinned" with coal, he falls to the ground weeping (294). With the blackening of his face, the last of Miss Dent's animosity toward Blake dissipates. His dirtying allows her now to "wash her hands" of him, as she claims to have discovered "some kindness, some saneness in me that I can find and use."[71] He listens to her footsteps as she walks away, raising himself up from the dust to catch a final glimpse of her boarding a train back to the city. Judging "by her attitude, her looks, that she had forgotten him, that she had completed what she wanted to do, and that he was safe," Blake stands up and walks home.[72]

This ending is simultaneously climactic and anticlimactic. Dent's concluding act of coerced blackface feels transgressive given blackness's complete absence from the stories in *Housebreaker*. In forcing Blake to wear the mask of blackness, Dent illuminates Shady Hill's more general traffic in racial masquerade. An uncovering rather than a putting on, his coal-skinned countenance reminds us of Shady Hill's own investment in racial masks, refracting its residents' discursive disavowal of race within its own autumnal light. Yet Miss Dent is ultimately left unsatisfied by Blake's compelled performance of racial alterity. Her demand is seemingly improvised, representing the best strategy she can come up with in the moment for making Blake feel her powerlessness, humiliation, and misrecognition. But the brevity of his discomfort emphasizes just how little impact this encounter is likely to have. After all, Blake already announces himself "safe" by the story's close, indicating the unlikeliness that this confrontation will result in anything like a reckoning. As Aubry notes, "Blake returns to his suburban life, having learned, it seems, nothing" and reminding the reader of the "various class, race, and cultural boundaries" that prevent him from learning any lesson that might imperil his own subject position.[73] Miss Dent's name further suggests the limits of her capacity to meaningfully impact the world of either Blake or Shady Hill. Her ultimate failure to disrupt the functioning of either Blake or his town reinforces the notion accumulating across the collection that whiteness is not just a matter of skin but an investment; singular encounters aiming to change the hearts and minds of its residents prove inadequate to dismantling the financial incentives encouraging not just homeownership but the racial exclusion on which the market value of their homes and Shady Hill's notion of security depends.

Yet it is the combined effect of Blake's concluding action of getting up and returning to his home and Miss Dent's departure from Shady Hill, presumably to forge a home elsewhere, that we must weigh. No matter how great their disillusionment with Shady Hill's insularity becomes, the majority of its residents in *Housebreaker* remain there.[74] And Cheever never rebukes those who stay. Cheever's compassion for his characters, on which Baldwin and other have dwelled, intersects with his depiction of his characters' astonishment at ending up in such a place. Despite the prevailing understanding of white flight as the willful abandonment of darkening cities, the bewilderment that Cheever's protagonists feel in and toward Shady Hill reflects the vexed feelings suburbanization and its alleged securities provoked. While pointing to the forms of racial exclusion undergirding Shady Hill's promises of pleasant refuge, Cheever also makes it hard to censure its residents for being dazzled by them.

But even as Cheever puts us in a position to process alongside these suburbanites the kinds of performances, identities, and suppressions this form of dwelling they've opted into demands, he also peppers the collection with peripheral figures that push the reader to reassess the value of these trade-offs through acts of rebellion or self-exile. Miss Dent, for instance, neither falls in love with Shady Hill's light nor imagines how nice it would be to raise kids there. Temporarily swapping its white faces for dark ones is ultimately not enough to redeem this community for her. In her disillusionment with Shady

Hill, she joins characters like the "dark" Marx-reading Marcie Flint fighting for a public library despite its unpopularity and the fatherless teenager Clayton Thomas, who diagnoses Shady Hill as futureless, rebuking the energy his neighbors spend on "perpetuating the place—in keeping out undesirables."[75] The possibility of forging other visions of dwelling that do not reproduce the forms of homeownership, exclusion, and insulation required to sustain Shady Hill remains palpable throughout *Housebreaker*. Cheever's stories suggest both the difficulties of disinvesting in Shady Hill and the whiteness around which it coheres while also never foreclosing the possibility that the intrusions upon this idyll might soon become too persistent to ignore.

That only one other critic has read Miss Dent's final act in "The Five Forty-Eight" as a redeployment of blackface attests to both Cheever's success in working within the suburbs' own rhetorical racial idiom as well as the limits of his mastery, allowing his light touch to be taken frequently for evasion. Consider, for instance, the enduring misreading of Cheever originated by literary critic Irving Howe in his 1959 review of *Housebreaker*. Howe argues that while "Cheever really knows a great deal about suburban life," he ultimately cheats in representing it.[76] Charging Cheever with "systematically refus[ing] to face the meaning of the material he has himself brought to awareness and then suppressed," Howe finds that the author "connives in the cowardice of contemporary life; the resignation which constitutes his stock wisdom is nothing but advice to his readers that, dying slowly, they also die quietly."[77]

But Howe, in collapsing the experiences Cheever scripts for his protagonists with Cheever's own, also collapses his description of atmospheres inducing and incentivizing suppression with suppression itself. In seeking an overt structural condemnation of the suburbs from the Shady Hill stories, Howe overlooks Cheever's attention to the muddled and disassociated ways his characters experience these structures. It is important that readers do not confuse Cheever's representation of his characters' disavowals with his own; his characters' systematic refusal to face, name, or own their investment in whiteness is part of what it meant to invest in—and describe—whiteness in this period. But by deploying older literary tropes of passing and blackface that have been historically used to draw attention to race as something one *becomes* rather than something one merely *possesses*, Cheever's stories function as accounts of racial formation even when his characters fail to mark this accounting themselves. Resuscitating the version of Cheever who claimed in 1960 that "the only possible position for a writer now is negation" allows us to rethink the affirming qualities of his suburban descriptions as part and parcel of the discourse of racial disavowal Cheever so cannily captured. While Baldwin stops short of detailing exactly why he was so fond of Cheever's depiction of "lost suburbanites," I would hazard that his admiration had something to do with Cheever's recognition of their being lost, allowing him to capture the amnesia and aphasia accompanying his characters' racial investments within these expanding third spaces.

Disentangling the rhetorical silence around whiteness in *Housebreaker* from its structural importance to the collection confirms Toni Morrison's long-standing call in *Playing in the Dark* to attend more closely to "the signs, the codes, the literary strategies designed to accommodate" encounters with what she calls the Africanist other.[78] Morrison prompts us to consider race as a descriptive problem all American writers necessarily confront, a problem made manifest by reading not for race's description but for its function. Carrying out her prescriptions in relation to midcentury literature is complicated not only by the rhetorical invisibility of whiteness, particularly within suburban literature, but also by the literary canons created for its study. Cheever is undoubtedly a writer of white flight, but he also wrote in the wake of the Great Migration and its literary tradition, a fact we limn by reading him both with and against a broader canon of movement and migration populated by black and white writers alike. What we consider to be suburban literature, in fact, might start to look quite differently when returned to the fuller literary, regional, residential, and racial contexts in which this category came of age.

George Murchison's Property Lessons in *A Raisin in the Sun*

I think housing is so important I wrote a play about it.
 —LORRAINE HANSBERRY, 1963[79]

While residential segregation became more bureaucratic and even polite in its execution at midcentury, the economic and emotional pain black Americans experienced when denied or exploited through property did not hurt any less. In fact, the systemic uptake of residential segregation could hurt a whole lot more. Whereas racists could be compelled either by law, culture, or sentiment to change their behavior, dismantling the housing market built on the "truth" of black illiquidity—a system upheld just as easily by liberals as by segregationists—was harder to conceptually tackle (more on this in the next chapter). Moreover, the belief in an alternative to the property system sustaining and radicalizing Americans across the color line just a few decades prior was also harder to publicly hold in this period.[80] Gone were the raucous rent parties of the 1930s where blacks practiced living joyously in excess of property. So, too, were the Cultural Front's heyday of the 1930s and '40s now past. In Cold War America, where Jim Crow seemed fated to be replaced by more impersonal structures of discrimination, doubling down on the dream of property and its attendant rights appeared to many black Americans as the only viable path to the good life as well as to equality, dignity, and justice.

Richard Wright's transformed approach to property in the 1950s underscores this shift. As discussed in Chapter 3, Wright praised the black folk in the 1930s and '40s for failing to be "blinded by the hunger for possessions."[81] This group's "social vision and deep social consciousness," he argued, distinctively equipped them to avoid "the handicaps of false ambition and property."[82] But the Wright of 1951 had a more personal story to tell about his own dashed property ambitions. In his unpublished essay "I Choose Exile," Wright describes how his experience of discrimination while trying to buy a house became "the last personal event which resolved me to leave America."[83] He goes on to tell an all-too-common story of midcentury housing discrimination filled with disappointing runarounds and deferrals managed by a stalling if polite relator. While waiting to hear if his $6,000 cash offer (roughly $85,000 today) on a house in New England would be accepted, Wright suddenly realizes—if oddly belatedly—that "the dreadful issue of 'race' was hovering somewhere over those beautiful snow-clad hills of New Hampshire."[84] Upon confronting his realtor about the delay, Wright learns that "the 'truth' turned out to be that the white owner did not want to sell his house to a Negro." On the train ride back to New York, home unpurchased, Wright describes how "a feeling welled up in me, springing from the depths of my life." It is then that he decides to "get out of it" and "go to France at once."[85] Once in Paris, Wright contrastingly notes his ease in acquiring an apartment despite the postwar housing crunch. Not only did he find "the apartment of my choice," he notes, but he even had tea with his prospective landlord while working out the terms.

Of the many forms of anti-black violence and discrimination Wright had experienced in his life up to this point—threats of lynching, race-based wage exploitation, limited educational opportunities, humiliation at the hands of whites expecting his submission—it is this most innocuous if pervasive experience of housing discrimination, Jim Crow with an apologetic Northern lament, that ultimately drives Wright to give up on America for good. Occurring only a few years after the apex of his fame as the most successful black author in America, Wright's thwarted efforts to buy a house prove to him that no amount of wealth or fame would insulate him from either the economic or emotional costs of being black in America. Despite the twelve years he spent as a member of the Communist Party, he nonetheless narrates the heartbreak of ownership's unattainability as the source of tremendous pain.

Wright was, of course, merely one of many former communists whose politics shifted in the steely light of the Cold War at midcentury. It's tempting to understand this shift in terms of mere contradiction.[86] But as one activist recalled of housing struggles in this period, "Communists, Uncle Toms, preachers and everybody had to pull together. Where you were born wasn't the issue, but where you could go was the problem."[87] Wright's description of his affective dejection in the face of his dashed property aspirations speaks to the difficulties of disentangling oneself from the feelings yoked to homeownership, no matter one's ideological orientation. What Wright hoped to purchase in New England was not just a home but broader residential respite from the civic and social forces of anti-blackness. The final dissolution of his lingering faith that somewhere in America, he, too, could buy his way into protection and peace opens a wellspring of emotion in Wright that he cannot stanch. He is thrown not only by the shattering of this residential possibility, but by the kindly nature of its destruction. He is not spit upon, threatened, or called out of his name during his negotiations—rather the revelation of its racial core upsets all involved. When Wright finally asks to see his real estate agent in person to get to the bottom of the delay, Wright describes the "hurt, stunned look" in the man's "brooding eyes," delivering "the truth before he spoke."[88] The inability of Wright's realtor to hide his own feelings during this encounter—one imagines the agent would have preferred to keep deferring by phone until Wright lost interest or got the message—denies Wright even the righteousness of his rage. Everyone involved feels bad—Wright, his white hosts, the realtor. Yet no amount of feeling can change the outcome: that Wright cannot buy the home he desires because he is black.

Although Wright viscerally described redlining and its harms in his earlier books, his intellectual and aesthetic work failed to prepare him for his own confusing and tumultuous experience of housing discrimination. But the unspecified, if no less racking, "feeling" it triggers in him—seeming to mark both the depth of his longing for property as well as the world-shattering pain of its denial—is oddly underdescribed. Though this feeling is so powerful that it causes him to leave the U.S. forever, Wright can only gesture to its form as a "feeling" without any further elaboration of its tenor beyond a sense of "depth." For a writer much experienced in representing interiority, particularly of those racked with despair, Wright's occlusion of the substance of this feeling leading to his permanent exile is noteworthy. Was the experience of property found and lost so distinctive a feeling that it defied description? Or was it so common a sensation that this final instance was merely the last straw?

Wright does not answer these questions, rendering his feeling for property as something immense if unrepresentable. But another writer working in the 1950s would make black midcentury attachments to property the central subject of her literary investigation. In her 1959 play, *A Raisin in the Sun*, Lorraine Hansberry explores the force of property's affective power, the difficulty of dissolving one's feeling for it, and the uneven consequences of severing those attachments. Like Cheever's Shady Hill stories privileging neighborhood formation, Hansberry seeks to represent the diverse experiences of property attachment across a varied community of black Chicagoans. But whereas Cheever depicts neighborhood formation as a process of racial formation, Hansberry focuses on the neighborhood deformations catalyzed by redlining and what new raced imaginaries of liberation might emerge in its wake. Hansberry sits with her characters' property aspirations to better understand the fullness of what was at stake in this faith and the possibility for reorienting or troubling it without destroying their will for progress in the process. As I'll argue in this section, the tenderness with which Hansberry renders and carefully troubles her characters' feelings for property is best understood by attending to one of the play's least considered characters—the smug, well-off, but undeniably knowing George Murchison.

Hansberry is undergoing a much-deserved renaissance. A queer radical miscast for much of her life—and death—as an accommodationist making middle-of-the road art, her work has been long overdue for reexamination. Much recent work on Hansberry emphasizes how much more there was to her work beyond *A Raisin in the Sun*—a text at the heart of the canons of both twentieth-century theater and African American literature.[89] Both Soyica Diggs Colbert and Imani Perry have recently attended to *Raisin* in fresh ways while simultaneously painting a fuller picture of Hansberry's output. But the need to go beyond *Raisin* to find the real Hansberry remains central to their missions. And Perry and Colbert are in good company. Their desire to transcend *Raisin* is an old one, dating back to the play's early days of mass popularity when fans and critics of the play were equally stymied by and stuck on its immense reach. As Mollie Godfrey's collection of interviews with Hansberry reveals, in the early years of the play's reception, interviewers and reviewers incessantly questioned its hype even as they continued to feed it. Even Hansberry expressed weariness of the juggernaut of *Raisin*, affirming in a 1960 note in all caps, "I AM BORED TO DEATH WITH *A RAISIN IN THE SUN*."[90]

And yet, the unfinished business of this play lingers—a work easy to underestimate when removed from the context of Hansberry's life and politics, concurrent debates about the place of liberalism and radicalism in the struggle for black liberation, and the recent reign of mass homeownership remaking race and its perceptual norms. Rather than attempting to recuperate the play's radical interventions to be more in line with Hansberry's politics or insisting on the play's interstitial place within her fuller oeuvre, I read *Raisin* as Hansberry's attempt to understand the complexities of feelings for and about property and its capacity to serve as both tether and tinder for black visions of liberation. And few were better equipped than Hansberry to capture the specific hue of cruel optimism endemic to black property relations at midcentury. The child of one of the most successful black property dealers in the Midwest, Hansberry blamed her father's early demise at age fifty on the bitterness he experienced in the wake of capitalism's broken promises underwritten by white supremacy.[91] Residential property failed to save Carl Hansberry Sr. from the yoked pains and limitations of racism and capitalism further maintained by the real estate market through which he earned his substantial living.

Reading the play both with and against the grain of Hansberry's own statements and her family's ongoing ties to the real estate industry post-*Raisin*, this section looks for Lorraine—and her theorizations about the place of property in black freedom struggles—in a figure we have yet to really see: *Raisin*'s white-shoed, silver-spooned George Murchison. Although a minor character, Murchison, as a representative of the black bourgeoisie, bears the most biographical resemblance to Hansberry. Yet it would have been easy for Hansberry to reduce Murchison to an incorrigible villain. Such a choice would have been in keeping with the tradition of Western mortgage melodramas in which landed characters mercilessly wield their leverage over the dispossessed. But while a figure of farce, George is no villain or even a major antagonist. Hansberry paid for this choice, which contributed to the brutal critiques by those on the left who accused *Raisin* of fetishizing property as the cure for all that ails black life.

But I find in Hansberry's portrayal an unshakable if ever-so-slight tenderness toward George Murchison, a small emotional slant we might wield as a lens for seeing Hansberry's careful navigation of black attachment to property. Hansberry takes these emotional bonds seriously while also constructing alternative visions of sovereignty, inheritance, and desire with the potential to dislodge property's centrality to black freedom dreams dating back to Emancipation's promises of forty acres and a mule. In rebalancing Walter, Lena, and Beneatha's feelings about property's possibilities with a focus on Murchison's property realities, we see the fuller picture the play paints of black property feeling in the age of mass homeownership. Hansberry experiments with how such feelings might be managed, remade, or replaced, while refusing to dismiss or reject them outrightly as the swift puncturing of the Younger's property yearnings may prove even more harmful for the long-term prospect of radical politics. One cannot build new visions of uplift, Hansberry warns, without reckoning with the afterlives of preceding infrastructures for black liberation even as they dry, fester, stink, crust over, and perhaps explode as Langston Hughes's eponymous poem suggests.

A Play About Real Estate

It irked Lorraine Hansberry when critics referred to *A Raisin in the Sun* as a play about real estate. While this might seem like a fairly neutral description to us today, reducing the play to this thematic was a tactic that critics on the left used to dismiss *Raisin* as nothing more than bourgeois melodrama. Take the critiques launched by then-LeRoi Jones, who deemed *Raisin* a "middle class" play fetishizing "moving into white folks' neighborhood"; Nelson Algren, who called it nothing more than a "good drama about real estate" about "how good it would be for everybody if white property owners and investors would let a certain quota of Negroes into the game"; Jonas Mekas, who denigrated *Raisin* in the *Village Voice* for positing that the "ideal of the Negro is to get into one of those suburban houses advertised in the *Saturday Evening Post*, with lawns, good neighbors, and rosy kitchens"; or Harold Cruse, who dismissed the work as "an 'all-Negro' play about a family in the throes of integrating into a white community."[92] In her 1961 article for the *Village Voice*, "Genet, Mailer, & the New Paternalism," Hansberry strikes back at such readings of *Raisin* as "a play about 'insurance money' and/or 'real estate'" as guilty of "absurdity," a crime made "a little less frightening only by the knowledge that there are people who sincerely believe that *Othello* is a play about a handkerchief."[93]

Despite Hansberry's recoil from this framework, it seems possible to reclaim *Raisin* as a play about real estate without also implying it is inherently trivial, melodramatic, or liberal in its politics. Given the entanglement of property and the construction of race from the Enlightenment forward, this reclamation is not meant to dismiss the play but to wield it as a lens to better understand this historic entanglement amid its late-1950s inflection when the successful racial project of mass homeownership had begun to remake racial experience, definition, and perception. To approach *Raisin* as a play about real estate in these terms is to resituate the play's efforts to work through the deep aporias attending the relationship between property, race, feeling, and rights in the period. While some critics preferred to scoff at the desires of the black bourgeoisie and its pretenders, Hansberry approached black attachments to property—financial, familial, and affective in nature—as the deadly serious affairs they were and continued to be for many, including to those whom Hansberry personally knew and loved. Despite her own more radical horizons, she warns, we dismiss black attachment to property at our peril.

To reclaim the play as being "about" real estate, moreover, is to recognize Hansberry's own knowledge of this industry despite the touchiness of this subject for her for much of her life. The broad strokes of the Hansberrys' property dealings are well-known. The real-life landmark 1940 Supreme Court case centering on the right of the Hansberry family to occupy the home they purchased in the white Chicago neighborhood of Woodlawn informed the Youngers' integration plotline. Lorraine's father, Carl Hansberry Sr., earned his modest wealth enabling his family's act of integration by flipping and managing Chicago kitchenette buildings akin to the one the Youngers are desperate to escape. Lorraine thus knew firsthand about the housing profits to be reaped across the color line. Carl Hansberry's legacy remains vexed—he provided housing to a black population desperately in need of it due to redlining's confining commandments while building a business profiting from these exploitative conditions.[94]

Hansberry Enterprises survived Carl Hansberry's 1946 death manned by Lorraine's siblings. When she was named in a suit the city of Chicago filed against the company in 1958 charging forty-two counts of building code violations, the Hansberry family immediately moved to protect Lorraine, then in the middle of supervising *Raisin*'s early previews and on the brink of success, by having her removed as a defendant. Although she would come to relinquish all shares of the company—assets that helped support her during her early days in New York—the letters Lorraine continued to receive from her siblings after her formal exit from the company kept her in the loop about their maneuvers. As late as 1962, Lorraine's family asked her to supply a statement of assets, which she speculated in a letter to her lawyer was a way for her siblings to demonstrate "'credit strength' to somebody with regard to the purchase of some property of consequence."[95] Though she did not "wish to be associated with any of their purchases or enterprises," her lawyer nonetheless complied with this request on her behalf. Lorraine might have been legally clear of Hansberry Enterprises, but both *Raisin* and her family correspondence speak to her ongoing aesthetic, familial, and financial ties to the family business.

Locating Hansberry's subject position in *Raisin* has been a popular critical pastime since the play's debut. Beneatha is most often pegged as Hansberry's surrogate given their shared restlessness, followed closely by her other suitor, Asagai, whose commitment to thinking black struggle in diasporic terms mirrors Hansberry's own position. But in terms of upbringing, Hansberry's biography most mirrors that of George Murchison. In fact, in a contentious 1959 interview with Mike Wallace, Hansberry indicates just this. In response to Wallace's question "Is there none of you in your play?" Hansberry answers, "George Mur— the young suitor, you know"—responding as if she was unsure as to whether George's name would even register to Wallace given the smallness of his role in the play.[96] Wallace responds to Hansberry with seeming disbelief, "The young suitor?" causing Hansberry to respond: "The college student." Wallace then goes on to openly disagree: "I thought the young college girl, Beneatha," citing a previous interview where Hansberry referred to Beneatha as "me eight years ago," an association Hansberry goes on to also acknowledge and explain, without any further mention of George.[97]

But George is more complex than his minor status in the play requires. Viewers might expect the ostentatious Murchison to serve as the show's archvillain given ages of theatrical precedent pitting the propertied against precarious lessees. But Hansberry refuses this trope. By the play's first act, Beneatha rules out marrying George, dashing notions that their union would fuel the Youngers' future social mobility. The Murchison family, moreover, wields no direct power over the Youngers. Though they earn their living from property, the Murchisons do not hold the lease to the kitchenette where the Youngers have lived for decades. In fact, the play withholds the building owner's identity—a canny omission on Hansberry's part.[98] Making the owners of the Youngers' kitchenette black, a choice reflective of her father's status, would have tilted the play's focus away from the broader exploitation of the Youngers at the hands of a housing system designed to keep them in place. Rendering the building's owners white, however, would have elicited accusations of hypocrisy given Carl Hansberry's kitchenette empire. So she sidesteps this decision entirely, leaving the Murchisons to more mutedly register class difference within the black community next to the Youngers.

Beyond the Murchison family's role as fraught figures of aspiration for the Youngers, leading to their treatment as both models and punching bags, critics have found few reasons for their existence in *Raisin* at all. As Hansberry biographer Charles Shields argues of George Jr., "Murchison actually serves no serious purpose in the play except as a straw man to make a point" about the dangers of black consumerism.[99] When this character has garnered attention, critics have generally applauded Hansberry's skilled deflation of his airs. Houston Baker refers to George Murchison's appearance in the play as "masterfully satirized," while Amiri Baraka deemed "the clash between Walter Lee and George one of the high points of class struggle in the play and a dramatic tour de force," giving us "the dialogue between the sons of the house and of the field slave."[100] Because George "thinks he is 'cool,'" as Baraka writes, "he does not understand he is corny."[101] Helene Keyssar more pointedly frames George as an interloper within the Youngers' inner sanctum who baits the audience to turn on him, thus bringing them closer to the Youngers. "His presence is as unwelcome and inappropriate in this world as would be the sudden entrance of the corporation—General Motors—that his initials signify."[102]

In the archive that Hansberry's ex-husband, Robert Nemiroff, kept of her own materials as well as critical responses to her work after her death, he placed a question mark and exclamation mark next to Keyssar's reading of Murchison.[103] In keeping with his larger annotation habits, these marks seem to signify his bemused befuddlement at Keyssar's assessment. Much in the play supports Nemiroff's skeptical response. Casting Murchison as the play's ultimate outsider does a disservice to his actual reception by the Youngers in the play. Beneatha refers to George as a "fool"—a term marking his status as a social climber interested in pedigree over substance, credentials over actual knowledge, who is clearly mismatched with the searching Beneatha.[104] But despite being introduced in the play as beautiful, wealthy, and shallow—called an "assimilationist Negro" to his face during his first scene onstage—George falls short of full roguedom.[105] He may be a fool, but he is not guilty of ignorance; he can name as many African tribes and empires as Beneatha, for instance, proving he is as aware of the debates and discourses that enchant her even if they bore him. And although Walter and George spar, Walter continues to advocate for George as a suitor up until *Raisin*'s end. He even uses his second-to-last utterance in the play to implore Beneatha, if with a provoking smile, to reconsider his strengths as a husband. George may be a fool, but Hansberry ultimately seems to suggest there are bigger, more systemic and global fish to fry when understanding the Youngers' plight.

This position tracks with Hansberry's other statements about the relationship between working- and middle-class African Americans in which she downplays the idea of a large chasm between these two groups while defending the black middle class against critiques that their growing consumerism was a lamentable sign of spiritual and social decay—a critique Hansberry found demeaning and a distraction from more pressing issues of white supremacy and colonialism facing black diasporic subjects.[106] In Hansberry's assessment, shaped by E. Franklin Frazier's 1955 study, *The Black Bourgeoisie*, racism's limitations blunted the distance between the black middle and lower classes, rendering white faux concern about black bourgeois consumerism an act of bad faith purposefully overlooking the gulf between the opportunities afforded to the middle class across the color line.

If George is a distraction, he's one that the play insists we reckon with by making him more than just a villain or a buffoon. Whereas the Youngers are replete with self-delusion, George has a sharp sense of himself and others, even if one disagrees with his positions. The possessor of a keen social and aesthetic sensorium, George's minor presence in *Raisin* helps illuminate both the possibilities and limitations of the black property imaginary within the play in concert with the divergent property sensibilities of the Youngers. The Murchisons' property prowess can't be easily dismissed, just as Walter's unceasing hunger for their prestige and trappings fail to easily recede. Given her own radical commitments, Hansberry understood that the road to black liberation might not run through the terrain of property rights. But neither would black liberation be won (or be taken) by ignoring property's hold on the black imaginary as the path to the good life. Hansberry acknowledges the cruel optimism of black property dreams by tuning us in again and again to the painful tenor of its cruelty. Long before Walter's compromised if no less important choice to move to Clybourne Park at the end of Act 3, the pain of choosing property as well as the powerlessness to choose elsewise haunts the play. The shallow depths of George Murchison prove key to producing this cumulative atmosphere.

The wealth of the Murchisons enters the play before George does. When George is first referred to in Act 1 as Beneatha's date for the following evening, the word *rich* appears in this short burst of dialogue six times. Although heavily referenced, the source of the Murchisons' wealth is not disclosed until Act 2, when George first appears onstage. Walter reveals this information when he asks George about his "old man" before alluding to speculation that his family is "going to buy that big hotel on the Drive."[107] Though we are told little else about the nature of the Murchisons' business, this detail leads us to assume the family deals in real estate. The close parallels between the Murchisons' fictional hotel purchase and the concurrent efforts of Hansberry Enterprises further support this correlation. At the time of *Raisin*'s writing, Lorraine's oldest brother, Carl Jr., was working to acquire the Pershing Hotel on the South Side of Chicago. Lorraine's sister, Mamie, wrote her early in 1961 about the ongoing deal: "It appears that the Pershing Hotel from our correspondence and phone conversation with Carl will eventually be a *Raisin* success, although there are growing pains with this venture."[108] Mamie followed up about the hotel in a letter a few weeks later: "As luck would have it the Hotel was our best bet and gave us very good credit on the West Coast along with being *Raisin*'s sister which hit about right."[109] But the deal, which Mamie signals is entangled with her sister's hit play in both metaphoric and material terms, would soon sour. Hansberry Enterprises fell behind on utility payments and abandoned the Pershing to their creditors.

Despite Mamie's optimism, Hansberry's past experiences with the family business likely led her to intuit this outcome for the Pershing. Reading the correspondence between Hansberry and her siblings gives one the impression that their frantic proclivity for "big plans" that more often than not end poorly is more in keeping with the blinding ambition of Walter Younger than the cool stability associated with the Murchisons.[110] The ongoing enmeshment of not just Lorraine but her play in Hansberry Enterprises' real estate schemes—as Mamie's letter demonstrates, it was common for her siblings to use the play for cultural and, at times, economic collateral in the funding of new property development opportunities—underscores the tension between her family's attachment to the business of property and her wish to live elsewise.[111]

Hansberry's play thus didn't just represent the drive for black homeownership; rather, the success of *Raisin* helped the Hansberry siblings fund further residential business opportunities, with or without Lorraine's explicit endorsement. While the play has been both lauded and critiqued for the ability of the Youngers' ownership plight to touch white viewer's hearts enough to reconsider their stance on residential integration, we might consider the play's other, more brass-tacks, takeaway: that a large subset of black renters sought to flee the black belt at any cost, a desire backstopped by deep cultural attachments to property's significance in excess of its financial sensibility. This is the knowledge that developers like the Hansberrys as well as blockbusters, realtors, and lenders across the color line had already capitalized upon to great recompense. Despite Karl Lindner's attempt toward the end of the play to disentangle emotion from segregation by offering the Youngers what he considers a generous deal that would also spare them from experiencing the ire of their new neighbors, the play suggests that black attachment to property exceeds either economic or social circumstance and that white faith in the "rule" of black devaluation is similarly hard to dislodge. No matter their means—whether desperate and with little capital as the Youngers have lived, or as a generationally propertied family that has been both hurt and rewarded by residential investment—a keenness for ownership saturates the Youngers, Murchisons, and Hansberrys across their class positions.

Though Walter Younger particularly longs to command property in the manner of the Murchisons, the two families approach the value of residential property differently. Just as Big Walter's absence haunts the play as a defining presence, with his death financing the surviving Youngers' financial opportunities, so too does the absent elder Mr. Murchison hover over *Raisin*. Walter fetishizes this unseen figure as someone who "knows how to operate," "thinks big," and is the one man "on this whole South Side who understands my kind of thinking."[112] If the Murchisons' portfolio was anything like that of Hansberry Enterprises, this "big thinking" largely took the form of residential property deals including hotels but also rental properties, flipped kitchenettes, and new black housing developments that Lorraine's brother Perry Hansberry worked on in Compton, California, in the early 1960s. Like the Hansberrys, *Raisin* suggests that the Murchisons approached the residential as a site of speculation with the potential for large profit margins. Although the play doesn't tell us where the Murchisons live—we presume they have a higher quality of life than the Youngers wherever they reside—it makes a point of establishing that their means for making a living is tied to residential investments.

The Murchisons' entrepreneurial approach to the residential is a far cry from how members of the Younger family consider such spaces. Let's begin with Walter, who, for much of the play, fails to view his mother's home purchase as a financial asset. While both the house in Clybourne Park and the liquor store he longs to own are both investments that could rise in value over time, Walter only understands the liquor store in these terms. Not only is Walter unable to see homeownership as an investment, but he approaches it as a loss of capital taking resources away from his speculative endeavor. To Walter, Mama's choice to invest in Clybourne Park is a choice to not invest in him. Perhaps Walter's job as a chauffeur, whose meager spoils have amounted to "stories about how rich people live," as he insists, has made it hard for him to think the residential outside of his own experiences of limitation.[113] But gender also seems to shape Walter's narrow view of residential investment. His wife, Ruth, suggests as much when she mockingly insists to him, "So you would rather *be* Mr. Arnold than be his chauffeur. So—I would rather be living in Buckingham palace."[114] Though she aggrandizes their divergent ambitions, these lines point to the core distinction between her dream of the good life and Walter's. Ruth's aspirations are anchored by residential living, while Walter's revolve around the active performance of "doing business" in "downtown offices." Walter leans into the gendered nature of their viewpoints, chastising Ruth as a stand-in for "the colored woman in this world" in general who "don't understand about building their men up and making 'em feel like they somebody."[115] If the home remains the horizon of black ambition, Walter warns, the race will fail to advance. "Colored people ain't never going to start getting ahead till they start gambling on some different kinds of things in the world—investments and things."[116] Walter best sums up his economic philosophy in Act 2: "Invest big, gamble big, hell, lose big if you have to."[117] To Walter, the owned home is a spoil of enterprise, not its source.

But Mama and Ruth also fail to view the home as an investment. They describe seeking somewhere to live where they can garden and with fewer rats, but not necessarily a longing to own a home or for the long-term equity it might accrue. Due to the fragile protections offered by the mortgage form, buying presents the family with their best and most affordable chance of escaping the redlined enclosure of the black belt and its attendant lack of resources. Despite their recent windfall, buying a home in a black neighborhood remains out of reach. "Them houses they put up for colored in them areas way out," Mama explains, "all seem to cost twice as much as other houses."[118] If renting or public housing allowed them decent dwelling and the ability to tend a garden, the Youngers might have just as eagerly jumped at those opportunities to escape their kitchenette. Mama's brief reflections on her initial residential aspirations further point to her non-actuarial approach to homeownership. She recalls her and Big Walter plan upon arriving in Chicago in the 1920s to "buy a little place out in Morgan Park," located on Chicago's far South Side. "We had even picked out the house," she notes, before admitting it "looks right dumpy today."[119] This house no longer has the same sheen, but

Mama nonetheless fondly recalls to Ruth "the dreams I had 'bout buying that house and fixing it up and making me a little garden in the back."[120] Though the house might have ultimately been a bad bet—her acknowledgment of its current "dumpy" appearance suggests that either her original judgment of the home was wrong, or the home has depreciated in the decades since she dreamed of owning it—her ownership dream was never about investing in a specific property but in the kind of life it afforded the family in terms of space, beauty, privacy, and peace.[121] Unlike Walter's individualist dream of business prowess making homeownership a secondary asset in his eyes, Mama and Ruth associate the residential with the family's collective security. The owned home falls short as a form of "big investment" for Walter, while Ruth and Mama see the home as a site of comfortable stasis that may not earn them anything in the long run other than the pleasure, dignity, and safety they derive from its occupancy.

The Clybourne Park home becomes understood by Walter as an investment only after he has lost the rest of the insurance money. When Walter first reveals his intentions to accept the Clybourne Park Improvement Association's offer to "buy the house from you at a financial gain to your family," marking Walter's emotional nadir in *Raisin*, he describes himself as "going to do business."[122] This phrase, dripping with irony, finds Walter framing homeownership as a financial asset only in his darkest and most desperate hour. Far from the kind of business he dreamed of conducting, his willingness to make a deal with Lindner points to how far he has fallen. And yet, under different circumstances, accepting the buyout offer could be viewed as a successful act of speculation, the exact result of the kind of business "gamble" Walter admires. As detailed in the previous chapter, speculative "blockbusters" across the color line were doing just this on a scaled-up level, purchasing properties in "vulnerable" white neighborhoods to force spooked neighbors to buy them out or push other white sellers to sell cheaply and flip the neighborhood entirely. The black neighborhoods in which the Youngers still cannot afford to buy were likely created in just this way. In the long term, given the likelihood Clybourne Park would "change over" with the Youngers' occupancy—a change historically followed by massive disinvestment in South Side neighborhoods—taking Linder's deal might have ultimately resulted in the best economic outcome for the Youngers.[123] Someone with the property orientation of the Hansberrys or the Murchisons might have accepted the offer with no hard feelings, using the profit from the Clybourne Park home to flip a home or kitchenette elsewhere.

But despite Lorraine Hansberry's own politics, she commits to the necessity of Walter's defense of the Youngers' homeownership dreams. His Act 3 refusal to sell also signals Walter's conscious rejection of wealth-seeking as the horizon of his aspirations, leaving the door open for other, more communally formed priorities. In her 1959 *Village Voice* essay "Willie Loman, Walter Younger, and He Who Must Live," Hansberry reflects on the insufficiency of Walter's options at this moment in the play by elaborating on his limited courses of action. After losing the insurance money, Walter could "don the saffron robes of acceptance and sit on a mountain top all day contemplating the divine justice of his misery," Hansberry writes. Or he "might wander down to his first Communist Party meeting," as one of *Raisin*'s theatrical predecessors, Theodore Ward's 1937 *Big White Fog*, posits as its resolution.[124] But she insists that for someone of Walter Lee's background, "revolution seems alien to him and his circumstances, and it is easier to dream of personal wealth than of a communal state wherein universal dignity is supposed to be a corollary."[125] The only other realistic alternative for Walter's redemption in the play, Hansberry suggests, is for him to "take his place on any one of a number of frontiers of challenge. Challenges (such as helping to break down restricted neighborhoods) which are admittedly limited because they most certainly do not threaten the basic order."[126]

For all the limitations surrounding Walter's choice to reject Lindner's offer, Hansberry frames his ability to make this final decision as distinguishing Walter's enlivening position at *Raisin*'s end from Willy Loman's choice to take his own life in Arthur Miller's 1949 play, *Death of a Salesman*. Walter's choice to move to Clybourne Park does not necessarily serve him personally—he never really wanted the house after all—but he makes it on behalf of his family. In arriving at this decision, Walter draws on what Hansberry describes as "the strength of an incredible people who, historically, have simply refused to give up."[127] "The symbolism of moving into the new house," she admits, "is quite as small as it seems and quite as significant."[128] But in his "tiny moment" of refusing Lindner's offer, Walter catches "that sweet essence which is human dignity," which Hansberry further extrapolates as his acceptance of an Ellisonian "American responsibility."[129] Ever the realist, Hansberry was not interested in a dogmatic ending whose sudden prescription of socialism would have rung untrue for the Youngers and those like them whose faith in property as a symbol and a sanctuary is not so easily dashed. For the Youngers, selling their home for profit to whites seeking their exclusion would be a tacit acknowledgment of their inferiority. As Mama says, "I come from five generations of people who was slaves and sharecroppers—but ain't nobody in my family never let nobody pay 'em no money that was a way of telling us we wasn't fit to walk the earth. We ain't never been that poor. We ain't never been that—dead inside."[130] This genealogical line spanning from the agricultural to the residential is yoked by an enduring commitment to a progressive vision of equality steered by increasing property rights. In these terms, as Hansberry limns, accepting money to abandon property that should rightfully be yours is a form of suicide.

With the Soviet Union's fading power as an aspirational alternative to American liberalism and the winning of key civil rights victories, Hansberry seemed to recognize that persuading black Americans to give up on property's promises in this moment was a losing feat. "I deliberately chose the class background of the people who are the characters in *A Raisin in the Sun*," Hansberry explained to Mike Wallace, "because my own particular point of view is that most of what we hope for as a people, most of what we hope for, our ultimate stature as a people, is going to come from these people who are the base, the backbone of our people."[131] Like Richard Wright before her, Hansberry recognized that the Youngers and those they represent—as opposed to the Murchisons or the Hansberrys—were the engines of black liberation. But whereas the Richard Wright of 1941 found revolutionary potential in the black folk's alienation from property, forcing them to forge other forms of community, both Hansberry and Wright by the 1950s accepted private ownership's integral role within the structure of black aspiration and, by extension, struggle. Hansberry chose to acknowledge black attachments to property as the current terrain of battle rather than dismissing this terrain or those who found it meaningful. Understanding and mobilizing the black base, she suggests, requires understanding the symbolic power of property once tethered to land but increasingly being refastened to residential homes. Such an approach is the difference between waiting for a dream deferred to explode—destroying the dreamer in the process—or mapping the structure of the dream to gradually work from within it to remold its parameters.

This is not to say that Hansberry fully cedes a critique of property in *Raisin* or gives up on limning other forms of dignified living. Take, for instance, the alternative ending to *Raisin* she considered. Rather than concluding with the Youngers joyously, if anxiously, packing their belongings for the move to Clybourne Park, Hansberry entertained flashing forward to the family's armed entrenchment within their new home. Likely too dark for her Broadway backers despite reflecting her own recollection of her mother's armed defense of their Woodlawn home, this scrapped ending points to the possibility of black radicalization *through* ownership—it is the dream attained rather than the dream deferred that explodes—forcing black owners to meet violence with violence. Hansberry was often pushed in interviews in this period to denounce more militant strands of black nationalism, and she didn't shy away from these provocations—as she said to Mike Wallace, "people who are just coming into their own in the world must be as dramatic about it as they possibly can, must embrace all causes, must embrace all methods."[132] As her scrapped ending suggests, seeing the property faith of the Youngers through to its violent conclusion has the potential to give way to an even more militant position when it turns out that the price of the Youngers' faith is ever-more-steeled battle.

But other alternatives to the American Dream emerge in the play beyond this amended ending. Soyica Diggs Colbert powerfully attests to the play's attention to the price of their ticket out of the black belt—Big Walter's death. That the family's sole economic opportunity comes from their patriarch's untimely demise reveals that "inhabiting freedom, in a property ownership model requires death and exploitation."[133] "The system of inheritance, the legal structures that protect it and the property rights that install it," Colbert continues, "demand not only the death of the one that bequeaths but also the extraction of resources from all of those that lead to the accumulation of wealth."[134] As Colbert argues, "Hansberry does not offer desegregation as the ultimate answer to segregation, but rather as a necessary step toward what she envisioned as 'a socialist organization of society as the next great and dearly won universal condition of mankind.'"[135] The Youngers' choice to move to Clybourne Park at the play's conclusion is not inherently a win; rather, it is Walter's ability to make the decision that best honors the values of his people that Hansberry allows the audience to celebrate while still recognizing the compromised nature of his choice. While the American Dream anchored by property may ultimately mean the deferral of dreams of black liberation beyond property, the move to Clybourne Park at least gives the Youngers the emotional energy to fight another day. But this choice is not without cost. "Motivated but not limited by her father's legacy," Colbert writes, "Hansberry produced the shadow figure of Big Walter to personalize the physical losses that accrue through freedom movements to emphasize that transfer of property does not amount to liberation." She concludes that "in Hansberry's play, the transfer of property functions as a freedom practice that positions the Youngers to struggle in a complicated terrain."[136]

Asagai is also key to limning this terrain. As Hansberry described to Mike Wallace, "Walter Lee Younger and his family are necessarily tied to this international movement. Whether they have consciousness of it or not they belong to an affirmative movement in history."[137] Asagai's description of his relationship to his home village serves to further reposition the Youngers' struggles. As Colbert points out, the exchange between Beneatha and Asagai in Act 3 features the play's most explicit acknowledgment of the limits of the property system, with Asagai gently insisting in reference to Big Walter, "isn't there something wrong in a house—in a world—where all dreams, good or bad, must depend on the death of a man?"[138] If "equal access to private property—either through inheritance or purchase—has proven a stumbling block in Black freedom struggles" as Colbert concludes, Asagai's long-view orientation toward emancipation evokes the possibility of another approach.[139] He advocates not for a specific vision of progress but for forward motion itself, no matter how uneven and erratic its tempo may be or how unpredictable its immediate content. The work Asagai envisions carrying out in his home village will effect change both "slowly and swiftly," sometimes seeming as if "nothing changes at all . . . and then again the sudden dramatic events which make history leap into the future. And then quiet again"[140] The outcome of these actions is unknown and he risks his own ruin in the process; yet, Asagai insists, one must fight to move forward nonetheless despite this unknowability. It is in moving toward change, whatever the goal or speed, that prevents the deadening stasis of accepting the conditions of the present. While Walter's choice is limited and desegregation is a compromised accomplishment, it is nonetheless enlivening as a form of motion. If finding an out to the property system was less viable in the 1950s than in preceding decades, Hansberry suggests, one must work within the limits of that system until the next opening emerges. This is not a choice of liberalism over radicalism, but rather a recognition of the erratic time stamp of revolutionary struggle.[141]

In line with such an approach, even the George Murchisons of the world have a role to play. Following Asagai's lesson in the broad and erratic landscape of struggle, we can return to George to consider his contributions within this widened terrain. Though the two are positioned as foils for much of *Raisin*, Asagai gives us the tools for envisioning George's possible contributions within this longue durée of struggle. Enter George's queer vision, which has the potential to exceed, complicate, or warp his immediate property attachments. George's sexuality is mentioned once in the play, in a context designed to insult him. When George refuses to drink with Walter, Walter vindictively responds through a form of studied menace. He begins by studying Murchison "from head to toe," an act of visual scrutiny Hansberry fleshes out in her stage directions detailing George's "carefully casual tweed sports jacket over cashmere V-neck sweater over soft eyelet shirt and tie, and soft slacks, finished off with white buckskin shoes."[142] Walter uses this sartorial inventory to insult George: "Why all you college boys wear them faggoty-looking white shoes?"[143] Though he softens his critique by indicting Beneatha's fashion choices as well, noting that George's shoes "look as funny as them black knee socks Beneatha wears out of here all the time," Walter's reproach of his sister lacks the same spiteful tenor of his remark about George's sexuality designed to also question his masculinity.[144]

George's sartorial performance of assimilation, materializing the fault line of class that divides the black community, turns into a proxy fight about sexuality. George's stoicism in the face of his goading is worth noting. George does not recoil following Walter's slur. Nor does he butch up his self-presentation, return the insult, or deny Walter's insinuation in any way. He simply ignores Walter. For the rest of the scene, George is described as treating Walter with "boredom," "indifference," and "distaste" while appearing "a little above it all." Walter's remaining lines to George in the scene, by contrast, come out "bitterly, hurt," "passionately and suddenly," "intently," and "violently." Critics like Houston Baker and Amiri Baraka have relished Hansberry's satirical representation of George, leaving it unclear as to whether they cosign her portrait of George or Walter's homophobic representation of his difference. Others have dwelled on the audience's alleged lack of sympathy for George. But this moment in *Raisin* seems to defy both readings. Walter's erratic emotionality across the play underscores his own fragile sense of his masculinity—a point that Walter himself continually insists upon in the play—while George's solid performance of impassivity in the form of homophobic baiting, while underscoring the privilege enabling his indifference, also points to George's quiet strength. His interaction with Walter doesn't drive him away from the Youngers; he returns to their apartment a few weeks later to continue to court Beneatha. Maneuvering the depths of Walter's pain is the price of his entanglement with the Youngers.

Whether George's sexuality is in any real question in the play following Walter's comment is unclear. His later efforts to kiss Beneatha in private signals his romantic interest in her, but whether this fully defines his sexuality is ambiguous. George is, moreover, the play's foremost aesthete. Though we know relatively little about George, the glimpses we receive of him in the play most strongly attest to the intensity of his cultural commitments. He is a lover of theater in both Chicago and New York (where he goes "a few times a year"), he doesn't like beer, his insults come by way of Greek mythology and classic Hollywood cinema ("Good night, Prometheus" to Walter, "Drop the Garbo routine" to Beneatha), and he is the first to see the chic appeal of Beneatha's natural hair ("I like it. It's sharp—it really is").[145] George's stylish, potentially effete taste renders him lacking in the eyes of Walter, while serving as the primary source of connection between him and Beneatha when they seem to share little else. Though George's sexuality remains unresolved within the play, there is a queerness to George—a way of being yoked to his class status but also in excess of that status alone—to which both Walter as character and Hansberry as playwright differently attend in the play.

When viewed as the queer progeny of a black property mogul, George Murchison's connections to Lorraine Hansberry grow stronger, especially in light of what we now know about Hansberry's exploration of her own queerness in this period as well her unwillingness to do so publicly. But George's final substantial lines in the play declaring his instrumental relationship to education ("You read books—to learn facts—to get grades—to pass the course—to get a degree. That's all—it has nothing to do with thoughts") also underscore their differences.[146] Though George is certainly no hero in the play, he is no more of a villain than Walter. Like most of her characters, Hansberry prefers to illuminate George than judge him. But following the expanded terrain of struggle invoked by Asagai, the play urges us to consider to what other uses might George's keen eye and canny sensibility be put. While George has the least developed diasporic imaginary in the play (see his insistence to Beneatha that "your heritage is nothing but a bunch of raggedy-assed spirituals and some grass huts!") he seems genuinely interested in Beneatha, dating her despite the friction derived from their class difference.[147] One imagines George's life would certainly have been eased by dating someone of his own status, yet he remains persistent in his pursuit of Beneatha. His love of culture coupled with his disinterest in discussing his family's business deal, moreover, points to the prickliness surrounding his own relationship to his propertied family. Though George represents the black bourgeoisie, the nature of his enjoyment of this status seems to derive from the aesthetic opportunities it grants him more than a particular enjoyment of property or its management. What could both Walter and George become in a world where ownership didn't overdetermine their future trajectories? Hansberry doesn't answer this question, but the paucity of choices attending both their situations allows *Raisin*'s audience to wonder how else their varying skills and passions might be deployed if freed from the correlated limitations of economic, sexual, and gender inequality preventing more expansive forms of solidarity from taking hold.

With *Raisin*, Hansberry recognizes the reignited power of property at midcentury overdetermining the terrain of black struggle in comparison to the relative nadir of property's hold on the black imaginary during the Cultural Front years of the 1930s and '40s. Her play maps a way forward within the constricted and residentially oriented terms of the present that doesn't leave either the Youngers or the Murchisons behind. Unlike Richard Wright or even her friend James Baldwin, exile was not a viable response to American racism in Hansberry's eyes. Nor was lambasting the black bourgeoisie or the bourgeois-adjacent desires of the black working class, as Baraka and Cruse at times advocated. Like her friend and fellow author Paule Marshall, whose 1959 novel, *Brown Girl, Brownstones*, similarly turns a critical if empathetic eye to the property aspirations of her parents' generation, Hansberry prioritizes capturing the depth of feeling surrounding black property attachment and the correlated struggles for dignity, sovereignty, self-determination, and equality that property rights have come to stand in for.[148] It is only in recognizing all that property signifies that one can start to imagine disentangling these other values from the right to own, which is fundamentally the right to exclude. Understanding the depth and nature of black attachment to property across class, gender, generations, and orientations, Hansberry suggests, is a necessary first step to mobilizing this attachment for revolutionary struggle beyond the immediate frontier of redlining and the right to own. The play's melancholic ending—characterized by the joy of Walter's dignity-bestowing choice mingled with the anxiety encircling their move to Clybourne Park, foreshadowed at several times in the play to portend bombings and unrest—points to the ongoing battles still to be fought by the Youngers. The spoils of private property will not result in their equal treatment within the social, economic, or legal regimes. But while this tragic truth hovers over the play's conclusion, Hansberry refuses to disrespect her characters' visions of the good life and the optimism they harbor for it. Though their disillusionment with the promises of the residential as a black family is likely imminent, this immediate victory is key to their ability to weather the coming storm and perhaps find their way to other kinds of attachments when this one fails.

Though this section has primarily focused on George Murchison, I want to conclude by turning to the two characters in the play who harbor the greatest faith in residential homeownership's transformational power—Mama and Ruth. As I have already traced, all of *Raisin*'s other major characters locate their ambitions elsewhere. Walter's primary attachment is to business, George's is to culture, while Beneatha and Asagai place their faith in a long-term if incremental commitment to a vision of progress whose content may vary over time. Only the mothers in the play seem deeply invested in the residential good life. Their attachment derives from their commitment to reproductive futurity via the family unit—both Ruth and Mama point to Travis, the youngest Younger, as the foremost beneficiary of the move—while also reflecting the traditionally gendered split between the domestic and public spheres.[149] Though her immediate priority is Travis, Mama is also careful to situate her achievement of homeownership within the larger trajectory of her ancestors when she cites the "five generations of people who was slaves and sharecroppers" as a reason they must refuse Lindner's offer and move.

Yet Mama is not without doubts about this decision. In fact, her final onstage appearance in the wake of the Youngers' residential triumph echoes Richard Wright's reaction to his ownership denial. Like Wright, Mama experiences an upsurge of emotion in the face of her residential future whose visceral quality seems to overwhelm its content and source. Mama is alone onstage in *Raisin*'s closing scene, taking in the apartment she has lived in for the last forty years one last time. Hansberry describes Mama as feeling something "suddenly, despite herself" in this moment, a sensation Hansberry proceeds to flesh out as "a great heaving thing rises in her" that she "puts her fist to her mouth to stifle."[150] Whether one has, like Wright, been rebuffed by redlining or, like Mama, has managed to break through its formidable obstacles, the prospect of homeownership for both of these figures produces a feeling of such vehemence that it seems to defy explanation or description. As with Asagai's vision of progress, the content of Wright's and Mama's immediate displays of emotion at the prospect of homeownership vary. But the force of its expression overrides its signification, marking the depth of the attachment to property as both a source of incredible optimism and tremendous and unrelenting burden.

What Does Institutional Racism Look Like? The Investigative Aesthetics of Fair Housing

IN A LETTER DATED NOVEMBER 20, 1962, Leroy M. McLean wrote to the executive director of the New York City Commission on Human Rights (CCHR) to describe "the role played by so-called legitimate banks" in housing discrimination.[1] McLean wrote to the CCHR in response to its recent study of blockbusting—the practice of manipulating white owners into selling their homes cheaply out of fear of racial invasion to resell those homes to blacks at high prices. But as McLean insists, "no study on blockbusting would be complete without revealing the role played by so-called legitimate banks in this whole sorry business." "The main reason that blockbusters are able to sell at fantastic mark-ups," McLean continues, "is because they are ready and willing to finance at inflated prices while legitimate banks consistently refuse financing, even at reasonable and property selling prices, to Negroes and Puerto Ricans." He goes on to share his personal experience of lending discrimination. "Some years ago when I attempted to get a mortgage loan on an excellent property, not only did the legitimate banks turn down the request for a loan, but the mortgage officer of one attempted to steer me to one of the most notorious speculators in the area."

With his letter, McLean enclosed the loan rejections he had received from the Brevoort Savings Bank, the Dime Savings Bank of Brooklyn, and Equitable Savings and Loan Association between February and April of 1958.[2] The three short letters are nearly identical in content, with each informing McLean that his request for a mortgage loan for 1272 Park Place has been denied. They cheerfully thank him for his application and express their hope they can be of service for other banking matters in the future. None explain why his loan was denied.

McLean, whose home address is listed in these documents as 1270 Park Place, was looking to buy the home immediately next door and was well acquainted with the property and the neighborhood at large. A bit of sleuthing reveals these homes to be attached brownstones located in the Weeksville neighborhood in Brooklyn, first founded by African American freedmen in the 1830s. The neighborhood's historical legacy had largely faded by the 1950s and most of its original homes had fallen into disrepair, a condition most likely tied to the inability of residents like McLean to get loans to maintain or improve local homes.[3]

In his letter to the president of the Dime Savings Bank of Brooklyn, which he also forwarded to the CCHR, McLean makes his unhappiness with his loan denial known. Requesting to close his accounts, McLean explains, "I am convinced that you are no longer interested in serving the legitimate needs of the small property owner in this community."[4] "Although you still maintain offices in this area," he continues, "and even recently conducted an extensive campaign for new depositors in this area, attempts to secure mortgage loans from you are met with replies such as 'we are not lending mortgage money on homes in this area.'" Although he never explicitly accuses the bank of racial discrimination in his letter, McLean's reference to the bank's refusal to serve the immediate community suggests as much. But McLean is more explicit about his suspicion of the racial nature of his loan denials in a letter he sent to the black newspaper the *New York Amsterdam News* in May 1958. There McLean describes many of the banks in the city as having "a policy of not granting any substantial business or mortgage loans to Negro applicants."[5] "This policy is designed to throw the Negro into the hands of unscrupulous money lenders, Funding Corporations and loan sharks where they will be charged high rates of interest on pre-discounted loans."

In his letter to the *Amsterdam News*, McLean includes a compiled list of common responses blacks often received when rejected for a loan:

> The following may sound familiar to any Negro who has ever attempted to secure mortgage money from legitimate sources:
> 1) We are not lending in this area
> 2) We only lend on new construction
> 3) We don't lend on two family houses
> 4) We don't lend on brownstone or older houses
> 5) Our mortgage portfolio is closed at this time.

McLean seemingly accepts he will find no smoking gun proving that race—either his race or the racial makeup of the surrounding neighborhood—was the primary reason for his loan denials.[6] But his efforts to archive and circulate the paper trail of his rejections—sending copies of these materials to the CCHR four years after his original loan denial—as well as his efforts to compile the varying rationales lenders provided black loan seekers for their denials suggests the depth and breadth of his study of this more indirect if no less pervasive form of discrimination.[7]

In assembling his own bureaucratic archive and reading strategies for detecting the occluded processes of discrimination they index, McLean fashioned himself into a barometer of bureaucratic racism. The responses he amassed might not set off alarms when read in isolation, but the racial motivation behind these denials becomes legible in their aggregation by McLean and other black consumers. Although these courteous denials avoided the violence and intimidation associated with more publicized civil rights struggles in the South, we see McLean making the case that even though the loan officers address him as "Sir" and "Mr. McLean," detecting the racism of the housing market premised on a belief in black illiquidity called for methods superseding the documentation of immediately egregious encounters dominating the representational canon of racial oppression. One must instead learn to recognize racism's broader aggregate patterns, which could take any number of mannered forms while still culminating in an inevitable denial for those outside of whiteness.[8]

Leroy McLean knew in 1962 what Dr. Martin Luther King Jr. would come to harshly learn for himself when mounting his own Northern campaign a few years later. In the winter of 1966, King moved to Chicago to begin his first extended civil rights action outside of the American South. Following the passage of the 1964 Civil Rights Act and the 1965 Voting Rights Act, King sought new terrain upon which to fight against the inequities black Americans continued to face despite these key legislative victories. The Watts riots of the summer of 1965, moreover, had placed the state of black lives in Northern urban centers on the nation's radar. Chicago activist Albert Raby and James Bevel, a director of the Southern Christian Leadership Conference (SCLC), convinced King that Chicago would be the ideal next front for bringing attention to the distinct set of issues facing black urbanites as highlighted by the Watts uprising—specifically, equal access to housing and municipal services.[9]

From the start, King sensed this Northern campaign would need to take a different approach than his previous Southern actions. As Coretta Scott King described in her memoir, King realized during his preliminary visits to the city in the fall of 1965 that it was "in a sense harder for Northern blacks to pinpoint their grievances than for those of us in the South who had as obvious villains the Wallaces, the Jim Clarks, the Bull Connors."[10] Like McLean before him, King would need to construct a representational strategy for not only pinpointing those grievances but displaying and mobilizing them for the purpose of redress. But as Leroy McLean's earlier entreaties also suggest, redlining's effectiveness derived precisely from its representational slipperiness—its lack of obvious villains was integral to its operation. Private rating maps in secret circulation quantified and depersonalized disinvestment and steering, while lenders and realtors framed residential segregation as an unchangeable market truism, no matter how they personally felt about the matter. King would need to figure out how to direct public outrage toward a villain who was neither singular nor spectacular given the discrimination undergirding the housing market's functioning at almost every entry point. How do you mobilize around a bias that can only be inferred through the compilation of mundanely polite form letters? What good were direct actions targeting specific realtors and lenders when the free market enshrined whiteness as a neighborhood's signal amenity and blackness as a sign of property's inevitable decline? King, like McLean, would wrestle with how to make institutional racism legible as well as how best to strike against such an elusive foe.

King's first task in assembling a representational strategy for making housing discrimination visible and addressable in Chicago was finding a place to live that would allow him to better understand the plight of Chicagoans while also painting the most evocative, newsworthy picture of this plight as possible. As King told reporters, "you can't really get close to the poor without living and being here with them." "A West Side apartment," he continued, "will symbolize the slum-lordism that I hope to smash."[11] Already, we hear King struggling to find the right discursive language for redressing housing discrimination. He evokes the empathetic documentarian language of the 1930s and the '40s (seeking to "really get close with the poor") while also announcing his intent to use this proximity to fashion a symbolic portrait of black housing capable of catching the attention of journalists, politicos, and liberals writ large as he had previously done in the South. King eventually settled on a ninety-dollars-a-month two-bedroom railroad flat on the topmost floor of a run-down building in the Lawndale neighborhood, located on the city's West Side, as most optimal for these dual missions of deep intimacy and system-smashing symbolism. Lawndale, a neighborhood that had been 87 percent white in 1950, had in ten years' time flipped to a 90 percent black occupancy rate—a figure representative of how quickly communities "turned over" in the city following residential integration. Although the neighborhood was severely overcrowded, no new private housing had been planned there and the housing stock that did exist was in awful shape. Lawndale's black residents, furthermore, had trouble finding work in their own neighborhood, with local industries (including the corporate campus for Sears & Roebuck) employing mostly former white residents who increasingly commuted to the neighborhood from the suburbs.[12]

The Kings moved into their Lawndale apartment, located two blocks from the headquarter for the Vice Lords street gang, on a cold January day. With no lock on the front door, a packed-dirt floor in the foyer that smelled of urine, a refrigerator that didn't keep food cold, and a gas stove that failed to warm them, the Kings struggled to settle into their new Northern headquarters. The apartment was originally rented by King's assistant; when the landlord realized King was the real occupant, he sent over a crew of plasterers, painters, and electricians to fix up the apartment. But only so much could be done to mask its shabby conditions.[13] Though a fair housing ordinance had been passed in the city several years earlier, living in Lawndale revealed to King the failures of such actions to improve access to housing stock or resources. As he told a New York newspaper about what he was learning from his new neighbors, "The non-violent movement of the South has meant little to them, since we have been fighting for rights that theoretically are already theirs."[14] The problem in Chicago in 1966 wasn't the law per se—it was its limited enforcement as well as its relative toothlessness in the face of the free market's legitimation of the notion that black space was inherently and perpetually devaluating, rendering black neighborhoods and residents as perpetually bad bets.

Nonetheless, King wasted no time in attempting to translate the conditions he was experiencing into headlines useful for igniting public interest and, by extension, public pressure. In February, King and his staff donned their work clothes and, accompanied by a crew of reporters and photographers, set out to refurbish a tenement at 1321 South Homan Avenue, a few blocks from the apartment occupied by the Kings. "There was no heat, and there were babies wrapped in newspaper 'cause there were no blankets," as SCLC executive director Andrew Young recalled of the building.[15] A week later, King led a group of two hundred people to the same building and announced that the Chicago Freedom movement was to assume "Trusteeship" of the property on behalf of the tenants, collecting their rent to go to repairs rather than landlords. For the next few months, King helped organize rent strikes, tenant unions, and nonviolence workshops for local black youths and business boycotts. But these actions received little media coverage. Mayor Richard J. Daley, hyperaware of the potential for bad press and insistent on not becoming the next Bull Connor, avoided confrontations with King and would strategically (if temporarily) redirect city resources to the areas King targeted. King, moreover, held little traction with local ministers and religious leaders who had thrown their lot in with the Daley machine and were not so keen on joining ranks.

After a largely uneventful winter in terms of results, King decided to escalate his efforts by generating "creative tension" in the city. He orchestrated this tension by leading a series of summer marches through white neighborhoods, beginning with Gage Park. King's residential marches were met by hundreds of angry white neighborhood residents. During one march in Marquette Park, King was hit in the head by a fist-sized rock, making clear the threat he posed to the neighborhood's racial identity and, by extension, economic status. With this violent reception, Mayor Daley moved to end King's Chicago campaign once and for all. The two met on August 26, 1966, and struck a deal—King would stop marching and City Hall and the Chicago Real Estate Board pledged to do more to promote fair housing and more equal lending. The pact was not legally binding and many interpreted King's deal as a surrender rather than a win. King himself eventually hinted at a more sober assessment. "In all frankness," he said a few months after the agreement was signed, "we found the job greater than even we imagined."[16]

By most accounts, King's Chicago campaign was, at best, a modest intervention setting the stage for later federal housing legislation and, at worst, a failure.[17] Some have described King's Chicago efforts as laying the ground for the 1968 Fair Housing Act, making it illegal for landlords, realtors, insurers, and lenders to discriminate against tenants or buyers on the basis of race, religion, or national origin. However, it was King's death rather than his life that proved the most potent catalyst for the bill's passage, signed into law the day after his funeral. Up until that point, Northern members of Congress had been reticent to pass civil rights legislation directly affecting their own constituents.[18] But the 150 urban uprisings during the summer of 1967 followed by the riots that broke out in nearly one hundred cities after King's 1968 murder swayed enough members of Congress that immediate action was necessary.

It seems safe to say that King's Chicago campaign continues to be peripheral to King's legacy, remaining little known compared to his appearances in Selma, Montgomery, or Washington, D.C. We might contextualize King's inability to gain either representational, political, or legal traction in Chicago in several ways. Images of King performing light handiwork in a Lawndale building seem out of place in comparison to the more known images of King delivering speeches, marching, in jail, or under physical attack. King's Chicago photographs depict instead a more domestic image of this icon as he dwells in one decrepit Chicago building while fixing up another. Most compelling is a series of photographs of King hammering a window frame, a powerful analogy for the way he attempted to use the public interest in his own magnetizing body as a frame for the plight of blacks in Lawndale and other parts of Chicago's South and West Side boxed into inadequate housing.

But more than being out of place in relation to King's more canonical presentation within the public sphere, these images of King more pertinently underscore his *belatedness* to the representational canon of black housing. After all, black modernists had been representing black housing conditions in the North for over fifty years by the time King entered the fray. Part of King's failure in Chicago derived from his inability to innovate in relation to the powerful corpus of material already seeking to represent the distinctive cadence of housing inequities. King's images simply could not do more than those created by Richard Wright, Lorraine Hansberry, Gwendolyn Brooks, Ann Petry, Paul Laurence Dunbar, Claude McKay, Frank London Brown, James Weldon Johnson, Ralph Ellison, Lloyd Brown, Chester Himes, Langston Hughes, Gordon Parks, James Baldwin, or Dorothy West long testifying to the fact of the devaluation of black residential life. Even next to a lost historical figure like Leroy McLean, King's Chicago campaign appears late to the game.

FIGURE 6. Martin Luther King Jr. helps renovate an apartment at 1321 South Homan Avenue in Chicago on February 24, 1966.

Source: Chicago Tribune/TCA.

In light of this heady list of figures depicting the devaluation of blackness inherent to American residential space, we might modify James Smethurst's claim in *The African American Roots of Modernism* positing Jim Crow as central to "American notions of modernity—and, ultimately, modernism."[19] Adjacent to Jim Crow but not reducible or identical to it, the often less spectacular efforts to represent the lack of privacy, disrespected domesticities, exploitative financing, and pressure-filled migrations shaping experiences of residential segregation in the twentieth century undergird a large subset of aesthetic work. Given the aesthetic and social innovation emerging from this residential canon spanning modernist, realist, and naturalist genres, King's contributions appear not just late but almost rearguard. During his time in Chicago, King neither discovered or publicized any new evidence of housing discrimination, nor did he find new strategies for residential segregation's representation or reproach. Rather, his efforts in Chicago largely entailed King wielding his magnetic presence to try to magnify what everyone already knew—that American residential space was hostile to black life. Moreover, who was responsible for these conditions—the individual, the state, the market—was something King never articulated or successfully pressed. In fact, images of King performing maintenance in Lawndale may have hindered rather than helped his redressive efforts. By suggesting that the poor housing besetting black communities could be rectified through intra-community uplift like that performed by the Kings, these images belie the economic, legal, and state forces perpetuating the active disinvestment in black space across the color line that no amount of neighborly pitching-in could alone remedy.[20] King appears within these photographs attending to the decrepit outcomes of residential discrimination rather than their less imageable source—the bureaucratic infrastructure maintaining segregation.

King failed in Chicago due to what he and his wife had already intuited and what Leroy McLean had earlier marked—that housing discrimination's lack of "obvious villains" and smoking guns made it difficult to represent and, by extension, combat. King proved unable to find a new or generative representational strategy for either "pinpointing the grievances" of Northern blacks via housing or helping whites to understand how these grievances structure their own economic, moral, or existential being. He finally had to resort to more overt tactics—marching through white neighborhoods to elicit violence, even getting struck by a rock—to get any mass coverage and bring Mayor Daley to the table. Only by transforming the more furtive harms of housing segregation into brash menace to better resemble the violence associated with the Jim Crow South did King bring about any action at all.

The form of discrimination McLean described in his 1962 letter to the CCHR and that King struggled to bring into a representational form falls under the umbrella of what Stokely Carmichael and Charles Hamilton first named in 1967 as institutional racism.[21] In fact, when defining institutional racism for the first time in their book, *Black Power: The Politics of Liberation*, housing anchors the second of two explanatory examples. Their first example juxtaposes the "overt" racism of the 1964 Birmingham church bombing killing four black girls with the "covert" institutional racism of differential health care access resulting in the deaths of "five hundred black babies each year" in the same city.[22] The second centering housing works similarly, with Carmichael and Hamilton opposing the overt racism of a black family "stoned, burned or routed out" of a white neighborhood with the "institutional racism that keeps black people locked in dilapidated slum tenements, subject to the daily prey of exploitative slumlords, merchants, loan sharks and discriminatory real estate agents."[23]

For Carmichael and Hamilton, overt individual racism encompassed acts of violence that resulted in immediately observable damage to the body or its property caused by identifiable actors, whereas covert institutional racism named forms of slow death and accumulating inequality lacking a specific agent or a spectacular scene. As Carmichael and Hamilton write, overt racism "can be recorded by television cameras; it can be frequently observed in the process of commission," whereas its institutional strains may be "less identifiable in terms of specific individuals committing the acts," but are "no less destructive of life."[24] Their reference to the televisual here seems to nod to the ready circulation of images of black bodies being physically harmed that contributed to the civil rights movement's successes in the court of first public then legal opinion, begging the question of the possibility of institutional racism's representation in such a mediascape.[25] Carmichael had expertise in this arena given the media firestorm provoked by his own divergences from the mainstream civil rights movement in his call for Black Power. Carmichael's attention to institutional racism in *Black Power* was informed by his differences with King and the SCLC, and perhaps King's more specific failures in Chicago, where his tactics of nonviolence proved less efficacious for opposing racism's more covert forms. Black Power as a mantra and praxis—adopted most prominently in Northern cities in the 1960s and 1970s—emerged from an understanding of more pervasive if at times more benign-seeming forms of racism baked into society's systemic functions. Despite being known for its blunt rhetorical style, Black Power emerged as a response to the persistent if often less spectacular forces of white supremacy—including within the housing market—largely untouched by the civil rights legislation of the mid-1960s.[26]

Whereas Leroy McLean, Martin Luther King Jr., and Stokely Carmichael and Charles Hamilton encountered and diagnosed the difficulties of representing institutional racism from varying positions along the political spectrum, Matthew Fuller and Eyal Weizman give us a name for an approach to its detection and representation: investigative aesthetics. Applicable to the apprehension of not only institutional racism but other forms of state, corporate, and economic violence whose evidence may be covert, partial, or under erasure, investigative aesthetics is an "anti-hegemonic" approach to case-building inquiry that centers on "drawing out and combining individual recordings until they become collective—a commons."[27] It is "an intrinsically aesthetic practice" because it relies on sensing and sense-making as the locus of what it seeks to both analyze and expose.[28] Investigative aesthetics depends not on a single eyewitness's account but on the aggregation of signals, be it from people or satellites, soil analysis or open-source code. Its findings are assembled as much for the art gallery as the courtroom, striving across these spaces toward the construction of a new common sense.

Fuller and Weizman's understanding of the aesthetic is informed by Jacques Rancière's definition of aesthetics as "the system of a priori forms determining what presents itself to sense and experience."[29] For Rancière, aesthetics is intimately connected to politics as it "revolves around what is seen and what can be said about it" as well as "who has the ability to see and the talent to speak."[30] Fuller and Weizman similarly figure aesthetics as a perpetually adaptive set of processes involving the "careful attunement and noticing extending to the elaboration of precise means of sensing and sense-making."[31] Focused primarily on more contemporary instances of corruption, human rights violations, environmental crimes, and secret surveillance, Fuller and Weizman propose investigative aesthetics as a strategy for assembling and reading the "weak signals and faint traces" left behind by forces, events, and systems designed to operate covertly and appear agentless.[32] Investigative aesthetics, as applicable to the analysis of letters and photographs as to surveillance videos, geotags, and malware, is the practice of "paying close attention to the accounts of people, matter, and code."[33]

In cases where discrimination may be the covert rule of record, where there may not be a specific villain but rather layers of bureaucratic or technocratic mediation, investigative aesthetics involves attuning to perceptual, embodied, and material details to sense the covert through modes of aggregation, assemblage, and re-presentation. Investigative aesthetics puts a name to what Leroy McLean had already begun to pioneer in the 1960s by assembling an archive and detecting patterns of lending rejection, no matter how polite, to make institutional racism sensate to others. In producing his archive of aggregated rejections, McLean sought in his own way to "combine individual recordings until they become collective—a commons." The case he builds to apprehend the racism of the housing market involves gathering collective experience, recognizing patterns, and producing aggregated knowledge of institutions and how they make sense of people.[34] The covert racism of the housing market elicited new ways of paying attention and other ways of attuning one's sensorium, aspects King, McLean, and Carmichael variously theorized, sensed, and slammed up against at midcentury.

Joining them in the consideration of residential segregation's distinguishing qualities were the drafters of the 1968 Fair Housing Act. While Senator Walter Mondale, one of the bill's legislative sponsors, aspired for the law to encourage "truly integrated neighborhoods" in addition to criminalizing discrimination, this more proactive and transformational aspect of the law has generally gone ignored or proved difficult to achieve for much of its history.[35] But even its more limited charge—curbing discrimination—has proven complicated to see through. As Keeanga-Yamahtta Taylor observes, "the suggestion that Black equality in the real estate market could be achieved by the formal end to housing discrimination failed to take into account the very ways that racial inequality was structured and embedded within the architecture of the system of buying and selling real estate in the United States."[36]

Even within the limits of what reform-minded legal action can achieve, the Fair Housing Act's efficacy has been strained. In addition to the individuated nature of the law privileging those affluent enough to press their case, the varying legal approaches to discrimination's definition and detection have further stifled the law's applicability. The ability to enforce the Fair Housing Act fluctuates according to whether housing discrimination must be proven to be intentional—requiring concrete evidence demonstrating that a lender or realtor did not lend to someone based on their race—or if proof of disparate impact—that an institution or policy produced discriminatory outcomes, whether intended or not—is enough.[37] As McLean, Fuller, and Weizman all mark, detecting and challenging covert racism requires not just amassing evidence but a reassessment of what counts as such as well as expanding modes of sense-making necessary for this evidence's legibility and redress. And yet, as George Lipsitz notes, the Fair Housing Act, "a law written deliberately and cynically to be weak," has generally been enforced from "a perspective that envisions discrimination to be temporally discrete, to have one clear moment of origin and finite period of injury, to consist of one unambiguous act committed against one identifiable victim by one identifiable perpetrator."[38] As Lipsitz warns, "the dominant framework fails to recognize the ways in which discrimination is systemic and structural, impersonal and institutional, collective, cumulative, and continuing"—not a series of discrete acts but a "continuous general condition."[39]

Following this wide range of theorists, activists, and politicians confronting the institutional, bureaucratic, and systemic conditions of residential discrimination, the rest of this chapter takes up experiments in investigative aesthetics by writers and organizations in the midcentury interested in bringing the covert racism of the housing market into a representational form. While Carmichael and Hamilton described the institutional racism germane to housing as empirically slippery, lacking direct agents, and hard to represent, let alone combat, the Fair Housing Act was largely designed to address only its most overt and individualized forms. As a result, the legacy of this legislation—now over a half century old—has been decidedly mixed. But the Fair Housing Act was only one effort to try to codify, detect, and represent the covert institutional racism of the housing market. If institutional forms of racism determining residential outcomes were, by Carmichael and Hamilton's

1967 definition, "less identifiable in terms of specific individuals committing the acts," how did narrative and figurative genres—which at their core are organized around acts by specific individuals—learn, or fail to learn, to bring the institutional racism of the housing market—designed to work impersonally and as a non-event—into representation? And what might these representational efforts tell us about both the utility and the limit of institutional racism as a political, legal, and representational term in the immediate wake of its coining in the late midcentury?

To answer these questions, I first turn to a set of public materials produced by two New York–based fair housing organizations suggesting the difficulties of finding an aesthetic form for rendering the systemic nature of housing discrimination. The second half of the chapter will turn to two works released on either side of the Fair Housing Act's passage—Kristin Hunter's 1966 novel, *The Landlord*, and its 1970 film adaptation, written by Bill Gunn and directed by Hal Ashby—to consider the ways these works narrated the forms of racism organizing the American housing market. The largely faulty truism that property value heavily depended on the racial makeup of a neighborhood—despite being challenged as early as the 1950s—enabled even the most liberal lenders, realtors, renters, buyers, and sellers to understand themselves as helplessly subject to a discriminatory property market that they had no choice but to participate in. How, then, do accusations of racism inadvertently produce systems that further impersonalize and bureaucratize discrimination, making its appearance even more diffuse? Representations of housing as a raced commodity falling on either end of the Fair Housing Act allow us to see the ways race and racism are ever-evolving constructs differently calibrated across historical periods but also in relation to shifting physical and financial space.

Residential Segregation's Banal Dance

For the battle against institutional racism to enter the terrain of politics, it needed to find fitting forms of representation. And many at midcentury were on the case. While Leroy McLean presented himself as a lone concerned citizen, the tactics he used to detect and publicize lending discrimination were being taken up by a broad network of midcentury fair housing activists and organizations. In New York City, groups such as the Brooklyn chapter of the Congress of Racial Equality (CORE), the Harlem Mortgage and Improvement

Council (HMIC), and the Committee on Civil Rights in Metropolitan New York (CCRM) sought to study, describe and broadcast aspects of housing discrimination designed to escape detection or elude fault.[40] In fighting for equal housing resources, increased legal protections were not necessarily these groups' primary aim. As Wendell Pritchett notes, by the late 1950s, "fair housing laws covered a majority of the dwellings in New York City" across public and private housing, rentals, and home sales.[41] But this legislation had limited efficacy due to its reliance on individuals having the resources to file complaints as well as the chronically understaffed agencies tasked with investigating them, all while new suburban developments continued to subsidize white movement out of the city, relocating residential segregation beyond urban jurisdictions. More fully addressing the inequities of the housing market would require better understanding how racial discrimination was normalized across its multiple parts—lending, federal programs and subsidies, realtors and developers, and the ideologies of buyers and renters. Such understandings could be used to either advocate for more precise, proactive laws addressing discrimination or to push for more radical housing solutions in the face of systemic injustice and the devaluation of blackness via the free market that discrimination laws alone—or laws or markets more broadly— would never fully address.[42]

While some at midcentury limned the limits of antidiscrimination legislation to achieve fair housing, the paucity of these legislative solutions would not be fully grappled with until decades later. In the meantime, fair housing groups set out to work with the legislation they had to prosecute discriminatory entities where they could. One strategy for rendering discrimination explicit at midcentury was known as "shopping" or, more commonly, "testing."[43] This tactic involved sending black and white potential tenants of similar economic standing to either view, rent, or purchase a home or acquire a home loan and compiling the results.[44] Testing enabled organizations to prove race-based discrimination as an empirically discernible phenomenon. While the ability for testers to legally sue under the Fair Housing Act was only upheld by the U.S. Supreme Court in 1982, it has been used as a tactic by individuals and organizations to prove and protest discrimination as an observable and repeatable offense since at least the midcentury. Martin Luther King Jr., for instance, participated in testing actions during his Chicago campaign, helping to organize residents to test a realtor's willingness to show them housing in majority-white neighborhoods. As King explained in a speech during the campaign, "Every time Negroes went in, the real estate agent said, 'Oh I'm sorry we don't have anything listed.' And then soon after that we sent some of our fine white staff members into those same real estate offices and the minute those white persons got in, they opened the book. 'Oh yes, we have several things, now what exactly do you want.'"[45]

While interracial testing was one of the most successful tactics for making the covert discrimination of the housing market overt, it did not necessarily generate gripping visuals or narratives. Testing is a matter of steady observation and repeatable results proving bias. Testers, moreover, are meant to be reducible to types, made interchangeable. Cases do not revolve around the tester's personal experience being particularly gripping, noteworthy, or exceptional—lending and realty professionals may be polite, apologetic, or helpful when dealing with black or white customers. The evidence of bias derives instead from repeated testing of realtors and lending agencies to assess the divergent outcomes for those otherwise similar. Because of the mundanity of the testing process—designed to be anti-narratival given its interest in producing aggregative results unyoked to the subjective experience of individuals—testing has failed to produce much in the way of representation. I've found no literature featuring testing as a central representational point. Not designed to tug at the heartstrings or expand the limits of the sensible, testing is merely meant to produce unassailable evidence of discrimination. With the Supreme Court's 1982 ruling that testing was legally admissible evidence in proving violations to the federal Fair Housing Act, moreover, its procedures became even more standardized.[46]

Testing's reliance on nonspecific abstraction finds visual representation in at least one early effort to publicize such work. The Committee on Civil Rights in Metropolitan New York, or CCRM, founded in 1950, sought to compare "public practices in public accommodations, housing, employment, health and other fields in which all human beings are entitled to equal treatment as prescribed by the principles of equality embodied in the American Constitution."[47] To further their focus on housing, CCRM formally launched the Partnership Apartment Seekers' Experiment, or PASE, in 1960. PASE paired white volunteer checkers and black apartment seekers to test for racial bias at buildings across the city. The recruitment brochure for the program features two illustrations—one of a black family entering an apartment building from the street level as movers unload furniture from a truck behind them while another features a black couple at a desk facing a white man on the other side.[48] Capturing the physical and bureaucratic settings of the housing market—a residential complex and the office of either a lender or a realtor—the figures within these scenes appear featureless, not much more visually realized than stick figures. Though the illustrator has taken care to suggest the middle-class appearance of the black figures through the rendering of their clothes, the generally abstract appearance as representative black residents mirrors the logics of testing itself. The PASE brochure describes testing as "a simple plan that gets results" in a market where "housing discrimination is stubborn and deeply ingrained."[49] The simplicity of the process is mirrored in these illustrations that depict the straightforward work of testing as well as the efficacy of its results—acquiring an apartment for black residents who might have otherwise been turned away.

"Each time a PASE team goes out," the brochure proclaims, "someone—broker, agent, apartment manager, landlord, superintendent—is brought to a moral crossroads."[50] At this juncture, "either he gives the would-be tenant an even break—or faces up squarely to the fact that he is a lawbreaker, deliberately blocking a citizen from equal treatment because of color or national background."[51] The banal work of testing, the CCRM insists, brings about transformation either through revelation or, if necessary, legal punishment. But how exactly testing evidence brings offenders to "a moral crossroads" is not described. The brochure presents this possibility in terms that most resemble blackmail—either the offender has a change of heart when confronted with the evidence of testing leading to a just outcome, or the law will force this conversion upon them by punishing them as a "lawbreaker." We might claim testing as a practice of investigative aesthetics due to its efforts to use compiled data to confront offenders with the specificity of their own racism. But framing this possibility as a "moral crossroads" does not seem quite right; not only does it presume that the offender is unaware of their biased actions, but it overlooks the likelihood that any quick change of heart was as likely to be motivated by money and convenience, given the costliness of litigation, as by one's conscience.[52] While testing may catch individual lenders and realtors

FIGURES 7 AND 8. Brochure produced by the Committee on Civil Rights in Metropolitan New York (CCRM) to publicize testing.

From: **CCRM**
THE COMMITTEE ON CIVIL RIGHTS
IN METROPOLITAN NEW YORK-
an organization of volunteers dedicated
to eliminating discrimination in housing

To: **APARTMENT SEEKERS**

You can raise the odds of finding the right home for you and your family by enrolling today in PASE (Partnership Apartment Seeking Exchange).

White volunteers team up with non-white apartment seekers
...pinpointing discrimination if it occurs
...helping New Yorkers put fair housing laws to work.

It's a simple plan that *gets results*. Here's how...

Source: Manuscripts, Archives and Rare Books Division, Schomburg Center for Research in Black Culture, The New York Public Library.

CALL AND TELL US YOUR NEEDS

Telephone CCRM: CI 7-6343.

Arrange to stop in at our office: 225 West 57 Street, Room 403.

Hours: 9-5 weekdays; appointments may be made for evening visits.

Describe the size, price and neighborhood of the apartment you need, and the searching you have already done on your own.

SIGN UP FOR THE NEXT PASE TRAINING SESSION

One evening session provides a group of white and non-white teammates with valuable tips on the techniques of partnership home-seeking:

* What to look for
* How to approach landlords and renting agents
* How to cope with rebuffs
* How to work effectively with your partner-checker
* How to report your findings

You'll have a chance to act out situations that may arise in encounters with landlords or renting agencies. You'll be given a special form for reporting your experiences in detail.

PASE IMPROVES YOUR CHANCES FOR SUCCESS

The PASE program, attracting several hundred applicants a year, has helped many people secure apartments. Here's one example:

> A Negro couple, Mr. and Mrs. A, who for more than a year had been searching for a home in Brooklyn, paired up with the B's, white volunteers. Seeing an attractive ad, the A's arranged to meet the B's in the neighborhood.
>
> First the A's approached the superintendent and were told the apartment was not available. Then the B's saw the super; they were shown the apartment and looked it over carefully, noting every detail they knew the A's needed to know. Now the A's were able to register a well-documented complaint with the city agency charged with enforcing anti-discrimination laws. A month later the Negro family moved in to live quietly and amiably in the neighborhood of their choice.

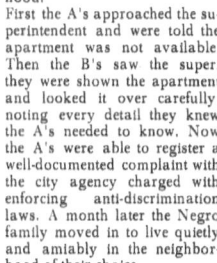

To get the best results, we need your cooperation. If you meet discrimination, you should be prepared to *follow through*. Present the full, documented facts to one of the official agencies — either the City Commission on Human Rights or the State Commission for Human Rights — charged with enforcing New York's laws against discrimination. We'll help you. Partnership apartment-seeking gives you the kind of evidence these offices need.

YOU CAN HELP ROOT OUT INJUSTICE

Housing discrimination is stubborn and deeply ingrained. Partnership apartment-hunting strikes at the very root of the problem. Because each time a PASE team goes out, someone — broker, agent, apartment manager, landlord, superintendent — is brought to a moral crossroads. Either he gives the would-be tenant an even break — or faces up squarely to the fact that he is a lawbreaker, deliberately blocking a citizen from equal treatment because of color or national background.

Success does not always come easily. But everyone who works through PASE has a good chance of finding housing and is adding important evidence needed by officials if they are to enforce New York's laws against discrimination.

engaged in racist practices red-handed—and could prove incredibly effective in integrating specific buildings—the CCRM's framing of discrimination as an individual moral issue rather than one of economy, policy, or even ethics neglects the larger forces making institutional racism profitable. In this way, although testing is an investigative practice, it did not generally strive to make an aesthetic intervention reshaping common sense. Although a hasty "moral" reckoning might lead to a black resident gaining access to housing, testing results ultimately needed to be translatable into standardized formats that could stand up in a court of law if morality failed. Moreover, midcentury organizations soon encountered the limits of testing and other forms of direct action to produce systemic change on the broader housing market. As one CORE organizer insisted, "People were solving these cases but they weren't solving the problem."[53] PASE's testing illustrations—representing residential and bureaucratic settings populated by interchangeable types—point to this tactic's legal utility but also its aesthetic limitations in its capacity to expand arenas of sense and sense-making enshrining discrimination as an economic necessity.

Although the Harlem Mortgage and Improvement Council (HMIC) did not engage in testing, its efforts to render the bureaucratic racism of the lending market faced similar representational challenges. The HMIC was founded in June 1950 to "devise an effective program to combat the lack of mortgage credit in the Harlem area from institutional sources."[54] The council produced well-researched studies of mortgages inequities in Harlem, educated and assisted Harlem property owners and borrowers, and encouraged local owners and managers to maintain and improve their properties. The group's most notable action was the publication of a hallmark report analyzing the policies of Manhattan savings banks regarding mortgage loans on properties in Harlem between 1945 and 1950. Although Harlem had been predominately African American for decades by the 1950s, the HMIC did not foreground racial discrimination as a root cause of its mortgage inequities in its materials. In one of its flyers advertising their services to Harlemites, the HMIC visualizes this race-neutral approach via cartoon figures whose racial identities are ambiguous at best.[55] The HMIC flyer depicts the process of discrimination almost like a dance diagram, using big swooping arrows to suggest the repetitious nature of this embodied rejection and the runaround faced by unwanted residents seeking housing. And yet, in both the visual rendering of loan rejection and

FIGURE 9. Flier produced by the Harlem Mortgage and Improvement Council (HMIC).

Source: Manuscripts, Archives and Rare Books Division, Schomburg Center for Research in Black Culture, The New York Public Library.

accompanying text, racial identification or description is absented—a choice perhaps in keeping with the HMIC's commitment to being a "non-partisan, non-political" organization. Unlike the CCRM's abstract rendering of bodies that nonetheless preserve the race of its figures, the HMIC flyer racially abstracts its figures so as to dislodge housing discrimination from the discourse of racial grievance entirely, representing its figures instead as subject to a universalizable form of bureaucratic fatigue.

Despite their different visual approaches to rendering race, both the HMIC and CCRM materials draw from a limited visual language of office desks to present the mundane if no less impactful scene of residential discrimination. But the HMIC gave housing inequities a more colorful face in its booster publication, the *Home and Housing Journal*. Its editors describe the publication's mission in its inaugural issue as bringing attention to "perhaps one of the best kept 'secrets of our time'"—"the amazing strides that Negro America is making in the province of home ownership; and the role that Negro real estate agents, builders, developers, and their affiliates are playing in this inspiring growth."[56] Designed to rival the National Association of Realtors' trade journal, which largely addressed itself to white realtors, the *Home and Housing Journal* addressed itself to "YOU, the apartment dwellers, the prospective buyer, the home owners, the displaced businessman, the agent, the builder, the mortgagee," and, more generally, "the Negro wage earner and home owner who is often misguided, exploited, and robbed" and, as a result, ignorant of the laws, tips, and products "which will save him minutes, migraine—and money" on the housing market.[57] While featuring occasional stories on racial tensions in housing complexes and enclaves, the publication more prominently featured items like its Miss Home and Housing Journal contest glamorizing black homeowners and aspirants. The 1959 winner, who received 329,000 votes, appears in *Home and Housing* photographed in her gown and title-bearing sash.[58] Designed for strivers looking for help in breaking into the property game, the journal openly embraced a rhetoric of self-determination.

But it was far easier for the HMIC to glamorously represent black brokers and owners in its pages as striving icons who helped themselves than to find a visual language for the undazzling and less spectacular aspects of lending disparities and governmental policies that, despite their bureaucratic inanity, harmed a large swath of Harlemites—whether they had ownership dreams or not. Neither the CCRM nor the HMIC was able to overcome the representational problem at the heart of institutional racism—how to render a form of bias "less identifiable in terms of specific individuals committing the acts" in order to bring a system rather than actors into view.[59] While relying heavily on practices of investigation, these groups did not generally traffic in

FIGURE 10. "Helen Horne Wins Journal Contest Title," from *Home and Housing Journal*, Summer 1959.

during the last session and signed into law by Governor Rockefeller on April 21, the Limited Profit Housing Mortgage Corporation is being established to stimulate the construction of middle income housing throughout the State and is intended to triple the amount of housing that can be built with available State Loan funds.

The Board of Directors members represent insurance companies, savings banks, commercial banks and one representing the public at large. They will serve without compensation, have the responsibility of electing officers and conducting the corporate affairs until the members elect a permanent board.

90 PER CENT OF COST

The Corporation and the State will make loans to limited profit

(Continued on Page 2)

Helen Horne Wins Journal Contest Title

Although Philadelphia's Helen Horne was the latest starter in the Home and Housing Journal Sweepstakes, she pulled the surprise of the year by hitting the tape ahead of all of the other eleven contestants vying for the title of "Miss Home and Housing Journal," with a final tabulation of 329,600 votes.

Josephine Fox, who led until the final tabulation, copped second place, 125,600 votes behind the winner.

Almost as elated at Miss Horne are her sponsors, Delores and

(Continued on Page 2)

MISS HOME AND HOUSING JOURNAL — Attractive Helen Horne, late entry in the Journal's sweepstakes, copped coveted title of "Miss Home and Housing Journal" from ten other contestants. Philadelphia lass was sponsored by Tucker and Tucker Real Estate Co.

Source: Manuscripts, Archives and Rare Books Division, Schomburg Center for Research in Black Culture, The New York Public Library.

forms of investigative aesthetics seeking to disrupt the economic and bureaucratic common sense preserving housing discrimination's financial value that proved largely impervious to individual moral reckonings. But a midcentury novel would attempt to render the tension between bureaucratic racism and individual transformation, deploying the form of the epiphanic bildungsroman as a red herring of sorts for bringing the system enshrining racial inequity within the housing market on an atmospheric level into view.

The Landlord Circa 1966

There may not have been any novels or films about racial testing on the housing market, but there were plenty of narratives written about residential discrimination writ large. While most of these works were earnest protest novels like those described in Chapter 4, there were a few generic outliers. Perhaps the strangest—and funniest—novel to foreground residential discrimination was Kristin Hunter's 1966 novel, *The Landlord*. Little read today, *The Landlord* has more in common with Paul Beatty's 2015 satirical novel, *The Sellout*, than its more immediate predecessor, Lorraine Hansberry's *A Raisin in the Sun* (1959). Predating more well-known satires by black writers like John Oliver Killens's *The Cotillion: or, One Good Bull Is Half the Herd* (1971), Fran Ross's *Oreo* (1974), and Ishmael Reed's *Mumbo Jumbo* (1972) and *Flight to Canada* (1976), Hunter's psychoanalytically inflected seriocomic romp was seemingly before its time. *The Landlord* was the second novel written by Hunter, who also taught writing at the University of Pennsylvania for most of her career. She belonged to the broader illustrious group of black women writers working in this period, including Lorraine Hansberry, Nikki Giovanni, Audre Lorde, Alice Walker, Toni Cade Bambara, Toni Morrison, Alice Childress, and Kathleen Collins, to name a few—almost all more well-known than Hunter today.

Whereas Hunter's first novel, *God Bless the Child* (1964), was a dramatic tale about the intergenerational struggles of black women, *The Landlord* is a very different book. Best described as a piercing satire maintaining great sympathy for its characters, *The Landlord* is told from the point of view of its titular figure, Elgar Enders, the thirty-four-year-old scion of a wealthy white family who believes his foray into property management will solve his psychic instability. Suffering from crippling anxiety despite his vast inheritance and good looks, Elgar is so fragile that he moves his psychoanalyst into his building for easier access. The building upon which Elgar has staked his fragile identity is in a black neighborhood most often described as a slum and home to a long-standing group of black tenants including an aging blues singer, a former beauty queen who makes her money from faking falls, her Black Nationalist husband variously claiming black and indigenous identities, a queer college dean who sells degrees, and an ancient couple rarely glimpsed outside their apartment. Most of the novel details Elgar's relationship with his tenants as they first outsmart his rent collection efforts, then allow his limited assimilation into the life of the building, and ultimately work with him when the building is slated through urban renewal for demolition set to displace everyone but Elgar.

Though widely reviewed, the novel was largely received with perplexity. The *New York Times* review by critic Andrew Sarris situated the novel in relation to the black literature of its time, predicting that "the White Liberal reader, still lolling lasciviously under the lash of James Baldwin and LeRoi Jones, will be somewhat disappointed by Kristin Hunter's relatively urbane view of race relations."[60] Despite underscoring the significance of the novel's dedication to Chester Himes, whom Sarris describes as "an underrated and under-publicized Negro novelist who tempers anger with humor," the reviewer ultimately insists that the novel's "fantasy becomes too frothy, the merriment too merciful."[61] The effectiveness of Hunter's satire was also questioned by Dudley Randall, who, in his review for *Negro Digest*, despite noting that "Hunter has a distinctive voice, of humor and gaiety, which even while laughing scores some shrewd hits," laments that her "characters are more cardboard creatures with labels than human beings."[62] "Although this book does not stir the emotions," Randall concludes, "it rouses the risibilities."[63] But these more mixed official reviews of the novel sit in contrast to the assessment of at least one key reader: singer and actress Pearl Bailey. Describing Hunter's novel as "the funniest book I ever read," Bailey would insist on being cast as the character of Marge when the book was eventually adapted for film.[64]

The Landlord is, in many ways, the antithesis of Lorraine Hansberry's 1959 breakout hit, *A Raisin in the Sun*, which perhaps further contributed to its critical illegibility. Gone is the noble Mama, striving Beneatha, and the wounded Walter and Lena deciding whether to leave behind their kitchenette for more residential pastures using money exceptionally begotten from the death of the family patriarch. Whereas Walter is ultimately schemed out of a good chunk of their inheritance, the tenants in *The Landlord* are the hustlers who band together to not just outsmart their naïve landlord but ultimately form bonds with him that make his planned exploitation of them more challenging. Moreover, while *A Raisin in the Sun*, along with a good deal of property dramas at midcentury, focused on the obstacles blacks faced when attempting to move to white communities, Hunter's novel is about the struggle of black urban tenants to stay put as forces of urban renewal and gentrification work to displace them. That displacement rather than enforced segregation anchors Hunter's novel may suggest that by the time the federal government passed the Fair Housing Act in 1968 criminalizing the blatant steering of blacks into segregated enclaves, these enclaves had already entered into a new phase of co-option and predation designed to unlock their newfound value as black access to other housing markets became theoretically eased.

Hunter's commitment to protagonist Elgar's point of view as he goes from loving (and lusting after) his tenants to hating them to ultimately forging a new relation with them that isn't idealized or exploitative but premised on reciprocity and advocacy is clear-eyed and uproarious. Elgar is an easy target, but the novel's most effective satire—like most memorable satires of the twentieth century—is aimed at systems and their rhetoric rather than individuals. At the center of *The Landlord* is what the novel names at one point as "the machinery of dispossession" targeting urban black residents for capitalist exploitation, financial undervaluation, and state interventions.[65]

In fact, we might read *The Landlord* as positing satire as an answer to Carmichael and Hamilton's implied question about how to represent institutional racism's covert and less empirically visceral strains. Hunter's novel is anchored by Elgar's personal befuddlements and breakthroughs that drive forward its plot. But his individual awakening takes place within the omnipresent atmosphere of the real estate industry, whose various bureaucrats and state agents working to maintain existing property relations continually puncture and punctate the novel's narrative world. The machinery of dispossession atmospherically saturates the novel, persistently working as a check on Elgar's earnestly framed emotional journey threatening to overtake the novel with his blatant neediness. Hunter's satire works through the juxtaposition between Elgar's faith in what his emotional transformation can achieve and the novel's efforts to continually make visible all the entities operating alongside Elgar to at times enforce his property rights but to also work at cross-purposes to him when he tries to disrupt this machinery's racialized functionality. Institutional racism is brought into representation by contrasting its saturating uneventfulness with Elgar's earnest and absorptive self-concern, which Hunter sets us up to emotionally invest in while simultaneously poking fun at his (and perhaps our own) naïveté. While Dudley Randall framed *The Landlord*'s capacity to "rouse the risibilities" rather than "stir the emotions" as a failing, it is precisely Hunter's wielding of risibility to upend the norms of the sensible—at the expense of tugging at canonical heartstrings—that drives its investigative aesthetics.[66] Hunter's version involves teaching readers to pay attention to the minor details reiterating the omnipresence of the machinery's presence despite Elgar's understanding of himself as the star of the show. Elgar's exceptional coming-to-consciousness is the red herring against which Hunter plots the nonstory of the "continuous general condition" of black devaluation, to cite George Lipsitz once more, pervading all aspects of the housing market.

The Landlord was published in 1966, two years after the Civil Rights Act and two years before the Fair Housing Act. And while I'm cautious of too strongly reading the novel as a mirror of this specific context, *The Landlord* deals with the exact circumstances left unregulated by the Civil Rights Act of 1964—discrimination within the private property market. Housing's centrality to articulating the problem of institutional racism is present from the term's inaugural use by Carmichael and Hamilton in 1967 and tracks more generally onto the ways activists described housing discrimination's modus operandi as early as the 1940s. *The Landlord* describes instances in which race factors into both the marketing of the building to Elgar as well as developers' intentions for the neighborhood after its "clearance." And while the eventual passage of the 1968 Fair Housing Act did not stop racial discrimination—and perhaps only made its discriminatory activities more covert, as Keeanga-Yamahtta Taylor charts—it did make it actionable in cases when discrimination was overt enough to be documented.

But even as we might read this novel in anticipation of the 1968 Fair Housing Act, which would become the definitive legalistic solution to housing discrimination in the U.S., *The Landlord* proves far more interested in the extralegal quandary in which Elgar and his tenants find themselves, locked into racialized social scripts of owner and occupant that operate in excess of the verifiable, explicit, and directly agential overt racism that the 1968 act limits itself to addressing. Elgar can either extract himself from the life of the building to more smoothly fleece his tenants, as almost all his peers instruct him to. Or he can lose money to his tenants, who both exploit and suspect his liberal bleeding heart. His tenants have similarly limited options—they can either participate in their continued exploitation by a property system stacked against them or they can embrace Elgar as an exception to a system they have long distrusted (despite knowing he originally planned to evict them). In other words, the novel is interested in the limits of love, like, or even understanding to redress or erase experiences of racism that can't be located in an exchange with a particular individual but are no less saturating. The novel most precisely encapsulates this quandary in a passage towards its end:

> Elgar stared at his assembled tenants, the "family" he had hoped to belong to at last, and realized how fantastic that illusion had been. . . . In spite of their highly vocal complaints, his tenants' dissatisfaction did not spring from tangible things like leaky plumbing and worn linoleum. The sophisticated DuBois had hinted at deeper reasons—old hostilities, deeply buried suspicions, murky race-memories of injustice and treachery—things dark and formless and slippery as the invisible insides of a drain.[67]

In the figure of DuBois—who profits from the college credentials he sells while gleefully playing the role of bourgeoisie academic—Hunter certainly invites associations with W. E. B. Du Bois. Whether this link marks this character's social striving or is meant as a gentle ribbing of W. E. B. Du Bois's classism is ambiguous. But DuBois the character's articulation of murky, buried, and formless feelings without direct origin or tangible cause that inform his sense of racial injury seems directly indebted to his namesake's idea of the racial veil as a ghostly phenomenon. While DuBois's feelings here of deep-seated racial pain are less about institutional racism in the present and more about racial wounds of the past, they nonetheless demonstrate why Elgar's personal breakthroughs regarding racial inequity fail to earn the trust of his tenants, who believe his revelations will do little to change race relations or property relations in any era.

Similar to Elgar, his tenants also find it easier to reduce the machinery of dispossession to a single immediate foe than to face its enormity. As one tenant insists, "It is extremely difficult to deal with this Landlord. He refuses to be an abstraction, which would make it easy to hate him."[68] Although Elgar is the novel's boldest fantasist, when he refuses to play the role of mean landlord, he ends up disrupting his tenants' own fantasies of localizable injury. This opens them up to the more painful truth that their living conditions are not traceable to a single cruel man but rather a broader network precisely designed to impersonally profit from their immobility and neglect. Their focus on eluding Elgar leaves his tenants even more vulnerable when the building is ultimately slated for demolition by the state.

Even as Hunter's characters never explicitly invoke institutional racism in name, the recurring intrusion of property relations into the narrative continually blunts the impact of Elgar's racial bildungsroman. His love for his tenants cannot offset the fact that realtors and financiers view him as a "real asset to the community" while they view his tenants as a symptom of its sickness—a notion pedaled within real estate since the 1920s as a matter of financial and social fact.[69] We see this, for instance, when a developer argues that the neighborhood requires an "economic transfusion" to attract "property-maintaining people"—code for whites—even while insisting that "racial bias has nothing to do with the subject matter" since it is "strictly a matter of dollars and cents."[70] Hunter's parroting of the open secret of racism's role in real estate, which this rhetoric need only barely mask, sits in direct tension to Elgar's awakening.

But despite the constant reminders across the novel of the many bankers, realtors, developers, and state agents invested in depleting black neighborhoods, Hunter ends the novel with a surprisingly sunny ending dependent on Elgar's revelations. He ultimately invests both in his residents, funding their individual talents, as well as the greater neighborhood with the help of a newly founded Department of Housing and Urban Development, or HUD, established in 1965, proving that a community of low-rental apartments can make money without displacing black residents. Elgar can finally embrace the title of "landlord" after redefining its role as caretaker rather than exploiter.[71]

This cheery ending feels, however, like the most far-fetched moment of the whole novel despite its many moments of absurdity and farce. Elgar's exceptionality in possessing both the time and the wealth to invest in his new home suggests just how extraordinary an ending this really is. That Elgar's change of heart is tied to his ability to make his investments turn a profit points to

Hunter's ultimate faith in the capacity of the free market to right itself if only one could change the hearts and minds of enough wealthy liberals. Since so much of the novel challenges individualist solutions to the institutional conditions perpetuating slums, it is jarring, to say the least, when everything falls perfectly into place for its characters at its conclusion.

Yet, even as Hunter seems to abandon satire in *The Landlord*'s reformist ending, the racialized presence of the "machinery of dispossession" punctuating the novel up to this point reminds the reader again and again of all that Elgar's breakthrough cannot achieve. Despite largely sticking to Elgar's point of view, Hunter offers readers frequent glimpses into the ways his tenants have learned to stay afloat as various bureaucrats, realtors, and developers have devalued their block largely from a distance. The forms of numbness, mental illness, and self-harm that the tenants exhibit across the novel result not from fighting a few crummy landlords but from the larger network of property relations profiting from discrimination. That this small building of tenants ultimately thrives due to the efforts of a wealthy white patron is gratifying. But *The Landlord*'s ending also brings to mind the many more tenants in slum housing not fortunate enough to have an Elgar Enders wake up and pay attention while still turning a profit.

The Landlord Circa 1970

While the happy ending of Hunter's version of *The Landlord* could be said to reflect the optimism of 1966 following the passage of the Civil Rights Act, such an ending might have been a harder sell two years later following the riots of 1967 and King's assassination in 1968. The optimism of this recent past is precisely what appealed to Norman Jewison, who would most strongly steer the novel's 1970 film adaptation. Jewison was a Hollywood director and producer known for making humanistic films about overcoming racial impasse, including, most notably, the 1967 Oscar-winning film *In the Heat of the Night*. Although Jewison bought the rights to Hunter's novel a month after its 1966 publication, his investment in its themes of interracial cooperation must be understood in relation to the post-1968 moment when the film was made. Moreover, given that the drastic rewriting of Hunter's plot that Jewison authorized further simplified its story of cross-racial redemption, the takeaways of 1970's *The Landlord* significantly differ from those of its source material.

Further distinguishing the context of the novel's production from that of the film was the 1968 passage of the Fair Housing Act. I posit that the housing bill's ratification enabled the film's producers and writers to more easily shift their focus away from the "machinery of dispossession" central to Hunter's novel and constantly in tension with Elgar's individual wrestling with racism. By excising the book's emphasis on the institutional racism undergirding property relations in urban centers, the film can more fully devote itself to Elgar's individual transformation, buoyed by the personal attachments he accrues across the color line. Whereas the novel juxtaposes Elgar's story with the experiences of his tenants' stasis propagated by varying private and public institutions, the film focuses on Elgar at the expense of this broader network maintaining racialized property relations, dismantling the satirical investigative aesthetics of satire so vital to the novel.

Jewison's preference for Elgar's story was present from the first draft of the screenplay by Erich Segal—the Ivy League scholar of comparative literature who eventually wrote the book and film *Love Story*.[72] In a letter to Jewison, Segal drew a connection between Hunter's novel and Jewison's previous movies centering on a "kooky confrontation" between "supposed enemies" that ultimately leaves "the world just a little bit better."[73] Jewison, to his credit, realizing how perilous it might be to trivialize race relations as a set of "kooky encounters," given the current national climate, scrapped Segal's version. He then called upon black playwright and novelist Bill Gunn to draft the script that director Hal Ashby ultimately used to shoot in the summer of 1969.

Film scholar Christopher Sieving has done the most thorough job of situating the film in relation to Hunter's novel as well as other "racial impasse" films from the 1960s. Against the backdrop of Sieving's elaboration of these broader contexts, I want to focus on what *The Landlord* as film can tell us about the possibilities for representing the relationship between race, racism, and property in the post–Fair Housing Act era. The film gives us a window into how artists were learning to newly present the relationship between race and housing in the wake of this new federal legalistic solution that, in criminalizing discrimination, helped to cement ownership as an unquestionable asset now that housing discrimination was theoretically outlawed. With the Fair Housing Act largely completing the state's formal actions to redress racism in the housing market, *The Landlord* suggests how this story would be told moving forward now that the civil rights component of housing was largely deemed over and done with.

Kristin Hunter's reported displeasure with the film is a good place to start. As reported by a Philadelphia newspaper, Hunter took issue with four changes the filmmakers made to her original plot: the new focus on Elgar's wealthy family, the decision to cut both his psychoanalysis (a large part of how he learns to better attune himself to the world around him) as well as the urban renewal plot, and, most egregiously, the flattening of its black characters. "I found the blacks in the movie more stereotyped than I had made them," Hunter lamented.[74] Her stated disappointments all generally stem from the filmmakers' decision to center the film around a simplified Elgar at the expense of the tenants' more complex representation.

Nowhere is this choice more evident than in the robust attention the film pays to Elgar's romantic entanglements. While Elgar's love life in the novel serves as an index of his inner chaos, it never alone drives the plot. Elgar's attachments to people in general are rapacious and suffocating, be they romantic or platonic in nature. In Hunter's original text, Elgar has an affair with his married tenant, Fanny. When she becomes pregnant, it is unclear whether Elgar is the father or Fanny's husband, Copee. While Elgar is ultimately not the father, a fact revealed when the child is born, his potential siring of a mixed-race child is one of many elements within the novel that draw him deeper into the emotional world of the building.

But in the film, Elgar's love life takes up a majority of its screen time. Early on in the movie, Elgar meets and starts dating the mixed-race Lanie (a minor figure in the novel). Upon sleeping with Fanny and believing he has impregnated her, his relationship with Lanie becomes strained. But unlike in the novel, Elgar does turn out to be the father of Fanny's child, driving her husband to a psychotic break. In one of the film's most memorable scenes, Fanny demands soon after giving birth that Elgar place their child up for adoption as white so he can "grow up casual like his father."[75] The film ends with Elgar leaving the deed of the building to her and ultimately choosing to leave with his son to raise him elsewhere. The film's final scene features Elgar and child arriving at Lanie's apartment building to enlist her help in this task.

In the film's revised ending, the building's fate is largely an afterthought. Elgar casually announces its new ownership while storming out of the building for good as his tenants stare him down. The pregnancy story line now becomes the plot mechanism that forces Elgar's maturation. Yet the question of how exactly to resolve the film's property plotline remained an ongoing issue in the screenplay's drafting. Bill Gunn toyed with two different endings for the building—in one, a group of black nationalists blow it up to protest Elgar's relationship with Fanny.[76] Another draft includes a climactic scene in a lawyer's office in which Elgar leaves the building to all the remaining tenants.[77] The resolution Ashby ultimately filmed feels far less substantial than either of these possibilities as Elgar's paternity eclipses the building as a point of interest.

Although the building had multiple fates in earlier drafts, Jewison had always planned to steer the film away from what he termed "the Urban Renewal thing" that ends Hunter's novel.[78] In the novel's original ending, Elgar decides to stay in the neighborhood and invest in better housing that allows his tenants say, too. As Sieving observes, Jewison's notes on the novel end halfway through, suggesting his disinterest in Hunter's ending from the start.[79] Given Jewison's desire to, in his words, "bring to the screen in this country, a real, genuine, warm comedy with a mixed cast," he seemed to have decided early on that wading into fraught policies about the forced demolition of black neighborhoods would not a "warm comedy" make.[80]

The filmmakers decided instead to make Elgar's new mixed-race family the vehicle for demonstrating his newfound social responsibility. This is not to reduce the complexity of how the film tackles this subject. In one of its most surreal scenes, a rotating cast of black characters deliver a shared monologue to Elgar at a party concluding with the following line: "You whites scream about miscegenation and you done watered down every race you ever hated!" That Elgar goes on to unthinkingly sleep with Fanny in the next scene suggests, however, his inability to engage this accusation.[81] Elgar's final decision to adopt the child of this union and raise him with Lanie is clearly meant to mark his new capacity to take responsibility for his actions. But it is also true that this resolution frames responsibility as something inherently familial rather than as extending to those who one isn't tied to either by blood or lust. The novel's complex questions about what constitutes an ethical property relation are largely excised in the film. Elgar's responsibility to his very narrowly defined family now sits front and center. Long gone are the dispossessive ecstasies of the pop-up rent party I discussed in Chapter 2 privileging forms of community-making beyond the family. In the film version of *The Landlord*, the unit of the building once dominating the social imaginary of the rent party must be dismantled in order for the family unit—the only sustainable mechanism for racial integration in the film—to survive.

While the film's new ending most significantly signals its disinterest in institutional racism's covert and unspectacular ordering of property relations, a casting choice reinforces this choice in a telling fashion. Hunter's novel makes the "machinery of dispossession" continually felt in the form of minor characters including realtors, developers, constables, bankers, urban renewal experts, and businessmen who pop up across its plot. Their purpose is seemingly to underscore the commonplace view that Elgar's investment in a building in a black neighborhood is risky and can only be made profitable through the ruthless pursuit of rent. In the novel, for instance, Elgar correctly gathers the meaning of his white realtor, who insists that while he wouldn't have minded selling the building to its tenants, he "prefers dealing with a businessman."[82] Elgar follows this by rightly inferring, "A white man, you mean."[83] The novel marks the confusion Elgar generates when he starts to buck the commonplaces of racialized property management and the behavior expected of him as a white slumlord.

But instead of a white realtor signaling his racial solidarity with his white client, the realtor appearing in the 1970 film version is played by a black woman who would have been quite recognizable in certain circles: activist Florynce Kennedy, one of the first black women to graduate from Columbia Law School and cofounder of the National Black Feminist Organization, known for her signature cowboy hat.[84] Kennedy appears as Enid the realtor in a short scene lasting under a minute and never appears in the film again. She is the lone face of realty in the film.

This scene reads differently depending on whether the viewers recognizes the realtor as Florynce Kennedy. When Kennedy's presence is known, the scene seems to wink at the viewer by inviting them to bask in its ironies. Impersonating a slick realtor profiting from gentrification while purposefully underpreparing Elgar for his coming difficulties, Kennedy's willingness to play against type makes the film's satire all the more tangible. Her presence

FIGURES 11 AND 12. Florynce Kennedy playing Elgar's realtor in *The Landlord*, 1970.

Source: Hal Ashby, *The Landlord*, 1970.

signals to the audience that they should mistrust the desire to sympathize with Elgar's predicament, reminding the viewer that Elgar's ability to buy this building is symptomatic of the power, privilege, and willful ignorance his race and gender have bestowed upon him—imbalances Kennedy fought fiercely to address in real life. Kennedy's presence potentially also serves as a seal of approval, assuring us of the filmmakers' left credibility.

But if the viewer does not recognize Flo Kennedy, the casting of the realtor generates another set of potential readings. In making a black woman not only the face of real estate but also the force behind the neighborhood's gentrification, the film also gestures toward the multiracial business of property exploitation further eased by the Fair Housing Act. As historian N. D. B. Connolly has shown, some middle- and upper-class African Americans reaped financial benefits from discrimination allowing black and white landlords alike to charge higher prices to blacks contained to concentrated areas where they generally paid far more rent than their white counterparts for far worse housing.[85] We might read the transposition of the realtor's race in particular in the film as a representation of the black middle class's exodus and increasing distance from inner-city neighborhoods accelerated by the Fair Housing Act.[86] Enid's complicity in Elgar's purchase evokes this expanding intra-racial class gap through property. Her presence points to the profit to be had by both blacks and whites alike on the predatory multiracial housing market extracting value from the black urban poor. On the other hand, Enid manipulates Elgar in much the same way his tenants do, underscoring the connections between her property hustle and their rent hustle rather than their differences.

But given Jewison's reluctance at representing "the Urban Renewal thing" from Hunter's novel and his broader interest in stories depicting the overcoming of racial impasse, a more likely read of this scene is that the casting of the realtor as a black woman paints the exploitation of the black poor with a multiracial sheen—avoiding any further reflection on how assumptions of the inherent devaluing effect of black occupation undergird the housing market itself. To return to the novel, the interaction between Elgar and his white realtor offers the reader a window into what Hunter terms the "odious chumminess" of business-as-usual within the housing market in which the realtor treats Elgar as the building's rightful possessor while lamenting the "ignorance" of the building's tenants for having "paid enough rent to buy the house four times over."[87] (Even as their "ignorance" is later revealed to be cunning when we observe the tactics the tenants have honed to avoid paying rent or the inflated mortgages they would have likely paid if they had purchased their apartments.)

Whereas this transaction in the novel between Elgar and his white realtor demonstrates how blacks were locked out of the housing market before they even have a chance to be denied, the film's rendering of this character as a black woman effectively circumvents conversations about forms of racism central to the housing market before and after the Fair Housing Act. Making a black woman the face of the real estate industry serves the film's efforts to emphasize Elgar's capacity for change over any broader story of how racism has shaped property relations in the U.S., allowing for an all-black slum to exist in the first place. Jewison's desire to make a "real, genuine, warm comedy with a mixed cast" precludes depicting the impersonal and uneventfully saturating racism on which much of the American residential market had been built and maintained in the twentieth century.

Kristin Hunter's 1966 novel ultimately imagines an optimistic property future at the novel's end in which Elgar transforms his impersonal property relations premised on debt into relations increasingly social and ethical in nature. And while Hunter ultimately valorizes ownership and the free market as the sole means through which these transformations can be achieved in the novel's conclusion, she nonetheless remains committed to exploring the malleability of property relations and their capacity to beget other kinds of intimacies and collaborations. Even as the novel humorously follows Elgar's conversion from spoiled heir to someone having a real emotional and ethical stake in the community he buys into, it also shows the larger real estate apparatus preventing more Elgars from having similar revelations.

The film adaptation of *The Landlord*, however, concludes with Elgar's ultimate abdication of any relationship with his tenants at all. Elgar decides to instead invest his energies in his newborn child, whom he will raise as white, far away from the unsalvageable black block. Whereas Hunter's vision for the neighborhood's future is highly idiosyncratic in relation to the rest of the novel, it nonetheless imagines a future for the neighborhood that includes its black characters. Four years later, the same neighborhood would be abandoned by both Elgar and the film version at large, ultimately suggesting that new life can only flourish beyond its borders. With the passage of the Fair Housing Act satisfying public outrage that the state no longer sanctioned overt individual discrimination, *The Landlord* insists it is okay for its viewers to turn their attentions elsewhere as the individual overcoming of racism through sex overshadows addressing or even representing its less exciting, if more immobilizing, institutional forms.

The Property Imagination Post-1968

Both versions of *The Landlord* invented strategies to variously represent and evade the representation of institutional racism before and after the 1968 Fair Housing Act. Whereas Hunter's novel uses satire to bring housing discrimination's ongoingness into view at a time when both covert and overt forms of racism in the private market were still legally sanctioned on the federal level, the 1970 film adaptation of *The Landlord* suggests how the Fair Housing Act, addressing only the most overt forms of discrimination, relieved some of the pressure to represent housing discrimination as a systemic condition. The Fair Housing Act's passage, in fact, may have helped to erode the urgency of Carmichael and Hamilton's 1967 call to both represent and redress the forms of covert racism central to the housing market's operation to the broader American public. While writers in midcentury openly grappled with the relationship between homeownership and racism, the 1968 Fair Housing Act proffered a legal solution to discriminatory practices while failing to dismantle the financial structures dependent on racism's entrenchment. It has been argued, moreover, that the Fair Housing Act inadvertently cleared the way for homeownership to finally become the normative state of dwelling in the U.S., increasing the number of total homebuyers on the private market while removing the last hurdle preventing the broader embrace of homeownership as the solution to economic and, now, racial disparity. As Keeanga-Yamahtta Taylor has studied at great length, "racial discrimination persisted in the new market because it was good business," leaving blacks open to what she terms "predatory inclusion" sanctioned by state agencies in the post–Fair Housing Act era.[88]

But novels like *The Landlord*, openly referring to real estate as the "machinery of dispossession," would become less prevalent in the decades that followed. Coming after not just the passage of the Fair Housing Act but also the continued waning faith in the transformative possibilities of public housing, we find future writers focusing less intently on homeownership's pitfalls as a property relation. Disenchantment with homeownership, of course, does not dissipate in the 1970s—later works by Gloria Naylor, Richard Ford, John Edgar Wideman, Jonathan Franzen, Chang-rae Lee, Mat Johnson, and Angela Flournoy attest to the sustained interest by fiction writers into the present in the complications of homeownership across the color line. But in literature written after the 1970s, there is a greater sense of resignation to homeownership as a normative aspiration. Disgruntlement with one's living situation supersedes more specific attention to housing as a financial mechanism dictating how one lives. With the majority of Americans investing a good deal of their wealth and aspirations into their homes, walking away or forsaking this option seems harder to entertain even in fiction.

I want to conclude, then, by briefly retrieving two aspects from the two versions of *The Landlord* that point to how the story of race and housing would come to be increasingly told as well as the motifs and ideas increasingly less available to the post-1970s housing imaginary. Let's start with a telling omission from both versions of *The Landlord*. For all the differences between Hunter's 1966 novel and Ashby's 1970 adaptation, both center the culture clash between Elgar, a blue blood of remarkable wealth, and his down-on-their-luck poor black tenants who despite their various talents must devote most of their energy to figuring out how to avoid eviction. The interchange between these two extremes of the American social and racial landscape certainly makes for a dramatic fish-out-of-water story that neither version can resist. Yet this conflict between Elgar, the white blue blood, and the black working poor absents the population that largely drove the American real estate market at midcentury: the white middle class, encouraged by the private-public partnership managing residential real estate's development to buy newly built homes in the suburbs. The best mortgage rates were given to white homeowners purchasing in mass-developed whites-only middle-class suburbs that were themselves constructed using state subsidies requiring their ongoing segregation.

By taking the wealthy Elgar as their protagonist, both the novel and the film avoid having to wade into the complex motivations, subsidies, and ideologies that encouraged middle-class whites and, after the 1948 *Shelley v. Kraemer* decision dismantling the legal enforcement of racial covenants, middle-class blacks as well to leave urban neighborhoods to largely become the domain of the black urban poor. By rendering property exploitation as a matter of wealthy whites exploiting the black poor, both versions obscure the engine of homeownership in the U.S. after 1950: the multiracial middle class. Read in this context, *A Raisin in the Sun* is not the story of black pioneering as a general possibility but as an option selectively open to the newly cash-rich Youngers and other upwardly mobile black families, even as they generally paid more than their white middle-class counterparts for the privilege of ownership. If the black realtor of the 1970 film version of *The Landlord* helps to obfuscate the white supremacy at the heart of real estate's "machinery of dispossession," she also points to the profit to be had by both blacks and whites on the discriminatory housing market at the expense of the black working poor. Both versions of *The Landlord* forecast the difficulties of telling this more complex story of how mass homeownership produced new definitions of both race *and* class increasingly tethered to property.

But I want to close with another moment from Hunter's novel suggesting what would be increasingly expelled from the American housing imaginary in the years following its 1966 publication. This moment revolves around another minor character, Old Man Mose, who runs a magazine stand down the street from where Elgar and his tenants reside. While Elgar remains oblivious to the multiple signs that the neighborhood is being slated for urban renewal, Mose is keenly aware that "when the Blighters come"—his name for the developers and so-called reformers arriving to decry the neighborhood's worn state—"the bulldozers ain't far behind."[89] Although Elgar remains oblivious to the changes all around him, Mose pontificates on his future given the impending signals of urban renewal:

> "I been on this corner fifty years, man and boy," Old Man Mose said. "Guess I ought to be glad I'm not a property owner like you. Yep, that's one thing to be thankful for. I can always pick up my stand and move on, sell my papers somewhere else. But just the same, I'll sure hate to see this neighborhood go."[90]

The humor in this scene comes from the juxtaposition of Mose's sage awareness of his coming displacement with Elgar's failure to see what is so obviously taking place. ("Elgar did not understand a word of this," Hunter notes).[91] And yet, while Mose most explicitly articulates the consequences of urban renewal for him and the neighborhood's other black occupants, his status as unpropertied somewhat insulates him from its effects.

Mose's relief at not being a property owner recalls the earlier astonishment expressed by Elgar's white realtor that the building's tenants did not themselves jump at the chance to buy it despite having "paid enough rent to buy the house four times over." In these two instances, Hunter has the novel's black characters suggest either in word or deed the limitations of embracing property ownership as the horizon of either personal, economic, or political possibility. Given the state's attempts to confiscate much of the neighborhood through eminent domain, Hunter suggests that Mose and his neighbors are wise to be weary of ownership as a fix-all granting them permanence, sovereignty, or recognition. Even though she ultimately renders capitalist enterprise (with an assist from HUD) as the remedy to the neighborhood's exploitation and neglect, Hunter's scripting of these other countervailing moments in which her characters spurn ownership for the possibility to "move on" and be "somewhere else," to cite Mose, offers another vision of dwelling that does not conflate civil rights with property rights.

This line of thought is reminiscent of Richard Wright's assessment twenty-five years earlier in *12 Million Black Voices*. Here, as I gloss in Chapter 3, Wright casts Reconstruction not as a moment of lost possibility for black sovereignty ended by the violent retrenchment of white supremacy with the rise of Jim Crow, as W. E. B. Du Bois does in 1935's *Black Reconstruction*. Wright devotes only two slim paragraphs of *12 Million Black Voices* to Reconstruction. Rather than casting this era as one of tragically thwarted potential, he presents it instead as a moment when blacks could bask in the glories of being liberated from the land after having been confined to it for centuries through enslavement: "Just as a kitten stretches and yawns after a long sleep," Wright insists, "so thousands of us tramped from place to place for the sheer sake of moving, looking wandering, landless upon the land."[92] Wright's definition of black freedom as freedom from property appears as a minor chord in Hunter's novel twenty-five years later. But such visions of a life well lived unanchored by property as well as aesthetic strategies for representing them would be increasingly harder to find in the post-1968 U.S. literary imagination. Investigative aesthetics can only read the past that it uncovers in trace glimpses. Going beyond retrieval to revive freedom dreams untethered from property requires more positive methods of resuscitation, reanimation, and reimagining across investigative and aesthetic forms.

Epilogue
Resurrection City and Beverly Hills, Chicago

THE HOUSING MARKET REMAINS BUILT around the perception of racial difference. Far from ending discriminatory residential practices, the Fair Housing Act of 1968—as described in Keeanga-Yamahtta Taylor's *Race for Profit: How Banks and the Real Estate Industry Undermined Black Homeownership*—led lenders, realtors, and policy makers to move from strategies of racial exclusion and toward predatory forms of racial inclusion continuing to disadvantage black resident and neighborhoods. But while the structural entrenchment of residential discrimination was once an open secret, national news stories attesting to its depths now seem to appear every few weeks.[1] This coverage largely points to one enduring fact: the belief that black presence makes property inherently more illiquid, and that whiteness is a neighborhood's most valued amenity, continues to undergird the housing market. Despite the illegality of housing discrimination, black homes today are still appraised lower than white homes, and black neighborhoods valued less than white ones.[2] Predatory lending and other exploitative real estate practices have made it easier for blacks to buy *and* lose property, causing the black homeownership rate to remain far below that of white Americans. In 2022, 74.6 percent of white households in the U.S. owned their homes, compared to 45.3 percent of black households, a gap wider now than it was in 1960, before the passage of the Fair Housing Act.[3] "Even when no discernable discrimination is detected," as Taylor writes, "the fact that Black communities and neighborhoods are perceived as inferior means that African Americans must rely on an inherently devalued 'asset' for maintenance of their quality of life."[4]

Because the home remains the largest investment most white Americans will make in their lifetime, and because the perceptual assumptions made on behalf of white homebuyers continue to anchor practices of lending and realty, the residential sensorium still dominates how we see and know race. As the age of mass homeownership stretches on, the residential sensorium becomes harder to locate as a distinct set of perceptual practice because it has become so synonymous with the racial sensorium writ large. The culling of racialized language from real estate processes since the midcentury, moreover, has made the racialization of the residential sensorium all the harder to acknowledge or describe outside of either individual experience or aggregated data about homeownership's enduring inequalities. But redlining patterns established nearly a century ago persist; majority-black neighborhoods experience worse social outcomes than those who live almost anywhere else.[5]

Given this ongoing history, the declining black homeownership rate is indicative not just of the ravages of predatory inclusion, but also perhaps of the hesitancy potential black homebuyers have learned to develop toward this asset that their very presence devalues. It tracks that blacks would be wary of investing in a homeownership system that has not only paid less dividends to them, but which is organized around the premise that black property—or any form of investment in black residential living—has less inherent value. Stories abound of the disappointment and pain accompanying ongoing encounters with the racialized housing market. Writers like Sarah Broom, Natalie Moore, and Angela Flournoy describe living in and caring for black-owned homes worn down after years of structural disinvestment and environmental racism, struggles with structures that cannot be renovated or sold except at a steep financial loss, and the failures of home equity to produce generational wealth. These writers suggest that black homeownership may not be a story to pass on, to cite Toni Morrison, marking both the difficulty of giving up on ownership but also the necessity of finding other forms other than the home to invest in and hand down.[6]

Yet, as this book has also shown, experiments in learning to differently see and feel for forms of dwelling in excess of assumptions of black illiquidity and whiteness as a universal amenity have always emerged to challenge visions of homeownership's good life. At this book's close, I find myself drawn to a cluster of housing actions and imaginaries fashioned and pursued where the previous chapter leaves off in the late 1960s, all of which seemed to sense the inadequacies of the Fair Housing Act to substantially remake the racialized housing market while charting their own alternative visions for dwelling. Some of these plans involved reclaiming the land as a viable place to live and work. Fannie Lou Hamer founded the Freedom Farm Cooperative in 1969 on forty acres of land in Rueville, Mississippi, to improve nutrition for black communities, create opportunities for fair profit distribution, and offer affordable housing.[7] The New Afrikan Independence Movement formed in 1968 to "free the land" in order to build an independent black nation stretching across Louisiana, Mississippi, Alabama, Georgia, and South Carolina. Other projects aspired to make space for black self-determination in more residential settings.[8] Using the pathways created by the wake of the Fair Housing Act, Floyd McKissick, a former head of CORE, began developing Soul City, a combined residential development and economic corridor in North Carolina dedicated to black economic empowerment.[9] Though these actions varied in strategy and political philosophy, they point to the ongoing desire to reimagine the relationship between race and housing in anticipation of and response to the failures of legal reform to do so alone.

But I'm most drawn to a housing action from this period even more fleeting than even these relatively short-lived projects. Resurrection City was located on the National Mall in Washington, D.C., for a few weeks in the spring of 1969. First conceived by Martin Luther King Jr. and the Southern Christian Leadership Conference (SCLC) in 1967, Resurrection City was designed to be the centerpiece of the Poor People's Campaign and a bold pivot in King's political trajectory.[10] After the mixed results King achieved in Chicago as well as his desire to counteract the growing appeal of the Black Power movement, he began to envision a multiracial alliance dedicated to economic justice. Through the Poor People's Campaign, King and the SCLC intended to focus on building power through electoral politics, labor unions, and economic boycotts. It was housing, however, that would come to dominate the campaign's representational strategy as the SCLC planned for thousands of the nation's poor to convene on its capital city to build and occupy a highly visible encampment from which they would hold rallies while making demands upon government officials. The planned visibility of Resurrection City reflected the foundational role of housing in any vision of economic justice. But the decision to not just rally on the National Mall, but to also build and occupy a city there, was also canny media strategy. While yet another March on Washington might not turn heads, a newly built enclave located in the middle of nation's front lawn would be harder for the city and, by extension, the wider public to ignore.

Amid the midcentury proliferation of neighborhood description in literature, reportage, and real estate charted by this book, Resurrection City would not only make poverty visible, as the SCLC aimed; it would also offer Americans a glimpse of a different residential model whose value did not depend on seeing and appraising the racialized value of its residents. This does not mean that it was to be a color-blind endeavor. Ralph Abernathy described his aspirations for the encampment to be a place where "American Indians, Puerto Ricans, Mexican-Americans, white poor Americans from the Appalachian area of our country and black Americans will all live together here in this city of hope."[11] Resurrection City would bring together various civil rights movements organized around racial identity to imagine what other forms of solidarity and political aspirations might emerge when property—which has historically relied on racial distinctions to generate value—did not overdetermine practices of dwelling or movement building. Though the Poor People's Campaign's was focused on redress from the state, the interracial occupancy and communal aspirations of Resurrection City would demonstrate an approach to the residential untethered from either ownership or racial appraisal—central tenets of the housing market propped up by the state if not reducible to state support alone.

But things did not go as planned. The Poor People's Campaign's spring launch was thrown into disarray by King's assassination in April 1968, just weeks before caravans from across the country were set to start the journey to Washington. The SCLC, now helmed by Ralph Abernathy, decided to move forward with the May action to capitalize on both the grief and determination catalyzed by King's death. While King had not planned on asking permission from the state to occupy the land—he was more concerned with getting consent from Native peoples who he hoped would also join them in the occupation—the SCLC sought and received a five-week permit from the National Park Service to build an encampment along sixteen acres of the western end of the National Mall. A team of architects led by John Wiebenson hurriedly coordinated the site selection, planning, and design of Resurrection City to be safe and habitable while also best serving the Campaign's political mission. In designing Resurrection City as an unowned interracial community, as Mabel Wilson notes, its midcentury architects "went against their training, which had promoted large-scale modernist urban design projects" that had largely resulted in "the demolition of poor Black neighborhoods to make way for modernist mid- and high-rises housing mostly white middle class residents."[12] Here was an opportunity to imagine building and living differently. With few materials—promised donations never arrived—and little time, the team designed working water, electricity, and sanitation systems suitable for weeks of occupation organized around a central "Main Street" with public amenities that would functionally and symbolically bind its four large residential compounds.

But Resurrection City was no utopia. Constructed and inhabited during an unusually rainy period, the muddy grounds made for difficult living. The rain exasperated an already challenging experiment in co-management among thousands of strangers with few resources and little time for planning, while movement members reeled from the shocks of King's murder in April shortly followed by Robert F. Kennedy's assassination in June. Meeting the higher-than-anticipated demand for housing as residents arrived—more than three thousand at its peak—and managing the site's structural and safety needs after residents began departing provided further challenges. The senior leaders of the campaign never lived in Resurrection City, preferring instead to stay in hotels nearby, leading to a leadership vacuum on the ground. In the words of one historian, the encampment was "a crushing weight" for the SCLC and a "perfect failure."[13] "By allowing itself to become bogged down in running a city, the SCLC surrendered all its best protest weapons: imagination, spontaneity, and élan." Built on principles of bootstrap self-reliance and unable to deliver on promises of participatory governance, the occupation, as Mabel Wilson further notes, ultimately fell back on "already existing sociospatial relations of private property, rather than new forms of community by design."[14] Resurrection City was officially closed on June 24 after police offers, responding to reports of youths throwing rocks nearby, teargassed the complex and cleared it out for good, arresting 288 demonstrators, including Ralph Abernathy.

Despite Resurrection City's problems, efforts to cast it as a failure by the press at the time but also by historians shaping its long-term interpretation have papered over the exuberance, imagination, and, most importantly, the desire of its planners and participants to undertake this residential experiment in the first place. As Resurrection City's leading architect, John Wiebenson, wrote of the project, "If, finally, Resurrection City did not show how people should live, it did show the problems too many have in how they do live."[15] Part of this demonstration revelation came from the space's own structural and organizational failures; but Resurrection City also revealed these problems through its residents' willingness to participate in this ad hoc formation, propelled by the belief that there must be a better way to live beyond the forms that had so far failed them. Addressing "the problems too many have in how they do live" was not a matter of more and better ownership, as the residents' presence and demands suggested, but of rethinking the residential outside the tenets of exclusion underwriting private property itself. Like the rent parties of earlier years, Resurrection City showcased its occupants' commitment to trying out, for better or for worse, a different mode of residential living not rooted in possession.

Indeed, some tenants found their temporary structures superior to their permanent accommodations at home.[16] Others saw doctors, nurses, and dentists for the first time while visiting Resurrection City's health facilities. A resident hung a sign outside one of their domiciles stating, "We have lived in many houses. This is our first home. Welcome."[17] A photograph of the encampment shows a man proudly holding a sign reading "Happiness is: a warm dry house; no rats or roaches, lots of good food."[18] In other photos, residents pose proudly next to their residential structures, some of which have been decorated while others appear to be almost bare. Nowhere in the action's imagery is ownership pronounced, described, or represented as an aspiration. If operating Resurrection City blunted the campaign's broader capacity for imagination, spontaneity, and élan, the concentration of these qualities within the occupation remains of value. As Wiebenson wrote afterward, "though temporary, Resurrection City is a useful model of the community development process in action."[19]

The spirit of Resurrection City lives on—if not in the historical record, where its memory has largely faded—in the contemporary literary imagination increasingly more interested in the Resurrection Cities of the world than its Levittowns. If novels of white residential diaspora, to again cite Catherine Jurca, dominated American literary fiction from 1922's *Babbitt*, to 2001's *The Corrections*, the residential imaginary of the twenty-first century has been eager to chart other forms of living. While the ownership bug continues to persist for much of the American public, the stalwart setting of the single-family home at the center of much American literature in the twentieth century has increasingly been challenged by fictional representations of tent cities, refugee camps, military encampments, public housing, and reservations. The literature of dispossession—which has always shadowed residential literature in the age of mass homeownership, as I've argued—increasingly defines literary production in the twenty-first, suggesting the fragility of ownership's hold on both dreamworlds and realities across the color line.

Given the mutually constituted histories of race and property as concepts, transformations in thinking with regard to one inevitably impact and reshape thinking the other. To that end, the significance of the literary imagination's shift away from the racialized trials and tribulations of homeownership to explore other modalities of dwelling may point toward coming transformations in both the racial and residential sensoriums. But rather than trying to forecast the future from these aesthetic tea leaves, I close this book with one last look back to the work of Gwendolyn Brooks, one of our most canny observers of residential observeration. Brooks's poem "Beverly Hills, Chicago," published in 1949, follows a carful of Chicagoans who travel from their own neighborhood to take a leisurely evening drive through the nearby and relatively better-off Beverly neighborhood, the residents of which seem to live so well that even their trash exudes a sheen of "neat brilliancy." Though the race of those within the car and the people they observe in Beverly—a real Chicago neighborhood that was majority white at the time—is left unmarked within the poem, by 1949 the segregation that was increasingly endemic to residential settlement did not need explicit naming.[20] The different parts of the city those inside the car—likely Bronzeville—and those outside of it called home were treated by the housing industry and Americans writ large as oppositional units of value defined by race, even as the vocabulary for marking and describing race on the block was becoming more strategically evasive.

But Brooks subverts the reader's expectation of a chasmic gulf separating black and white aspirations for residential living. Those who live in Beverly and those driving through it seem to want the same kinds of creature comforts, even as *where* they live shapes *how* they live in ways both major and minor. Those in the car imagine those in Beverly Hills to likely drink nicer tea and sleep more peacefully without the interference of too-near neighbors, and that their work upon waking is likely less exhausting than those whose livings are "to be made again in the sweatingest physical manner." While Brooks's speakers admit that such luxuries will not shield Beverly's residents from all hardship, their experience of "trouble with a gold-flecked beautiful banner" will allow them to survive it for longer and with more tranquility: "they make excellent corpses, among the expensive flowers." Akin to the SCLC's approach to Resurrection City almost twenty years later, Brooks wields the residential as a lens for visualizing and measuring inequity writ large.

While observation and comparison inform the poem's first half, its second half pivots to those in the car trying to make sense of all they've seen. Her speakers insist that "it is only natural that we should look and look" within this residential milieu—a repetition emphasizing both the labor and duration of their eager watching. There is an air of defensiveness to their observational rationale, a posture that could derive from their sense that their act of racial tourism is somewhat macabre, rubbing salt in the already painful wounds of discrimination. And this pain, indeed, lingers as the occupants of the car struggle to imagine its repair. "We do not want them to have less," they insist, and yet "it is only natural that we should think we have not enough." This seemingly modest formulation is also a devasting stalemate. Are these observers confronting an impossible arithmetic? Can their residential advancement only come from the residential decline of others? Or is this very framework of scarcity the problem?

Perhaps the issue is having itself. Brooks's attention to looking and wanting as naturalized desires refracts the two founding principles of American residential space examined by this book: that the best Americans innately desire to own their own home and that desiring ownership itself is a fundamentally racialized proclivity. In the poem's stalemate about whether one can have more without someone else having less, "Beverly Hills, Chicago" skirts the longer history of race, ownership, and feeling rendering homeownership a zero-sum game. Black residential gains, real estate professionals argued, *could* only be won at the expense of declining property values for whites. By 1949, the idea that black presence devalued all homes in its proximity had been fully embraced as an economic truism that no amount of feeling, protest, or reformist legislation could seemingly budge.

Yet Brooks leaves open as a question the possibility of imagining other distributive residential equations in which wanting more may not depend upon someone else having less—or having at all. The lyric speakers limn the shortcomings of contemporary residential logic positing black advancement as a threat to white possession, but they do not yet have an alternative maxim with which to replace it. The poem's collective speakers naturalize the sense that they do not *have* enough, yet Brooks falls short of endorsing either more or better having as the solution to the inequality they perceive or that it is natural to feel so in the first place. In the speakers' assertion that it is "only natural that we should think we have not enough," their recourse to the natural seems to mask their uncertainty, an overcompensation suggesting that *wanting to have* might not actually be as innate as they claim it to be. When those in the car finally speak to one another, the dissatisfaction of this impasse leaves an air of bad feeling betwixt those in the car, taking the form of "gruff" speech. Their experience of residential observation has not only left them unsettled, but it has also diminished their solidarity with each other. The desire to see beyond their own residential environs—and their lack of frameworks for explaining its difference beyond possession—has only left them feeling worse.

But whereas Brooks's car-bound speakers only begin to voice the contorted logic framing their residential desires as a threat to white possession and sovereignty, this book has charted how others in the age of mass homeownership across a wide spectrum of disciplines and genres joined Brooks in giving a range of shapes to this logic while challenging ownership's position as the natural horizon of citizenship, security, or investment. It is this broader range of gruff voices—those singing the racial praises of homeownership and those calling for other modes of dwelling in excess of possession and reconstruction from the nation's rent parties and Resurrection Cities—that this book has tried its best to hear.

Notes

Introduction

1. For more on the racial sensorium and racial perception, see Adrienne Brown, *The Black Skyscraper: Architecture and the Perception of Race* (Baltimore: Johns Hopkins University Press, 2017).

2. See *Chasing the American Dream: New Perspectives on Affordable Homeownership*, William M. Rohe and Harry L. Watson, eds. (Ithaca, NY: Cornell University Press, 2007), and Thomas Sugrue, "The Right to a Decent Home," in *To Promote the General Welfare: The Case for Big Government*, Steven Conn, ed. (New York: Oxford University Press, 2012).

3. For more on the impact of 1917 on the real estate industry, see LeeAnn Lands, *The Culture of Property: Race, Class, and Housing Landscapes in Atlanta* (Athens: University of Georgia Press, 2009), 117.

4. It's also worth noting the role of academic research—particularly in regards to land economics—in helping to create and shore up arguments for homeownership as a specific vehicle for white sovereignty that would help ensure its survival. For more on the academic support for residential segregation, see David Freund, *Colored Property: State Policy & White Racial Politics in Suburban America* (Chicago: University of Chicago Press, 2007); Elaine Lewinnek, *The Working Man's Reward: Chicago's Early Suburbs and the Roots of American Sprawl* (New York: Oxford University Press, 2014); Margaret Garb, *City of American Dreams: A History of Home Ownership and Housing Reform in Chicago, 1871–1919* (Chicago: University of Chicago Press, 2005); and Benjamin Wiggins, *Calculating Race: Racial Discrimination in Risk Assessment* (New York: Oxford University Press, 2020).

5. The story of American homeownership would also not have been possible without the ongoing dispossession of native land. This framework has so far not been central to how mass homeownership in the twentieth century has been studied by housing scholars and it's one I only begin to plumb here. For a more policy-oriented study of contemporary Native housing in the U.S., see David Listokin, *Housing and*

Economic Development in Indian Country: Challenge and Opportunity (New York: Taylor & Francis, 2018), funded by the Fannie Mae Foundation.

6. Reinhold Martin, "Real Estate Agency," in *The Art of Inequality: Architecture, Housing, and Real Estate: A Provisional Report*, Reinhold Martin, Jacob Moore, and Susanne Schindler, eds. (New York: Temple Hoyne Buell Center for the Study of American Architecture, 2015), 92.

7. Michael Omi and Howard Winant, *Racial Formation in the United States*, 3rd ed. (New York: Routledge, 2014), 125. I seek to slightly modify George Lipsitz's insistence that "the racial projects of U.S. society have always been spatial projects" to insist more specifically that racial projects are always projects of property. See George Lipsitz, *How Racism Takes Place* (Philadelphia: Temple University Press, 2011), 52.

8. Brenna Bhandar, *Colonial Lives of Property: Law, Land, and Racial Regimes of Ownership* (Durham, NC: Duke University Press, 2018), 8. I forward Bhandar's more muscular articulation of the mutual reliance of these concepts on one another, building from Cheryl Harris's articulation of the "interaction" of "conceptions of race and property" as playing "a critical role in establishing and maintaining racial and economic subordination." Cheryl I. Harris, "Whiteness as Property," *Harvard Law Review* 106, no. 8 (June 1993): 1716.

9. See, for instance, Michael Heller, "Three Faces of Property," *Oregon Law Review* 79, no. 2 (2000): 417–34.

10. Carol Rose, *Persuasion Revisited: Vision and Property* (New York: Routledge, 1995), 278.

11. Judith Butler and Athena Athanasiou, *Dispossession: The Performative in the Political* (Cambridge: Polity, 2013), 13.

12. See John Locke, *A Second Treatise on Government* (Indianapolis: Hackett, 1980), 19, and Adam Smith, "Moral Sentiments," in *The Essays of Adam Smith* (London: Alex, Murray & Son, 1869). As Tyler Stovall puts it, "The issue of property was central to the emergence of white freedom, so the fact that protecting individual property rights became a major issue for the construction of liberal democracy in the 19th century underscored its centrality to modern ideas of liberty." Tyler Stovall, *White Freedom: The Racial History of an Idea* (Princeton, NJ: Princeton University Press, 2021), 140.

13. Debates about whether property was a natural right would be invoked in arguments as to whether suffrage should be limited to property owners in the U.S. See Jacob Katz Cogan, "The Look Within: Property, Capacity, and Suffrage in Nineteenth-Century America," *Yale Law* Review 107, no. 473 (1997): 473–98.

14. Smith, "Moral Sentiments," 77.

15. William Blackstone, *Commentaries on the Laws of England, Volume 2: A Facsimile of the First Edition of 1765–1769* (Chicago: University of Chicago Press, 1979), 2.

16. Bhandar, *Colonial Lives of Property*, 3.

17. Ibid., 4.

18. As Maximillian C. Forte writes, "both race and place are ways of making the Indigenous visible and, paradoxically, are also ways to minimize indigeneity when they

are used as objectified markers of authenticity" (24). *Who Is an Indian? Race, Place, and the Politics of Indigeneity in the Americas* (Toronto: University of Toronto Press, 2013).

19. As Joanne Barker notes, "the erasure of the sovereign is the racialization of the 'Indian.'" Barker, "For Whom Sovereignty Matters," in *Sovereignty Matters: Locations of Contestation and Possibility in Indigenous Struggles for Self-Determination*, Joanne Barker, ed. (Lincoln: University of Nebraska Press, 2005) 17.

20. I am also indebted to Cheryl Harris's articulation of this relationship: "Although the systems of oppression of Blacks and Native Americans differed in form—the former involving the seizure and appropriation of labor, the latter entailing the seizure and appropriation of land—undergirding both was a racialized conception of property implemented by force and ratified by law." "Whiteness as Property," 1715.

21. John Locke, *Two Treatises of Government* (Cambridge: Cambridge University Press, 1988), 213.

22. Cited in Stuart Banner, *How the Indians Lost Their Land: Law and Power on the Frontier* (Cambridge, MA: Harvard University Press, 2007), 152.

23. *Messages of the Presidents of the United States* (Columbus, OH: Jonathan Phillips, 1841), 92.

24. Aileen Moreton-Robinson, *The White Possessive: Property, Power, and Indigenous Sovereignty* (Minneapolis: University of Minnesota Press, 2015). See also Robert Nichols, *Theft Is Property: Dispossession and Critical Theory* (Durham, NC: Duke University Press, 2020), for more on the relationship between dispossession, sovereignty, and the creation of property.

25. Locke, *A Second Treatise on Government*, 19. For more on Locke's own financial and managerial connections to slavery as they informed his philosophical work, see David Armitage, "John Locke, Carolina, and the Two Treatises of Government," *Political Theory* 32, no. 5 (October 2004): 602–27.

26. Nicholas Buccola, *The Political Thought of Frederick Douglass: In Pursuit of American Liberty* (New York: New York University Press, 2013), 29.

27. William Harper, *On Slavery, Read Before the Society for the Advancement of Learning of South Carolina, at Its Annual Meeting at Columbia* (Charleston, SC: James S. Burges, 1838), 14. For more on the centrality of property rights to the defense of slavery, see Simon J. Gilhooley, *The Antebellum Origins of the Modern Constitution: Slavery and the Spirit of the American Founding* (New York: Cambridge University Press, 2020).

28. Ibid., 5.

29. Ibid., 38.

30. George Fitzhugh, *Sociology for the South: Or, The Failure of Free Society* (Richmond, VA: A. Morris, 1854), 267. Fitzhugh's disdain for Locke's concept of natural rights informed his description of the philosopher as a "presumptuous charlatan."

31. W. E. B. Du Bois, *Black Reconstruction in America: 1860–1880* (New York: Free Press, 1935), 700. See also David Roediger, *The Wages of Whiteness: Race and the Making of the American Working Class* (New York: Verso, 1991).

32. Howard Odum, *Social and Mental Traits of the Negro: Research into the Conditions of the Negro Race in Southern Towns* (New York: Columbia University Press, 1910), 225.

33. Ibid., 224.

34. Ibid.

35. Alfred Holt Stone, "The Economic Future of the Negro: The Factor of White Competition," *Publications of the American Economic Association* 7 no. 1 (February 1906): 246.

36. H. T. Kealing, "The Characteristics of the Negro People," in *The Negro Problem*, Booker T. Washington, ed. (New York: James Pott, 1903), 176.

37. Ibid.

38. Ibid., 174. In the same volume, W. E. B. Du Bois and Charles Chesnutt positively focus on the "three hundred million dollars worth of real and personal property" accumulated by Negroes in the U.S. to date (81, 47).

39. Stone, "The Economic Future of the Negro," 294.

40. Ella Myers, "Beyond the Psychological Wage: Du Bois on White Dominion," *Political Theory* 47, no. 1 (2019): 6–31; W. E. B. Du Bois, "The Souls of White Folks," in *Darkwater: Voices from Within in the Veil* (New York: Harcourt, Brace, 1920), 30.

41. Ibid., 31.

42. Ibid.

43. William James, *The Principles of Psychology* (New York: Henry Holt, 1890), 293–94.

44. Ibid., 291.

45. Paige Glotzer, *How the Suburbs Were Segregated: Developers and the Business of Exclusionary Housing, 1890–1960* (New York: Columbia University Press, 2020), 5.

46. This is in explicit conversation with David Freund's focus on the more general arguments made in the 1910s and 1920s citing biological hierarchies of race to resist residential integration. *Colored Property: State Policy & White Racial Politics in Suburban America* (Chicago: University of Chicago Press, 2007).

47. Sean Illing, "The Sordid History of Housing Discrimination in America," *Vox*, May 5, 2020, https://www.vox.com/identities/2019/12/4/20953282/racism-housing-discrimination-keeanga-yamahtta-taylor.

48. Keeanga-Yamahtta Taylor, *Race for Profit: How Banks and the Real Estate Industry Undermined Black Homeownership* (Chapel Hill: University of North Carolina Press, 2020), 7.

49. Rose Helper, *Racial Policies and Practices of Real Estate Broker* (Minneapolis: University of Minnesota Press, 1969), 65. Realtors singled out recent Southern migrants in particular, accusing them of not knowing "how to use modern buildings, plumbing" and lacking the know-how to "look after property" (64).

50. Ibid., 96.

51. Alfred A. Ring, *The Valuation of Real Estate* (Englewood Cliffs, NJ: Prentice Hall, 1963), 71.

52. Illing, "The Sordid History of Housing Discrimination in America."

53. John Irving Romer, "Suburban Versus City Life," *The Suburbanite* 1, no. 1 (April 1903): 2.

54. Ibid.

55. See Kevin Fox Gotham, *Race, Real Estate, and Uneven Development: The Kansas City Experience, 1900–2000* (Albany: State University of New York Press, 2002), 27.

56. Cited in Sonia Hirt, *Zoned in the USA: The Origins and Implications of American Land-Use Regulation* (Ithaca, NY: Cornell University Press, 2015), 1.

57. Ibid., 13. Hirt goes on to compellingly claim that "far from being exceptional as a nation of homeowners," the United States is exceptional in being a "nation of homezoners" (14).

58. William Dean Howells, *Suburban Sketches* (Boston: James R. Osgood, 1872), 71.

59. Glotzer, *How the Suburbs Were Segregated*, 59.

60. See Kenneth Jackson, *Crabgrass Frontier: The Suburbanization of the United States* (New York: Oxford University Press, 1985); Nell Painter, *The History of White People* (New York: Norton, 2011); Matthew Frye Jacobson, *Whiteness of a Different Color: European Immigrants and the Alchemy of Race* (Cambridge, MA: Harvard University Press, 1999); David Roediger, *Working Toward Whiteness: How America's Immigrants Became White* (New York: Basic Books, 2005); David Freund, *Colored Property: State Policy & White Racial Politics in Suburban America* (Chicago: University of Chicago Press, 2007); Dianne Harris, *Little White Houses: How the Postwar Home Constructed Race in America* (Minneapolis: University of Minnesota Press, 2013); Karen Brodkin, *How Jews Became White Folks and What That Says about Race in America* (New Brunswick, NJ: Rutgers University Press, 1998); Elaine Lewinnek, *The Working Man's Reward: Chicago's Early Suburbs and the Roots of American Sprawl* (New York: Oxford University Press, 2014); George Lipsitz, *The Possessive Investment in Whiteness: How White People Profit from Identity Politics* (Philadelphia: Temple University Press, 2006); Deborah Dash Moore, *To the Golden Cities: Pursuing the American Jewish Dream in Miami and L.A.* (Cambridge, MA: Harvard University Press, 1994); Eric Avila, *Popular Culture in the Age of White Flight: Fear and Fantasy in Suburban Los Angeles* (Berkeley: University of California Press, 2006).

61. Homer Hoyt, *One Hundred Years of Land Values in Chicago* (Chicago: University of Chicago Press, 1933), 316.

62. For more on the distinctions between models of whiteness organized around Anglo-Saxonism versus Nordicism, see Ewa Barbara Luczak, *Breeding and Eugenics in the American Literary Imagination: Heredity Rules in the Twentieth Century* (New York: Palgrave, 2015).

63. Helper, *Racial Policies and Practices of Real Estate Broker*, 75.

64. *The Suburbanite* 3, no. 4 (July 1905): 16.

65. Jacque Le Fevre, "The Camera in the Suburbs," *The Suburbanite* 3, no. 3 (June 1905): 24.

66. Ibid., 25.

67. Ibid.

68. Adrienne Brown, *The Black Skyscraper: Architecture and the Perception of Race* (Baltimore: Johns Hopkins University Press, 2017).

69. Winthrop E. Scarritt, "Jersey—The Automobilist's Paradise," *The Suburbanite* 1, no. 1 (April 1903): 3.

70. "The Apartment House and Race Suicide," *The Suburbanite* 1, no. 10 (January 1904): 22.

71. Ibid.

72. Ibid., 23.

73. Harriet Westman, "The Real Blessing of the Suburbs," *The Suburbanite* 2, no. 4 (August 1904): 14.

74. Freund, *Colored Property*, 8.

75. Dianne Harris, *Little White Houses: How the Postwar Home Constructed Race in America* (Minneapolis: University of Minnesota Press, 2013), 18.

76. Matthew Pratt Guterl, *Seeing Race in Modern America* (Chapel Hill: University of North Carolina Press, 2015), 3; Carol Rose, *Persuasion Revisited: Vision and Property* (New York: Routledge, 1995), 296.

77. Catherine Jurca, *White Diaspora: The Suburb and the Twentieth-Century American Novel* (Princeton. NJ: Princeton University Press, 2001), 9.

78. Richard H. Sander, Yana A. Kucheva, and Jonathan M. Zasloff, eds. *Moving Toward Integration* (Cambridge, MA: Harvard University Press, 2018), 40.

79. Ibid., 53.

80. As Avila writes, white flight was "a renegotiation of racial and spatial identities, implying a cultural process in which an expanding middle class of myriad ethnic backgrounds came to discover itself as white." *Popular Culture in the Age of White Flight: Fear and Fantasy in Suburban Los Angeles* (Berkeley: University of California Press, 2004), 26.

81. Following the publication of Richard Rothstein's *The Color of Law: A Forgotten History of How Our Government Segregated America* (New York: Norton, 2017), scholars of housing and political economy have debated how much the state is to blame for residential discrimination as opposed to the free market within racial capitalism. As Destin Jenkins writes, "with government as the vehicle, and capitalism in the driver seat, suddenly the racial segregation of the past century makes dreadful sense." See Destin Jenkins, "Who Segregated America," Public Books, December 21, 2017, https://www.publicbooks.org/who-segregated-america/; David Imbroscio, "Race Matters (Even More Than You Already Think): Racism, Housing, and the Limits of *The Color of Law*," *Journal of Race, Ethnicity and the City* 2, no. 1 (December 2020): 29–53; and Keeanga-Yamahtta Taylor, *Race for Profit: How Banks and the Real Estate Industry Undermined Black Homeownership* (Chapel Hill: University of North Carolina Press, 2019).

82. Cheryl Harris, "Whiteness as Property," *Harvard Law Review* 106, no. 8 (June 1993): 1714.

83. Ibid., 1736.

84. Ibid.

85. Ibid.

86. For more on the racialization of space more broadly see Kevin Fox Gotham, *Race, Real Estate, and Uneven Development: The Kansas City Experience, 1900–2000* (Albany: State University of New York Press, 2002); and Rashad Shabazz, *Spatializing Blackness: Architectures of Confinement and Black Masculinity in Chicago* (Champaign: University of Illinois Press, 2015).

87. American Institute of Real Estate Appraisers, *The Appraisal of Real Estate* (Chicago: Lakeside Press, 1951), 103.

88. Ibid.

89. Richard Brooks and Carol Rose talk about similar dynamics differently, tracking how white neighbors used covenants and other signals of segregation to "establish a form of collective ownership, asserting that they informally 'owned' the neighborhood as a whole, to the exclusion of nonwhite persons" (7). But the language of amenity better captures the difference between the economic and aesthetic investment in one's own home versus the kinds of upkeep required of a neighborhood needing to accommodate for some differences in aesthetic and social values while understanding whiteness (rather than the neighborhood itself) as the foremost stabilizer of value. *Saving the Neighborhood: Racially Restrictive Covenants, Law, and Social Norms* (Cambridge, MA: Harvard University Press, 2013).

90. Benjamin Looker writes extensively about the neighborhood unit in *A Nation of Neighborhoods: Imagining Cities, Communities, and Democracy in Postwar America* (Chicago: University of Chicago Press, 2015). Looker focuses more extensively on the urban than I do in his efforts to capture the "divergent notions over the meaning of neighborhood ties and experiences" that "constantly reemerged into American public discourse" during the twentieth century(2).

91. Glotzer, *How the Suburbs Were Segregated*, 13.

92. Elaine Lewinneck defines the "the mortgages of whiteness" in explicit conversation with W. E. B. Du Bois and David Roediger as "expectations about white property values." *The Working Man's Reward: Chicago's Early Suburbs and the Roots of American Sprawl* (New York: Oxford University Press, 2014), 13.

93. Helper, *Racial Policies and Practices of Real Estate Broker*, 79.

94. Taylor, *Race for Profit*, 31.

95. This is not to suggest that notions of black illiquidity replaced understandings of black racialization as "the mark that renders subjects as suitable for hyper exploitation and expropriation," to cite Jackie Wang in *Carceral Capitalism* (122). Rather, it is to bring more precision to the racialized operation of the liberal housing market—dictated by the economic logic of elimination—versus the liberal labor market, where exploitation and expropriation reigned. Perceptions of black illiquidity also fueled the racialized expropriations of the rental and lending markets where blacks paid far more to rent and lend in segregated districts. Wang, *Carceral Capitalism* (South Pasadena, CA: Semiotext(e), 2018).

96. Wendy Cheng, *The Changs Next Door to the Díazes: Reamapping Race in Suburban California* (Minneapolis: University of Minnesota Press, 2013), 17.

97. Henry James, *The Art of the Novel: Critical Prefaces* (Chicago: University of Chicago Press, 2011), 46. As Anna Kornbluh writes, "for James, realism works architecturally because it projects coherent spaces independent of preexisting spaces but dependent upon laws of composition—because, in short, it evinces a formalistic regard for world-making." *The Order of Forms: Realism, Formalism, and Social Space* (Chicago: University of Chicago Press, 2019), 33.

98. James, *The Art of the Novel*, 46.

99. Ibid.

100. Ibid.

101. Ibid., 47.

102. I credit Adam Fales for his insights on the looniness of the metaphor itself.

103. Kornbluh, *The Order of Forms*, 33.

104. Chad Luck, *The Body of Property: Antebellum American Fiction and the Phenomenology of Possession* (New York: Fordham University Press, 2014), 6, 12.

105. John David Rhodes, *Spectacle of Property: The House in American Film* (Minneapolis: University of Minnesota Press, 2017), 45.

106. In this, I build on Catherine Jurca's attention in *White Diaspora* to the "uniform, unlocatable" suburbs as they challenged the regional associations of some of the genre's most famous authors. Like Jurca, I am drawn to the residential as type appearing across and complicating regional categorizations. But I find critical attention to the literary suburbs to have obscured residential typologies containing but also exceeding the suburb where racial definitions and perceptual norms were being altered and reformed. Jurca, *White Diaspora*, 13–14.

107. Koritha Mitchell, *From Slave Cabins to the White House: Homemade Citizenship in African American Culture* (Urbana: University of Illinois Press, 2020), 14.

108. Saidiya Hartman, *Wayward Lives, Beautiful Experiments: Intimate Histories of Riotous Black Girls, Troublesome Women, and Queer Radicals* (New York: Norton, 2019), xv. I also acknowledge Keeanga-Yamahtta Taylor's observation in *Race for Profit* of the key role black women continued to play in debates about homeownership as well as in housing activism after the Fair Housing Act of 1968.

Chapter 1

1. *Public Papers of the Presidents of the United States: Herbert Hoover, Containing the Public Messages, Speeches, and Statements of the President, January to December 31, 1931* (Washington, DC: U.S. Government Printing Office, 1976), 572.

2. Ibid., 573.

3. Ibid.

4. For more on the early public-private promotion of mass homeownership see Gail Radford, *Modern Housing for America: Policy Struggles in the New Deal Era* (Chicago: University of Chicago Press, 1996); Janet Hutchison, "The Cure for Domestic Neglect:

Better Homes in America, 1922–1935," *Perspectives in Vernacular Architecture* 2 (1986) 168–78; James L. Greer, "The Better Homes Movement and the Origins of Mortgage Redlining in the United States," in *Statebuilding from the Margins: Between Reconstruction and the New Deal*, Carol Nackenoff and Julie Novkkove, eds. (Philadelphia: University of Pennsylvania Press, 2014); Chloe N. Thurston, *At the Boundaries of Homeownership: Credit, Discrimination, and the American State* (New York: Cambridge University Press, 2018); and Lawrence Vale, *From the Puritans to the Projects: Public Housing and Public Neighbors* (Cambridge, MA: Harvard University Press, 2000).

5. See Destin Jenkins's "Who Segregated America" for an overview of recent debates about the usefulness of understanding redlining as a product of the state, the market, or both. Public Books, December 21 2017, https://www.publicbooks.org/who-segregated-america/.

6. For more on this period in Hoover's career see George Nash, *The Life of Herbert Hoover: The Humanitarian, 1914–1917* (New York: Norton, 1988).

7. In this, my argument shares an affinity with Brenna Bhandar's *Colonial Lives of Property: Law, Land, and Racial Regimes of Ownership* (Durham, NC: Duke University Press, 2018), and Paige Glotzer's *How the Suburbs Were Segregated: Developers and the Business of Exclusionary Housing, 1890–1960* (New York: Columbia University Press, 2020), works also interested in uncovering the racialized roots of property and development in earlier periods and through more international frameworks than is usually the focus of housing scholarship

8. Richard Crawford, *America's Musical Life* (New York: Norton, 2001), 177.

9. The song's availability in the public domain—its initial publication in the U.K. meant it could not be copyrighted in the U.S.—further bolstered its American popularity. That "Home, Sweet Home" could not be claimed the exclusive property of any one American publisher makes Hoover's eventual deployment of the song as the ultimate evidence of ownership's sacred virtues particularly ironic: his very ability to claim the song as reflective of shared sentiment depended on its failure to be privately owned. Crawford, *America's Musical Life*, 179.

10. Crawford, *America's Musical Life*, 180.

11. Clari's status as a woman, moreover, throws even more cold water on the notion that ownership intensifies one's feeling for home. In 1823, only unmarried white women possessed regularly recognized property rights in the U.S. The first laws extending property rights to married white women were not passed until 1839 and only became normalized in 1848, while women of color had an even more tenuous claim to property for long after. Even if Clari had been American, she most likely longed for a home belonging to her father or brother.

12. As Thomas Sugrue similarly notes of most Americans in the nineteenth century, "Home Sweet Home did not lose its sweetness because someone else held the title." Thomas Sugrue, "The Right to a Decent Home," in *To Promote the General Welfare: The Case for Big Government*, Steven Conn, ed. (New York: Oxford University Press, 2012).

13. See Nell Painter, *The History of White People* (New York: Norton, 2010).

14. George Fitzhugh, *Sociology for the South: Or, The Failure of Free Society* (Richmond, VA: A. Morris, 1854), 267.

15. Brenna Bhandar, *Colonial Lives of Property: Law, Land, and Racial Regimes of Ownership* (Durham, NC: Duke University Press, 2018), 4.

16. For more on Hoover's work as international mining engineer, see George Nash, *The Life of Herbert Hoover, Volume 1: The Engineer, 1874–1914* (New York: Norton, 1983).

17. Herbert Hoover, *Principles of Mining: Valuation, Organization, and Administration* (New York: McGraw-Hill, 1909), 163.

18. Hoover similarly analyzed the innate capacity of the Chinese, positing whites to be the natural bearers of prized affective and personality traits against which the Chinese perpetually fell short. Arguing that "the Chinaman does not possess the executive instinct," Hoover used the evolutionary rhetoric of his day to insist that "the capacity for departmental organization and execution" is "often difficult enough to secure among our own people who have evolved the mental processes underlying it during the past 2000 years," resting on "an intrinsic honesty, a conscientiousness in service, foreign to the Chinese mind." Cited in Nash, *The Life of Herbert Hoover, Volume 1*, 506.

19. For more on the global history of private property and settler colonialism and its connections to domestic settlement in the U.S. in the twentieth century, see Andro Linklater, *Owning the Earth: The Transforming History of Land Ownership* (New York: Bloomsbury USA, 2015).

20. My use of the term *white diaspora* here differs from Catherine Jurca's use. Jurca uses it to lay bare "a fantasy of victimization that reinvents white flight as the persecution of those who flee," turning "material advantages into artifacts of spiritual and cultural oppression" so as to sympathetically treat "affluent house owners as the emotionally dispossessed" (8–9). My use of the term *white diaspora* indexes the emergence of the category of Anglo-Saxon in the nineteenth century to name, gather, and valorize white settlers around the globe whose alleged racial superiority was used to justify these incursions.

21. The song appears in several lyrical compilations and soldier songbooks from World War I.

22. Joanne O'Connell, *The Life and Songs of Stephen Foster* (Lanham, MD: Rowan & Littlefield, 2016), 129. See also Crawford, *America's Musical Life*, 217.

23. Ibid., 130. See also Susan Key, "Sound and Sentimentality: Nostalgia in the Songs of Stephen Foster," *American Music* 13, no. 2 (Summer 1995): 145–66.

24. This is not to deny the centrality of Native Americans to American understandings of property. As Stuart Banner writes, the false belief that Indians were not farmers by nature was used to legally dispossess Indians of their land by insisting on their failure to ever actually own it, leading to the legal understanding of Indians as occupants but not owners of the land. The ease with which this history goes unmarked within not only Hoover's version of the American songbook but the broader discourse

of modern real estate at large points to the minimal threat realtors believed Native Americans posed to the project of mass homeownership in the twentieth century—versus the growing danger of blacks moving to the urban centers where homeownership was meant most rapidly take hold held in the mind of these figures. *How the Indians Lost Their Land: Law and Power on the Frontier* (Cambridge, MA: Harvard University Press, 2009).

25. Clarissa Rile Hayward, *How Americans Make Race: Stories, Institutions, Spaces* (New York: Cambridge University Press, 2013), 123.

26. As historian Jeffrey M. Hornstein writes, "realtors would play a central role both in organizing federal housing policy to favor the private sector and in opposing attempts to develop more robust public-sector approaches to low-income housing." *A Nation of Realtors: A Cultural History of the Twentieth-century American Middle Class* (Durham, NC: Duke University Press, 2005), 145. As Richard Rothstein further notes in *The Color Of Law*, the conference's documents were "written and endorsed by some of the nation's most prominent racial segregationists." (New York: Norton, 2017), 61.

27. Today, a different real estate organization uses the acronym NAREB—the National Association of Real Estate *Brokers*, a trade organization of minority professionals in the real estate industry.

28. Hornstein, *Nation of Realtors,* 31.

29. Jeffrey Hornstein, "The Rise of the Realtor: Professionalism, Gender, and Middle-Class Identity, 1908–1950," in *The Middling Sorts: Explorations in the History of the American Middle Class*, Robert D. Johnston, ed. (New York: Routledge, 2001), 222.

30. The association was concerned with distinguishing the reputable realtor from the "curbstone broker" or "real estate shark" who lacked an office or a license and had a reputation. Aiming to rehab the nineteenth-century image of the realtor as a huckster, the association eventually formalized official licensing procedures while its journal coached members on matters of professionalization from advertising to sales. As historian Jeffrey M. Hornstein writes of the NAREE's formation, "through national-level organization, they sought to join what the historian Robert Wiebe called the 'national class'—the new middle class of educated, cosmopolitan men and women, bound loosely by a consciousness of their 'unique skills and functions,' who would achieve a 'revolution in values' in the early twentieth century" (2).

31. Hornstein, *Nation of Realtors,*10.

32. Ibid., 29.

33. Paige Glotzer, *How the Suburbs Were Segregated: Developers and the Business of Exclusionary Housing, 1890–1960* (New York: Columbia University Press, 2020), 116.

34. Glotzer focuses on the songs and tours at NAREB conference delegations where realtors "repeatedly affirmed their own personal and professional status through performing whiteness and masculinity" (11). I build from her argument to attend to the repackaging of those materials alongside the other articles and theories the NAREB

circulated in its trade journal as seeking not only a performative activation of whiteness but an empirical one rooted in both science and aesthetics.

35. See Thomas Philpott, *The Slum and the Ghetto: Neighborhood Deterioration and Middle-Class Reform, Chicago, 1880–1930* (New York: Oxford University Press, 1978), 190–92, and Richard Brooks and Carol Rose, *Saving the Neighborhood: Racially Restrictive Covenants, Law, and Social Norms* (Cambridge, MA: Harvard University Press, 2013), 121.

36. Margaret Garb, *City of American Dreams: A History of Home Ownership and Housing Reform in Chicago, 1871–1919* (Chicago: University of Chicago Press, 2005), 3.

37. Ibid.

38. Charles H. Israels, "New York Apartments Houses" *Architectural Record* 2 (July 1901): 477–508.

39. Ibid., 508.

40. Charlotte Perkins Gilman, "The Passing of the Home in the Great American Cities," *Cosmopolitan*, December 1904, 140.

41. As Margaret Garb writes in *City of American Dreams*, "as property in investment produced increasingly great wealth and grandiose styles of life, the purchase of a family home became, for those with income that stretched beyond daily necessities, just one of several option for investing surplus capital" (4).

42. Sugrue, "The Right to a Decent Home," 105.

43. "Glenn Frank Gives Realtors a Challenge" *National Real Estate Journal* (1928): 51. Frank's speech came in the wake of several articles in the 1920s encouraging Americans to "colonize" allegedly "vacant" land in prairie states, a continuation of the association's original aim to serve rural areas as well as metropolitan ones. Given that the last homesteading claim was in 1980, several *NREJ* articles mostly in the 1910s and 1920s promoted the allegedly "open lands" for farmers to claim.

44. B. F. Faast, "The Settlement of New Farm Lands," *NREJ* (June 18, 1923): 22.

45. W.W. Hannan, "City Planning," *NREJ* 4, no. 1 (September 15, 1911): 28–32.

46. Adom Getachew, *Worldmaking After Empire: The Rise and Fall of Self-Determination* (Princeton, NJ: Princeton University Press, 2019), 22.

47. Charles G. Little, "The Torrens System of Land Transfers: Its Essential Features as in Operation in Cook County Illinois," *NREJ* 1. no. 4 (June 15, 1910): 157.

48. Brenna Bhandar, *Colonial Lives of Property: Law, Land, and Racial Regimes of Ownership* (Durham, NC: Duke University Press, 2018), 82.

49. "Famous Old Laws and Decisions," *NREJ* 5, no. 6 (August 15, 1912): 472.

50. "Weyburn—The Saskatchewan Type," *NREJ* 5, no. 6 (August 15, 1912): 486.

51. Ibid., 488.

52. "Modern Real Estate Advertising: Address by Mr. Allen D. Albert of the Minneapolis Tribune at the Convention of the Na. Assoc of Real Estate Exchanges, Louisville KY, June 20 1912," *NREJ* 6, no. 2 (October 15, 1912): 110.

53. J. A. M. Aikins, K.C.M.P., "The Hudson's Bay Co. and Western Development," *NREJ* 9, no. 1 (September 15, 1913): 38.

54. James S. Cruse, President of the Indianapolis Real Estate Board, Indianapolis, Indiana, "Why Real Estate is a Better and Safer Investment than Stocks and Bonds," *NREJ* 10, no. 5 (November 15, 1914): 359.

55. Thomas Forsyth Hunt, "The Relation of a Permanent Agriculture to Social Welfare," *NREJ* 12, no. 2 (August 15, 1915): 66.

56. Ibid., 67.

57. Ibid., 65.

58. "New York Adopts the Divisional Plan," *NREJ* (November 5, 1923): 50.

59. Ibid.

60. The journal also published two articles by land economist Richard Ely in the 1920s featuring eugenic lines of argumentation. Like Hunt, Ely advocated for settling more Americans on farmland but insisted that selecting the right settlers for regional lands was key to this endeavor's success. See Richard T. Ely, "Private and Public Colonization," *NREJ* (March 12, 1923): 47.

61. Cheryl I. Harris, "Whiteness as Property," *Harvard Law Review* 106. no. 8 (June 1993): 1707–91, 1713.

62. Ibid.

63. See also David Freund, *Colored Property: State Policy and White Racial Politics in Suburban America* (Chicago: University of Chicago Press, 2007).

64. See Ronald Schaffer, *America in the Great War: The Rise of the War Welfare State* (New York: Oxford University Press, 1991), 69–70.

65. For more on the policy road to public housing see Gail Radford, *Modern Housing for America: Policy Struggles in the New Deal Era* (Chicago: University of Chicago Press, 1996), and Lawrence Vale, *From the Puritans to the Projects: Public Housing and Public Neighbors* (Cambridge, MA: Harvard University Press, 2000).

66. As Lawrence Vale writes, "especially during periods of international strife, actual or imagined, the house could be lauded as proof of the superiority of individualism to anarchosyndicalism or other socialist or communist movements." *From the Puritans to the Projects*, 120. Perhaps the most famous articulation of this sentiment occurred during the run-up to the Cold War when developer William Levitt said in 1948 that "no man who owns his own house and lot can be a Communist" because "he has too much to do." Eric Larrabee, "The Six Thousand Houses That Levitt Built," *Harper's*, September 1948, 84. But the exact sentiment appeared in the *NREJ* in the immediate wake of the Russian Revolution.

67. William M. Garland, President of the NAREB, "Realtors Urge Construction," *American Contractor* 40, no. 2 (January 11, 1919): 20.

68. "The 'Own Your Home' Movement and the Crying Need of the Nation," *NREJ* 17, no. 6 (June–July 1918): 252.

69. LeeAnn Lands, *The Culture of Property: Race, Class, and Housing Landscapes in Atlanta* (Athens: University of Georgia Press, 2009), 117.

70. Henry L. Freking, "Editorial," *NREJ* 14, no. 1 (March 1919): 7; L. F. Eppich, "Who Owns the Home," *NREJ* 21, no. 14 (July 5 1920): 5–6; Herbert Hoover, "The Home

Owner," *NREJ* (Septemberf 24 1923): 29; "Do You Own Your Own Home," *NREJ* (November 27, 1924): 37.

71. Robert E. Simons, "Constructive Housing Suggestions," *NREJ* 21, no. 23 (November 8 1920): 7.

72. "The 'Own Your Home' Movement and the Crying Need of the Nation," *NREJ* 27, no. 6 (June–July 1918): 252.

73. James S. Curse, "Why Real Estate Is a Better and Safer Investment Than Stocks and Bonds," *NREJ* (November 15, 1914): 359.

74. "National Association of Real Estate Boards," *NREJ* (November 1919): 3.

75. "The 'Own Your Home' Movement and the Crying Need of the Nation," 252.

76. Leo Bozell, "Formal Discussion Opened," *NREJ* 21, no. 16 (August 2, 1920): 8

77. "The Publisher's Page," *NREJ* 32, no. 4 (February 16, 1931): 7.

78. "Roanoke, VA," *NREJ* 5, no. 6 (November 15, 1912): 197.

79. "Uncle Sam's New Empire," *NREJ* 2, no. 2 (October 15, 1910): 82–84.

80. In 1910, African Americans made up nearly 30 percent of the Southern population, with several Southern states having black majorities.

81. "Contents," *NREJ* 5, no. 17 (May 1918): 199.

82. "Activities of Various Real Estate Boards—New Orleans," *NREJ* (March 1918): 143.

83. Ibid.

84. This is not to say this was a position universally adopted by all entities committed to the promulgation of homeownership in this period. See the efforts by the Better Homes in America movement, sponsored in part by then-secretary Hoover's Department of Commerce, to promote homeownership across the color line and award prizes to homes in Gullah communities in St. Helena, South Carolina, demonstrating excellence in design and efficiency in the 1920s, before and after the contest became segregated by race. Janet Hutchison, "Better Homes and Gullah," *Agricultural History* 62, no. 2 (Spring 1993): 102–18.

85. Carol Rose, *Property and Persuasion: Essays on the History, Theory, and Rhetoric of Ownership* (Boulder, CO: Westview Press, 1994), 267.

86. "Louisiana State Convention: First Annual Meeting Displays Great Interest in License Law," *NREJ* (November 22, 1920): 23–24.

87. "Race Riots and Real Estate," *NREJ* (September 1919): 31.

88. Ibid.

89. Realtors most often punted on this question of black urban housing in the pages of the *NREJ*. One exception is a 1924 article arguing that "the proper housing of the colored man in Northern cities will naturally fall within the province of the Realtor to solve, we should consider the problem very carefully." But though this writer insists that "it would seem a mistake to ignore the fact that the colored man is entitled to live in comfortable and respectable quarters," he counters that "it would, at the same time, seem a greater mistake to believe that a miscellaneous mixture of whites and blacks is desirable upon the part of either race" (44). "Ohio Convention Accomplishes Much Through Conference Plan," *NREJ* (October 20, 1924): 44–45.

90. This also attests to Paige Glotzer's important work to "push back the chronology of suburban housing segregation, from its putative origins in the New Deal to the 19th century" by tracing the place of racial segregation in the projects of the earlier developers of planned suburbs, focusing primarily on the Roland Park development in Baltimore, Maryland (3). *How the Suburbs Were Segregated: Developers and the Business of Exclusionary Housing, 1890–1960* (New York: Columbia University Press, 2020).

91. Sinclair Lewis, *Babbitt* (New York: Signet Classic, 1922), 6.

92. *Babbitt* is a key text for Jurca's argument about suburban literature's adoption of spiritual dispossession as its signal affect, effacing the precarity of those facing real material precarity in relation to housing. Jurca recovers "the role of the novel in promoting a fantasy of victimization that reinvents white flight as the persecution of those who flee, turns material advantages into artifacts of spiritual and cultural oppression, and sympathetically treats affluent house owners as the emotionally dispossessed. Such fraudulent identifications are treated as the birthright of the suburbanite and are the hallmark of the suburb's luxury and privilege (9). *White Diaspora: The Suburb and the Twentieth-Century American Novel* (Princeton, NJ: Princeton University Press, 2001).

93. H. L. Mencken, "Portrait of an American Citizen," *Smart Set* 69 (October 1922): 138–39.

94. James M. Hutchisson, "'All of Us Americans at 46': The Making of Sinclair Lewis' 'Babbitt,'" *Journal of Modern Literature* 18, no. 1 (Winter 1992): 95–114.

95. Robert Herrick, "Our Super-Babbitt," *The Nation* 131 (September 30 1931): 60–62.

96. Lewis, *Babbitt*, 38.

97. Ibid.

98. Hutchisson, "All of Us Americans at 46," 100.

99. Ibid.

100. James S. Miller, "Zoning the Past: Brokers, Babbitts, and the Memory Work of Commercial Real Estate," *Journal of American Studies* 44, no. 2 (May 2010): 287–311.

101. Ibid., 303.

102. National Association of Real Estate Boards, "Code of Ethics," June 6, 1924, 3.

103. Ibid., 7.

104. See N. D. B. Connolly, *A World More Concrete: Real Estate and the Remaking of Jim Crow South Florida* (Chicago: University of Chicago Press, 2014).

105. Lewis, *Babbitt*, 46.

106. Catherine Jurca also notes the consequences of black marginality in Zenith on Babbitt's personal sense of spiritual persecution: "In Babbitt, the assault on his well-being is not from a city of dark-skinned people from without, but from the self-destructive excesses of the suburbanite within. . . . In the absence of a territory that needs immediate defending, Babbitt perceives himself as requiring protection from it" (45).

107. Glotzer, *How the Suburbs Were Segregated*, 142.

108. M. W. Folsom, *A Home of Your Own—And What It Means to You* (Chicago: National Association of Real Estate Boards, 1922).

109. See, for instance, Gail Bederman, *Manliness and Civilization: A Cultural History of Gender and Race in the United States, 1880–1917* (Chicago: University of Chicago Press, 1995), as well as Kyla Schuller, *The Biopolitics of Feeling: Race, Sex, and Science in the Nineteenth Century* (Durham, NC: Duke University Press, 2018).

110. See also Adrienne Brown, "1922–1968: The Disenchanted Literature of Homeownership" in *Timelines of American Literature*, Christopher Hager, ed. (Baltimore: Johns Hopkins University Press, 2019), 37–52.

111. F. Scott Fitzgerald, *Three Novels of F. Scott Fitzgerald* (New York: Charles Scribner's Sons, 1953), 94.

112. Ibid., 131.

113. See Walter Benn Michaels's claim in *Our America: Nativism, Modernism, and Pluralism* about Gatsby's status as not entirely white (Durham, NC: Duke University Press, 1993), 25.

Chapter 2

1. Kendrick A. Clements, *The Life of Herbert Hoover: Imperfect Visionary, 1918–1928* (New York: Palgrave Macmillan, 2010), 184. Allan's penchant for jazz would continue at least through 1929, when the then-twenty-two-year-old Harvard student, visiting his family at the White House over the holidays, threw a dance for a hundred guests featuring a "private dance orchestra" supplementing the Marine Dance Band. See the *Brainerd Daily Dispatch,* December 30, 1929.

2. See Ted Gioia, *The History of Jazz* (New York: Oxford University Press, 1997).

3. See Kathy J. Ogren, *The Jazz Revolution: Twenties America and the Meaning of Jazz* (New York: Oxford University Press, 1992), and Ted Gioia, *The History of Jazz* (New York: Oxford University Press, 1997).

4. As David Madden and Peter Marcuse note, while "the idea of crisis implies that inadequate or unaffordable housing is abnormal, a temporary departure from a well-functioning standard," "for working-class and poor communities, housing crisis is the norm." *In Defense of Housing*, David Madden and Peter Marcuse, eds. (London: Verso, 2016), 9. For more on the connection between the plantation economies of the South and the emergence of the urban ghetto in the North, see Saidiya Hartman, *Wayward Lives, Beautiful Experiments: Intimate Histories of Riotous Black Girls, Troublesome Women, and Queer Radicals* (New York: Norton, 2019).

5. Richard H. Sander, Yana A. Kucheva, and Jonathan M. Zasloff, *Moving Toward Integration: The Past and Future of Fair Housing* (Cambridge, MA: Harvard University Press, 2018), 53.

6. Ibid., 61. This story has also been told in a number of other places, including by Richard Rothstein, *The Color of Law: A Forgotten History of How Our Government Segregated America* (New York: Norton, 2017); David Freund, *Colored Property: State Policy and White Racial Politics in Suburban America* (Chicago: University of Chicago

Press, 2007); and Paige Glotzer, *How the Suburbs Were Segregated: Developers and the Business of Exclusionary Housing, 1890–1960* (New York: Columbia University Press, 2020).

7. The exception was in the wake of riots like those in Chicago in 1919, where housing discrimination would get direct attention from the public and private spheres as a direct cause of racial unrest followed largely by inaction.

8. Nannie Burroughs and Charles S. Johnson, *Negro Housing: Report of the Committee on Negro Housing* (Washington, DC: National Capital Press, 1932), 73.

9. Ibid., 72.

10. Ibid., 79.

11. Ibid., 86.

12. For more on the ways the black middle class embraced class-based models of ownership at the detriment of promoting housing affordable to all, see Preston H. Smith II, *Racial Democracy and the Black Metropolis: Housing Policy in Postwar Chicago* (Minneapolis: University of Minnesota Press, 2012).

13. Not that they had much choice in the matter—the committee was, after all, assembled by the federal government seeking to endorse homeownership as a civic virtue and an economic necessity for both the nation and its residents. The outcome—an endorsement of homeownership—was likely inevitable given Hoover's embrace of mass homeownership as a state project.

14. We could put this version of indexicality in conversation with another shifting index later described by Charles Abrams in 1955's *Forbidden Neighbors: A Study of Prejudice in Housing*, focusing not on housing type but on the surrounding neighborhood: "It is no longer the type of house but the type of neighborhood which reflects social standing. This is now true in America's little towns as in its Middletowns and Bigtowns. Fine looking homes in Chicago may be still as fine looking but are considered blighted when Negroes or other minorities live in the neighborhood." As Abrams continues, "the neighborhood one lived in became a main index and new protections had to be devised to resist any assault upon it. The suburb and the quest for status are shaping the American personality of the future as the frontier once shaped the American personality of the past." (New York, Harper Brothers, 1955), 139–40.

15. David Levering Lewis, *When Harlem Was in Vogue* (New York: Oxford University Press, 1989), 107. As jazz musician Benny Carter notes, "We in music knew there was much going on in literature, for example, but our worlds were far apart. We sensed that the black cultural as well as moral leaders looked down on our music as undignified." Cited in Ted Gioia, *The History of Jazz* (New York: Oxford University Press, 1997), 81.

16. Ibid.

17. Langston Hughes, *The Big Sea: An Autobiography* (New York: Knopf, 1940), 151.

18. Ibid., 156–57.

19. James Agee, *Let Us Now Praise Famous Men* (New York: Houghton Mifflin, 1939), 10.

20. "The Harlem Sketch-Book," *New York Amsterdam News*, August 20, 1930, 9. The context of this poem is noteworthy, appearing as a preface to Wallace Thurman's guest takeover of theater critic Theophilus Lewis's "The Harlem Sketch Book" column. As Lewis writes following their contributions, "With the leading cinnamon poet and novelist and the playwright whom the theater must perforce confirm in the title of 'The Father of Negro Drama' . . . the Sketch Book indisputably becomes a big-time column."

21. For more on Hughes's cabaret poems, see Shane Vogel, "Closing Time: Langston Hughes and the Queer Poetics of Harlem Nightlife," *Criticism* 48, no. 3 (Summer 2006): 397–425.

22. Saidiya Hartman usefully speculates on the relationship between scenes of black dance and the cabaret and the cinematic image: "In the cabaret scene, black virtuosity is on display. . . . The dance scene is crucial, the movement of bodies, the chorus as well as the ordinary folks crowding the floor, reveal the other lineages of black cinema, understood broadly as a rendering of black life in motion in contrast to the arrested and fixed images that produce and document black life as a problem. The cabaret scene illuminates the indebtedness of the moving picture to the limbo dance (which, practiced on the slave ship, was 'the gateway to or threshold of a new world and the dislocation of a chain of miles'), and to the ring shout danced in the clearing." *Wayward Lives*, 196.

23. Katherine Hazzard-Gordon, *Jookin': The Rise of Social Dance Formations in African-American Culture* (Philadelphia: Temple University Press, 1990), 115.

24. Ibid., 97.

25. Moore framed Harlem's exorbitant rents not as a matter of affordability, as historian Shannon King notes, but of capitalist exploitation. See Shannon King, *Whose Harlem Is This, Anyway? Community Politics and Grassroots Activism During the New Negro Era* (New York: New York University Press, 2015), 113.

26. *The Tenant Movement in New York City, 1904–1984*, Mark Naison and Ronald Lawson, eds. (New Brunswick, NJ: Rutgers University Press, 1986), 114.

27. Naison and Lawson describe the Sugar Hill strikes as giving way to a professional class of housing advocates largely working for the black middle class. "Harlem's unique housing conditions enabled people with legal and organizational skills to pursue tenant advocacy as a career. Harlem's landlords, their rents inflated by discrimination, could afford to make substantial concessions without sacrificing 'reasonable' profit; organizers with the talent to extract such concessions could find a large market for their services, especially among middle class blacks." *The Tenant Movement in New York City*, 114.

28. Naison and Lawson note that eviction resistance proved a far more powerful tool than rent strikes, which were often difficult to organize: "Eviction resistance did not require active support from the population or even the political sympathy of the victim. Given the overextended schedules of marshals and police, a handful of Party

cadre could move the furniture back, provided the rest of the neighborhood was sympathetic or indifferent." Ibid., 101.

29. Joshua Clover, *Riot. Strike. Riot: The New Era of Uprisings* (New York: Verso Books, 2016), 3. While the strike is generally associated with formally organized Marxist action, Clover notes that "those who have accorded the riot the potential for an insurrectionary opening onto a social rupture come generally from intellectual and political traditions indifferent or even antithetical to the command of state and economy, most famously (but not exclusively), those of some strands of anarchism" (3).

30. Ibid., 4.

31. See James F. Wilson, *Bulldaggers, Pansies, and Chocolate Babies: Performance, Race, and Sexuality in the Harlem Renaissance* (Ann Arbor: University of Michigan Press, 2010); Martin Summers, *Manliness and Its Discontents: The Black Middle Class & the Transformation of Masculinity, 1900–1930* (Chapel Hill: University of North Carolina Press, 2005); Stephen Robertson, Shane White, Stephen Garton, and Graham White, "Disorderly Houses: Residences, Privacy, and the Surveillance of Sexuality in 1920s Harlem," *Journal of the History of Sexuality* 21, no. 3 (September 2012): 443–466; Fred Moten, "Air Shaft, Rent Party," in *Stolen Life* (Durham, NC: Duke University Press, 2018); Shane Vogel, "The Sensuous Harlem Renaissance: Sexuality and Queer Culture," in *A Companion to the Harlem Renaissance*, Cherene Sherrard-Johnson, ed. (New York: Wiley, 2015), 267–84.

32. Vogel, "The Sensuous Harlem Renaissance," 268.

33. Ibid., 276.

34. Ibid., 277.

35. Moten, "Air Shaft, Rent Party," 190.

36. Ibid., 189.

37. Clover, *Riot. Strike. Riot*, 46.

38. Building from Moten and Vogel's emphasis on the rent party's "critical sensuousness" and its capacity to trouble the feeling of singular embodiedness itself in relation to physical space, we might consider how his term could be deployed not only in relationship to the queering of domestic and social space but the ideological space of private property more broadly, especially given homeownership's centrality to state-sponsored conceptions of citizenship. The rent party's critical sensuousness kindled an alternative sensorium of property simultaneous to the emergence of state projects such as the racial survey underwriting redlining and Hoover's brand of affective boosterism linking homeownership to innate and cultivated feeling.

39. Willie "The Lion" Smith with George Hoefer, *Music on My Mind* (New York: Doubleday, 1964), 156.

40. Joel Vance, *Fats Waller: His Life and Times* (Chicago: Contemporary Books, 1977), 40.

41. Richard Bruce Nugent, *Gentleman Jigger: A Novel of the Harlem Renaissance* (Boston: Da Capo Press, 2008), 174.

42. Maurice Waller and Anthony Calabrese, *Fats Waller* (Minneapolis: University of Minnesota Press, 1977), 31.

43. W. T. Ed Kirkeby, *Ain't Misbehavin: The Story of Fats Waller* (London: Peter Davies, 1966), 41.

44. Alyn Shipton, *Fats Waller: The Cheerful Little Earful* (London: Continuum, 1988), 7.

45. Paul Machlin, *Stride: The Music of Fats Waller* (New York: Palgrave Macmillan, 1988), 11.

46. Whereas the growth of wage-based employment outside of the home in the late nineteenth century helped precipitate the dropping homeownership rate in the U.S., the rent party bucked this trend. The means of production for the city's most-heralded jazz musicians originated within the domestic spaces of the rent party before moving to the more public spaces of clubs, cabarets, theaters, and, ultimately, recording studios producing content for radio and phonographs to be consumed at home. Stride pianists working rent parties would take the songs they honed on the circuit and sell them for astonishingly cheap to song publishers. Fats Waller is notable in this regard, selling a good deal of musical compositions for next to nothing.

47. For more on Gladys Bentley, see Wilson, *Bulldaggers, Pansies, and Chocolate Babies.*

48. Ibid..

49. Hartman, *Wayward Lives*, 61.

50. Ibid., xv.

51. T. R. Poston, "Socialist Uncovers Something New in Harlem: The House Rent Party," *New York Amsterdam News*, March 16 1935, 2.

52. Ira D. Reid, "Mrs. Bailey Pays the Rent," in *Ebony and Topaz: A Collectanea* Charles S. Johnson, ed. (New York: Opportunity and National Urban League, 1927), 144–48.

53. For more on Reid's style as a sociologist, see Francille Rusan Wilson, *The Segregated Scholars: Black Social Scientists and the Creation of Black Labor Studies, 1890–1950* (Charlottesville: University of Virginia Press, 2006), 115–72.

54. His more ambivalent stance emerges in the first few paragraphs when he rejects purely economic explanations for the rent party by foregrounding its origins in similar Southern soirées. "The truth seemed to be," Reid asserts, "that the old-party of the South had attired itself á la Harlem" (145). In his account, the rent party cannot be reduced to either hedonistic impulse or economic need but must be attributed instead to a mix of motives and conditions.

55. Reid, "Mrs. Bailey Pays the Rent" 147.

56. Ibid.

57. W. Edwin Blair, "Do You Own Your Own Home?" *NREJ* (November 17 1924): 37.

58. Reid, "Mrs. Bailey Pays the Rent," 147.

59. Ibid.

60. This is resonant with Robert Nichols's cautions about dispossession as a mobilizing term in both indigenous and black studies given that the term often "appears to presuppose a commitment to possession," be it of the land of "self-ownership or property in the person" (118). "Since self- possession remains an uncertain ideal within Black political thought, dispossession remains a fraught weapon of critique" (131). *Theft Is Property: Dispossession and Critical Theory* (Durham, NC: Duke University Press, 2020).

61. Ibid.

62. Ibid.

63. Ibid., 148.

64. Moten, "Air Shaft, Rent Party," 188.

65. Following Nash, we can situate Reid within the longer trajectory of black feminist theory described by her as "a tradition that has railed against capture and instead has envisioned other forms of relationality, knowledge-production and worldmaking." The figures in this chapter follow Nash in their efforts to think "about what it might mean for black feminism to be animated by ways of thinking and being that are about non-ownership." See Jennifer C. Nash, "Response to James Bliss," in "Symposium on *Black Feminism Reimagined*," Shoniqua Roach, ed., Syndicate, November 11, 2019, https://syndicate.network/symposia/literature/black-feminism-reimagined/.

66. Wallace Thurman, *The Collected Writings of Wallace Thurman: A Harlem Renaissance Reader*, Amritjit Singh and Daniel M. Scott III, eds. (New Brunswick, NJ: Rutgers University Press, 2003), 74.

67. Vogel, "The Sensuous Harlem Renaissance," 279.

68. Wallace Thurman, "Negro Life in New York's Harlem: A Lively Picture of a Popular and Interesting Section," in *The Collected Writings of Wallace Thurman*, 53.

69. Theophilus Lewis, "Trailing the Spotlight," *Inter-State Tattler*, January 25, 1929, 8.

70. Questions of ownership also surround Thurman and Rapp's collaboration. Amritjit Singh and Daniel M. Scott III, the editors of Thurman's collected works, theorize Thurman likely drafted the overall story, dialogue, and scenic details while Rapp, the more experienced playwright, provided the work with its structure and flow. Thurman's friends Arna Bontemps and Langston Hughes mark his dissatisfaction with the play due to the transformations it underwent to appeal to theatrical producers.

71. Wallace Thurman, "Cordelia the Crude," *Fire!!*, November 1926, 5.

72. *The Collected Writings of Wallace Thurman*, 307. James Wilson describes this pressure in detail: "Rapp and Thurman were advised to rewrite the ending of Harlem to make it more palatable for Broadway audiences and the New York censor. Ben Hecht and Charles MacArthur, the playwrights of the smash hit *The Front Page* (1928), and the latter the cowriter of *Lulu Belle*, offered a detailed scenario for the recommended revision. According to Rapp and Thurman, Hecht and MacArthur suggested 'the play should show Cordelia Williams going on and on along her sinful career and finally ending up disastrously, say, in Paris'" (77). *Bulldaggers, Pansies, and Chocolate Babies:*

Performance, Race, and Sexuality in the Harlem Renaissance (Ann Arbor: University of Michigan Press, 2010).

73. R. Dana Skinner, "The Play," *Commonweal* 18 (March 6 1929): 514.

74. Wallace Thurman and William J. Rapp, *Harlem*, in *The Collected Writings of Wallace Thurman*, 316.

75. Ibid.

76. Ibid., 315.

77. Ibid., 316.

78. Ibid., 317.

79. Ibid., 319.

80. Ibid.

81. Ibid., 320.

82. Ibid., 325.

83. Ibid., 326.

84. Ibid., 330.

85. Ibid., 322.

86. Ibid., 323.

87. "National Association of Real Estate Boards," *NREJ* (November 1919): 3.

88. Saidiya Hartman, "The Anarchy of Colored Girls Assembled in a Riotous Manner," *South Atlantic Quarterly* 117, no. 3 (2018): 466.

89. Ibid.

90. Thurman and Rapp, *Harlem*, 332.

91. Ibid., 337.

92. Ibid.

93. Vogel, "The Sensuous Harlem Renaissance," 278.

94. Carol Rose, *Property and Persuasion: Essays on the History, Theory, and Rhetoric of Ownership* (Boulder, CO: Westview Press, 1994), 278.

95. Wilson, *Bulldaggers, Pansies, and Chocolate Babies*, 72.

96. Ibid., 71.

97. Performance scholar James Wilson traces a debate among the play's contemporary critics about whether to classify its depiction of Harlem as authentic and naturalist or melodramatically excessive. The critic for the *New York Telegraph* deemed *Harlem* "the most accurate of the photographs made at Seventh avenue and 132d street," for instance, while the *Chicago Defender*'s critic proclaimed "it is not realism, it is exaggeration." Thurman and Rapp's stage directions in this specific scene, however, portray the rent party as a place to escape mimesis entirely. Wilson, *Bulldaggers, Pansies, and Chocolate Babies*, 71–72.

98. Thurman and Rapp, *Harlem*, 369.

99. Stephen Best's conclusion to *None Like Us: Blackness, Belonging, Aesthetic Life* resonates here: "it is not the recovery of an impossible community but, rather, the making of a world that will no longer have me that is at stake. I said, too, that whatever blackness or black culture is, it cannot be indexed to a 'we'—or if it is, that 'we' can

only be structured by and given in its own negation and refusal. There is no mutuality, no witnessing, no acknowledgement to be discovered in the archive (understood, as one final reminder, not as a repository, but as a Foucauldian 'knot of conflicted interdependence'). In the archive, we discover not who we are but how 'we' are not." (Durham, NC: Duke University Press, 2018), 132.

100. Richard O. Boyer, "Hot Bach," *New Yorker*, July 1, 1944, 26. Jazz critics have since argued that Ellington's song "Harlem Air Shaft" was not, in fact, crafted as an indexical representation of this space as he proclaims here, insisting this was a retrospective origin story Ellington produced long after the song's creation. For more on this, see Edward Green, "'Harlem Air Shaft': A True Programmatic Composition?" *Journal of Jazz Studies* 7, no. 1 (Spring 2011): 28–46.

101. Boyer, "Hot Bach," 26–27.

102. Moten, "Air Shaft, Rent Party," 187.

103. See A. H. Lawrence, *Duke Ellington and His World* (New York: Routledge, 2004), 229, and Harvey G. Cohen, *Duke Ellington's America* (Chicago: University of Chicago Press, 2010), 250. As Lawrence writes of the visit, "despite the fact that the meeting was publicized in the press, it never took place. Ellington biographer John Edward Hasse said that Herbert Hoover's presidential papers revealed that the meeting was stopped because the man who set it up, Charles Lucien Skinner, had a police record. Nonetheless, Ellington posed for photographers on the White House grounds without anyone from the presidential staff. The African American press at that time fired blistering salvos at President Hoover, accusing him of being afraid to be photographed with black visitors, given the fact there would be a presidential election the following month" (229).

Chapter 3

1. See *Housing and Mortgage Markets in Historical Perspective*, Eugene N. White and Kenneth Snowden, eds. (Chicago: University of Chicago Press, 2014); Gail Radford, *Modern Housing for America: Policy Struggles in the New Deal Era* (Chicago: University of Chicago Press, 1996); Frederick Lewis Allen, *Only Yesterday* (New York: Blue Ribbon Books, 1931); David Kennedy, *Freedom from Fear: The American People in Depression and War, 1929–1945* (New York: Oxford University Press, 1999); Cheryl Lynn Greenburg, *To Ask for an Equal Chance: African Americans in the Great Depression* (Lanham, MD: Rowman & Littlefield, 2009).

2. See Rose M. Stein, "More Homes or More Mortgages?" *New Republic*, September 7, 1932, 88–90; "Housing vs. Ownership," *New Republic*, December 16, 1931, 122–23; Stuart Chase, "The Case Against Homeownership," *Survey Graphic* 27, no. 3 (May 1938): 261–67; Langdon Post, *The Challenge of Housing* (New York: Farrar & Rinehart, 1938); and Dorothy Rosenman, *A Million Homes a Year* (New York: Harcourt, Brace, 1945). The concerns of these reformers also overlap with the arguments being made in the period for robust public housing. See H. Peter Oberlander, *Houser: The Life and Work of Catherine Bauer, 1905–64* (Vancouver: University of British Columbia Press,

2000), and *From Tenements to the Taylor Homes: In Search of an Urban Housing Policy in Twentieth-Century America,* John F. Bauman, Roger Biles, and Kristin M. Szylvian, eds. (University Park: Pennsylvania State University Press, 2000).

3. Stein, "More Homes or More Mortgages?" 90.
4. Chase, "The Case Against Homeownership," 267.
5. Ibid.
6. Post, *The Challenge of Housing,* 243.
7. Ibid., 75.
8. Ibid., 3.
9. Richard Wright, *Native Son* (New York: Harper & Row: 1939), 200.
10. The two Betty Boop cartoons are 1934's "She Wronged Him," in which her farm is first metaphorically then literally underwater, and 1932's "Betty Boop's Ups and Downs," with Boop this time enduring a residential foreclosure that not only leaves her out on the street but expands to the planet. The Broadway plays include Samuel Shipman's *Creoles* (1927), Louis Weitzenkorn's *First Mortgage* (1929), Lawton Campbell's *Solid South* (1930), Channing Pollock's *The House Beautiful* (1931), and Stephen Gross's *One Good Year* (1935). The first novel to reference the HOLC was Josephine Lawrence's *If I Have Four Apples* (New York: Frederick A. Stokes, 1935).
11. This is especially true in comparison to concurrent novels of the period reinforcing the racial differences attending more recent waves of immigrants.
12. W. E. B. Du Bois, *Darkwater: Voices from within the Veil* (New York: Verso Books, 2016), 18.
13. Walter Stein, *California and the Dust Bowl Migration* (Westport, CT: Greenwood Press, 1973), 49.
14. Michael Denning, *The Cultural Front* (London: Verso, 1997), 267.
15. Mollie Godfrey, for instance, posits Steinbeck as using the language of white supremacy to interrupt its utility for capitalist exploitation. Mollie Godfrey, "'They Ain't Human': John Steinbeck, Proletarian Fiction, and the Racial Politics of 'The People,'" *Modern Fiction Studies* 59, no. 1 (Spring 2013): 107–34.
16. Charles Cunningham, "Rethinking the Politics of *The Grapes of Wrath,*" *Cultural Logic: An Electronic Journal of Marxist Theory and Practice* 5 (2002): 18. See also Kevin Hearle, "These Are American People: The Spectre of Eugenics in *Their Blood Is Strong* and *The Grapes of Wrath,*" where he raises the possibility that "Steinbeck's racially tinged discourse is a calculated strategy in which he consciously plays to the prejudices of his audience in order to elicit action from white America to help save the Okies." *Beyond Boundaries: Rereading John Steinbeck,* Susan Shillinglaw and Kevin Hearle, eds. (Tuscaloosa: University of Alabama Press, 2002), 248. See also Sarah Wald's claim that "the novel relies on migrants' whiteness to indict those who deny them land." *The Nature of California: Race, Citizenship, and Farming Since the Dust Bowl* (Seattle: University of Washington Press, 2016), 53. Shane Lynn reads the racial politics of *The Grapes of Wrath* as evidence that Steinbeck was "a product of the ethos of Roosevelt's New Deal" before going on to reclaim *Tortilla Flat* as a "celebration of

paisano culture and the ethnic diversity of Monterey and its environs, although these essentially light-hearted comedies are scarcely intended to be serious racial commentaries." "'A Room of Experience into which I Cannot Enter': John Steinbeck on Race," *Steinbeck Review* 12, no. 2 (2015): 152. Milton Cohen even goes so far as to suggest that Steinbeck in *Grapes* merely "simplified the microscopic sample, making them all white" so as "not to deflect his study with ethnic prejudices of his characters and readers." *The Pull of Politics: Steinbeck, Wright, Hemingway, and the Left in the Late 1930s* (Columbia: University of Missouri Press, 2018), 23.

17. Bryan Yazell, "Steinbeck's Migrants: Families on the Move and the Politics of Resource Management," *Modern Fiction Studies* 63, no. 3 (Fall 2017): 518.

18. John Steinbeck, *Working Days: The Journals of The Grapes of Wrath*, Robert DeMott, ed. (New York: Penguin, 1990), 14.

19. Ibid., 43.

20. As one Steinbeck scholar suggests, the novel's "concern for families who had lost their land may have partly assuaged his guilt, if not his sense of irony, as he was about to make the biggest property purchase of his life." Steinbeck, *Working Days*, 15.

21. Ibid., 61.

22. Ibid., 64.

23. Ibid., 76.

24. Jay Parini, *John Steinbeck: A Biography* (New York: Henry Holt, 1996), 5.

25. John Steinbeck, "I Remember the Thirties," first published in *Esquire* in June 1960, republished in *The Thirties: A Time to Remember*, Don Congdon, ed. (New York: Simon & Schuster, 1962), 23–26.

26. Joseph Fontenrose, *John Steinbeck: An Introduction and Interpretation* (New York: Holt, Rinehart & Winston, 1963), 56.

27. Michael Hogan, "A Study of John Steinbeck's Treatment of Property" (MA thesis, Oklahoma State University, 1966), 2.

28. For the former claim, see Warren French, *John Steinbeck* (New York: Twayne, 1961), 110. For the latter, see Joseph Henry Jackson, *Why Steinbeck Wrote The Grapes of Wrath* (New York: Limited Editions Club, 1940), 4.

29. John Steinbeck, *The Short Novels of John Steinbeck* (New York: Penguin Classics, 2009).

30. The *New York Times* review noted that the work "comes closer, perhaps to the novels that deal in a spirit of charm and amused sympathy with the manners and vagaries of Southern Negroes," noting in its conclusion that "we doubt if life in Tortilla Flat is as insouciant and pleasant and amusing as Mr. Steinbeck has made it seem." Fred T. Marsh, "Life in a California Shantytown: 'Tortilla Flat' Is an Amusing Novel about the Lighter Side of a Community Made Up of Mixed Races," *New York Times*, June 2, 1935, 42. Edmund Wilson referred to *Tortilla Flat* in the *New Republic* as a "comic idyll, with the simplification almost of a folk tale," before going on to insist that "the paisanos of *Tortilla Flat* are really not quite human beings: they are cunning little living dolls who amuse us like pet guinea-pigs or rabbits." Edmund Wilson, "The

Californians: Storm and Steinbeck," *New Republic*, December 9, 1940, 784–87. See also Thomas Fensch's introduction to the Penguin edition of the novel, *Tortilla Flat* (New York: Penguin Classics, 1997).

31. See Francisco E. Balderrama and Raymond Rodriguez, *Decade of Betrayal: Mexican Repatriation in the 1930s* (Albuquerque: University of New Mexico Press, 2006), and Fernando Saúl Alanís Enciso, *They Should Stay There: The Story of Mexican Migration and Repatriation During the Great Depression* (Chapel Hill: University of North Carolina Press, 2017).

32. Steinbeck later regretted his portrayal of this community, noting that "it did not occur to me that paisanos were curious or quaint, dispossessed or underdoggish." "If I have done them harm by telling a few of their stories," he wrote, "I am sorry." John Steinbeck, *Tortilla Flat* (New York: Modern Library, 1937).

33. Louis Owens, "'Grampa Killed Indians, Pa Killed Snakes': Steinbeck and the American Indian" *MELUS* 15, no. 2 (Summer 1988): 87. "In this somewhat remote, exotic form," Owens continues, "for Steinbeck, the Indian need not actually be dealt with as anything more than impulse, a shadowy presence."

34. Ibid.

35. See Vine Deloria, *The Nations Within: The Past and Future of American Indian Sovereignty* (New York: Pantheon, 2013).

36. Ibid., 127.

37. Ibid., 153.

38. John Steinbeck, *Conversations with John Steinbeck*, Thomas Fensch, ed. (Jackson: University Press of Mississippi, 1988), 32.

39. Denning, *The Cultural Front*, 267, and Arthur Pettit, *Images of the Mexican American in Fiction and Film* (College Station: Texas A&M University Press, 1981), 192. Arguing that "Steinbeck's characterization of the paisano universe was tied to his profound disenchantment with the machine-mad, corrupt Anglo world," Pettit suggests that Steinbeck's fictional paisanos served as a brownface mirror for reflecting the ills of white America, including the undying fealty to homeownership, back to itself.

40. Studs Terkel, *Hard Times: An Oral History of the Great Depression* (New York: New Press, 2011), 5.

41. Ibid., 81.

42. Colleen Lye, *America's Asia: Racial Form and American Literature, 1893–1945* (Princeton, NJ: Princeton University Press, 2005), 148.

43. Romani immigration to the U.S. intensified like much other immigration from Europe in the late nineteenth and early twentieth centuries.

44. John Steinbeck, *Their Blood Is Strong* (San Francisco: Simon J. Lubin Society of California, 1938), 3.

45. Ibid.

46. Ibid.

47. Ibid. Chester E. Eisinger tracks this ethos back to its agrarian roots. The idea that "occupying the land and devoting one's labor to it are the criteria of ownership,

and that these transcend the legal right to the land represented by title," traces back to the "the natural right argument current in the eighteenth century: men had a natural right to such land as they could profitably use. This natural right assumption gave sanction to the squatter whose heritage passed down into the nineteenth century, and even into the twentieth" (152). "Jeffersonian Agrarianism in *The Grapes of Wrath*," *University of Kansas City Review* 14 (Winter 1947): 149–54.

48. Sarah Wald locates the power of *The Grapes of Wrath* in "its affirmation of the Dust Bowl migrants' whiteness and its contention that white Americans should be farmers, not farmworkers," a sentiment underwritten by the novel's guiding racial logic that "white citizens deserve land" (54). While I share Wald's commitment to thinking the Joads' whiteness in relationship to land relations, I argue here that Steinbeck's formulation of the "land men" beginning in *Their Blood Is Strong* and bleeding into *Grapes* is less invested in tying whiteness to actual ownership status but understands the desire for land—sentiment itself—as the hallmark of white racial identity. Wald, *The Nature of California*.

49. Steinbeck, *Their Blood Is Strong*, 3.

50. Ibid.

51. See Theodore Roosevelt, *The Naval War of 1812* (New York: G. P. Putnam's Sons, 1900), 35, and "The Expansion of the White Races," in *National Edition: The Works of Theodore Roosevelt*, ed. Hermann Hagedorn, vol. 18 (New York: Charles Scribner's Sons, 1926).

52. Ibid. Kevin Hearle understands Steinbeck's reference to the Okies' status as a new race as a positive attribute, arguing that "the implication is that migration has made a new race of them and it has strengthened their blood" (252). I read Steinbeck's declaration as more unstable and unsure than this, marking the precarity of their white racialization in the face of their recent and ongoing exploitation within the California context that the rest of the articles will go on to restabilize and rescue.

53. Steinbeck, *Their Blood Is Strong*, 3

54. While Steinbeck seems to suggest the Midwest land man's racialization is new, this division potentially runs deeper. It could also distinguish the "they" of the Jeffersonian yeoman of the East and Midwest and the more recent white settlers arriving West in the late nineteenth and early twentieth centuries, where the consolidation of the land by midsize-to-large farming operations by the 1870s presented a different historical terrain of racialization. Steinbeck's own lineage bears out this distinction. Unlike the Dust Bowl migrants, Steinbeck was not one of the "descendants of the middle west who won their lands by fighting." Rather, both of his grandfathers immigrated to the Eastern US in the mid-nineteenth century before moving to California to settle, skipping the Midwest and the direct settlement of indigenous land altogether. And yet, though they were not yeoman "old American" stock, Steinbeck and his forefather nonetheless understood themselves as "land men," to which their various histories of homesteading in Ireland, the U.S., and Palestine attest.

55. As Bryan Yazell writes, "concerned with the future of migrant labor, Steinbeck deploys this racial terminology to distinguish among different populations of people. He therefore implicitly produces a timeline during which certain populations wither while others—in this case the white migrant farmer—enter the center of society through a combination of their own so-called natural talents and specific government." "Steinbeck's Migrants: Families on the Move and the Politics of Resource Management," 503. The only thing I would add is that Steinbeck seems to more than implicitly produce this timeline—it is explicitly built into the structure of the essay itself in terms of the progression of the argument and its rhetoric.

56. Steinbeck, *Their Blood Is Strong*, 3

57. One could also connect Steinbeck's interest in land to the mythos within his family of his grandfather's dispossession of land in Palestine that he had claimed as part of a messianic farming colony. The death of his brother and the sexual assault of his brother's wife and her mother preceded his arrival in the U.S. in 1858, when he changed the family name from Großsteinbeck to Steinbeck.

58. This reading is very much in line with Colleen Lye's reading of the images that accompanied *Their Blood Is Strong* in its pamphlet form. "The message their look sends is clear: despite hardship and deprivation, a genetic superiority promises a future." *America's Asia*, 188.

59. "The emphasis on the new migrants' mythic Anglo-Saxonism," as Colleen Lye notes, "makes a pointed allusion to the foreignness of old migrants" of Chinese, Japanese, Filipino, and Mexican descent who had worked the same fields prior to the Dust Bowl migrants. Lye, *America's Asia*, 188.

60. Ibid., 145.

61. Ibid., 190.

62. Steinbeck, *Their Blood Is Strong*, 6.

63. Ibid.

64. Ibid.

65. Ibid., 9.

66. Ibid., 15.

67. Ibid.

68. Ibid., 25.

69. Ibid.

70. Ibid., 25.

71. Ibid. Steinbeck paints the next wave of Japanese settlers in a nearly identical light. Of the Japanese, Steinbeck writes that "the history of their activities was almost exactly like that of the Chinese: a low standard of living which allowed them to accumulate property while at the same time they took the jobs of white labor" (25). As with the Chinese, Steinbeck depicts the relationship between the Japanese and the land in the sterilely economic language of accumulation, framing their acquisition of the land as merely tactical and thus differentiating them from the "descendants of the middle west" whose predilection for the land leads them to desire it even in excess of its profitability.

72. Steinbeck, *Their Blood Is Strong*, 28.
73. Ibid.
74. Ibid.
75. Ibid., 30.
76. "Address of Dr. Ray Lyman Wilbur, Secretary of the Interior and Joint Chairman of the Conference at the Closing Session of the President's Conference on Home Building and Home Ownership," in *Housing Objectives and Programs: General Sessions of the Conference*, John M. Gries and James Ford, eds. (Washington, DC: National Capital Press, 1932), 16.
77. Ibid.
78. Ibid.
79. Ibid.
80. Ibid., 8.
81. For more on Lyman Wilbur's relationship to eugenics, see Ben Maldonado, "Eugenics on the Farm: Ray Lyman Wilbur," *Stanford Daily*, November 18, 2019.
82. Stanford University, *Tentative findings of the Survey of race relations, a Canadian-American study of the Oriental on the Pacific coast, prepared and presented at the findings conference at Stanford University, California, March 21–26, 1925* (Palo Alto, CA: Stanford University, 1925), 15.
83. "Address of Dr. Ray Lyman Wilbur" 16.
84. Toni Ann Alexander, "From Oklahomans to 'Okies': Identity Formation in Rural California" (PhD diss., Louisiana State University and Agricultural and Mechanical College, 2004).
85. John Steinbeck, *The Grapes of Wrath* (New York: Penguin Classics, 2006), 304.
86. I build here from Sarah Wald's recognition that while "there are no black characters in *Grapes of Wrath*," "Steinbeck, however, repeatedly references the specter of slavery through the owners' comparison of the white Dust Bowl migrants to blacks in the South and through the Dust Bowl migrants' affirmation of their whiteness through joking and derogatory reference to blackness" *The Nature of California*, 57.
87. Crooks, as Michael Denning insists, "is not the descendent of slaves, he tells Lennie, but of landowners" (267).
88. Steinbeck, *Grapes of Wrath*, 8.
89. Because of its settlement history, Oklahoma had a large number of white sharecroppers. But by 1900, three-fourths of all sharecroppers in Oklahoma were white and by 1935, the state had the highest rate of white tenancy in the country. https://www.okhistory.org/publications/enc/entry.php?entry=TE009&l=.
90. Steinbeck, *Grapes of Wrath*, 10.
91. Ibid., 17.
92. The home ultimately fails, moreover, as a haven from the lung-clogging dust at the heart of the ecological crisis, with dust soon penetrating the homes of Oklahomans through cracks and seams. Not only do homes fail to provide physical shelter

from the dust, but they also fail to shield families from the emotional and financial distress of the Dust Bowl.

93. Steinbeck, *Grapes of Wrath*, 29.
94. Ibid., 33.
95. Ibid.
96. Ibid.
97. Ibid.
98. Their occupation of the land, the novel suggests, will be marked in scant material traces and folklore—the form in which black and Native peoples largely appear in the Midwestern sections of the novel. While black presence is made manifest through the mediated form of a vulgar poetic fragment, Native Americans largely turn up in the Oklahoma sections of the novel in the form of decorative objects punctuating what remains of the Joads' fading material world. The remnants of indigenous peoples captured in paper and pillows seem to forebode that the Joads' remaining tie to the land will take a similarly ornamental form. This image of the "vanishing Indian" who lives on only in white culture rendered invisible the large population of indigenous peoples who lived and continue to live in Oklahoma.
99. Steinbeck, *Grapes of Wrath*, 88.
100. Ibid.
101. Ibid., 37.
102. As Florian Freitag writes in *The Farm Novel in North America*, "ultimately, Steinbeck shows, owning (or keeping), the land is indispensable to the farmer's physical and spiritual survival. For indeed, the most immediate consequence of the loss of the land is death." (Rochester, NY: Camden Press, 2013), 247.
103. Steinbeck, *Grapes of Wrath*, 78.
104. Ibid., 230.
105. Michael Szalay aptly includes Pa Joad within a larger constellation of "vanishing men" within *Grapes*. Whereas Connie and Tom Joad "depart to engage abstract collectives," leaving women like Ma Joad and Rose of Sharon to deal with the "quotidian responsibilities these men leave behind with less than utopian force," Pa Joad physically stays put as part of the family group. Michael Szalay, *New Deal Modernism: American Literature and the Invention of the Welfare State* (Durham, NC: Duke University Press, 2000), 168.
106. Bryan Yazell further fleshes out Ma Joad's growing role as not just family leader but a model for the migrants' broader incorporation into the nation-state given her faith in the family structure and her lingering belief in the American Dream. While Yazell casts Ma Joad's efforts to keep the family together as "the first step toward solidifying this demographic as both a political and workforce," this reading overlooks the fissures both within the family as well as the broader migrant community about the residential ends to which this solidification should be put. "Steinbeck's Migrants," 515.
107. Steinbeck, *Grapes of Wrath*, 188.

108. When Tom echoes the kernel of his father's vision, asking a group of returning migrants fleeing California whether "a fella got work an' saved, couldn' he get a little lan," his query solicits mournful laughter in his conversation partners (206).

109. Steinbeck, *Grapes of Wrath*, 338.

110. Ibid., 423.

111. For more on Pa's melancholy, see George Henderson, "John Steinbeck's Spatial Imagination in *The Grapes of Wrath*: A Critical Essay," *California History* 68, no. 4 (1989): 210–223.

112. Steinbeck, *Grapes of Wrath*, 423.

113. Ibid., 91.

114. Milton Cohen has paid the most attention to residential nature of Ma Joad's dream, noting that "the dreams of these migrants, although vaguely expressed, are also individual, symbolized by the small white house amid the orange trees" (200). Cohen further observes how the family's "individual dream and the rugged individualism of the pioneering farmers do not cohere well with Steinbeck's major theme of privileging collective action both as a means to achieve the migrants' aim and as a mode of living preferable to the divisive selfishness of individual self-interest" (181). But while Cohen insists that "what they want are individual small farms, the kind they had worked before they migrated" (201), attending to the divergences of their residential imaginaries reveals the range of differing dwelling desires that individual Joads possess. *The Pull of Politics: Steinbeck, Wright, Hemingway, and the Left in the late 1930's* (Columbia: University of Missouri Press, 2018).

115. Steinbeck, *Grapes of Wrath*, 134.

116. Ibid., 148.

117. Ibid., 204.

118. When Al mentions his new dream of living in a mobile trailer, Ma doubles down on her original vision, insisting "I ruther have a little house. Soon's we can, I want a little house" (305).

119. Ibid., 307.

120. Ibid.

121. There is much more to say about the place of Jules, the lone Native American character to appear and speak in *Grapes*. It could be said that Steinbeck toys with Jules's incorporation into the same residential imaginary as the Joads because he is a "half blood" who shares their "land man" pedigree to a certain degree. Jules's status as a "land man" who seeks out land and the sensorium of property is ultimately tied to his whiteness, negating his native blood. For more on Jules and Steinbeck's representation of indigeneity, see Owens, "Grampa Killed Indians, Pa Killed Snakes,", 87.

122. Steinbeck, *Grapes of Wrath*, 165.

123. Ibid., 424.

124. Ibid., 233.

125. Ibid., 282.

126. Ibid., 152.

127. Ibid., 230.

128. By the early 1940s, as Walter Stein reports in history of Dust Bowl migration to California, "migrants no longer stopped first in the agricultural valleys before moving on to the cities: they went directly to the war industries centers" (280). *California and the Dust Bowl Migration* (Westport, CT: Greenwood Press, 1973).

129. This quote comes from a letter written by a Californian to President Roosevelt. Cited in Marilyn Wyman, "Affirming Whiteness: Visualizing California Agriculture," *Steinbeck Studies* 16, nos. 1–2 (Spring 2005): 32–55.

130. Becky Nicolaides, *My Blue Heaven: Life and Politics in the Working-Class Suburbs of Los Angeles, 1920–1965* (Chicago: University of Chicago Press, 2002), 187.

131. Gregory, *American Exodus*, 176.

132. Nicolaides describes in depth how "the FHA began deeply impacting the L.A. housing market by the 1940s" (189).

133. Gerald D. Nash, *The American West Transformed: The Impact of the Second World War* (Bloomington: Indiana University Press, 1985), 40. As Nash further notes, the number of Californian suburbanites was likely even larger given that the statistics reflect the census's rule at the time to classify suburbs only as "rural non-farm areas," overlooking the suburbs more closely yoked to urban areas.

134. Darren Dochuk, *From Bible Belt to Sunbelt: Plain-Folk Religion, Grassroots Politics, and the Rise of Evangelical Conservatism* (New York: Norton, 2011), 106.

135. Cited in Gregory, *American Exodus*, 172. This article was by Oliver Carlson, "Up from Dust," *U.S.A.* (August 1952): 97–104

136. W. E. B. Du Bois, "Hopkinsville, Chicago and Idlewild," *The Crisis*, August 1921, 158–60.

137. W. E. B. Du Bois, *The Autobiography of W. E. B. Du Bois* (New York: Oxford University Press, 2007), 192.

138. Christopher Reed echoes this sentiment in his history of the Depression on Chicago's South Side, noting that blacks "did not have as much to lose in a material sense, as they had begun feeling the worst effects of the economic depression earlier" (11). *The Depression Comes to the South Side: Protest and Politics in the Black Metropolis, 1930–1933* (Bloomington: Indiana University Press, 2011).

139. Cheryl Lynn Greenberg, *To Ask for an Equal Chance: African Americans in the Great Depression* (Lanham, MD: Rowman & Littlefield, 2009), 22.

140. Ibid., 23.

141. Guy B. Johnson, "Does the South Owe the Negro a New Deal?" *Social Forces* 13 (October 1934): 100–103.

142. Greenberg, *To Ask for an Equal Chance*, 93.

143. As Robin Kelly reminds us, "For most black rural and urban working people, the New Deal led to greater inequalities and outright dispossession." This was largely achieved through federally subsidized crop reductions that, despite being designed to be fairly distributed to sharecroppers, were in actuality largely kept by landlords who evicted tenant farmers to then hire them back as cheap wage laborers (xx). *Hammer*

and Hoe: Alabama Communists During the Great Depression (Chapel Hill: University of North Carolina Press, 2015). Moreover, as James Gregory notes, black workers were often the first fired during the Great Depression. James N. Gregory, *The Southern Diaspora: How the Great Migrations of Black and White Southerners Transformed America* (Chapel Hill: University of North Carolina Press, 2005), 98.

144. Efforts to organize black sharecroppers and farmworkers, of course, continued during the 1930s as Robin Kelley, Nell Painter, and others have documented, and produced tangible effects and outcomes in terms of the history of left politics. But the structural efforts to keep blacks in peonage in the South remained deeply effective.

145. As Nikhil Singh notes, "many of these younger intellectuals and activists—Du Bois's erstwhile radical critics—would become strong supporters of the New Deal state, even as the old race man continued to resist its blandishments, growing ever more restive in his radicalism" (79). *Black Is a Country: Race and the Unfinished Struggle for Democracy* (Cambridge, MA: Harvard University Press, 2005).

146. W. E. B. Du Bois, *Black Reconstruction in America: 1860–1880* (New York: Free Press, 1935), 367.

147. Ibid., 368–69. It should also be noted that Du Bois largely ignores the land claims of Native Americans who continued to be pushed west and dispossessed of land in this period in *Black Reconstruction*.

148. Homer Hoyt, *One Hundred Years of Land Values in Chicago* (1933), 315–16.

149. In fact, the Google Books Ngram viewer shows the phrase "standards of living" and its variants skyrocketing in usage during the 1930s.

150. Ibid., 67.

151. Ibid., 67.

152. Ibid., 602.

153. Nikhil Singh in *Black Is a Country* offers an alternative reading of the lesson of *Black Reconstruction*: "The use of a phrase like 'dictatorship of the proletariat' (to describe the early taxation schemes and land-redistribution efforts of black dominated Reconstruction governments in states like South Carolina), needed to be understood as an effort to convey that the unconditional democratic demands by blacks had a larger significance, one that pointed to the superseding of capitalist property relations in general" (94). While I agree that Du Bois sees in black land hunger the possibility for a mass ownership superseding capitalist property relations, Du Bois is also interested in simultaneously insisting that blacks did indeed desire to own and had the capacity to do so—a claim that has its own history of denial within racist science and philosophy. Du Bois both wants to write the Negro back into the category of the "land man" even as he is mourning the democratic and collective ends to which that category might have been put had land redistribution been achieved.

154. Richard Wright, *12 Million Black Voices: A Folk History of the Negro in the United States of America* (London: Lindsay Drummond, 1947), 10.

155. Ibid., 35.

156. Ibid., 36.

157. Ibid.

158. Moynihan argued that many black family structures exhibited a "tangle of pathology." "In essence, the Negro community has been forced into a matriarchal structure which, because it is to out of line with the rest of the American society, seriously retards the progress of the group as a whole, and imposes a crushing burden on the Negro male and, in consequence, on a great many Negro women as well." Daniel Patrick Moynihan, *The Negro Family: The Case for National Action* (Washington, DC: Department of Labor, 1965).

159. Wright, *12 Million Black Voices*, 61.

Part II

1. This is based on the U.S. Census Bureau calculation of homeownership rate as the percentage of homes that are owner-occupied, which involves dividing the number of homes that are owner-occupied by the total number of occupied households. Because this rate is not determined by how many adults own a home but, rather, how many homes are occupied by the owner, it does not account for various forms of cohabitation. For instance, if an adult lives at home with their parents, it is counted as one owner household. And if five adults rent an apartment together, it is tallied by the census as one renter household rather than five discrete renters. Given this accounting system, the percentage of adults who own may be much lower than the official homeownership rate, especially in the current moment given the number of adult children living at home and the housing crunches within major metropolitan areas creating large renting households. See John Asmis, "The Homeownership Rate Is Misunderstood," Landed, October 26, 2017, https://www.landed.com/blog/the-homeownership-rate-is-misunderstood.

2. Kenneth Jackson, *Crabgrass Frontier: The Suburbanization of the United States* (New York: Oxford University Press, 1987), 203.

3. As Gene Slater puts it, "realtors were so integral to FHA, they came to view it as their agency of the federal government." *Freedom to Discriminate: How Realtors Conspired to Segregate Housing and Divide America* (Berkeley, CA: Heyday Books, 2021), 104.

4. Robert Weaver, *The Negro Ghetto* (New York: Russell & Russell, 1967), iv.

5. David Freund, *Colored Property: State Policy and White Racial Politics in Suburban America* (Chicago: University of Chicago Press, 2007), 132.

6. Slater, *Freedom to Discriminate*, 105.

7. As David Freund writes, "the debate over integration, whites insisted, no longer turned on questions about race, ideology, or personal preference. What counted was a person's relationship to places and to property, and a person's ability to function properly in what was assumed to be a free market for both." *Colored Property*, 19.

8. This phrasing is indebted to Eduardo Bonilla, *Racism without Racists: Color-Blind Racism and the Persistence of Racial Inequality in America* (Lanham, MD: Rowman & Littlefield, 2014).

9. Here is Charles Abrams's assessment in his 1955 book, *Forbidden Neighbors: A Study of Prejudice in Housing* about the additive costs for of residential segregation: "The Negro has been forced to pay too much for his houses; land is so far from the source of employment that he spends more for automobile and bus transportation than he can afford; he pays duress prices for his land; sites often lack the benefit of schools, streets, and city services; land often entails inordinate outlays for improvements and utilities; cities penalize him with a high assessment when he has moved out of his place; he pays usurious premiums for building loan money, if he can get it at all, and excessive interest on his permanent loan; oppressive zoning ordinances or other kinds of official opposition prevent him from completing the house or carrying it; FHA officials set appraisals so low that the Negro cannot put up the extra cash required." (New York: Harper & Brothers, 1955), 173.

10. Freund, *Colored Property*, 19.

Chapter 4

1. As William J. Collins and Robert A. Margo note, "The white owner-occupancy rate rose by about 34 percentage points between 1940 and 1980, with the gains concentrated before 1960." "Race and Home Ownership from the End of the Civil War to the Present," *American Economic Review* 101, no. 3 (2011): 355–59.

2. James Baldwin, "The Image of the Negro," *Commentary*, April 1948, 378.

3. Ibid.

4. Ibid., 380.

5. Ibid.

6. For more on Rockwell's civil rights paintings, see Bridget R. Cooks, "Norman Rockwell's Negro Problem," *Cultural Critique* 105 (Fall 2019): 40–79.

7. For assessments of this image's optimism, see Jennifer Dasal, *ArtCurious: Stories of the Unexpected, Slightly Odd, and Strangely Wonderful in Art History* (New York: Penguin, 2020), 73, and Gregory D. Squire, *The Fight for Fair Housing: Causes, Consequences, and Future Implications of the 1968 Federal Fair Housing Act* (New York: Taylor & Francis, 2017), 7.

8. Many neighborhoods either remained segregated or "changed over" swiftly after initial black occupancy. As W. Edward Orser notes, "flight appeared to be more common than overt resistance" *Blockbusting in Baltimore: The Edmondson Village Story* (Lexington: University Press of Kentucky, 1994), 68.

9. This argument follows N. D. B. Connolly's claim in *A World More Concrete: Real Estate and the Remaking of Jim Crow South Florida* that "Americans, immigrants, and even indigenous people made tremendous investments in racial apartheid, largely in an effort to govern growing cities and to unleash the value of land as real estate" (Chicago: University of Chicago Press, 2014), 3.

10. See, for instance, the difficulties the NAACP faced in even acquiring a copy of the FHA's Underwriting Manual to build a case regarding the explicit role race played in its property valuations. As Chloe Thurston recounts, it took the NAACP over a year

and much plotting just to obtain a copy in the late 1930s. But the NAACP's lack of access to the FHA's materials belies the eased and frequent circulation of racial information and guidelines between government agencies and private real estate and lending partners, as Benjamin Wiggins illustrates, suggesting just how successful appraisers were at both hiding their processes from hostile audiences and widely circulating their findings to the specific bureaucratic institutions charged with quietly carrying them out. See Chloe Thurston, *At the Boundaries of Homeownership: Credit, Discrimination, and the American State* (New York: Cambridge University Press, 2018).

Benjamin Wiggins, *Calculating Race: Racial Discrimination in Risk Assessment* (New York: Oxford University Press, 2020), 74.

11. Frederick Babcock, *The Appraisal of Real Estate* (Urbana-Champaign: University of Illinois Press, 1924), 71.

12. Nicole Fleetwood, *Troubling Vision: Performance, Visuality, and Blackness* (Chicago: University of Chicago Press, 2011), 7.

13. See Wiggins, *Calculating Race*, and Colin Koopman, *How We Became Our Data: A Genealogy of the Informational Person* (Chicago: University of Chicago Press, 2019), for more on the birth of real estate value.

14. As Keeanga-Yamahtta Taylor writes, "the contrived sciences of real estate brokerage and appraisal were developed in the shadow of a eugenic pseudoscience in which fatalistic assumptions linked biology, race, and ethnicity." *Race for Profit: How Banks and the Real Estate Industry Undermined Black Homeownership* (Chapel Hill: University of North Carolina Press, 2020), 147.

15. As Benjamin Wiggins writes of the notorious HOLC security maps in *Calculating Race*, it is more generative to think of these documents as "reflective of the practice of redlining rather than foundational to it" (58).

16. Koopman, *How We Became Our Data*.

17. For more on the emergence of the field of appraisal, see Norman G. Miller and Sergey Markosyan, "The Academic Roots and Evolution of Real Estate Appraisal," *Appraisal Journal* 71, no. 2 (2003): 172–84; and Jennifer Light, "Discriminating Appraisals: Cartography, Computation, and Access to Federal Mortgage Insurance in the 1930s," *Technology and Culture* 52, no. 3 (2011): 485–522.

18. Federal Housing Administration, *Underwriting Manual: Underwriting and Valuation Procedure under Title II of the National Housing Act with Revisions to April 1, 1936* (Washington, DC), pt. 2, sec. 2, Rating of Location.

19. Wiggins, *Calculating Race*, 57.

20. Homer Hoyt, *One Hundred Years of Land Values in Chicago* (Chicago: University of Chicago Press, 1933), 316.

21. Ibid., 315. Jennifer Light has traced how this list ended up guiding the land value maps whose production Hoyt supervised late at the FHA in "Nationality and Neighborhood Risk at the Origins of FHA Underwriting," *Journal of Urban History* 36, no. 5 (September 2010): 653.

22. Kerry D. Vandell, "FHA Restructuring Proposals: Alternatives and Implications," *Housing Policy Debate* 6, no. 2 (1995): 307.

23. Carl Nightingale, *Segregation: A Global History of Divided Cities* (Chicago: University of Chicago Press, 2012), 346.

24. As Andrew Wiese notes, contemporary estimates suggest that less than 3 percent of FHA-insured mortgages during this period went to nonwhite Americans. *Places of Their Own: African American Suburbanization in the Twentieth Century* (Chicago: University of Chicago Press, 2004), 140.

25. Light, "Discriminating Appraisals," 515.

26. Light, "Nationality," 640.

27. Nightingale, *Segregation*, 347.

28. Freund, *Colored Property*; Jackson, *Crabgrass Frontier*. Geographer Amy Hillier has suggested that the role of the HOLC's maps in redlining has been overstated, arguing that they do not match up with differences in lending practices and weren't widely distributed. "Redlining and the Home Owners' Loan Corporation," *Journal of Urban History* 29, no. 4 (May 2003): 394–420. Freund counters, however, that one cannot deny that "the HOLC was inextricably linked to extensive institutional networks that created and disseminated appraisal practices" rooted in race.

29. Jennifer Light notes "the disappearance from agency records of any completed applications for mortgage insurance and with them the data for a systematic analysis of how nationality factored into the FHA's risk-rating equations" (*Nationality*, 642). Light uses GIS to reconstruct these equations after the fact to determine race's influence on appraisal applications.

30. Drawing hard distinctions between the "objective" measure of building condition and the "subjective" nature of its appeal and character is dubious. Benjamin Wiggins, for instance, describes the subjective elements shaping the "Report of the Architectural Inspector" from the FHA's *Underwriting Manual* valuing, as he describes, "uniformity, conformity, typicality, and other normalized prompts" privileging "the standards of an imagined, presumably white, family of prospective homeowners." Inspectors were asked to not only rate the "character" of the property but whether the "arrangement and design" of a property would "appeal to a typical family." *Calculating Race*, 66.

31. David Roediger makes the case in *Working toward Whiteness* that *ethnicity* is an ahistorical term in this period. The term *ethnic*, he insists, does not become a systematized term of analysis distinct from race until the 1940s. See Roediger, *Working toward Whiteness: How America's Immigrant's Became White: The Strange Journey from Ellis Island to the Suburbs* (New York: Basic Books, 2005).

32. See Adrienne Brown, *The Black Skyscraper: Architecture and the Perception of Race* (Baltimore: Johns Hopkins University Press, 2017).

33. Frederick Morrison Babcock, *The Appraisal of Real Estate* (New York: Prentice-Hall, 1946), 77.

34. Robert Thorley and William H. Stickney, *Real Estate Forms* (New York: Prentice Hall, 1926), 103.

35. Stanley L. McMichael, *McMichael's Appraising Manual* (New York: Prentice-Hall, 1937), 40.

36. Ibid.

37. Wiggins, *Calculating Risk*, 55.

38. Harry Grant Atkinson, *Fundamentals of Real Estate Practice* (New York: Prentice-Hall, 1946), 34.

39. Ibid.

40. Ibid.

41. Earl Teckemeyer, *How to Value Real Estate: The Foremost Factor in Selling* (Englewood Cliffs, NJ: Prentice-Hall, 1956), 77.

42. Ibid., 77–78.

43. Alfred A. Ring, *The Valuation of Real Estate* (Englewood Cliffs, NJ: Prentice-Hall, 1963), 71.

44. Ibid., 72.

45. Norris Vitchek, "Confessions of a Block-Buster," *Saturday Evening Post*, July 14, 1962, 16.

46. Ibid.

47. Jane Jacobs, *The Death and Life of Great American Cities* (New York: Vintage Books, 1961), i.

48. Peter Laurence importantly notes the care with which Jacobs approached her methods and their presentation in *Becoming Jane Jacobs* (Philadelphia: University of Pennsylvania Press, 2016), 255.

49. Jacobs, *Death and Life*, 9.

50. Ibid.

51. Ibid.

52. Jacobs notes this herself when, later in the book, she describes meeting a North Ender who points out to her a three-story row house whose owners had spent $20,000 modernizing it. This resident tells Jacobs, "That man could live anywhere. Today he could move into a high-class suburb if he wanted to" (284).

53. See Stefano Luconi, "Frank L. Rizzo and the Whitening of Italian Americans in Philadelphia," in *Are Italians White? How Race Is Made in America*, Jennifer Guglielmo and Salvatore Salerno, eds. (New York: Routledge, 2003), and Jeanine Bell, *Hate Thy Neighbor: Move-In Violence and the Persistence of Racial Segregation in American Housing* (New York: New York University Press, 2013). Ronald P. Formisano's *Boston Against Busing: Race, Class, and Ethnicity in the 1960s and 1970s* importantly notes that opposition to busing in the North End was "relatively restrained" compared to the more raucous resistance found in East Boston for instance (Chapel Hill: University of North Carolina Press, 1991), 128.

54. Jacobs, *Death and Life*, 71–72.

55. Ibid., 299.

56. Ibid., 72.

57. Ibid.

58. Jamie Creed Rowan situates Jacobs's vision of urban sociality as part of a "rich, but somewhat dispersed, intellectual tradition" focused on relationality in *The Sociable City: An American Intellectual Tradition* (Philadelphia: University of Pennsylvania Press, 2017), 153.

59. This is also in line with Eric Avila's reading of the inherent conservatism undergirding Jacobs's urban advocacy. Jacobs "railed against the interventions of government and its audacious figureheads but said nothing about the radical forces of capitalism that ravaged her neighborhood, pushing out factories, affordable housing, and struggling artists while enforcing broader disparities of race, wealth, and poverty. Her color-blind polemic altogether ignored these patterns of rising inequality, even as they made a starker imprint on the landscape of the postwar American city." *The Folklore of the Freeway: Race and Revolt in the Modernist City* (Minneapolis: University of Minnesota Press, 2014), 67.

60. Robert Farnsworth, "The World of Gwendolyn Brooks," in *On Gwendolyn Brooks: Reliant Contemplation*, Stephen Caldwell Wright, ed. (Ann Arbor: University of Michigan Press, 2001), 35.

61. John Barlow Martin, "The Strangest Place in Chicago," *Harper's*, December 1950, 86.

62. Brooks would return to Martin's piece in her own ode to the Mecca Flats, 1968's "In the Mecca," citing Martin in the work's epigraph. Brooks first began writing "In the Mecca" as a novel in the 1950s, and it is likely that "They Call It Bronzeville" came out of the original version of the project.

63. Gwendolyn Brooks, "They Call It Bronzeville," *Holiday*, October 1951, 61.

64. Ibid.

65. Ibid., 116.

66. This question is in line with Preston H. Smith's efforts in *Racial Democracy and the Black Metropolis: Housing Policy in Postwar Housing* (Minneapolis: University of Minnesota Press, 2012), to trace how African American elites in Chicago prioritized the fight against racial segregation while neglecting working-class African Americans' plight for housing.

67. For more on the specifics of the GI Bill's raced distribution, see Glenn C. Altschuler and Stuart M. Blumin, *The G.I. Bill: A New Deal for Veterans* (New York: Oxford, 2009).

68. Brooks, "They Call It Bronzeville," 116.

69. Ibid.

70. Sarah Wasserman, *The Death of Things: Ephemera and the American Novel* (Minneapolis: University of Minnesota Press, 2020), 146.

71. Thomas Pynchon, "A Journey into the Mind of Watts," *New York Times Magazine*, June 12, 1966.

72. Ibid.

73. Sally Bachner, *Prestige of Violence: American Fiction, 1962–2007* (Athens: University of Georgia Press, 2011), 49.

74. David Seed, in *The Fictional Labyrinths of Thomas Pynchon* (Iowa City: University of Iowa Press, 1988), reprints a letter Pynchon wrote in response to a graduate student's queries about the materials on southwestern Africa he consulted when writing the novel. In a footnote to this letter where Pynchon suggests the student "read Lewis Mumford or talk to someone in the city planning department here," Seed notes that "although Pynchon has denied reading any Mumford, . . . he actually consulted Jane Jacobs' *The Death and Life of Great American Cities* (1961)" (263).

75. For more on Pynchon's readerly relationship to James Baldwin but also Ralph Ellison, see David Witzling, *Everybody's America: Thomas Pynchon, Race, and the Cultures of Postmodernism* (New York: Routledge, 2008). There is less tangible evidence Pynchon was reading Gwendolyn Brooks, but this is, of course, hard to say.

76. James Baldwin, "A Negro Assays the Negro Mood," *New York Times*, March 12 1961, 25.

77. James Baldwin, "Fifth Avenue, Uptown," *Esquire*, July 1960, 76.

78. Ibid.

79. Ibid.

80. Critic David Witzling argues the opposite of this piece—that Pynchon is continually "reminding readers of the presence of the (white), author." He insists Pynchon undergoes a "self-conscious staging of Watts," revealing the author's own biases. But it is hard to locate exactly where in this essay Pynchon expresses said self-consciousness or stages his own bias given Pynchon's repeated insistence on the puncturing work of beholding Watts. Witzling, *Everybody's America*, 141.

81. Ibid., 135. Witzling also insists the piece is "not particularly successful as reportage, but the direction Pynchon's writing took in the years following its publication suggests that its composition may have helped him to understand the ways in which social reality is always already a social construction" (134).

82. Pynchon, "A Journey into the Mind of Watts."

83. Ibid.

84. As Pynchon wrote about this story: "this is a hometown story, one of the few times I tried to write directly out of the landscape and the experiences I grew up with. I mistakenly thought of Long Island then as a giant and featureless sandbar, without history, someplace to get away from but not to feel very connected to. . . . Not only did I complicate this Long Island space, but I also drew a line around the whole neighborhood, picked it up and shifted it all to the Berkshires, where I still have never been." *Slow Learner: Early Stories* (New York: Back Bay Books, 1995), 20–21.

85. As Terry Reilly notes, "the name of the boys' imaginary friend, Carl Barrington, alludes to the nearby town of Great Barrington, the birthplace of W. E. B. Du Bois, one of the founders of the NAACP, who was born there in 1868" and who had recently died in 1963. See "'They Don't Know It, but We're Integrated': Thomas Pynchon's 'The Secret Integration' and The Saturday Evening Post," *Yale Review* 107, no. 1 (January 2019): 94–102.

86. Pynchon, *Slow Learner*.
87. Ibid., 188–89.
88. Ibid., 191.
89. Ibid., 192.
90. Ibid
91. Ibid
92. Ibid
93. Pynchon, "A Journey into the Mind of Watts."
94. Pynchon, *Slow Learner*, 22.

Chapter 5

1. John Cheever, "Moving Out," *Esquire*, July 1, 1960), 66–69.
2. Ibid., 69.
3. James Baldwin, "Fifth Avenue, Uptown," *Esquire*, July 1, 1960, 70–76.
4. Ibid., 76.
5. As Imani Perry writes in *Looking for Lorraine: The Radiant and Radical Life of Lorraine Hansberry* (Boston: Beacon Press, 2018), the Mount Airy section of Croton-on-Hudson was a popular outpost for leftist New Yorkers—so much so it was colloquially known as Red Hill (176). This may also explain why Hansberry was able to move there without much resistance, unlike many other predominately white neighborhoods in the country.
6. This point is informed in part by Timothy Aubry, "John Cheever and the Management of Middlebrow Misery," *Iowa Journal of Cultural Studies* 3 (2003): 64–83.
7. Kevin Kruse and Thomas Sugrue, eds., *The New Suburban History* (Chicago: University of Chicago Press, 2006).
8. This is reflected in recent work by urban historians and architectural scholars like Nancy Kwak, *A World of Homeowners: American Power and the Politics of Housing Aid* (Chicago: University of Chicago Press, 2015), and Paige Glotzer, *How the Suburbs Were Segregated: Developers and the Business of Exclusionary Housing, 1890–1960* (New York: Columbia University Press, 2020), reframing the international story of homeownership and suburbanization.
9. See Catherine Jurca, *White Diaspora: The Suburb and the Twentieth-Century American Novel* (Princeton, NJ: Princeton University Press, 2001).
10. Julius Lester, "James Baldwin—Reflections of a Maverick," in *Conversations with James Baldwin*, Fred R. Standley and Louis H. Pratt, eds. (Jackson: University Press of Mississippi, 1989), 28.
11. Ibid.
12. James Baldwin, "The Art of Fiction No. 78," interviewed by Jordan Elgrably, *Paris Review* 91 (Spring 1984).
13. The symposium took place over the course of three days, featuring a different writer's remarks on each of the three nights. Cheever was the headliner at Berkeley on Thursday, October 20; Philip Roth at Stanford on Friday, October 21; and James

Baldwin at San Francisco State on Saturday, October 22. Roth's remarks, titled "Writing American Fiction," were published in *Commentary* in March 1961, and Baldwin's were published as "Notes on a Hypothetical Novel" in his 1961 collection of essays, *Nobody Knows My Name*. Cheever's remarks were never published nor is there a recording publicly available.

14. In fact, the essays Cheever and Baldwin each published in *Esquire* a few months prior to the symposiums could have only bolstered expectations of their clashing.

15. Robert Gutwillig, "Dim Views Through Fog," *New York Times*, November 13, 1960, 68–69.

16. In his biography, *Cheever: A Life* (New York: Vintage, 2010), Blake Bailey laments that "Cheever is hardly taught at all in the classroom" (676), while Charles McGrath notes in a *New York Times Magazine* article, "The First Suburbanite" (February 27, 2009), that "Cheever has largely faded from the literary map" (36). If we understand Cheever as a suburban writer, this disinterest is par for the course given that this genre seems to have received relatively little critical attention in recent years. But if we consider Cheever in relation to Roth or Baldwin—whose work has been taken up with increasing frequency in the academy—Cheever's fortunes have precipitously fallen.

17. This is not to say that blacks did not buy homes at midcentury—they certainly did—but they often purchased them at far higher interest rates and were constrained in terms of the housing stock. In 1950, 34.5 percent of blacks in the U.S. owned their homes compared to 57 percent of whites. See U.S. Census Bureau, Housing and Household Economic Statistics Division, "Historical Census of Housing Tables," October 31, 2011.

18. I'm indebted to both Patricia Williams, *The Alchemy of Race and Rights* (Cambridge, MA: Harvard University Press, 1992), and Matthew Frye Jacobson, *Whiteness of a Different Color* (Cambridge, MA: Harvard University Press, 1998), for their models of understanding race alchemically, as something forged in the midst of a number of coinciding and often competing contexts and institutions.

19. Such novels include William Manchester's *City of Anger* (1953), David Karp's *Leave Me Alone* (1957), Keith Wheeler's *Peaceable Lane* (1960), Christopher Davis's *First Family* (1961), and John McPartland's *No Down Payment* (1957).

20. This is not to naturalize the neighborhood as a concept but to historicize its concretization both in reference to specific physical spaces and as a concept used to locate subjects. For a history of the neighborhood, see Benjamin Looker, *A Nation of Neighborhoods: Imagining Cities, Communities, and Democracy in Postwar America* (Chicago: Chicago University Press, 2015).

21. John Cheever, "The Trouble of Marcie Flint," in *The Stories of John Cheever* (New York: Ballantine, 1980), 346. Robert Beuka also makes note of the range of residential spaces populating Shady Hill in *SuburbiaNation: Reading Suburban Landscape in Twentieth-Century American Fiction and Film* (New York: Palgrave, 2004), 86–87.

22. John Cheever, "The Country Husband," in *The Stories of John Cheever*, 393.

23. John Cheever, "The Sorrows of Gin," in *The Stories of John Cheever*, 246.

24. Roediger, *Working Toward Whiteness*, 232.
25. Lipsitz, *The Possessive Investment in Whiteness*, viii.
26. Cheever, "The Country Husband," 392.
27. Cheever's father, a former sailor turned shoe salesman, was broke and an alcoholic by the mid-1920s. Much to the young Cheever's shame, his mother supported the family by running a small gift shop. Cheever dropped out of high school and published his first story in the *New Republic* in 1930, at age eighteen. In 1932, his family home—an eleven-room Victorian clapboard—was, like many homes at the start of the Great Depression, foreclosed on by the bank and razed to the ground. For these details, I draw from Bailey, *Cheever*, 33–62.
28. Quoted in Bailey, *Cheever*, 36.
29. Ibid.
30. Gatsby's status as racially other is described by Walter Benn Michaels in *Our America: Nativism, Modernism, and Pluralism* (Durham, NC: Duke University Press, 1995). Michaels argues that "Gatsby's love for Daisy seems to Tom the expression of something like the impulse to miscegenation" (25). See also William A. Gleason, *The Leisure Ethic: Work and Play in American Literature, 1840–1940* (Stanford, CA: Stanford University Press, 1999); Meredith Goldsmith, "White Skin, White Mask: Passing, Posing, and Performing in *The Great Gatsby*," *Modern Fiction Studies* 49, no. 3 (2003): 443–68; and James Smethurst, *The African American Roots of Modernism: From Reconstruction to the Harlem Renaissance* (Chapel Hill: University of North Carolina Press, 2011).
31. This is not to deny that Gatsby enjoyed the day-to-day advantages of whiteness, escaping the discriminatory treatment more visibly black subjects experienced under legal and cultural Jim Crow. But the fact that Gatsby's wealth is built on the black market in partnership with the Jewish gangster Wolfsheim suggests the relative limits of his access to whiteness when compared to someone like Nick, who despite having far less money has the right pedigree, earning him full access to circles and networks Gatsby could not.
32. Smethurst, *The African American Roots of Modernism*, 199.
33. Cheever, "Housebreaker," 300; Cheever, "The Trouble with Marcie Flint," 343.
34. John Cheever, "The Wrysons," in *The Stories of John Cheever*, 381; John Cheever, "Just Tell Me Who It Was," in *The Stories of John Cheever*, 437.
35. For more on the literary history of passing, see Gayle Wald, *Crossing the Line: Racial Passing in Twentieth-Century U. S. Literature and Culture* (Durham, NC: Duke University Press, 2000); Mary McAleer Balkun, *The American Counterfeit: Authenticity and Identity in American Literature and Culture* (Tuscaloosa: University of Alabama Press, 2006); and Kathleen Pfeiffer, *Race Passing and American Individualism* (Amherst: University of Massachusetts Press, 2002).
36. For more on the endurance of residential racial violence, see Jeannine Bell, *Hate Thy Neighbor: Move-In Violence and the Persistence of Racial Segregation in American Housing* (New York: New York University Press, 2013).

37. David Freund in *Colored Property: State Policy and White Racial Politics in Suburban America* (Chicago: University of Chicago Press 2007) captures the shift in racialized language within midcentury suburbs. He describes how polite rhetoric about protecting property values increasingly replaced more explicit language of racial animosity at midcentury, even as race continued to be the bedrock of residential migration. I extend Freund's point by suggesting that the displacement of both the language of racial animosity and race itself were a precursor to the discourse of color-blindness pervading the idea of multiculturalism later in the century. For more on the way color-blindness has been integral to the perpetuation of structural racism, see Eduardo Bonilla-Silva, *Racism without Racists: Color-Blind Racism and the Persistence of Racial Inequality in America*, 4th ed. (New York: Rowman, 2014).

38. See Richard Dyer, *The Matter of Images: Essays on Representation* (London: Routledge, 2002), and Ruth Frankenberg, *White Women, Race Matters: The Social Construction of Whiteness* (Minneapolis: University of Minnesota Press, 1993).

39. George Lipsitz, *The Possessive Investment in Whiteness: How White People Profit from Identity Politics* (Philadelphia: Temple University Press, 1998), 1.

40. Sara Ahmed, "Declarations of Whiteness: The Non-Performativity of Anti-Racism," *Borderlands* 3, no. 2 (2004). As Robyn Wiegman notes in *Object Lessons* (Durham, NC: Duke University Press, 2012), on the rise of critical whiteness studies in the 1990s: "of course, white identity had been studied before, as numerous scholars noted by citing Ethnic Studies in general or the black intellectual tradition that proceeded from W. E. B. Du Bois to James Baldwin, Frantz Fanon, and Toni Morrison in particular" (156). "But the academic press had not found the study of whiteness quite so interesting," she continues, "nor had publishers gone out of their way, as they did throughout the 1990s, to secure books on the topic."

41. Dyer, *The Matter of Image*, 127.

42. Catherine Jurca, *White Diaspora: The Suburb and the Twentieth-Century American Novel* (Princeton: Princeton University Press, 2001), 8.

43. Timothy Aubry, "John Cheever and the Management of Middlebrow Misery," *Iowa Journal of Cultural Studies* 3 (2003): 74.

44. Ibid.

45. For a recent iteration of this debate, see Lars Andersson, "Burglary in Shady Hill and Sarsaparilla: The Politics of Conformity in White and Cheever," *Australian Literary Studies* 22, no. 4 (2006), in which he insists that Cheever "ultimately endorses an affirmative view of suburbia that lacks the subversive analysis of society common to many forms of realism" (442). This view is challenged by Joseph George in "Suburbia's Alien Reek: Contract and Relation in John Cheever's *Bullet Park*," *Canadian Review of American Studies* 44, no. 3 (2014), who counters that Cheever continually illustrates his characters' "constant shortcomings" (529); Timothy Aubry, who writes that Cheever "implicates himself as a part of the company he is critiquing" (69); and Keith Wilhite, who emphasizes the "ambiguous position Cheever occupied in relation to

the suburbs" (216) in "John Cheever's Shady Hill, or: How I Learned to Stop Worrying and Love the Suburbs," *Studies in American Fiction* 34, no. 2 (Autumn 2006): 215–39.

46. James Baldwin, "On Being White . . . and Other Lies," in *The Cross of Redemption: Uncollected Writings* (New York: Pantheon, 2010), 137.

47. James Baldwin, "Introduction: The Price of the Ticket," in *The Price of the Ticket: Collected Non-Fiction 1948–1985* (New York: St. Martin's Press, 1985), xiv.

48. John Cheever, "O Youth and Beauty!" in *The Stories of John Cheever*, 258; Cheever, "The Country Husband," 388.

49. Cheever, "The Trouble with Marcie Flint," 350.

50. Cheever, "The Housebreaker of Shady Hill," 303.

51. Though I am not suggesting that "Housebreaker" explicitly cites *Native Son*, the careers of Wright and Cheever did dovetail early in the 1930s. In addition to sharing a lunch table at the New York WPA, they also allegedly shared a literary agent. For their histories with the WPA, see David A. Taylor, *Soul of a People: The WPA Writers' Project Uncovers Depression America* (New York: Wiley, 2009), 36. There is some controversy, however, about whether Cheever's agent, Maxim Lieber, also represented Wright. Arnold Rampersad claims that Lieber represented Wright in the 1930s, whereas Hazel Rowley argues that Lieber rejected Wright's submissions. See Hazel Rowley, *Richard Wright: The Life and Times* (Chicago: University of Chicago Press, 2001), 133, and Arnold Rampersad, *The Life of Langston Hughes, Vol. II: 1941–1967, I Dream a World*, 2nd ed (New York: Oxford University Press, 2002), 18.

52. Richard Wright, *Native Son* (New York: Perennial Classics, 1998), 304.

53. Jurca, *White Diaspora*, 103.

54. Wilhite, "John Cheever's Shady Hill," 224.

55. Cheever, "Housebreaker," 320.

56. Wilhite, "John Cheever's Shady Hill," 225.

57. Bailey, *Cheever: A Life*, 257.

58. John Cheever, "The Worm in the Apple," in *The Stories of John Cheever*, 338.

59. Ibid., 341.

60. Ibid., 342.

61. The only other reference to white skin in the entire collection applies to another marginal figure: the French maid of "The Country Husband," who is recognized by the story's protagonist as a Vichy collaborator.

62. Cheever, "The Worm in the Apple," 342.

63. Lynne Waldeland, *John Cheever* (Boston: Twayne, 1979), 71.

64. John Cheever, "The Five-Forty-Eight," in *The Stories of John Cheever*, 283.

65. Ibid., 286. Timothy Aubry has also pointed out Miss Dent's racialization, noting that the relationship between her and Blake is "constituted by a faintly articulated racial dimension" (75).

66. Ibid., 281.

67. Ibid., 291.

68. Ibid., 292.

69. Ibid., 290.

70. Ibid., 294.

71. Ibid.

72. Ibid.

73. Aubry, "John Cheever and the Management of Middlebrow Misery" 75.

74. For instance, a common occurrence across the stories is for a husband and wife to get in an argument and for one of them to start walking toward the train station in a gesture of self-exile; yet they never quite make it aboard the train, reconciling before either of them can leave.

75. Cheever, "The Country Husband," 401.

76. Irving Howe, "Realities and Fictions," *Partisan Review* 26 (1959): 131.

77. Ibid.

78. Toni Morrison, *Playing in the Dark: Whiteness and the Literary Imagination* (New York: Vintage, 1993), 16.

79. Diane Fisher, "Miss Hansberry and Bobby K: Birthweight Low, Jobs Few, Death Comes Early," *Village Voice*, June 6 1963, 3, 9, reprinted in *Conversations with Lorraine Hansberry*, Mollie Godfrey, ed. (Jackson: University Press of Mississippi, 2021), 173.

80. I very much subscribe to Mary Helen Washington's crucial insistence on extending the timeline of black cultural front activity through the late 1950s. This extension, however, also took place when the appeal and availability of leftism to the black masses was declining, as Washington also discusses. See Mary Helen Washington, *The Other Blacklist: The African American Literary and Cultural Left of the 1950s* (New York: Columbia University Press, 2014).

81. Richard Wright, *12 Million Black Voices: A Folk History of the Negro in the United States of America* (London: Lindsay Drummond, 1947), 61.

82. Richard Wright, "Blueprint for Negro Writing," in *Within the Circle: An Anthology of African American Literary Criticism from the Harlem Renaissance to the Present*, Angelyn Mitchell, ed. (Durham, NC: Duke University Press, 1994), 98.

83. Richard Wright, "I Choose Exile," Richard Wright Papers, JWJ-MSS 3, Box 6, Folder 10, Yale Collection of American Literature, Beinecke Rare Book and Manuscripts Library.

84. Ibid.

85. Ibid.

86. As Alan Wald writes regarding Richard Wright, "there is usually no bright red line clearly demarcating political orientations on the Left, and ideologies hardly remain static over time" (90), in *Richard Wright in Context*, Michael Nowlin, ed. (Cambridge: Cambridge University Press, 2021).

87. Shirley Ann Wilson Moore, *To Place Our Deeds: The African American Community in Richmond, California, 1910–1963* (Berkeley: University of California Press, 2000), 118.

88. Wright, "I Choose Exile."

89. As Soyica Diggs Colbert writes in her recent Hansberry biography, "disproportionate attention to *Raisin* not only limits Hansberry's impact during her life, it also causes misapprehension of her critical contribution to Black feminism as a theory and practice and to Afro-Modern political thought." Imani Perry marks the "neat" canonization of the play "as the story of a Black family fighting Northern segregation" as it was easily overlaid upon the arc of the civil rights movement. "Like Selma," Perry writes, "like Washington, *A Raisin in the Sun* sits static. Static things don't breathe. Or live. But Lorraine did. Deeply." See Soyica Diggs Colbert, *Radical Vision: A Biography of Lorraine Hansberry* (New Haven, CT: Yale University Press, 2021), 34, and Imani Perry, *Looking for Lorraine: The Radiant and Radical Life of Lorraine Hansberry* (Boston: Beacon Press, 2018), 2.

90. Colbert, *Radical Vision*, 98.

91. Charles Shields paints a more avaricious picture of the Hansberry fortune in *Lorraine Hansberry: The Life Behind A Raisin in the Sun* (New York: Henry Holt, 2022), noting Hansberry Enterprises' struggles with creditors and with the law at the expense of their tenants.

92. See Amiri Baraka, "'Raisin in the Sun's' Enduring Season," *Washington Post*, November 16, 1986; Nelson Algren, "Is 'Raisin in the Sun' a Lemon in the Dark?" *Tone*, April 1961, 6, 13; Jonas Mekas, "Movie Journal," *Village Voice*, April 6, 1961, 11–12; Harold Cruse, *The Crisis of the Negro Intellectual* (New York: New York Review of Books, 1967), 279.

93. Lorraine Hansberry, "Genet, Mailer, and the New Paternalism," *Village Voice*, June 1, 1961, 10, 14.

94. For more on Hansberry Enterprises see also Shields, *Lorraine Hansberry*, and Carol Rose, "*Raisin*, Race, and the Real Estate Revolution of the Early Twentieth Century," in *Power, Prose, and Purse: Law, Literature, and Economic Transformations*, Alison L. LaCroix, Saul Levmore, and Martha C. Nussbaum, eds. (New York: Oxford University Press, 2019).

95. Letter from Lorraine Hansberry to Sy Baldash, February 10, 1962, Box 2, folder 17, Lorraine Hansberry Collection, Schomburg Center for Research in Black Culture, New York.

96. Mike Wallace "Unaired Interview with Lorraine Hansberry," May 8, 1959, reprinted in *Conversations with Lorraine Hansberry*, Mollie Godfrey, ed. (Jackson: University Press of Mississippi, 2021), 67.

97. Ibid.

98. See Amani Morrison's forthcoming book, *Kitchenette Building: Representing Race, Space, and Housing in Chicago's Great Migration* for more on the curious absenting of the landlord from the play.

99. Shields, *Lorraine Hansberry*, 274.

100. Houston Baker Jr., *The Journey Back: Issues in Black Literature and Criticism* (Chicago: University of Chicago Press, 1980), 75; Baraka, "'Raisin in the Sun's' Enduring Season."

101. Baraka, "'Raisin in the Sun's' Enduring Season"

102. Helene Keyssar, *The Curtain and the Veil: Strategies in Black Drama* (New York: Burt Franklin, 1981), 130–31. Stephen Carter is the one critic to diverge from this line of thought, suggesting "Hansberry saw a grain of hope even in a George Murchison however," even as the character "remains almost as shackled to other forms of folly as he is to male chauvinism" for most of the play. "One of Hansberry's wishes (which her own example supported to the limited extent that any individual's can)," Carter continues, "was that the Murchisons of the future would, through the pressures of circumstance and the aspirations and actions of a multitude of Younger families, become closer in spirit to the Asagais of the late fifties and early sixties" (61). *Hansberry's Drama* (New York: Meridian, 1993), 59–60.

103. Keyssar, *The Curtain and the Veil*, Box 13, Lorraine Hansberry Collection, Schomburg Center for Research in Black Culture, New York.

104. Hansberry, *A Raisin in the Sun* (New York: Vintage Books, 2010), 97.

105. Ibid., 81.

106. For instance, in interviewing Hansberry, Mike Wallace cites the work of white social critic Vance Packard on the black middle class deeming this group "more desperately absorbed in surrounding themselves with limousines and mink coats, even than their white counterparts." In response, Hansberry insists "there is nothing peculiar or unique or exotic about people having middle class aspirations." "This particular group," she goes on to explain, "cannot come face-to-face with some of the more acute realities of what they are trying to overcome because they just don't get there, they don't become bankers in the larger sense. They don't get an opportunity to deal with those actual things." Wallace, "Unaired Interview with Lorraine Hansberry," 66, 68.

107. Ibid., 83.

108. Letter from Mamie Tubbs to Lorraine Hansberry, January 5, 1961, Box 2, folder 1, Lorraine Hansberry Collection, Schomburg Center for Research in Black Culture, New York. As Mamie also writes about Hansberry Enterprises' legal troubles in Chicago, "It appears that all the City pressure is off, the fines are paid, the properties liquidated (stolen), and nobody seems to be mad at us anymore since the bulk of the clan has made it (sic), exodus."

109. Letter from Mamie Tubbs to Lorraine Hansberry, January 30, 1961, Box 2, folder 3, Lorraine Hansberry Collection, Schomburg Center for Research in Black Culture, New York. Their optimism was ultimately misplaced. As Shields writes in *Lorraine Hansberry*, the family was sued by People's Gas and Light for nonpayment for utilities and the building was soon abandoned to creditors, leaving tenants with "no water, radiator heat, or telephone service that winter" (288).

110. Hansberry confirmed this connection between Walter's possessive hunger and at least one of her siblings in a 1959 interview with the *New York Post*. While her brother Perry "had the opportunity and accomplished the things Walter Lee vainly hoped to do," Hansberry notes that "the drive which impelled them both is the same." Ted Poston, "We Have So Much to Say," *New York Post*, March 22, 1959, M2, reprinted in *Conversations with Lorraine Hansberry*, 15.

111. Charles Shields in *Lorraine Hansberry* makes a similar observation, specifically about Hansberry's brother, Perry. "*A Raisin in the Sun* was her wish for her brother Perry, the more entrepreneurial of the two brothers to have a better life than their father." Shields goes on to note that "when Douglas Turner Ward later met Perry, he was 'shocked,' he said. 'Her brother was Walter Lee in the play!'" (233)

112. Hansberry, *Raisin*, 84.

113. Ibid., 34.

114. Ibid.

115. Ibid.

116. Ibid., 42.

117. Ibid., 84.

118. Ibid., 93.

119. Ibid., 45.

120. Ibid.

121. Mama and Ruth's vision of homeownership's benefits resonates with Andrew Weise's account of what drove black suburbanites to own in places outside of the city in the early twentieth century. As Weise writes, black residents of early suburbs "valued home ownership less as a long-term capital investment or as shelter for an idealized nuclear family than for its usefulness in cutting costs, providing supplemental income, and limiting dependence on a fragile wage." He also points to many residents' preference for "a bucolic landscape," including the possibility of tending gardens (93). *Places of Their Own: African American Suburbanization in the Twentieth Century* (Chicago: University of Chicago Press, 2004).

122. Ibid., 118, 141.

123. Carol Rose also notes the financial upside of Walter's acceptance of Lindner's deal: "The Clybourne Park neighbors would take a hit for their '**taste** for discrimination,'" while "the Youngers could use the money to buy a different house and still have some money left over for Beneatha's education, as Mama had planned before Walter squandered the insurance fund in his own dubious and duplicitous scheme" (303). Rose consequently ponders "why are none of these characters thinking about money," before suggesting that "the climactic scene of Walter Junior's refusal is certainly a much more satisfying experience for the play's audience, who have more or less been set up to take the short view and who are unlikely to care about the long-term possibilities of taking the money—no matter how advantageous those consequences might have been for families like the Youngers. But if none of these players onstage are thinking about money, in the real world the players in the real estate industry had money very much in mind" (304). "Raisin, Race, and the Real Estate Revolution of the Early Twentieth Century," in *Power, Prose, and Purse.*

124. Lorraine Hansberry, "An Author's Reflection: Willie Loman, Walter Younger, and He Who Must Live," *Village Voice*, August 12, 1959, 7–8, reprinted in *Conversations with Lorraine Hansberry*, 96.

125. Ibid.

126. Ibid.
127. Ibid., 97.
128. Ibid.
129. Ibid.
130. Hansberry, *Raisin*, 143.
131. Wallace, "Unaired Interview with Lorraine Hansberry," 67.
132. Ibid., 71.
133. Colbert, *Radical Vision*, 75.
134. Ibid.
135. Ibid., 85.
136. Ibid., 95.
137. Wallace, "Unaired Interview with Lorraine Hansberry," 70.
138. Hansberry, *Raisin*, 135.
139. Colbert, *Radical Vision*, 92.
140. Hansberry, *Raisin*, 135.

141. This reading diverges, for instance, from Mary Esteve's interpretation of the play's embrace of a liberal-oriented incremental realism: "Here, then, is a drama of rescue: an angry youngish man is encouraged to abandon his own will to destruction and instead to tether himself to the goals of developing familial wealth and stability over generations. . . . But Hansberry strongly implies that without a network of social, civic, and legal institutions to sustain their commitment to buying property, that the family has little chance of being integrated into the welfare state. Indeed, the bravery this family has collectively summoned to mount their incursion into a white neighborhood stamps them as liberal activists who insist these conditions be met" (79). I instead find Hansberry asking us to understand the family's commitment to buying property (and liberalism writ large), within the historical and material context of the midcentury that made this commitment seem like their best and only option, even as the play ultimate reveals the subtle but key differences in what constitutes a "commitment to property" embodied by the play's various characters. See *Incremental Realism: Postwar American Fiction, Happiness, and Welfare-State Liberalism* (Stanford, CA: Stanford University Press, 2021).

142. Ibid., 83.
143. Ibid.
144. Ibid.
145. Ibid., 82, 86, 96, 86.
146. Ibid., 97.
147. Ibid., 81.

148. For more on Marshall, see Adrienne Brown, "B-Sides: Paule Marshall's 'Brown Girl, Brownstones,'" Public Books, November 7, 2019, https://www.publicbooks.org/b-sides-paule-marshalls-brown-girl-brownstones/.

149. Asagai, too, offers his own rendition of "home" beyond the residential before leaving the play. In one of his last lines to Beneatha, he articulates his wish to bring her "home" to Nigeria, a home he represents not in terms of tended gardens and curtained

sills but "our mountains and our stars." Experiencing it involves "cool drinks from gourd" and learning "the old songs and the ways of our people" (137).

150. Hansberry, *Raisin*, 151.

Chapter 6

1. Letter from Leroy McLean to Madison Jones, Executive Director of the CCHR, November 20, 1962, Box 4, folder 1, Olivia Pleasants Frost Collection, Schomburg Center for Research in Black Culture, New York.

2. Letter from Edward Doyle, Mortgage Loan Officer at Equitable Savings and Loan, to Leroy McLean, February 11, 1958; letter from Marion T. Byrne, Mortgage Consultant, Dime Savings Bank of Brooklyn, to Leroy McLean, February 25, 1958; letter from William J. Wall, Mortgage Loan Department, Brevoort Savings Bank of Brooklyn, to Leroy McLean, February 7, 1958, Box 4, folder 1, Olivia Pleasants Frost Collection, Schomburg Center for Research in Black Culture, New York.

3. It wouldn't be until 1968 that Pratt University professors discovered four buildings occupied by the free African Americans who had settled in the area in the nineteenth century. These houses were eventually excavated and restored and are part of the Weeksville Heritage Center. See Corina Knoll and Morgan Jerkins, "Weeksville, a Haven for Free African-Americans Before the Civil War, Is Fighting for Survival," *New York Times*, May 10, 2019, https://www.nytimes.com/2019/05/10/nyregion/weeksville-brooklyn-crowdfunding-campaign.html.

4. Letter from Leroy McLean to George C. Johnson, President of Dime Savings Bank, April 26, 1958, Box 4, folder 1, Olivia Pleasants Frost Collection, Schomburg Center for Research in Black Culture, New York.

5. Letter from Leroy McLean to James Hicks, *New York Amsterdam News*, May 4, 1958, Box 4, folder 1, Olivia Pleasants Frost Collection, Schomburg Center for Research in Black Culture, New York.

6. It's unclear from his rejection letters whether McLean was rejected because of his race or whether the denials were based on the property's location in a predominately black neighborhood. Likely it was a combination of both. McLean's adamancy that the home he sought to purchase was an "excellent property" preempts the notion that he was denied due to the state of the property itself.

7. McLean pops up at least one other time as far as I know in the archive in relation to fair housing. He worked with Brooklyn's CORE branch in 1961 to organize on behalf of Eva McGuire, a black woman denied an apartment on the grounds, they suspected, of her race. Whether McLean was a professional organizer working on open housing or more of a "hobbyist" is hard to say but it seems clear that this issue mattered to him, and not just personally. See Brian Purnell, *Fighting Jim Crow in the County of Kings: The Congress of Racial Equality in Brooklyn* (Lexington: University Press of Kentucky, 2013), 71–75.

8. See Robert J. Sampson, *Great American City: Chicago and the Enduring Neighborhood Effect* (Chicago: University of Chicago Press, 2012).

9. See *The Chicago Freedom Movement: Martin Luther King Jr. and Civil Rights Activism in the North*, Bernard LaFayette Jr., James R. Ralph Jr., Mary Lou Finley, and Pam Smith, eds. (Louisville: University of Kentucky Press, 2016); James R. Ralph Jr., *Northern Protest: Martin Luther King, Jr., Chicago, and the Civil Rights Movement* (Cambridge, MA: Harvard University Press, 1993); Adam Cohen and Elizabeth Taylor, *American Pharaoh: Mayor Richard J. Daley—His Battle for Chicago and the Nation* (New York: Little, Brown, 2000); and David Bernstein, "Martin Luther King Jr.'s 1966 Chicago Campaign," *Chicago Magazine*, July 25, 2016, https://www.chicagomag.com/Chicago-Magazine/August-2016/Martin-Luther-King-Chicago-Freedom-Movement/.

10. Coretta Scott King, *My Life with Martin Luther King, Jr.* (New York: Henry Holt, 1993), 276.

11. Bernstein, "Martin Luther King Jr.'s 1966 Chicago Campaign."

12. Ibid.

13. Coretta Scott King described her experience of the Lawndale apartment as such in her memoir: "Our apartment was on the third floor of a dingy building, which had no lights in the hall, only one dim bulb at the head of the stairs." Inspecting the foyer, as King notes, "I realized that the floor was not concrete but bare dirt. The smell of urine was overpowering. We were told that this was because the door was always open (the front lock was broken), and the drunks came in off the street to use the hallway as a toilet. We walked up three rickety flights of stairs in gloom you could hardly see through, and into our new quarters.... The temperature outside was fifteen degrees, and the heat in the apartment was hardly noticeable." *My Life with Martin Luther King, Jr,* 276.

14. Bernstein, "Martin Luther King Jr.'s 1966 Chicago Campaign."

15. Ibid.

16. *The Chicago Freedom Movement*, xi.

17. Ibid.

18. As Walter Mondale insisted, while "a lot of civil rights was about making the South behave and taking the teeth from George Wallace," fair housing legislation "came right to the neighborhoods across the country. This was civil rights getting personal." Nikole Hannah-Jones, "Living Apart: How the Government Betrayed a Landmark Civil Rights Law," ProPublica, June 25, 2015, https://www.propublica.org/article/living-apart-how-the-government-betrayed-a-landmark-civil-rights-law.

19. James Smethurst, *The African American Roots of Modernism: From Reconstruction to the Harlem Renaissance* (Chapel Hill: University of North Carolina Press, 2011), 2.

20. We might further understand the representational shortcomings of King's campaign, in conversation with Myka Tucker-Abramson's *Novel Shocks: Urban Renewal and the Origins of Neoliberalism* (New York: Oxford University Press, 2018), as not only belated in relation to modernism but also as a presager of neoliberalism and the origins of "the renewed frontier imaginary that shaped and nourished the gentrification of US cities in the 1920s and 1980s that played a crucial role in forging

what Matthew Huber, following Michel Foucault, terms the 'entrepreneurial subject' of neoliberalism" (4).

21. A Google ngram search for this term confirms that it emerged sometime in the late 1960s. The term's invention likely evolved from the concept of "institutional bias" which first appeared in the 1950s but was not anchored in the particularities of racism. While I can't prove without a doubt that Hamilton and Carmichael were the first to use this phrase, I can say with certainty that Hamilton and Carmichael popularized it.

22. Stokely Carmichael and Charles V. Hamilton, *Black Power: The Politics of Liberation in America* (London: Jonathan Cape, 1968), 4.

23. Ibid.

24. Ibid.

25. Although institutional and bureaucratic racism may not be exactly identical, the claims Carmichael and Hamilton make about the difficulties of bringing institutional racism into representation apply to its bureaucratic forms. If both institutional and bureaucratic racisms are, by Carmichael and Hamilton's 1967 definition, "less identifiable in terms of specific individuals committing the acts," then both are difficult to bring into representation given that specific individuals committing acts are at the heart of narrative's more specific operation. And while narrative is just one representational genre among many, it seems to be the one Carmichael and Hamilton understood as having the most political purchase given their gesture to the televisual and their own choice of narrative genre in Black Power

26. See Peniel E. Joseph, *Waiting 'Til the Midnight Hour: A Narrative History of Black Power in America* (New York: Henry Holt, 2007).

27. Matthew Fuller and Eyal Weizman, *Investigative Aesthetics: Conflicts and Commons in the Politics of Truth* (New York: Verso Books, 2021), 4.

28. Ibid.

29. Jacques Rancière, *The Politics of Aesthetics*, Gabriel Rockhill, trans. (London: Bloomsbury, 2004), 8.

30. Ibid.

31. Fuller and Weizman, *Investigative Aesthetics*, 12.

32. Ibid., 2.

33. Ibid.

34. The increasing centrality of bureaucratic assemblage to contemporary art practices might also be presaged by Leroy McLean. See the collection and display of deeds, covenant, and real estate transactions by contemporary artists like Theaster Gates, Hans Haacke, and Cameron Rowland.

35. Justin P. Steil and Camille Z. Charles, "Sociology, Segregation and the Fair Housing Act," in *Perspectives on Fair Housing*, Vincent J. Reina, Wendell E. Pritchett, Susan M. Wachter, eds. (Philadelphia: University of Pennsylvania Press, 2021), 55.

36. Keeanga-Yamahtta Taylor, *Race for Profit: How Banks and the Real Estate Industry Undermined Black Homeownership* (Chapel Hill: University of North Carolina Press, 2020), 7.

37. See Hannah-Jones, "Living Apart"; Gregory Squires, ed., *The Fight for Fair Housing: Causes, Consequences, and Future Implications of the 1968 Federal Fair Housing Act* (New York: Routledge, 2017); and *Moving Toward Integration*, Richard H. Sander, Yana A. Kucheva, and Jonathan M. Zasloff, eds. (Cambridge, MA: Harvard University Press, 2018). Fair housing laws also disproportionately served those who could afford to pursue legal solutions. As Wendell Pritchett writes, "fair housing laws were, in principal, successful in securing the limited goals of opening up new resources for middle-class blacks that advocates hoped to achieve." "Where Shall We Live? Class and the Limitations of Fair Housing Law," *Urban Lawyer* 35, no. 3 (Summer 2003): 407.

38. George Lipsitz, "Living Downstream: The Fair Housing Act at Fifty," in *The Fight for Fair Housing*, 267.

39. Ibid.

40. As Martha Biondi notes, black New Yorkers did not necessarily fetishize residential integration but were instead committed to fighting for "unrestricted access to capital and residential space—in other words, to the economic opportunities of first-class citizenship" in whatever location they saw fit. *To Stand and Fight: The Struggle for Civil Rights in Postwar New York City* (Cambridge, MA: Harvard University Press, 2006), 223.

41. Pritchett, "Where Shall We Live?," 442. New York's 1958 Fair Housing Practices Law, or Local Law 80, was the first law in the nation to bar racial discrimination in private housing. Though the bill passed, it was not without controversy, as evidenced by the *New York Times*' opposition to the legislation as "the wrong way to a right end." The editorial insisted that change on the private housing market "must be a matter of education and spiritual growth rather than a consequence of legislation" (Pritchett, 439). As was the case in many Northern cities, fair housing laws were already on the books New York by the midcentury but were difficult to enforce. See Biondi, *To Stand and Fight*, 226, and Purnell, *Fighting Jim Crow in the County of Kings*, 61.

42. Critics of the Fair Housing Act's shortcomings have argued, as Pritchett notes, "that housing policy should focus less on directly combating discrimination and give more attention to increasing the supply of housing" as well as decoupling housing discrimination from residential segregation to instead focus on providing resources for black communities (469–70).

43. Sun Jung Oh and John Yinger, "What Have We Learned from Paired Testing in Housing Markets?" *Cityscape* 16, no. 3 (2015): 15–60.

44. Although applicable to a range of scenarios including employment, the practice was most associated with fair housing efforts.

45. Henry Hampton, director, *Eyes on the Prize: America's Civil Rights Movement*, Blackside, 1987, http://www.shoppbs.pbs.org/wgbh/amex/eyesontheprize/about/pt_202.html.

46. In 2003, HUD issued guidelines to its offices "to ensure that FHEO (Fair Housing and Equal Opportunity), investigators nationwide will adopt a uniform approach

to investigations where testing has been conducted with respect to the housing practices of a respondent." Testers are treated as anonymous witnesses, further de-particularizing their personal experience so they can better serve as data points. See the Fair Housing Institute, "Fair Housing Testers: The Fair Housing Insiders," https://fairhousinginstitute.com/fair-housing-testers/.

47. Amistad Research Center, "Committee of Civil Rights in Metropolitan New York, Inc.," http://amistadresearchcenter.tulane.edu/archon/?p=creators/creator&id=247.

48. Committee on Civil Rights in New York, "From: CCRM, To: Apartment Seekers," brochure, Box 5, folder 5, Olivia Pleasants Frost Collection, Schomburg Center for Research in Black Culture, New York.

49. Ibid.

50. Ibid.

51. Ibid.

52. Given the wealth generated by residential discrimination, moreover, a short-term penalty and some public embarrassment may in fact be worth being deemed a "lawbreaker."

53. Purnell, *Fighting Jim Crow in the County of Kings*, 75–76. As Purnell notes of Brooklyn CORE, following several victories using testing and direct-action protests, the chapter "decided to take on discrimination cases whose root causes were deeper than the decisions of just one person," but these efforts proved far less successful.

54. Harlem Mortgage and Improvement Council, *Harlem: A Neglected Investment Opportunity* (1951), 3.

55. Harlem Mortgage and Improvement Council, "Have You Found a Mortgage Loan Hard to Obtain in Harlem" flyer, Box 4, folder 1, Olivia Pleasants Frost Collection, Schomburg Center for Research in Black Culture, New York.

56. "Why a Home Journal: An Editorial," *Home and Housing Journal*, July 1957, 1, 4.

57. Ibid.

58. "Helen Horne Wins Journal Contest Title," *Home and Housing Journal*, June–July 1959, 1.

59. Carmichael and Hamilton, *Black Power*, 4.

60. Andrew Sarris, "Good Intentions," *New York Times*, April 24, 1966, 20.

61. Ibid.

62. Dudley Randall, *Negro Digest*, December 1966, 70.

63. Ibid.

64. A. H. Weiler, "Nice to Have You Back, Pearl," *New York Times*, April 20, 1969.

65. Kristin Hunter, *The Landlord* (New York: Charles Scribner's Sons, 1966), 213. Tucker-Abramson offers a key reading of shock's failure as a "resistant aesthetic strategy" for representing "the experience of the slum dweller who is excluded from society" given the ways shock had been "appropriated as a tool for the creative destruction of urban space, and the neutralization, appropriation, and commodification of black men" (*Novel Shocks*, 35).

66. As Darryl Dickson-Carr writes of the satire, "instead of denying a particular reality, satire necessarily depends upon and attempts to alter it" (121), while also having "the marked potential to be more aggressive than straight polemics" (122). *African American Satire: The Sacredly Profane Novel* (Columbia: University of Missouri Press, 2001), 121.

67. Hunter, *The Landlord*, 171.

68. Ibid., 168.

69. Ibid., 207.

70. Ibid., 204, 202.

71. We might understand this ending in relation to a genealogy of midcentury work traced by Tucker-Abramson that "depicted and responded to these new urban spaces as forms of traumatic 'shock' that required new aesthetic forms and political structures. These novels rejected older shock-based modernisms such as surrealism and naturalism and, like the urbanization projects they depicted, forged a new kind of modernism, one that transformed shock from a traumatic effect of urban modernity that disrupts the subject's psychic economy into a therapeutic force that helps strengthen and shape a more flexible, self-reliant, and resilient subject" (*Novel Shocks*, 4).

72. Christopher Sieving, *Soul Searching: Black-Themed Cinema from the March on Washington to the Rise of Blaxploitation* (Middletown, CT: Wesleyan University Press, 2011), 170.

73. Ibid., 172.

74. William Collins, "If You're Buying a Drink for Kristin Hunter, Say It's Because of Her Book," Box 8, folder 8, Bill Gunn Collection, Schomburg Center for Research in Black Culture, New York.

75. *The Landlord,* directed by Hal Ashby (Mirsch Company and Cartier Productions, 1970).

76. Bill Gunn, screenplay draft for "*The Landlord: A Black Comedy*," Box 8, folder 6, Bill Gunn Collection, Schomburg Center for Research in Black Culture, New York.

77. Bill Gunn, screenplay draft for *The Landlord: A Black Comedy*, page 34, Box 8, folder 5, Bill Gunn Collection, Schomburg Center for Research in Black Culture, New York.

78. Sieving, *Soul Searching*, 170.

79. Ibid.

80. Ibid.

81. Hunter, *The Landlord*.

82. Hunter, *The Landlord*, 9.

83. Ibid., 10.

84. For more on Florynce Kennedy, see Sherie M. Randolph, *Florynce "Flo" Kennedy: The Life of a Black Feminist Radical* (Chapel Hill: University of North Carolina Press, 2018).

85. N. B. D. Connolly, *A World More Concrete: Real Estate and the Remaking of Jim Crow South Florida* (Chicago: University of Chicago Press, 2014).

86. The fact of multiracial profiteering from residential apartheid, however, is not proof of the declining importance of racism to the housing market but, I would argue, of that racism's evolution to more specifically target the black poor. Moreover, given that the subprime lending preceding the 2008 crash was refined in minority neighborhoods suggests that they remain the most vulnerable to exploitation within the housing and lending markets.

87. Hunter, *The Landlord*, 9.
88. Taylor, *Race for Profit*, 6.
89. Ibid., 176.
90. Ibid.
91. Ibid.
92. Richard Wright, *12 Million Black Voices: A Folk History of the Negro in the United States of America* (London: Lindsay Drummond, 1947), 36.

Epilogue

1. For a smattering of coverage most recent to the publication of this book, see Debra Kamin, "Home Appraised with a Black Owner: $472,000. With a White Owner: $750,000," *New York Times*, August 18, 2022; Debra Kamin, "Widespread Racial Bias Found in Home Appraisals," *New York Times*, November 2, 2022; Colette Coleman, "Selling Houses While Black," *New York Times*, January 12, 2023; Debra Kamin, "Discrimination Seeps into Every Aspect of Home Buying for Black Americans," *New York Times*, November 29 2022; Jennifer Ludden, "Racial Bias in Home Appraising Prompts Changes in the Industry," *New York Times*, March 10, 2023.

2. Homes in black neighborhoods are valued on average 22 percent lower than they would be in non-black neighborhoods. See Jonathan Rothwell and Andre M. Perry, "How racial bias in appraisals affects the devaluation of homes in majority-Black neighborhoods," Brookings Institution, December 5, 2022, https://www.brookings.edu/research/how-racial-bias-in-appraisals-affects-the-devaluation-of-homes-in-majority-black-neighborhoods/. This same report notes that "neighborhoods with a majority of Latino or Hispanic, Asian American, or white residents do not experience home price devaluation, using the same model."

3. There have been major gains in Hispanic and Asian homeownership rates, but they too remain below white homeownership levels. In every state in the U.S., moreover, African American, Hispanic, Asian, and Native American households have lower rates of homeownership than white households except for Hawaii.

4. Keeanga-Yamahtta Taylor, *Race for Profit: How Banks and the Real Estate Industry Undermined Black Homeownership* (Chapel Hill: University of North Carolina Press, 2020), 261.

5. See Robert Sampson, *Great American City: Chicago and the Enduring Neighborhood Effect* (Chicago: University of Chicago Press, 2011), and Walter Johnson, *The Broken Heart of America: St. Louis and the Violent History of the United States* (New York: Basic Books, 2021).

6. Homeownership, too, plays a role in *Beloved*. Though Sethe and Denver live at house 124, even as Beloved spiritually possesses it, the home is owned by the white Mr. Bodwin, suggesting the line between abolitionism and the kinds of liberalism eventually begetting the middling reforms of the 1968 Fair Housing Act.

7. Irvin J. Hunt, *Dreaming the Present: Time Aesthetics and the Black Cooperative Movement* (Chapel Hill: University of North Carolina Press, 2022).

8. Edward Onaci, *Free the Land: The Republic of New Afrika and the Pursuit of a Black Nation-State* (Chapel Hill: University of North Carolina Press, 2020).

9. Thomas Healy, *Soul City: Race, Equality, and the Lost Dream of an American Utopia* (New York: Henry Holt, 2022).

10. For more on the planning and execution of Resurrection City see Mabel O. Wilson, "Lessons from Resurrection City," in *Radical Pedagogies*, Beatriz Colomina, Ignacio G. Galan, Evangelos Kotsioris, and Anna-Maria Meister, eds. (Cambridge, MA: MIT Press, 2022), 168–72; Robert Hamilton, *Dr. Martin Luther King Jr. and the Poor People's Campaign of 1968* (Athens: University of Georgia Press), 322; John Wiebenson, "Planning and Using Resurrection City," *Journal of the American Institute of Planners* 35, no. 6 (1969): 405–11; Charles Fager, *Uncertain Resurrection: The Poor People's Washington Campaign* (Grand Rapids, MI: Eerdmans, 1969); Gerald D. McKnight, *The Last Crusade: Martin Luther King, Jr., the FBI, and the Poor People's Campaign* (New York: Westview Press, 1998); Sylvie Laurent, *King and the Other America: The Poor People's Campaign and the Quest for Economic Equality* (Berkeley: University of California Press, 2018); and Alyosha Goldstein, *Poverty in Common: The Politics of Community Action During the American Century* (Durham, NC: Duke University Press, 2012).

11. Cited in Fager, *Uncertain Resurrection*, 36.

12. Mabel O. Wilson, "Lessons from Resurrection City," in *Radical Pedagogies*, 170.

13. McKnight, *The Last Crusade*, 107.

14. Wilson, "Lessons from Resurrection City" 172.

15. This quote is from John Wiesenborn's typed-up notes accompanying his published article, "Planning and Using Resurrection City," as made available by the Civil Rights Movement Archive at https://www.crmvet.org/docs/68_rescity_plan.pdf.

16. See Hamilton, *Dr. Martin Luther King Jr. and the Poor People's Campaign of 1968*, 174.

17. Ibid., 7.

18. Jill Freedman, *Resurrection City, 1968* (Bologna: Damiana, 2017).

19. Wiesenborn, "Planning and Using Resurrection City," 405.

20. I diverge here from Michael Clune's reading of this poem in which he insists that "a close description of environment replaces racial marking" (160). I would argue this is less a replacement than a strategic withholding given race's dominating role in structuring residential observation and valuation at midcentury. I further diverge from Clune in his claim that "what they see when they drive through the wealthy district is just what Americans always see when they drive through such areas," which

is "the difference between rich and not-rich" (161). Mass homeownership was already drastically changing this binary in this period, allowing the white not-rich new access to the Beverlys of the world at subsidized mortgage rates while locking most blacks across class backgrounds into very different residential and, by extension, economic circumstances. Clune's reading does not account for the ways in which racial vision overdetermined the work of residential observation and distribution relative class or homeownership's key role in changing the metrics of racial vision itself—the subject of this book. See Michael Clune, *A Defense of Judgment* (Chicago: University of Chicago Press, 2021).

Index

Note: Page numbers in *italic* type indicate illustrations.

Abernathy, Ralph, 308–9
abolitionism, 10
Abrams, Charles, 331n14
affect. *See* psychology/feelings
African Americans. *See* blackness/African Americans
Agassiz, Louis, 65
Agee, James, 92
Ahmed, Sara, 228
air shafts, 117–18
Albert, Allen D., 62–63
Algren, Nelson, 200, 245; *Chicago: City on the Make*, 199
American Dream, 1, 2, 6, 46, 256–57
American Eugenics Society, 145
American Institute of Real Estate Appraisers, 29, 184
American Lumberman (magazine), 66
Andersson, Lars, 356n45
Anglo-Saxon identity, 23, 50, 57, 60–63, 80, 82. *See also* whiteness
anti-Semitism, 63
apartments and tenements: African Americans' experiences in, 89; air shafts for, 117–18; physical and mental health dangers associated with, 16, 23, 89; popularity of, in early twentieth century, 58–59

appearance: assessment of neighborhoods and home values based on, 18–19, 90, 174–75, 178–80, 182–83, 188–90, 194–95, 276; as criterion of virtue and value of citizens, 90; race determined by, 18–19, 28, 39, 148, 174–75, 182–83, 189–90, 194–95, 223–24; urban reportage and, 199–204. *See also* observation
appraisal: appearances as basis for, 18–19, 90, 174–75, 178–80, 182–83, 188–90, 194–95; FHA and, 185–87; lending decisions based on, 187, 189; manuals for, 190–95; mechanisms of, 4, 182–83, 185; nationwide mapping studies undertaken for, 187–88; objective and scientific status imputed to, 40, 183–85, 189–94; professionalization of, 40, 184, 190; race linked to, 4, 40, 178, 184–95, 204–5, 349n10; role of personal and local mores and judgments in, 186–89, 191–93, 351n30. *See also* home/land values
Architecture Record (magazine), 58
Ashby, Hal, 41, 276, 293, 295, 301
Asian Americans, housing discrimination experienced by, 32

375

Asian immigrants: living conditions of, 142–43, 145; and property, 11, 140, 143; racial mixing restrictions advocated for, 145. *See also* Chinese immigrants; Japanese immigrants; migrants, foreign
Athanasiou, Athena, 7
Atkinson, Harry, *Fundamentals of Real Estate*, 192
Aubry, Timothy, 229, 237, 358n45, 359n65
Avila, Eric, 17, 27, 320n79, 353n59

Babcock, Frederick, 182–83, 185–86, 188, 190–91, 193; *The Appraisal of Real Estate*, 185, 190
Bachner, Sally, 206
Bailey, Blake, 233, 356n16
Bailey, Pearl, 287
Baker, Houston, 247, 258–59
Baldwin, James, 6, 177–79, 182–84, 206–7, 213, 216, 219–22, 228–30, 237, 239, 260, 269, 287, 355n13; "Fifth Avenue, Uptown: A Letter from Harlem," 199, 207–9, 216; "The Image of the Negro," 204; "A Negro Assays the Negro Mood," 207
Bambara, Toni Cade, 286
banks, 263–65, 282
Banner, Stuart, 324n24
Baraka, Amiri (formerly known as LeRoi Jones), 245, 247–48, 258–59, 287
Beatty, Paul, *The Sellout*, 286
Bentley, Gladys, 99
Best, Stephen, 336n99
Better Homes in America, 54, 328n84
Betty Boop cartoons, 126, 338n10
Beuka, Robert, 356n21
Bevel, James, 265
Bhandar, Brenna, 6–7, 8, 50–51, 61, 316n7, 323n7
"Bill Bailey, Won't You Please Come Home" (song), 101

Biondi, Martha, 368n40
blackface, 235, 236, 238
black nationalism, 256
blackness/African Americans: appearance and perception of, 18–19, 73, 148, 174–75, 178–80, 182–83; broken promises to, 11, 39, 125, 161, 163, 167, 243; in Cheever's stories, 235–36, 238; Depression's effect on, 39, 128, 161–63; Dust Bowl migrants compared to, 146–48, 150; exclusion of, as means of establishing whiteness, 1, 3–4, 16, 19, 27–28, 72–74, 77–78, 120, 156, 205, 227–28, 231; and homeownership, 4, 72, 86–87, 90–91, 161–66, 173, 175, 261–62, 305–6, 356n17, 363n121; housing needs of, 73, 77, 87–91, 94, 101, 328n89; middle-class, 248–49, 260, 298, 362n106; mortgage experiences of, 31, 263–65; one-drop rule of, 18, 175, 189, 224; and ownership, 218; and property, 6, 10–12, 14, 33, 162–69, 218–19, 239–62; real estate industry's attitude toward, 70–74; rental experiences of, 31, 77, 87, 94, 100, 162; in the suburbs, 363n121; as threat to home/land values, 4, 26–33, 46–48, 73, 77, 88, 90–91, 164–65, 173–74, 186, 193–94, 205, 266, 298, 305–6, 312. *See also* black women; Emancipation; housing discrimination; illiquidity; Jim Crow; race; rent parties; segregation
Black Popular Front, 218
Black Power, 272–73, 307, 367n25
Blackstone, William, 8
black women: documentary evidence of, 99; and feminism, 335n65; and homeownership, 37, 38; rent parties hosted or attended by, 37, 38, 87, 99–117, 121–22; rent strikes led by, 94; social and economic conditions for, 99–100

blockbusting, 3, 6, 19, 174, 181, 194, 199, 253, 263
blues music, 98–99
body, theory of property concerning, 7, 10
Bontemps, Arna, 335n70
Boston's North End, 196–98
Boyette, Raymond "Lippy," 118
Brand, Millen, *Albert Sears*, 177
Brevoort Savings Banks, 263
Brodkin, Karen, 17
Brooks, Gwendolyn, 6, 30, 37, 40, 175, 183, 195, 199, 206, 207, 209, 269; *Annie Allen*, 200; "Beverly Hills, Chicago," 41, 311–13, 370n20; "In the Mecca," 353n62; "They Call it Bronzeville," 184, 200–204
Brooks, Richard, 321n88
Broom, Sarah, 306
Brown, Adrienne, *The Black Skyscraper*, 22, 24, 32, 34
Brown, Frank London, 200, 269; *Trumbull Park*, 177
Brown, Lloyd, 269
bureaucratic racism, 211, 265, 271, 282–84, 286, 367n25. *See also* institutional racism
Bureau of Indian Affairs, 133
Burroughs, Nannie, 37, 89, 100

California Alien Land Law, 140
capitalism, 91, 150, 243. *See also* racial capitalism
Carmichael, Stokely, 272–76, 288, 289, 300, 367n21, 367n25
Carter, Benny, 331n15
Carter, Stephen, 362n102
CCHR. *See* New York City Commission on Human Rights
CCRM. *See* Committee on Civil Rights in Metropolitan New York
Central Railroad of New Jersey, 15

Chase, Stuart, 124
Cheever, John, 19, 40, 158, 175, 215–16, 218–39, 355n13, 357n27, 359n51; "The Country Husband," 225; "The Five-Forty Eight," 234–38; *The Housebreaker of Shady Hill*, 18, 40, 218–19, 221–39; "The Housebreaker of Shady Hill," 230–32; "The Sorrows of Gin," 223–24; "The Trouble with Marcie Flint," 230, 238; "The Worm in the Apple," 232–34
Cheng, Wendy, 32
Chesnutt, Charles, 318n37
Chicago, 200–201, 265–73, 277–78
Chicago Freedom movement, 268
Chicago Real Estate Board, 268
Childress, Alice, 286
Chinese immigrants, 137, 142–43. *See also* Asian immigrants
cities: migrations to, 58; senses/sensorium and, 20, 22
Civil Rights Act (1964), 265, 289, 292
civil rights movement, 5–6. *See also* Northern campaign
Clari (opera), 49
Clover, Joshua, 95, 96, 333n29
Clune, Michael, 372n20
Cohen, Milton, 160, 338n16, 345n114
Colbert, Soyica Diggs, 243, 256–57, 361n89
collective/communal living: in black experience after Emancipation, 168–69; Dust Bowl migrants and, 129, 142, 148, 151–55; race and, 133–34, 160; suburbs and, 156, 160
Collier, John, 133
Collins, Kathleen, 286
colonialism, 9, 50–51, 60–61
color-blind rhetoric, 358n37
Committee on Civil Rights in Metropolitan New York (CCRM), 277–84; brochure produced by, *280–81*

Committee on Negro Housing, 37
Commonweal (magazine), 109
Communist Party, 241, 254
Congress of Racial Equality (CORE), 276, 282, 365n7
Connolly, N. D. B., 298, 349n9
CORE. *See* Congress of Racial Equality
covenants: legality of, 16, 77; as pre-zoning measure, 16; racial/restrictive, 16, 57, 73, 76–77, 89, 159–60
Crawford, Richard, 49–50
Cruse, Harold, 245
Cultural Front, 240, 260
Cunningham, Charlie, 129

Daley, Richard J., 268, 272
dancing, 86, 87, 92, 99, 102–3, 107, 108, 113–16
Davis, Christopher, *First Family*, 177
Dawes Act (1887), 10
Denning, Michael, 129, 134
Depression. *See* Great Depression
desire. *See* sexuality and desire
developers. *See* real estate developers
Dime Savings Bank of Brooklyn, 263–64
discrimination. *See* housing discrimination
dispossession: in 1930s, 19, 33, 36, 123, 125, 128, 134–35, 345n143; concept of, 336n60; fictional accounts of, 125–27; Hunter's novel about the "machinery" of, 286–93, 296; literature of, 41, 311; Mitchell's *Gone with the Wind* and, 125; of Native American land, 1, 9–10, 50, 150, 315n5, 324n24; New Deal as source of, 346n143; race as factor in, 134–35; rent parties and, 37, 86, 87, 93, 95; in Steinbeck's *Grapes of Wrath* and *Tortilla Flat*, 128, 132–33, 150; structural conditions of, 135–36, 142; whites' feelings of spiritual,

25, 74–75, 324n20, 329n92, 329n106; whites not immune to, 128, 135–36, 150–51; whites' shame and guilt over, 135–36
Douglass, Frederick, 10
Du Bois, W. E. B., 10, 12, 30, 39, 78, 87, 128, 161–67, 169, 174, 290, 318n37; *Black Reconstruction in America*, 163–67, 303, 347n147, 347n153
Dunbar, Paul Laurence, 269
Dust Bowl migrants, 136–61: blackness in relation to, 146–48, 150; Californians' attitudes toward, 159; and collective/communal living, 129, 142, 148, 151–55; dignity of, 141–42, 155; foreign migrants contrasted with, 137–43; government aid to, 142; and homeownership, 130, 154–61; as land men, 138–61; ownership linked to, 19, 39, 128, 130, 139–44; reincorporation of, into whiteness, 19, 39, 127, 139, 143, 145–46, 148, 152, 156–60; sensorium of, 158–59; whiteness of, 19, 127–30, 136–61, 341n48
Dyer, Richard, 228

Eastern European immigrants, 3, 17–18, 88, 171
economy. *See* markets
Edison, Thomas A., 20, 22
Eisinger, Chester E., 340n47
Ellington, Duke, 38, 117–22, 121; "Harlem Air Shaft," 118, 337n100
Ellison, Ralph, 30, 183, 255, 269; "Harlem Is Nowhere," 199; *Invisible Man*, 94
Ely, Richard, 327n60
Emancipation: black living conditions after, 87; black ownership after, 10–11, 125, 218; Wright on the black experience of, 166–69
Enlightenment: and property, 3, 7–9, 12, 14, 60; racial theories of, 3, 8–9, 25;

real estate industry's use of theories of, 25
Equitable Savings and Loan Association, 263
Esquire (magazine), 207, 215, 220
Esteve, Mary, 364n141
eugenics: real estate industry and, 25, 64–65, 327n60; as sociocultural theme, 65, 145, 192; Steinbeck and, 129, 136–37, 146, 338n16; and white survival, 27, 64–65
Eugenics Research Association, 145
eviction resistance, 94–95, 332n28

Fair Housing Act (1968), 4, 35, 41, 177, 268–69, 274–78, 288–90, 293, 298–300, 305–7, 368n42
fair housing organizations, 276–86
Fair Housing Practices Law (Local Law 80), 368n41
Farm Security Administration, 166
Farnsworth, Robert, 200
Fauset, Jessie, 91
federal government: homeownership promoted by, 2, 45–46; housing discrimination practiced by, 3, 14, 39, 172–74; housing policy of, 54–55, 325n26; and racial theories of property and homeownership, 62, 186; real estate industry and, 54; segregation promoted by, 88–89, 164–65, 172–73, 181, 186, 271, 320n80
Federal Housing Administration (FHA), 17, 123, 164, 171–72, 181, 185–91, 202, 349n10
feeling. *See* psychology/feelings; senses/sensorium
feminism, black, 335n65
FHA. *See* Federal Housing Administration
fiction. *See* literature
Filipino immigrants, 129, 137, 142–43

Fitzgerald, F. Scott, *The Great Gatsby*, 18, 32, 38, 48, 74, 79, 81–84, 225–27, 357n30, 357n31
Fitzhugh, George, 10, 50
Fleetwood, Nicole, 183
Flournoy, Angela, 300, 306
Folsom, M. W., *A Home of Your Own and What It Means to You*, 79–82, 81, 84, 120
Ford, Richard, 300
foreclosures, 39, 46, 54, 123, 126
Forte, Maximillian C., 316n18
"forty acres and a mule," 11, 39, 128, 147, 149, 163, 167, 169, 244
Foster, Stephen, "My Old Kentucky Home," 52–53, 83
Frank, Glenn, 326n43
Frankenberg, Ruth, 228
Franzen, Jonathan, 300; *The Corrections*, 309
Frazier, E. Franklin, *The Black Bourgeoisie*, 248
Freedom Farm Cooperative, 307
Freitag, Florian, 344n102
Freund, David, 13, 17, 172, 174, 187, 318n45, 351n28, 358n37; *Colored Property*, 23, 190
Freund, Ernst, 15, 20
Fuller, Matthew, 273–75

Garb, Margaret, 58, 326n41
Gates, Theaster, 367n34
gentrification, 198
George, Joseph, 358n45
Gershwin, George, 85, 97
Getachew, Adom, 60
GI Bill, 70, 202
Gilman, Charlotte Perkins, 59
Giovanni, Nikki, 286
Glotzer, Paige, 13, 16, 30, 57, 79–84, 323n7, 325n34, 329n90, 355n8
Godfrey, Mollie, 243, 338n15

Index

Grant, Madison, 17
Great Depression: black experience during, 39, 128, 161–63; dispossessions brought on by, 2, 38–39, 46, 54, 123, 134–35; Dust Bowl migrants' experience after, 159–60; government response to, 144; housing market rebound after, 25–26, 59, 123, 127; literature and, 33, 36, 127, 166; Steinbeck's experience of, 131; Steinbeck's *Grapes of Wrath* and other writings on, 127, 130–31, 133–35, 146; whiteness strengthened as a concept during, 127, 129–30, 151
Great Migration, 26, 39, 88, 128, 162, 239
Greenberg, Cheryl Lynn, 162
Gunn, Bill, 41, 276, 293, 295
Guterl, Matthew, 24

Haacke, Hans, 367n34
Hamer, Fannie Lou, 307
Hamilton, Charles, 272–73, 275–76, 288, 289, 300, 367n21, 367n25
Hannan, W. W., 60
Hansberry, Carl, Jr., 250
Hansberry, Carl, Sr., 243, 246, 247
Hansberry, Lorraine, 6, 36, 37, 40–41, 175, 215–19, 239, 242–62, 269, 286; *A Raisin in the Sun*, 36, 40–41, 177, 215–19, 242–62, 286–88, 301; "Willie Loman, Walter Younger, and He Who Must Live," 254
Hansberry, Mamie, 250
Hansberry, Perry, 251, 362n110, 363n111
Hansberry Enterprises, 246, 249–51, 361n91
Harcourt, Alfred, 75
Harlem, New York, 91–119, 162, 207–8, 216, 282, 336n97
Harlem Mortgage and Improvement Council (HMIC), 276–77, 282–84; flier produced by, 283

Harlem Renaissance, 95, 100, 107
Harlem Tenants League, 94
Harper, William, 10
Harper's (magazine), 200
Harris, Cheryl, 24, 27–28, 66, 316n7, 317n19
Harris, Dianne, 17; *Little White Houses*, 13
Hartman, Saidiya, 37, 99–100, 106, 113, 332n22
Hazzard-Gordon, Katrina, 93–95
health, mental and physical: homeownership's positive effect on, 144; multifamily dwellings' negative effect on, 16, 23, 89
Hearle, Kevin, 338n16, 341n52
Hecht, Ben, 335n72
Hillier, Amy, 351n28
Himes, Chester, 269, 287
Hirt, Sonia, 319n56
HMIC. *See* Harlem Mortgage and Improvement Council
Hobbes, Thomas, 7
HOLC. *See* Home Owners' Loan Corporation
Holiday (magazine), 200, 203
"Home, Sweet Home" (song), 49–53, 63, 323n9
Home and Housing Journal, 284, 285
home/land values: blackness as threat to, 4, 26–33, 46–48, 73, 77, 88, 90–91, 164–65, 173–74, 186, 193–94, 205, 266, 298, 305–6, 312; future vs. present, 191; in Great Depression, 123; housing discrimination linked to, 13–14; importance of, 26–27; Mexican Americans as threat to, 164, 186; race linked to, 17–18, 27, 30–31, 46–48, 72, 180, 185–86, 192–93, 202, 276, 305; senses/sensorium as determining, 5, 72; suburban, 156; zoning linked to, 17. *See also* appraisal; illiquidity;

land men; property/property rights; value
homeownership: as American value, 1, 2, 6, 45–46; blackness and, 4, 72, 86–87, 90–91, 161–66, 173, 175, 261–62, 305–6, 356n17, 363n121; black women and, 37, 38; Cheever and, 215–16, 218–19, 221–39; criticisms of, 58–59, 123–24, 161, 163–69; decline of, in late nineteenth and early twentieth centuries, 17, 57–59, 123; Dust Bowl migrants and, 130, 154–61; federal government's promotion of, 2, 45–46; in fiction, 33–37; financing of, 2, 25–26, 58–59, 67–68, 70; Fitzgerald's *Great Gatsby* and, 81–84; growth of, 2–3, 127, 171, 221; Hansberry and, 215–16, 218–19; history of, 2–3; literature and, 74–84, 300–301; middle-class, 55, 57, 59, 67, 301–2; moral arguments for, 16–17, 46, 58, 68, 70, 72–73, 90, 96–97; patriotic motivations for promoting, 2, 45, 48, 66–74, 96, 144–45, 149, 327n66; physical and mental health benefits of, 144–45; as privileged form of ownership, 1; psychology of, 45–47, 63, 90, 124, 127, 131–32; race linked to, 1–4, 6, 13, 37–38, 40–41, 49–54, 62–63, 70–84; racialization of, 1–2, 13, 46–47, 51, 97; real estate industry's promotion of, 2, 16–17, 25, 38, 47–48, 55, 59–61, 67–74, 79–80; social reform and, 16, 70, 89–90; songs associated with, 45, 49–54, 62–63, 83; Steinbeck and, 130–31, 158; subjectivity linked to, 13; suburbanization linked to, 216–17; use value of, 58; whiteness linked to, 1–4, 17–19, 28–29, 47–49, 62–63, 80–84, 99, 130, 171, 175, 221, 225, 301, 305; women and, 103–4; zoning linked to, 16. *See also* home/

land values; mortgages; property/property rights; residential, the
Home Owners' Loan Corporation (HOLC), 123, 126, 187, 350n15, 351n28
Homestead Act (1862), 58
homogeneity: of neighborhoods/suburbs, 29, 127, 156, 198, 202, 210, 213, 217, 223, 229; of whiteness, 19
Hoover, Allan, 85, 330n1
Hoover, Herbert, 45–55, 62–63, 75, 83, 85–86, 89, 96, 120, 144–45, 324n18, 336n103; *Principles of Mining*, 51
Horne, Helen, 285
Hornstein, Jeffrey M., 55, 57, 325n26, 325n30
housing discrimination: attributed to impersonal and market forces, 13–14, 39, 172–74, 178, 182–83, 185, 190, 198, 266, 271, 274–76, 291–92; banks' role in, 263–65, 282; fair housing organizations' efforts against, 276–86; federal government's role in, 3, 13, 39, 172–74; King's Northern campaign and, 265–73, 277–78, 366n20; legal options against, 274–78, 282, 289, 300, 368n37, 368n41; literature on, 286; methods of exposing, 277–79; patriotic discourse linked to, 67–74; real estate industry's role in, 3, 13–14, 57, 67, 70–74, 77, 88–89, 291, 296–99; senses/sensorium linked to, 5; theories and justifications of, 31–32; value linked to, 13–14; Wright's experience with, 36, 240–42. *See also* institutional racism; segregation
housing market. *See* markets
Howe, Irving, 238
Howells, William Dean, 16, 20, 31
Hoyt, Homer, 19, 186–88, 191; *One Hundred Years of Land Values in Chicago*, 17, 164–65, 186
Huber, Matthew, 367n20

HUD. *See* US Department of Housing and Urban Development
Hughes, Langston, 91–93, 99, 244, 269, 335n70; *The Big Sea*, 91–92; "Rent Party Shout for a Lady Dancer," 92–93, 332n20
Hume, David, 7
Hunt, Thomas Forsyth, 64
Hunter, Kristin, 37, 175, 286, 294; *God Bless the Child*, 286; *The Landlord*, 41, 276, 286–96, 298–303
Hutchisson, James, 76

Illinois Institute of Technology, 200
illiquidity, blackness associated with, 31–33, 71, 76–77, 91, 173, 193–94, 205, 240, 265, 305, 321n94
Indian Reorganization Act (IRA), 133
indigeneity, 8–9. *See also* Native Americans
Industrial Workers of the World (IWW), 69–70
"inharmonious" groups, 17, 173, 188–90, 194, 199, 202, 227
institutional racism, 263–303; concept of, 272, 276, 367n21; fair housing organizations' efforts against, 276–86; and housing, 263–72; housing as example of, 289; obstacles to legal or critical challenges to, 274–76; representing the hidden nature of, 41, 263–303; urban reportage and, 199–204, 207–8. *See also* bureaucratic racism
integration: conceptualized as "invasion," 16, 174, 180, 188, 192–94, 227, 263; neighborhood turnover after, 194, 253, 267; as theme in literature and art, 177–82. *See also* blockbusting
Inter-State Tattler (newspaper), 108
In the Heat of the Night (film), 292
invasion, of residential space, 16, 174, 188, 192, 227, 263

investigative aesthetics, 273–75, 279, 282, 286, 289, 293
Irish immigrants, 3, 16, 17
Irving, Washington, 23
Italian immigrants, 3, 17–18, 88, 171, 196–97

Jackson, Kenneth, 17, 171, 187
Jacobs, Jane, 37, 40, 175, 195, 201, 203–4, 207, 213, 353n59; *The Death and Life of Great American Cities*, 184, 195–99, 201, 206
Jacobson, Matthew Frye, 17, 356n18
James, Henry, 33–34, 322n96
James, William, 12, 34
Japanese immigrants, 140, 142, 160, 342n71. *See also* Asian immigrants
jazz: Ellington and, 117–22; Hoover sons' affinity for, 85, 121; literature in relation to, 331n15; at rent parties, 85–86, 97–99, 334n46
Jeffersonian agrarianism, 2, 58, 148–49, 150, 152–53
Jenkins, Destin, 320n80
Jewison, Norman, 292, 295, 298, 299
Jews, 17–18, 171. *See also* anti-Semitism
Jim Crow regime, 76, 88, 162, 173, 189, 240, 241, 271, 272, 303, 357n31
Johnson, Guy B., 162
Johnson, James P., 97, 118–19
Johnson, James Weldon, 269
Johnson, Mat, 300
Jones, LeRoi. *See* Baraka, Amiri
Jurca, Catherine, 25, 74, 217, 229, 231, 309, 322n105, 324n20, 329n92, 329n106

Kealing, H. T., 11
Kennedy, Florynce, 296–97, 297
Kennedy, Robert F., 309
Keyssar, Helene, 248
Killens, John Oliver, *The Cotillion*, 286

King, Coretta Scott, 266, 271, 366n13
King, Martin Luther, Jr., 6, 41, 228, 265–74, *270*, 277–78, 292, 307–9, 366n20
Koopman, Colin, 185
Kornbluh, Anna, 34, 322n96
Kruse, Kevin, 217
Kwak, Nancy, 355n8

land. *See* home/land values; homeownership; property/property rights
Landlord, The (film), 41, 276, 287, 292–303, *297*
land men: African Americans as, 164–65, 167; concept of, 39, 127, 138, 148–49, 164, 341n48; Dust Bowl migrants as, 138–61; precarity of, 151; racialization of, as white, 39, 127–28, 138–61, 345n121; subjectivity of, 151, 165–66. *See also* property/property rights
Lands, LeeAnn, 68
land-use regulations, 15. *See also* zoning
land values. *See* home/land values
Lange, Dorothea, 161
Latina/o Americans, housing discrimination experienced by, 32. *See also* Mexican Americans
Lawrence, A. H., 337n103
Lawson, Ronald, 332n27, 332n28
Lee, Change-Rae, 300
Levitt, William, 327n66
Lewinnek, Elaine, 30
Lewis, David Levering, 91
Lewis, Sinclair: *Babbitt*, 32, 38, 48, 74–79, 309, 329n92; *Kingsblood Royal*, 78, 177
Lewis, Theophilus, 108, 332n20
liberalism: ethos of, 180; and property, 7, 13–14; silence on race as feature of, 13–14, 172–73
Life (magazine), 179, 230
Light, Jennifer, 187, 351n29
Lipsitz, George, 17, 224, 228, 275, 316n7

literature: of dispossession, 41, 311; and the Great Depression, 33, 36, 127, 166; homeownership as theme in, 74–84, 300–301; housing discrimination as theme in, 286; integration as theme in, 177–82; jazz in relation to, 331n15; and ownership, 33–37; racial feeling as theme in, 30, 36; and the representation of institutional racism, 286–303; residential, 36–37, 309–10; and social construction of race, 48–49; suburban, 217–19, 225, 229, 233, 239, 356n16. *See also* protest fiction; urban reportage
"Little Grey Home in the West" (song), 52–53
living standards. *See* standards of living
loans. *See* mortgages
Locke, John, 7, 9, 10, 60
Lockridge, Richard, 115–16
Look (magazine), 179–80
Looker, Benjamin, 321n89
Lorde, Audre, 286
Louisiana Real Estate Association, 73
Luck, Chad, 34
Lye, Colleen, 130, 136, 140, 148, 342n58, 342n59
Lynn, Shane, 338n16

MacArthur, Charles, 335n72
MacChesney, Nathan William, 57
Machlin, Paul, 98
Madden, David, 330n4
Madison, James, 9–10
Mad Men (television series), 158
Mailer, Norman, 219
Manchester, William, *The City of Anger*, 177
Marcuse, Peter, 330n4
markets: institutional racism of, 263–65, 276; psychological explanations supplanted by those grounded

markets (continued)
in, 13–14, 39, 172–74, 178, 182–83, 185, 205, 266, 276, 291–92; racialized basis of, 13, 306–7. See also home/land values
Marsh, Fred T., 339n30
Marshall, Margaret, 128
Marshall, Paule, *Brown Girl, Brownstones*, 260
Martin, John Barlow, "The Strangest Place in Chicago," 200–201, 353n62
Martin, Reinhold, 6
Marxism, 168
masculinity, 57, 80, 82, 99, 103, 258–59, 325n34
McClure, S. S., 65
McGrath, Charles, 356n16
McGuire, Eva, 365n7
McKay, Claude, 269
McKissick, Floyd, 307
McLean, Leroy M., 263–66, 269, 271–76, 365n6, 365n7, 367n34
McMichael, Stanley L., *Appraising Manual*, 191
Mecca Flats, Chicago, 200
Mekas, Jonas, 245
Mencken, H. L., 75
Mexican Americans: deportation of, 133; as farmworkers, 129, 137, 142–43, 145, 146; Steinbeck's *Tortilla Flat* and, 132–34; as threat to home/land values, 164, 186; and whiteness, 18. See also migrants, foreign
Michaels, Walter Benn, 357n30
middle class: black, 248–49, 260, 298, 362n106; homeownership for, 55, 57, 59, 67, 301–2; Lewis's *Babbitt* and, 74–75; songs suitable for, 52; Steinbeck's *Grapes of Wrath* and, 157; white, 301
Mies van der Rohe, Ludwig, 200

migrants, foreign, 137–43, 146. See also Asian immigrants; Dust Bowl migrants; Mexican Americans
Miller, Arthur, *Death of a Salesman*, 254
Miller, James, 76
minstrel songs, 52–53
Miss Home and Housing, 284, 285
Mitchell, Koritha, 37
Mitchell, Margaret, *Gone with the Wind*, 33, 125
modernism, 74, 271, 370n71
Mondale, Walter, 274, 366n18
Moore, Natalie, 306
Moore, Richard B., 94, 332n25
morality: and debt, 26, 59; and homeownership, 16–17, 46, 58, 68, 70, 72–73, 90, 96–97; and multifamily housing, 16; and property, 7–8; real estate industry's principles of, 57, 58; testing's appeal to, 279, 282
Moreton-Robinson, Aileen, 10
Morrison, Toni, 286, 306; *Playing in the Dark*, 239
mortgages: African Americans' and other non-whites' experiences with, 31, 88, 351n24; appraisal decisions affecting, 187, 189; discrimination in awarding of, 263–65; history of, 2–3, 25–26, 59, 70; insurance provided for, 171; post–World War II, 202; racial covenants linked to, 159–60; terms of, 26, 59
Moten, Fred, 95–96, 106, 119
Moynihan Report (1965), 168, 348n158
multifamily dwellings. See apartments and tenements
music. See jazz; songs
Myers, Ella, 12
"My Old Kentucky Home" (Foster), 52–53, 83

NAACP. *See* National Association for the Advancement of Colored People
Naison, Mark, 94, 332n27, 332n28
NAREB. *See* National Association of Real Estate Boards; National Association of Real Estate Brokers
Nash, Gerald D., 346n133
Nash, Jennifer, 107, 335n65
Nation (magazine), 75
National Association for the Advancement of Colored People (NAACP), 71, 349n10
National Association of Real Estate Boards (NAREB), 38, 48, 54–80, 99, 119, 171, 186–87, 325n30, 325n34. *See also* real estate industry
National Association of Real Estate Brokers (NAREB), 325n27
National Association of Realtors (NAR), 55
National Park Service, 308
National Real Estate Journal (NREJ), 25, 38, 48, 54–55, 56, 59–76, 83, 90, 103, 105, 113, 173, 328n89
National Urban League, 101
Native Americans: dispossession of, 9–10, 50, 150, 315n5, 324n24; Du Bois and, 347n147; and property, 1, 9–10, 50, 324n24; romanticization of, 133; and sovereignty, 133; Steinbeck's work and, 133, 344n98, 345n121
Naylor, Gloria, 300
Negro Digest (magazine), 287
Negro Housing Committee, 89–91, 120, 331n13
neighborhood improvement associations, 88
neighborhoods: assessment of, based on appearance, 18–19, 27, 90, 174–75, 178–80, 182–83, 188–90, 194–95, 276; in Cheever's stories, 40, 222; concept of, 29; homogeneity of, 29, 156, 198, 202, 210, 213, 217, 223, 229; mixed-race, 26, 31, 88; racial conception of, 28–30; as site of subjectivity, 222; social status linked to, 331n14; turnover in, after integration, 194, 253, 267; whiteness as amenity in, 28–29. *See also* appraisal; home/land values; residential, the; suburbs
Nemiroff, Robert, 248
neoliberalism, 366n20
New Afrikan Independence Movement, 307
New Deal, 13, 25, 39, 46, 54, 70, 123, 127, 159, 162, 171, 346n143
New Republic (magazine), 124
New York Age (newspaper), 104
New York Amsterdam News (newspaper), 92–93, 100–101, 264
New York City Commission on Human Rights (CCHR), 263–65
New Yorker (magazine), 25, 117, 222, 233, 234
New York Times (newspaper), 219–20, 287
New York Times Magazine, 205, 207
Nichols, Robert, 335n60
Nicolaides, Becky, 159, 346n130
Nightingale, Carl, 187
No Down Payment (film), 177
North: attitudes toward African Americans in, 26, 88; black housing opportunities in, 26, 31, 73, 87–89; black migrations to, 26, 39, 88, 162; migrations to, 108, 110–11; rent parties in, 25, 38, 87
Northern campaign, 265–73, 277–78, 366n20
nostalgia, homeownership associated with, 53, 59
NREJ. See National Real Estate Journal
Nugent, Bruce, *Gentleman Jigger*, 97–98

observation: Baldwin's urban reportage and, 207–8; Brooks's urban reportage and, 200–204; Jacobs's urbanism grounded in, 195–99; Pynchon and, 205–6, 208–14. *See also* appearance; appraisal
O'Connor, Flannery, 235
Okies. *See* Dust Bowl migrants
Omi, Michael, 6
one-drop rule, 18, 175, 189, 224
Orser, W. Edward, 349n8
Owens, Louis, 133, 340n33
ownership: blackness and, 218; critiques of, 167–69, 302–3 (*see also* rent parties as critique of); Dust Bowl migrants and, 19, 39, 128, 130, 139–44; homeownership as privileged form of, 1; innate vs. learned dispositions toward, 7, 10, 46–47, 54, 57, 61, 63–64, 66, 80–81, 137–38; literature and, 33–37; psychology of, 1, 3; rent parties as critique of, 6, 25, 86–87, 96–97, 100, 102–3, 117, 120; Steinbeck's "land man" and, 39; Thurman's *Harlem* as critique of, 109, 113, 117; whiteness linked to, 1, 3, 12, 39, 50, 54, 60, 130, 134. *See also* land men; property/property rights

Packard, Vance, 362n106
Painter, Nell, 17
Paris Review (journal), 220
Parks, Gordon, 269
Partnership Apartment Seekers' Experiment (PASE), 278–79, 282; brochure on practices of, *280–81*
passing, racial, 18–19, 83, 224, 226–27, 233, 235, 238. *See also* whiteness: performance of
perception. *See* senses/sensorium
Perry, Imani, 243, 361n89
Pershing Hotel, Chicago, 250

Petry, Ann, 269
Pettit, Arthur, 134, 340n39
Poor People's Campaign, 41, 307–8
Post, Langdon, 124
Preemption Act (1841), 58
President's Conference on Home Building and Home Ownership (1931), 37, 45–46, 54, 89, 144
primitivism, 74, 115, 134
Pritchett, Wendell, 277, 368n37, 368n42
property/property rights: blackness and, 6, 10–12, 14, 33, 88, 162–69, 218–19, 239–62; the body and, 7, 10; civil rights movement and, 5–6; colonialism and, 9, 50–51; Enlightenment thought about, 3, 7–9, 12, 14, 60; fictional accounts of, 125–27, 338n10; Great Depression and, 38–39; Hansberry's *A Raisin in the Sun* and, 242–62; indigeneity linked to, 8–9; Mitchell's *Gone with the Wind* and, 125–26; moral arguments for, 7–8; Native Americans and, 1, 9–10, 50, 324n24; political significance of, 7; psychology of, 7–12, 61, 131–32, 135, 138, 164, 167, 240–62, 341n48; race linked to, 6–15, 32, 69, 124–29, 147, 151, 192, 245; slavery and, 1, 10, 50–51, 60; Steinbeck and, 130–36; subjectivity and, 7–15, 151–52; suffrage in relation to, 316n13; theories and definitions of, 7–10, 27; whiteness linked to, 10, 27–28, 36, 38, 60–62, 66, 71, 125–29, 135–37; women's right to, 323n11; writers and, 36. *See also* appraisal; home/land values; homeownership; land men; ownership
protest fiction, 177–80, 204, 207, 213, 286
psychology/feelings: discrimination and, 13; dispossession and, 135–36; homeownership and, 45–47, 63, 90, 124, 127, 131–32; in literature, 30, 36;

neutral, impersonal, market-based explanations substituted for those based on, 13–14, 39, 172–74, 178, 182–83, 185, 190, 198, 205, 266, 275, 291–92; ownership and, 1, 3; property and, 7–12, 61, 131–32, 135, 138, 164, 167, 240–62, 341n48; racial grievances as source of, 290; racialization of, 9–15, 30, 36, 39, 324n18; segregation and, 239–40. *See also* senses/sensorium; subjectivity

public housing, 54–55, 67, 300

Pynchon, Thomas, 6, 30, 40, 183, 205–6, 354n74, 354n81; *The Crying of Lot 49*, 205–6; "A Journey into the Mind of Watts," 184, 199, 205–6, 208–9, 212–13, 354n80, 354n81; "The Secret Integration," 184, 210–14, 354n84, 354n85; *V*, 206

queerness, 95, 98–100, 104, 258–59, 333n38

Raby, Albert, 265

race: appearance as criterion for determining, 18–19, 28, 39, 73, 148, 174–75, 182–83, 189–90, 194–95, 223–24; appraisal and, 4, 40, 178, 184–95, 204–5, 349n10; categories and features of, 3–4; in Cheever's stories, 223–39; and collective/communal living, 133–34; dispossession linked to, 134–35; home/land values linked to, 17–18, 27, 30–31, 46–48, 180, 185–86, 192–93, 202, 276, 305; homeownership linked to, 1–4, 6, 13, 37–38, 40–41, 49–54, 62–63, 70–84; Hoover and, 51; indigeneity compared to, 8–9; "inharmonious" groups based on, 17, 173, 188–90, 194, 199, 202, 227; Jacobs' *The Death and Life of Great American Cities* and, 197–98; Lewis's *Babbitt* and, 78–79; as neighborhoods' most significant feature, 28–30; neutral, impersonal, market-based explanations substituted for those based on, 13–14, 39, 172–75, 185, 198, 205, 266, 271, 274–76, 291–92, 358n37; nuisance measures targeting, 17; one-drop rule of, 18, 175, 189, 224; property linked to, 6–15, 69, 124–29, 147, 151, 192, 245; real estate industry and, 29, 35, 38, 47–48, 57, 60–74, 77, 79–80; rent parties and, 98, 101; the residential linked to, 2, 4–5, 22–23, 30; senses/sensorium linked to, 1–2, 4, 18, 23–24, 39–40, 72–74, 174–75; social construction and malleability of, 4–5, 32, 276; Steinbeck and, 129, 136–61, 338n16. *See also* blackness/African Americans; bureaucratic racism; housing discrimination; institutional racism; Jim Crow; passing, racial; racialization; racism; segregation; whiteness

racial capitalism, 77, 136

racialization: of feelings, 9–15, 30, 36, 39, 324n18; of homeownership, 1–2, 13, 46–47, 51, 97; of markets, 13, 306–7; property as tool of, 9, 12, 32, 126, 147, 151; the residential as form of, 24; of standards of living, 140, 142–46, 151–52, 164–65; of the West, 146

racism: African Americans' housing needs afflicted by, 89; literary representations of, 204; overt vs. covert, 272; Pynchon's "The Secret Integration" and, 210–12; "scientific," 65. *See also* bureaucratic racism; institutional racism; Jim Crow; white supremacy

Rancière, Jacques, 273

Randall, Dudley, 287, 289

Rapp, William J., *Harlem* (with Wallace Thurman), 100, 108–9, 335n70, 335n72, 336n97

388 Index

Ray Miller Orchestra, 85
real estate. *See* home/land values; property/property rights; real estate industry
real estate developers, 174
real estate industry: code of ethics in, 57, 77, 88–89, 181; discrimination practiced by, 3, 13–14, 57, 67, 70–74, 77, 88–89, 291, 296–99; federal government and, 54; Hansberry's experience with, 243, 245–47, 249–51, 361n91; homeownership promoted by, 59–61; housing policy influenced by, 48, 54, 171, 325n26; Lewis's *Babbitt* and, 74–79; origins of, 55; professionalization of, 57, 75, 325n30; promotion of homeownership by, 2, 16–17, 25, 38, 47–48, 55, 59–61, 67–74, 79–80; and race, 29, 35, 38, 47–48, 57, 60–74, 77, 79–80; segregation efforts of, 88–89, 171–72, 181, 227, 271; self-conception of, 62, 66, 75, 77, 325n30; senses/sensorium as tool of, 72–74, 78–79; and whiteness/white supremacy, 57, 66, 77. *See also* markets; National Association of Real Estate Boards
real estate speculators, 194
Reconstruction, 11, 125, 161, 163, 166–69, 303
redlining, 3, 4, 6, 17, 46, 66, 185, 198, 218, 229, 242, 246, 262, 266, 306, 350n15
Reed, Christopher, 346n138
Reed, Ishmael: *Flight to Canada*, 286; *Mumbo Jumbo*, 286
Reid, Ira D., 87, 100–108, 117, 334n54, 335n65; "Mrs. Bailey Pays the Rent," 100–107, 120
Reilly, Terry, 354n85
rent parties: black women as hosts or attendees of, 37, 38, 87, 99–117, 121–22; cards associated with, 38, 87, 91–92, 99, 101; critique of ownership by, 6, 25, 86–97, 96–97, 100, 102–3, 117, 120; dancing at, 86, 87, 92, 99, 102–3, 107, 108, 113–16; and dispossession, 37, 86, 87, 93, 95; documentation of, 38, 91–93, 99, 122; Ellington and, 117–20; features of, 87, 91–92, 102–3; forms of resistance compared to, 94–96; history of, 87, 334n54; and housing needs/conditions, 6, 25, 38, 86–87, 96–97; Hughes and, 91–93; imitations of, 104, 105, 108; interpretations of, 93–95, 105–8, 119; interracial attendance at, 97–98, 101; jazz played at, 85–86, 97–99, 334n46; political character of, 93–97, 105; preparations for, 102; and queerness, 95, 98–100, 104, 333n38; reputation of, 91; senses/sensorium linked to, 86, 92–93, 95–96, 115, 333n38; social aspects of, 38, 99, 103, 104; and subjectivity, 96–97; violence at, 87, 92–93, 103–5
rent strikes, 94
"Report of Valuator" form, 188
reports. *See* appraisal; urban reportage
residential, the: Cheever and, 218–19; concept of, 15, 35; Hansberry and, 218–19; literature linked to, 36–37, 309–10; race linked to, 2, 4–5, 22–23, 30; representation of urban black experience of, 265–71; senses/sensorium linked to, 5, 15–25, 86, 173–75, 178, 199, 306; subjectivity associated with, 3, 19–20; as a way of life, 3, 15; whiteness linked to, 22–23, 174; zoning and, 15–17. *See also* homeownership; neighborhoods; suburbs
Resurrection City, National Mall, Washington, D.C., 41, 307–10
Reynolds, Malvina, "Little Boxes," 217
Rhodes, John David, 34–35
Ring, Alfred A., *The Valuation of Real Estate*, 193–94

riots, 95, 96, 265, 269, 292, 333n29
Robertson, Stephen, 95
Rockwell, Norman, 210; *New Kids in the Neighborhood*, 178–81, *179*
Roediger, David, 17, 224, 351n31
Romani, 137, 340n43
Roosevelt, Theodore, 50, 138, 228
Rose, Carol, 24–25, 72, 115, 321n88, 363n123
Ross, Fran, *Oreo*, 286
Roth, Philip, 220, 222, 355n13
Rothstein, Richard, *The Color of Law*, 320n80, 325n26
Rowan, Jamie Creed, 353n58
Rowland, Cameron, 367n34
Russian Revolution (1917), 2, 45, 48, 67–68, 96

San Francisco News (newspaper), 137
Sarris, Andrew, 287
Saturday Evening Post (magazine), 179, 210, 245
SCLC. *See* Southern Christian Leadership Conference
Scott, Daniel, 109
Sears & Roebuck, 267
Segal, Erich, 293
segregation: academic research's role in, 315n4; attributed to impersonal and market forces, 173–74, 178, 182–83, 185, 266, 271, 274–76; emotional experience of, 239–40; Fair Housing Act and, 35; federal government's role in, 88–89, 164–65, 172–73, 320n80; government role in, 27; history of, 329n90; legal challenges to, 16, 17, 29, 35; real estate industry's role in, 88–89, 171–72, 181, 227; self-, 26; urban reportage on, 200–204. *See also* housing discrimination
senses/sensorium: air shafts and, 117–18; and the city, 20, 22; Dust Bowl migrants and, 158–59; home/land values determined by, 5, 72; housing discrimination linked to, 5; ownership linked to, 1; racial, 1–2, 4, 18, 23–24, 39–40, 72–74, 174–75; real estate industry and, 72–74, 78–79, 181; rent parties and, 86, 92–93, 95–96, 115, 333n38; and the residential, 5, 15–25, 86, 173–75, 178, 199, 306; and suburbs, 20–22; and whiteness, 18–19. *See also* appearance; observation; psychology/feelings; subjectivity
sentiment. *See* psychology/feelings
sexuality and desire, 95, 98, 99, 108–17
sharecropping, 88, 138, 146–48, 150, 151, 154, 162, 167, 343n89, 346n143, 347n144
Shelley v. Kraemer (1948), 177, 301
Shields, Charles, 247, 361n91, 363n111
Sieving, Christopher, 293, 295
Simon J. Lubin Society, 137
Singh, Amritjit, 109
Singh, Nikhil, 347n145, 347n153
single-family homes, 16
Skinner, R. Dana, 109
Slater, Gene, 172
slavery, 1, 10, 50–51, 60
Smethurst, James, 226, 271
Smith, Adam, 7–8
Smith, Preston H., 353n66
Smith, Willie "The Lion," 97–98
socialism, 100–101
social reform, 16, 70, 89–90
songs, associated with homeownership, 45, 49–54, 62–63, 83
Soul City, North Carolina, 307
South: black property rights in, 88; racial mixing in, 78; real estate industry and, 71; rent parties' roots in, 87, 334n54
Southern Christian Leadership Conference (SCLC), 265, 268, 273, 307–9, 312

Soviet Union, 255
speculators. *See* real estate speculators
standards of living, 140, 142–46, 151–52, 164–65
Stein, Rose M., 124
Stein, Walter, 128
Steinbeck, John, 30, 39, 127–61, 165, 168, 192, 338n15, 338n16, 341n54, 342n57; *The Grapes of Wrath*, 33, 36, 39, 125, 127–31, 134, 136–61; "The Harvest Gypsies," 137–44; *Of Mice and Men*, 146, 147, 154; *Their Blood Is Strong*, 129, 136–37, 140, 146, 148, 157; *Tortilla Flat*, 132–36, 139, 146, 339n30, 340n32
Stickney, William H. *See* Thorley, Robert
Stoddard, Lothrop, 17–18
Stone, Albert, 12
Stovall, Tyler, 316n12
Stowe, Harriet Beecher, *Uncle Tom's Cabin*, 52–53
stride piano, 85, 97, 98, 335n46
subjectivity: homeownership linked to, 13; of land men, 151, 165–66; literature, 33–34; neighborhood as site of, 222; property and, 7–15, 151–52; race and, 3; rent parties and, 96–97; residential, 3, 19–20. *See also* psychology/feelings; senses/sensorium
Suburbanite, The (magazine), 15, 19–20, 21, 22–23
suburbs: African Americans in, 363n121; in California, 159; Cheever's work and, 219–39, 358n45; homeownership linked to, 216–17; home values in, 156; homogeneity of, 127; literature associated with, 217–19, 225, 229, 233, 239, 356n16; past history of residents of, 224–27; residents' unease with, 25, 237–39; scholarship on, 217–18; senses/sensorium linked to, 20–22; site selection for, 174; whiteness in relation to, 23, 217–18, 223–39. *See also* neighborhoods; residential, the
Sugrue, Thomas, 59, 217
Sullivan, James, 9
Summers, Martin, 95
Survey Graphic (magazine), 124
Survey of Race Relations (1925), 145
Szalay, Michael, 344n105

Taylor, Keeanga-Yamahtta, 4, 14, 31, 274, 289, 300, 305, 322n107, 350n14
Teckemeyer, Earl, *How to Value Real Estate*, 192–94
tenant farmers. *See* sharecropping
tenements. *See* apartments and tenements
Terkel, Studs, 135
testing, for discriminatory practices, 277–79, 280–81, 282, 368n46
Thorley, Robert, and William H. Stickney, *Real Estate Forms*, 190–91
Thurman, Wallace, 87, 91, 92, 107–17, 215, 332n20; "Cordelia the Crude," 108; *Harlem* (with William J. Rapp), 100, 108–17, 335n70, 335n72, 336n97
Thurston, Chloe, 349n10
True Romance (magazine), 230
Tucker-Abramson, Myka, 366n20, 369n65, 370n71
Twain, Mark, 210

University of California, Berkeley, 220
Updike, John, 219, 222
urban planning, 195–99
urban renewal, 287, 288, 294, 295, 296, 298, 302
urban reportage, 183–84; Baldwin and, 207–8; Brooks and, 199–204; Pynchon and, 205–6
US Department of Housing and Urban Development (HUD), 291, 303, 368n46
US Supreme Court, 16, 189, 245, 277, 278

Vale, Lawrence, 327n66
value. *See also* home/land values: racial, 83–84; of whiteness, 1–2, 4, 14, 26–33, 47, 66
Vice Lords, 267
Village Voice (newspaper), 245, 254
Vogel, Shane, 95–96, 99, 106, 107, 115
Voting Rights Act (1965), 265

Wald, Alan, 360n86
Wald, Sarah, 338n16, 341n48, 343n86
Waldeland, Lynne, 234
Waldman, Louis, 101, 104
Walker, A'Lelia, 215
Walker, Alice, 286
Wallace, Mike, 246–47, 255, 256, 257, 362n106
Waller, Maurice, 98
Waller, Thomas "Fats," 85, 87, 97–98, 334n46
Wang, Jackie, 321n94
Ward, Theodore, *Big White Fog*, 94, 254
Washington, Mary Helen, 360n80
Wasserman, Sarah, 205
Watts, Los Angeles, 205–6, 208–9, 212–13, 265
Weaver, Robert, 171
Weeksville, Brooklyn, 264, 365n3
Weise, Andrew, 363n121
Weizman, Eyal, 273–75
West, Dorothy, 269
West, Nathaniel, *A Cool Million*, 126
Wheeler, Keith, *Peaceable Lane*, 177
white diaspora, 324n20
white flight, 4, 27, 31, 181, 217–18, 237, 239, 320n79
Whiteman, Paul, 85
whiteness: as an amenity, 28–29, 266, 305; category/boundaries of, 3, 17, 28, 30–31, 88, 171, 189, 205, 226–29, 233; challenges to/fragility of, 33, 128–29, 135–36, 150–51, 156, 230; Cheever and, 221–39; concept of, 27–28; Du Bois's critique of, 12; of Dust Bowl migrants, 19, 127–30, 136–61, 341n48; exclusion as tool for establishing the meaning of, 1, 3–4, 16, 19, 27–28, 72–74, 77–78, 120, 156, 205, 227–28, 231; Fitzgerald's *Great Gatsby* and, 81–84; homeownership linked to, 1–4, 17–19, 28–29, 47–49, 62–63, 80–84, 99, 130, 171, 175, 221, 225, 301, 305; homogenization of, 19; invisibility/taken for grantedness of, 6, 78, 222, 228–29, 232, 239; masculinity associated with, 80, 99; middle-class, 301; moral duty for preservation of, 64–66, 77; ownership linked to, 1, 3, 12, 39, 50, 54, 60, 130, 134; performance of, 1, 4, 18–19, 28, 83, 227, 229, 238, 325n34; property linked to, 10, 27–28, 36, 38, 60–62, 66, 71, 125–29, 135–37; real estate industry and, 57, 66, 77; the residential linked to, 22–23, 174; scholarship on, 358n40; sensory perceptions of, 18–19; spiritual dispossession imputed to, 25, 74–75, 233, 324n20, 329n92, 329n106; in Steinbeck's *Grapes of Wrath* and other works, 127–30, 134–61; suburbs in relation to, 23, 217–18, 223–39; survival of, 27, 64–65, 228; as transnational identity, 50; value of, 1–2, 4, 14, 26–33, 47, 66. *See also* Anglo-Saxon identity; passing, racial; race
white supremacy: and capitalism, 243; global framework of, 51, 53, 60–62; and home/land values, 17; institutional racism as expression of, 273; racial comparisons and, 51; real estate industry and, 57, 66; Steinbeck's *Grapes of Wrath* and, 129, 338n15
Wideman, John Edgar, 300
Wiebe, Robert, 325n30
Wiebenson, John, 308, 309

Wiegman, Robyn, 228, 358n40
Wiese, Andrew, 351n24
Wiggins, Benjamin, 186, 351n10, 351n15, 351n30
Wilbur, Ray Lyman, 144–45, 149
Wilder, Laura Ingalls, Little House on the Prairie series, 126
Wilhite, Keith, 231, 232, 358n45
Williams, Patricia, 356n18
Wilson, James, 95, 115, 335n72, 336n97
Wilson, Mabel, 309
Wilson, Sloan, 222, 235; *The Man in the Gray Flannel Suit*, 158
Winant, Howard, 6
Witzling, David, 208, 354n80, 354n81
Wizard of Oz, The (film), 126
Wlson, Edmund, 339n30
women: concerns for protection of white, 101; and homeownership, 103–4; musicians, 98–99; property rights of, 323n11. *See also* black women
Wood, Maxine, *On Whitman Avenue*, 177
World War I, 45, 46, 52, 54, 67–68, 87
Wright, Richard, 36, 39, 128, 163, 183, 200, 240, 255, 260, 262, 269, 359n51, 360n86; "How Bigger Was Born," 199; "I Choose Exile," 240; *Native Son*, 126, 231–32; *12 Million Black Voices*, 163, 166–69, 199, 303
"Writing in America Today" (series of talks, 1960), 220, 355n13

Yates, Richard, 222
Yazell, Bryan, 129, 130, 342n55, 344n106
Young, Andrew, 268
Young, James O., 163

zoning, 15–17, 88–89

Patrick Whitmarsh, *Writing Our Extinction: Anthropocene Fiction and Vertical Science*

Rebecca B. Clark, *American Graphic: Disgust and Data in Contemporary Literature*

Palmer Rampell, *Genres of Privacy in Postwar America*

Joseph Darda, *The Strange Career of Racial Liberalism*

Jordan S. Carroll, *Reading the Obscene: Transgressive Editors and the Class Politics of US Literature*

Michael Dango, *Crisis Style: The Aesthetics of Repair*

Mary Esteve, *Incremental Realism: Postwar American Fiction, Happiness, and Welfare-State Liberalism*

Dorothy J. Hale, *The Novel and the New Ethics*

Christine Hong, *A Violent Peace: Race, U.S. Militarism, and Cultures of Democratization in Cold War Asia and the Pacific*

Sarah Brouillette, *UNESCO and the Fate of the Literary*

Sophie Seita, *Provisional Avant-Gardes: Little Magazine Communities from Dada to Digital*

Guy Davidson, *Categorically Famous: Literary Celebrity and Sexual Liberation in 1960s America*

Joseph Jonghyun Jeon, *Vicious Circuits: Korea's IMF Cinema and the End of the American Century*

Lytle Shaw, *Narrowcast: Poetry and Audio Research*

Stephen Schryer, *Maximum Feasible Participation: American Literature and the War on Poverty*

Margaret Ronda, *Remainders: American Poetry at Nature's End*

Jasper Bernes, *The Work of Art in the Age of Deindustrialization*

Annie McClanahan, *Dead Pledges: Debt, Crisis, and Twenty-First-Century Culture*

Amy Hungerford, *Making Literature Now*

J. D. Connor, *The Studios After the Studios: Neoclassical Hollywood (1970–2010)*

Michael Trask, *Camp Sites: Sex, Politics, and Academic Style in Postwar America*

Loren Glass, *Counterculture Colophon: Grove Press, the* Evergreen Review, *and the Incorporation of the Avant-Garde*

Michael Szalay, *Hip Figures: A Literary History of the Democratic Party*

Jared Gardner, *Projections: Comics and the History of Twenty-First-Century Storytelling*

Jerome Christensen, *America's Corporate Art: The Studio Authorship of Hollywood Motion Pictures*

The authorized representative in the EU for product safety and compliance is:
Mare Nostrum Group
B.V Doelen 72
4831 GR Breda
The Netherlands

www.ingramcontent.com/pod-product-compliance
Lightning Source LLC
Chambersburg PA
CBHW031844220426
43663CB00006B/496